Culture and Commitment

The American Culture

NEIL HARRIS—General Editor

CULTURE AND COMMITMENT 1929–1945

Edited,
with Introduction and Notes by
Warren Susman

George Braziller   New York

Published simultaneously in Canada by Doubleday Canada Limited

For information address the publisher:
George Braziller, Inc.
One Park Avenue
New York, N.Y. 10016

Standard Book Number: 0–8076–0631–6, cloth
                      0–8076–0630–8, paper

Library of Congress Catalog Card Number: 77–188361

First Printing
Printed in the United States of America

Acknowledgments

A scholar must count himself doubly blessed when good friends are equally brilliant critics: Loren Baritz, David Brion Davis, and Donald B. Meyer offered important responses to earlier efforts of mine to define the cultural history of the period covered in this volume. Former teachers who would never recognize, I suspect, anything of themselves in this work nevertheless, each in his own way, made me a cultural historian: Paul Wallace Gates, Curtis P. Nettles, Merle Curti, and most especially my dearest friend, the late Frederick J. Hoffman. And I have to acknowledge, joyfully, that my students, undergraduate and graduate alike, at Rutgers responded sharply, enthusiastically, and critically in ways always useful. While the Research Council of my university persistently refused to provide any support whatsoever on the grounds that I was no scholar and the work I did in no sense scholarship, I am nonetheless grateful to it because its constant negative response forced me all the harder to rethink what I was about.

Three younger colleagues were always of special service and much that is here depends on their efforts and understanding: Robert Berkowitz, Joseph Cusker, and Jerome Snider. While specific sources are indicated in connection with individual pictures, I want to make special mention of officials in the Prints and Photographs Division, Library of Congress, The Museum of Modern Art, Rockefeller Center and Radio City Music Hall, and most especially Brown Brothers for the extraordinarily generous help in securing pictures.

My greatest debt is, of course, offered in the form of that greatest cliché: to my wife Beatrice. Like our beloved Dilsey, she endured—but more, for her efforts physically made the manuscript possible and emotionally sustained me. This is in all ways, if she will have it, her book.

W. S.

Preface

"Do not tell me only the magnitude of your industry and commerce," wrote Matthew Arnold during his visit to the United States in the 1890's; "of the beneficence of your institutions, your freedom, your equality: of the great and growing number of your churches and schools, libraries and newspapers; tell me also if your civilization—which is the grand name you give to all this development—tell me if your civilization is *interesting*."

The various volumes that comprise THE AMERICAN CULTURE series attempt to answer Matthew Arnold's demand. The term "culture," of course, is a critical modern concept. For many historians, as for many laymen, the word has held a limited meaning: the high arts of painting, sculpture, literature, music, architecture; their expression, patronage, and consumption. But in America, where physical mobility and ethnic diversity have been so crucial, this conception of culture is restricting. The "interesting" in our civilization is omitted if we confine ourselves to the formal arts.

The editors of THE AMERICAN CULTURE, therefore, have cast a wider net. They have searched for fresh materials to reconstruct the color and variety of our cultural heritage, spanning a period of more than three hundred years. Forgotten institutions, buried artifacts, and outgrown experiences are included in these books, along with some of the sights and sounds that reflected the changing character of American life.

The raw data alone, however fascinating, are not sufficient for the task of cultural reconstruction. Each editor has organized his material around definitions and assumptions which he explores in the volume introductions. These introductions are essays in their own right; they can be read along with the documents, or they can stand as independent explorations into social history. No one editor presents the same kind of approach; commitments and emphases vary from volume to volume. Together, however, these volumes represent a unified effort to restore to historical study the texture of life as it was lived, without sacrificing theoretical rigor or informed scholarship.

NEIL HARRIS

Contents

VI THE WORLD OF TOMORROW AND TOMORROW THE WORLD

VII TOWARD AN ICONOGRAPHY OF THE PERIOD 1929–1947

Introduction

WARREN SUSMAN

I

An eminent British historian had a most effective rhetorical device for shaming his audience into easy acceptance of propositions some might have otherwise found original or even dubious. He would preface such statements with the phrase "every schoolboy knows" and those, often long out of school, who read him would blush and acquiesce, no matter what the initial ignorance or doubt. This is not the case here, for every schoolboy *does* know that in the period between the crash of the stock market and the surrender that marked the end of the second world war the American people suffered two extraordinary experiences: a prolonged and deep economic depression and the burdens of involvement in a protracted global war. He is also aware, albeit often more vaguely, that these experiences had a profound and often shattering impact on the lives of millions of Americans, with significant consequences for our history.

Yet in spite of what every schoolboy knows, the present book demonstrates little interest in those experiences. And since they are so central to most accounts of the period under study, some explanation is in order for what this volume does not do as well as for what it proposes. The current trends have tended to emphasize and perhaps even overemphasize the art of historical reconstruction to enable us to reexperience the experience of the past: What was it like, how did it feel? In its most popular forms such history becomes a kind of nostalgia; objects from the past allow us to relive our youth, or those who did not live it then to experience it now.

The cultural historian does not seek to know past experience, that is to reexperience it in any sense. Rather he seeks to discover the *forms* in which people have experienced the world—the patterns of life, the symbols by which they cope with the world. For no individual comes to an experience like some kind of Lockean *tabula rasa;* he comes conditioned to receive experience in certain ways, using certain patterns of response, certain established forms. Frequently in the course of such a confrontation with experience new forms are created or older patterns altered. The cultural historian keeps his eye on the changing shapes of these forms; he does not plunge into the experience itself bringing with him only his own culture, his own patterns, symbols, forms.

But the problem is a complicated one for the historian, for in order to do his job he must, as a matter of fact, also create forms so that he can best understand the forms which make up the culture he is studying. "Every work of history," the great cultural historian Johan Huizinga tells us, "constructs contexts and designs forms in which past reality can be comprehended. History creates comprehensibility primarily by arranging facts meaningfully and only in a very limited sense by establishing strict causal connections." Two interesting ideas follow. First, the historian deals with the culture he is studying very much like the culture itself deals with the experience with which it is confronted; in the effort to cope and make meaningful, people create culture, a set of forms, patterns, symbols with which to deal with experience. So, too, does the historian deal with his "experience," the culture under analysis. And secondly, the historian's contexts and forms are of course summoned out of his own ongoing culture and his history is thus part of that culture—part of its context and forms.

The present work thus concentrates on the forms, patterns, and symbols which largely middle-class America used to deal with the experiences of depression and war, and not on these experiences themselves. It deals, moreover, with these forms by arrangement of them in ways which prove meaningful to me within the general context constructed in this introduction. But just as I as historian find myself trying to make this cultural history "comprehensible" by designing forms and constructing contexts, so too I discover that in this period the people under study are trying to make their own world comprehensible by their self-conscious awareness of the importance of the idea of culture and the idea of commitment, their self-conscious search for a culture which will enable them to deal with the world of experience, and a commitment to forms, patterns, symbols that will make their life meaningful.

In 1926 the great historian of the Classic World Rostovtzeff asked a series of haunting questions at the end of his most extraordinary work:

But the ultimate problem remains like a ghost, ever present and unlaid: Is it possible to extend a higher civilization to the lower classes without debasing its standard and diluting its quality to the vanishing point? Is not every civilization bound to decay as soon as it begins to penetrate the masses?

And while these characteristic questions of the late 1920's and 1930's remain in mind, there are others raised by our particular study which specifically haunt this volume. What happens to a culture that suddenly discovers it is a culture? What are the consequences for culture of a self-conscious awareness not only of culture but of the *idea* of culture and the *idea* of commitment? What happens to a culture so rationalized that it seeks with full awareness for its own culture, its own commitments?

II

It was precisely the question of the relationship between experience and culture that fascinated a whole young generation of cultural critics from the years immediately preceding the first world war. Lewis Mumford's three path-breaking studies in American civilization and culture—*Sticks and Stones* (1924), *The Golden Day* (1926), *The Brown Decades* (1931)—might be viewed as a culmination of the concerns of a whole generation of intellectuals. By the end of the 1920's there was general agreement: America had indeed brought forth upon this continent a new civilization. In 1927 the distinguished French social scientist Andre Siegfried published a widely read and widely discussed analysis of that civilization, as hope and promise, as problem and menace. By 1929 his book *America Comes of Age* had gone through fourteen printings and its message found acceptance and general reinforcement in other developments; it was no longer simply the concern of a small group of intellectuals. It had become part of the general national consciousness. "Today," Siegfried announced, "as a result of the revolutionary changes brought about by modern methods of production, [America] has again become a new world. . . . The American people are now creating on a vast scale an entirely original social structure which bears only a superficial resemblance to the European. It may even be a new age. . . ."

Looking backward from their vantage point in 1936 Sheldon and Martha Cheney could declare that in 1927 "There was a spreading machine age consciousness." Other students since have pointed to some of the technological achievements of that year alone which heightened such consciousness: the establishment of radio-telephone service between New York and London, San Francisco and Manila; the development of the first national radio networks; the opening of the Holland Tunnel, the first underwater vehicular tunnel in the world; the introduction of talking films; the production of Henry Ford's fifteen-millionth automobile. The list of such developments alone seems almost endless for that year as Professor Robert A. M. Stern demonstrated in his important essay on 1927 as a turning point in the development of civilization.

As if the full consequence of living in a machine age—an age of an industrial civilization in which a new technology brought about changes in the material base of society that were altering patterns of social organization and structure—was not problem enough, there was also a growing awareness of subtle changes in the value structure as well, changes in part precipitated by the operations and needs of that very industrial civilization. Again writing from the perspective of the early 1930's, Malcolm Cowley shrewdly noted that the new ethical code first promulgated by the Bohemians of Greenwich Village in revolt against the "business-Christian ethic then represented by the *Saturday Evening Post*" had become necessary to the new industrial order itself by the end of the 1920's. In his *Exile's Return* (1934)—a classic work of the 1930's although a study of the 1920's—he points out that the prevailing ethic was, in fact, substantially a production ethic. "The great virtues it taught were industry, foresight, thrift, and personal initiative." But after World War I, the mature capitalism of the new industrial civilization demanded a new ethic, an ethic that encouraged people to buy, a consumption ethic. Without attempting to exaggerate the role of the Bohemians and certainly not trying to point to Greenwich Village as the source of the revolution in morality, Cowley stated:

It happened that many of the Greenwich Village ideas proved useful in the altered situation. Thus, *self-expression* and *paganism* encouraged a demand for all sorts of products, modern furniture, beach pajamas, cosmetics, colored bathrooms with toilet paper to match. *Living for the moment* meant buying an automobile, radio or house, using it now and paying for it tomorrow. *Female equality* was capable of doubling the consumption of products formerly used by men alone. Even *changing place* would help stimulate business in the country from which the artist was being expatriated: involuntarily they increased the foreign demand for fountain pens, silk stockings, grapefruit and portable typewriters. They drew after them an invading army of tourists, thus swelling the profits of steamship lines and travel agencies. Everything fitted into the business picture.

Americans were conscious of living in the machine age, a new era vastly different from the vision of an agrarian world in which America had been founded and in which her fundamental institutions and social structure had been molded. Charles and Mary Beard in their greatest popular success, *The Rise of American Civilization* (1927)—a book widely distributed among middle-class readers by the new Book-of-the-Month Club, which was to have significant impact on American thinking about its history for two decades—had in fact called the first volume "The Agricultural Era" and the second volume "The Industrial Era." But such awareness was further complicated by a sense of movement and conflict between an era of production and an era of consumption. Americans began to think and behave as consumers in a new way. No better symbol might be found for this shift than that offered by Henry Ford himself. In that same year, 1927, he ceased production of the old standard (and black) Model T and brought out the consumer-oriented (and available in many colors) high-styled Model A.

Thus a machine-age civilization could be seen in the physical world around Americans and could be sensed in a wide variety of social changes and patterns of living. Civilization, as Lewis Mumford had said, was "a material fact." But what of culture, which Mumford also defined in

The Golden Day (1926) as "the spiritual form"? "Civilization and culture
. . . are not," he assured his readers, "exclusive terms; for one is never
found without at least a vestige of the other." The point was clear: what
kind of culture would—and even more important what kind of culture
could—emerge on the basis of such a new machine-age civilization?
Initially a question that plagues intellectuals, more and more the whole
idea of culture and most especially an American culture began to take
hold in middle-class America. What did these obvious changes that had
occurred in the material base *mean* for life? More and more concern
grew over "ways of life," life-style, and as the debate moved on into the
1930's for what was to be called repeatedly "the American Way of Life."
That concept itself was a product of the debate and a leading cliché in
the debate itself in the post-Depression era: a search for forms in which
to organize and express the experiences of a machine age in such a way
that would lead (again in the 1926 words of Lewis Mumford) "to the
nurture of the good life; [to permit] the fullest use, or sublimation, of
man's natural functions and activities." The search for culture was the
search for meaningful forms, for patterns of living. That search began
in the 1920's; its culmination in the 1930's is one of the themes of this
volume.

By 1927 the words "modern" and "streamlined" were being used not
only in reference to design of particular objects but to a whole quality
of living, a whole life-style. They are in fact words of the new machine
order looking for a culture. In 1934 The Museum of Modern Art (founded
in 1929 and itself in a sense a product of the questions raised of culture
in an industrial era) held an important show it called "Machine Art."
Common household and industrial objects—stoves, toasters, kitchenware,
chairs, vacuum cleaners, cash registers, laboratory equipment—were displayed as *works of art*. One of the themes of that exhibition had been
provided by L. P. Jacks, the British social critic. "Industrial civilization
must either find a means of ending the divorce between its industry and
its 'culture' or perish." Alfred H. Barr, Jr., the Director of the Museum
elaborated:

It is in part through the aesthetic appreciation of natural forms that man has
carried on his spiritual conquest of nature's hostile chaos. Today man is lost
in the far more treacherous wilderness of industrial and commercial civilization. On every hand machines literally multiply our difficulties and point
our doom. If . . . we are to "end the divorce" between our industry and
our culture we must assimilate the machine aesthetically as well as economically. Not only must we bind Frankenstein—but we must make him
beautiful.

In April, 1935, an Industrial Arts Exposition opened fittingly enough in the new Rockefeller Center, which was planned in the late 1920's and built in the early 1930's and designed as a new form to meet the new needs of the city in the machine age. The exposition proposed to exhibit "industry's present solution of the practical, artistic, and social needs of the average man." The exhibitors demonstrated through a series of model rooms new ideas for the ordinary house in which low cost and efficiency, labor-saving devices, and new ways of decoration were stressed. There were new ways of heating, air-conditioning for the home, new models of efficiency in bathrooms and kitchens—even a model of Frank Lloyd Wright's "Broadacre City," the planned city of the future. Moreover, Roy L. Gray, of Fort Madison, Iowa, who had several years before been chosen as the Average American, was selected to head a committee of one hundred Average Americans to judge the show and present an award to the winning exhibitor.

Yet all Americans did not respond in quite the same way to this search for a life-style in the machine age. In the same year, for example, in 1935, a volume of some two hundred pages was published which hardly sounds like a book of the 1930's at all. It was called *A Brief and True Report for the Traveller Concerning Williamsburg in Virginia* and was issued in connection with the opening to the public of a project which had also begun in the late 1920's: the restoration of Williamsburg, the old colonial capital as it had existed in the eighteenth century. It, too, was a Rockefeller enterprise. The nonprofit corporation that made this unique effort not only to restore the old town physically but also to "re-create a living community" by showing living examples of crafts-men at their trade and hostesses wearing traditional garb of the era took as its motto "That the Future May Learn from the Past." It attempted to "tell the story of men of the 'middling sort' who conducted respectable though small businesses, and who provided support for the new nation in the making."

The restorers wanted not only to delight Americans with the charm of the place—considerably cleaned up socially (no real signs of slavery, for example) and physically (in order to get people to live and work there modern machine-age comforts such as electricity, indoor plumbing, camouflaged garages, screened porches, and the like had to be provided); they also wished to impress upon them a deeper significance by an "underlying appreciation of the moral and spiritual values of life" Williamsburg represented. Here, too, the stress was on the average man, defined as the small freeholder, although the restoration makes clear it was chiefly a planters' capital. The values the restorers sought to stress with the enormous and expensive work they undertook they clearly stated: the concept of the integrity of the individual; the concept of responsible leadership; the belief in self-government; the concept of individual liberty, and of opportunity. Not only were these eighteenth-century virtues, they were of "lasting importance to all men everywhere."

And yet it seemed to many, in the late 1920's and early 1930's while the project itself was underway, that many of these very values had in fact been threatened if not outmoded by the very advance of the United States into the machine age. Siegfried himself had insisted, for example, that the "magnificent material achievement" which was American industrial civilization had been possible only by "sacrificing certain rights of the individual." And one might ponder what meaning as culture or way of life such a Williamsburg could possibly have for a machine age. That did not stop the steady and increasing flow of visitors, nor did it eliminate the spell which led to an increased demand by American consumers of Williamsburg-type houses and furnishing—Williamsburg houses, that is, with all the "modern conveniences." There were those critics who found the Williamsburg restoration of Perry, Shaw, and Hepburn as reactionary an influence on architecture and culture as Louis Sullivan and others had found the Renaissance boom fostered by the designs at the Chicago Fair of 1893.

By 1930 the debate over the nature of culture was being held in magazines, journals, books, and even newspapers. The poet Alan Tate, whose 1927 "Ode to the Confederate Dead" called upon an older tradition as witness against the changes brought about by the newer order, joined eleven other distinguished Southern intellectuals at the end of the decade to issue a manifesto, *I'll Take My Stand*, questioning whether any culture could be created on the basis of industrialism and urging a reexamination of a culture based on a Christian-agrarian set of forms and patterns of living they presumably found buried in the South destroyed by the Civil War, that harbinger of industrialism. At about the same time the so-called New Humanists—primarily Irving Babbitt and Paul Elmer More—offered the sanctity of the great Classical civilizations as a cultural defense against the inroads of industrial barbarism. In 1931 Stuart Chase provided further ammunition in his *Mexico: A Study of Two Americas*. In this book, he compares two economic systems, handicraft and machine, and the resultant ways of life. He takes Tepoztlan, a village of 4000 people that had been carefully studied by the anthropologist Robert Redfield, and shows how this community of machineless men carried on, and how it compares with the Middletown studied by the Lynds. While by no means rejecting all of the achievements of the machine age, he does most effectively rejoice in the basic qualities of life and values projected in that world without machines. Not all could be said to have found the answer to their culture search in the world of the "modern" and the "streamlined."

Thus the American people entered an era of depression and war somehow aware of a culture in crisis, already at the outset in search of a satisfactory American Way of Life, fascinated by the idea of culture itself, with a sense of some need for a kind of commitment in a world somehow between eras. In 1927 the German writer Hermann Hesse reported a supposed remembered conversation with his hero Harry Haller in the introduction to his novel *Steppenwolf:*

Every age, every culture, every custom and tradition has its own character, its own weakness and its own strength, its beauties and cruelties; it accepts certain sufferings as a matter of course, puts up patiently with certain evils. Human life is reduced to real suffering, to hell, only when two ages, two cultures and religions overlap.

As early as the 1920's there were those who were beginning to see that in a sense they were between two eras; they were in a machine age and yet somehow not completely of it; they were caught between an older order and older values and a new order with its new demands. As early as the middle of the decade a citizen of the Lynd's Middletown could look at his fellow townsmen and sense: "These people are afraid of something; what is it?" That vague fear—in part at least of the consciousness of some suspension between two eras—was to be enormously elaborated under the threats imposed by the awesome experience of depression and war. But somehow, even before, there was already an ongoing sense that things were not quite right, in the natural order, in the moral order, in the technological order, and most especially in the relationships among them.

III

And the Depression did bring in its wake—in Harry Haller's words— "real suffering" to that group of Americans who most felt themselves suspended between two eras and who least expected their "progress" to yield such results: the enormous American middle class. For the story of American culture remains largely the story of this middle class. There is a tendency, when treating this period, for historians suddenly to switch their focus and concentrate on the newly discovered poor, the marginal men and women, migrant workers, hobos, various ethnic minorities deprived of a place in the American sun. There is equally a tendency to see the period in terms of the most radical responses to its problems, to see a "Red Decade" in which cultural as well as political life is somehow dominated by the Left. Yet the fact remains—and it is a vital one if we are to understand the period and the nature of American culture—that the period, while acknowledging in ways more significantly than ever before the existence of groups outside the dominant ones and even recognizing the radical response as important, is one in which American culture continues to be largely middle-class culture.

This is important because it is precisely the middle-class American for whom the experience of the Depression provided a special kind of shock and as a result a special kind of response. For those who were "marginal" in our society the Depression was in fact more of the same; suffering was not new to them since they had been denied a share in much of the progress and prosperity touted as characteristic of the achievement of American industrialism. If we keep our focus on the middle-class we may also be better able to understand why some shifts to the Left proved so temporary or even why the period proved in the end so fundamentally conservative as it concentrated on finding and glorifying an American Way of Life.

As early as 1944 the playwright Tennessee Williams could have his narrator in *The Glass Menagerie* define the period thusly:

The time, that quaint period when the huge middle class of America was matriculating from a school for the blind. Their eyes had failed them, or they had failed their eyes, and so they were having their fingers pressed forcibly down on the fiery Braille alphabet of a dissolving economy. In Spain there was revolution. Here there was only shouting and confusion and labor disturbances, sometimes violent, in otherwise peaceful cities, as Cleveland—Chicago—Detroit. . . .

But what is of crucial importance here is the characteristic response to the experience rather than the experience itself, for this determined the forms—that is to say, the culture. The initial response, as Franklin Roosevelt brilliantly saw, was fear. It was a kind of fear brought about by insecurity. To the already great confusions produced by the growing consciousness of living in a new machine age, the Depression (and to a lesser extent World War II) added new insecurities. "One thing everybody in Middletown has in common: insecurity in the face of a complicated world. . . . So great is the individual human being's need for security that it may be that most people are incapable of tolerating change and uncertainty in all sectors of life at once." So the Lynds report on their return to Middletown in the 1930's.

It would of course be a mistake to attribute such insecurity and such fear to the Depression alone. The very mobility, for example, provided to an increasing number of Americans by the machine age helped heighten the lack of security. Such mobility, long characteristic of civilization in the United States, became even more part of the way of life in the 1930's. Two Russian visitors to the United States in this period were overwhelmed with the image, not of cities and skyscrapers, not of monuments or hills or factories, "but the crossing of two roads and a petrol station against the background of telegraph wires and advertising billboards." For them, "America is located on a large automobile highway." Of all of the new words and phrases of the period none perhaps better symbolizes the problem that faced many Americans than the ironic idea contained in the concept of "mobile homes" and the growth of the whole trailer industry during the Depression years.

Such insecurity of course had its enormous consequences in the political and legislative history of the period. These have been profusely studied and documented. Less attention has been paid to the cultural consequences: middle-class Americans sought not merely political action and symbols; they readily attempted to translate these into more personally and easily identifiable cultural symbols as well. Witness, for example, the transformation of this sort in reference to President Roosevelt's political-economic objectives in the case of the famous Four Freedoms. When these were originally announced by the President in 1941 Freedom from Fear meant most specifically an effort to end by international agreement the frightening arms race and Freedom from Want was related to a search for trade agreements that would mean easier access of all nations to the raw materials and products of others. By 1943 when the popular painter Norman Rockwell executed his famous four paintings of the Four Freedoms for that middle-class magazine the *Saturday Evening Post*, "Freedom from Want" had become a healthy and ample American family seated around a well-stocked table being served an enormous, succulent stuffed turkey by an equally well-fed American mother, "Freedom from Fear" had become a sentimental visit to a children's bedroom with sleeping youngsters safely tucked in their comfortable bed, carefully watched over by kindly and loving parents. No other paintings ever so caught the American imagination or were so widely distributed in reproduction to eager American families.

Finding a sense of insecurity and a search for a pattern of culture and commitment to relieve such fears certainly provides no surprising discovery. But another overwhelming psychological reaction, even more important in analyzing the cultural developments of the period, may appear more unusual. A careful study of the evidence reveals an overwhelming sense of shame that seems to have engulfed so many of those middle-class Americans affected by the impact of the Depression—a shame felt by those who by no means starved but now found their accustomed way of life altered. So pervasive in fact was this sense that when Studs Terkel came some forty years after the event to interview the survivors of that era this feeling of shame, embarrassment, or even humiliation remained a vivid part of the remembering.

A well-to-do girl whose family could no longer pay her bills at a private boarding school: "I was mortified past belief." A girl who had lost her hair as a result of typhoid and could not afford a wig: "This was the shame of it." A middle-class suburbanite near Chicago: "Lotta people committed suicide, pushed themselves out of buildings and killed themselves, cause they couldn't face the disgrace. Finally, the same thing with me." Pauline Kael, the movie critic, remembering Berkeley in 1936: "There was embarrassment at college where a lot of kids were well-heeled." A distinguished theater producer and director: "I wonder if they remember the suffering and the agony and the shame they went through." A businessman: "Shame? You tellin' me? I would go stand on that relief line, I would look this way and that and see if there's nobody around that knows me: I would bend my head low so nobody would recognize me. The only scar that is left on me is my pride, my pride."

Such a brief sampling from Terkel's *Hard Times* can be duplicated many times over from this work alone as well as from our sources from the period. In an entirely different context the Lynds may have provided us with an explanation of why this particular kind of reaction, when they argue that when an individual "is caught in a chaos of conflicting patterns, none of them wholly condemned, but no one of them clearly approved and free from confusion; or where group sanctions are clear in demanding a certain role of man or woman, the individual encounters cultural requirements with no immediate means of meeting them." Perhaps in such a situation—and they see one existing in Middletown in the 1930's—the result is a sense of shame.

Terkel asks a distinguished psychiatrist in *Hard Times*, "Did any of the symptoms have to do with status in society, say losing a job and thus losing face . . . ? The psychiatrist answered:

No, it was internal distress. Remember the practice was entirely middle-class. I did a little field work among the unemployed. . . . They hung around street corners and in groups. They gave each other solace. They were loath to go home because they were indicted, as if it were their fault for being unemployed. A jobless man was a lazy good-for-nothing. The women punished the men . . . by withholding themselves sexually. By belittling and emasculating the men, undermining their paternal authority, turning to the eldest son. These men suffered from depression. They felt despised, they were ashamed of themselves. . . . Thirty, forty years ago, people felt burdened by an excess of conscience. An excess of guilt and wrongdoing.

And still another psychiatrist—by the middle of the 1930's as we shall see, psychiatry was to become an important part of the established culture, an aspect of the American Way of middle-class life—reported:

In those days everybody accepted his role, responsibility for his own fate. Everybody, more or less, blamed himself for his delinquency or lack of talent or bad luck. There was an acceptance that it was your own fault, your own indolence, your own lack of ability. You took it and you kept quiet. A kind of shame about your own personal failure. I was wondering what the hell it was all about. I wasn't suffering.

Against such a psychological background—fear and shame—we can begin better to understand the cultural responses of the period. We can begin, for example, to sense the importance of a certain type of comedy that played such a vital role whether in the writing of a Thurber, the leading radio comedy shows (perhaps like "Fibber Magee and Molly"), or the classic film comedies of Frank Capra. All, in some degree, depend initially on a kind of ritual humiliation of the hero, a humiliation that is often painful and even cruel but from which the hero ultimately emerges with some kind of triumph, even though it be a minor one. The theme, of course, is not new to comedy in this era; but this was to be a golden age of comedy in all media, and rather than simple escape it provided a special kind of identification for those whose self-image had become less than favorable. This was especially to be the case for the enormously swollen radio and movie middle-class audiences.

Walt Disney, one of the true geniuses of the age who often created its most important symbols (and used the science and technology of the machine age to do it) seemed to know precisely how to take American fears and humiliations and transform them in acceptable ways so Americans could live with them. From *Three Little Pigs* in 1933 to the "Night on Bald Mountain" (the terrors of the natural order), the "Sorcerer's Apprentice" (the terrors of the technological order), and episodes of *Fantasia* (1940) Disney proved a way to transform our most grotesque nightmares into fairy tales and pleasant dreams. It is perhaps no wonder, then, when Preston Sturges made his own remarkable film about film makers, *Sullivan's Travels* (1941) he told the story of a pretentious director of film comedy who decided, in response to the deplorable conditions in the world, to make a film of genuine social significance, "Brother, Where Art Thou?"

To do so he proposes to prepare himself by setting out as a vagrant to see "how the other half lives"—carefully attended at a distance by a huge staff following him in a trailer. Through a series of accidents near the end of the film, however, he does find himself in a real-life situation, falsely imprisoned in one of the most evil of prison situations. There he undergoes a singular experience. A black-people's church provides an occasion to share their poor happiness with the "less fortunate" prisoners: it invites them to attend a "picture show." The film is a typical Mickey Mouse cartoon. The director finds himself among the many laughing faces of the prisoners and the poor blacks, laughing with them. Thus he realizes at the end the enormous social importance of comedy. And perhaps we can also learn the cultural significance of the great comedies of the era if we realize the special kind of social role they were to play for a middle-class America frightened and humiliated, sensing a lack of any order they understood in the world around them and tending so often to internalize the blame for their fears, tending to feel shame at their inability to cope rather than overt hostility to a technological and economic order they did not always understand.

IV

Thus while political historians generally see the period as the age of Franklin D. Roosevelt, cultural historians are more likely to call it the age of Mickey Mouse, a culture-hero of international significance. The world of Walt Disney appears, initially, an absurd and even terrifying place; the inanimate become living things, men become artificial and nature human, accepted scientific laws thought to govern the world seem somehow no longer to apply, families are separated and children rarely have their real mothers. The Disney world is a world out of order: all traditional forms seem not to function. And yet the result is not a nightmare world of pity and terror, a tragic world, but a world of fun and fantasy with ultimate wish-fulfillment, ultimate reinforcement of traditional ways and traditional values. In *Fantasia,* for example, the terrors of the machine gone wild ("Sorcerer's Apprentice") is followed by the sweet vision of nature in "Pastorale" and the terrors of nature itself gone mad in "Night on Bald Mountain" are exorcised in the almost cloying religious sentimentalism of the "Ave Maria." No matter how disordered the world appears, Disney and his Mickey Mouse—any of his heroes or heroines—can find their way back to happy achievement by following the announced rules of the game.

Indeed, the leading games of the period stress this very fact: "Contract" Bridge, especially as it is developed into a fine art by Eli Culbertson, defies mere luck and chance in terms of the creation of an elaborate "system" of bidding and play; and "Monopoly," Parker Brothers' widely played board game of the period based on speculation in real estate, stressed at one and the same time the extremes of luck and chance (a roll of the dice) and the importance of a complex set of stern rules and even drastic moral obligations (one might be forced, by a roll of the dice, to "Go Directly to Jail," for example); the "pinball machine," ideal toy of the machine age with its spinning balls passing through a series of obstacle pins which meant points for the player if they met but at the same time the solemn injunction "Do Not Tilt" severely limited the player's opportunity to interfere with the chance movements of the balls.

Here, then, was the middle-class American—already made uneasy by the new set of roles he was assuming in the machine age and the conflict he was increasingly aware of because of the different roles he was required to play, suddenly faced with a set of circumstances in the society which often made him unable to fulfill many if not all of the roles his culture demanded of him, he found himself fearful and ashamed. His world in all its aspects seemed out of order; luck, chance, irrationality greeted him everywhere at a time when he was himself generally a convert to or a true believer in the vision of greater order and increased rationality in the world and especially his own social and economic system. And yet in spite of this he knew there were stern moral injunctions he had long been taught he could violate only at his own peril.

Such an American, witnessing what we might call an "alienation of all familiar forms," strove first of all to find a commitment or a system of commitments that would enable him to continue, that would provide him with a mechanism to overcome his fears and his profound sense of shame. The product of the machine age, the American did not surrender his faith in science and technology. Rather, he often attributed his difficulties to the failure to apply himself more rigorously to the creation of a culture worthy of such achievements in science and technology. Science in the nation's service became increasingly the challenge and the scientist even more the hero. In the Academy Award-winning *The Story of Louis Pasteur* (1936), one of the many screen biographies of the period (not a few of which dealt with men and women of science), Paul Muni's portrayal of the eminent scientist first displays his genius with a cure for anthrax, a disease destroying the sheep and therefore vital economic resources of France. His achievement is hailed (not, it is true, without a struggle) because of the service it clearly renders the whole nation. But his later work has a rougher time in winning recognition because not only does it go counter to professional opinion and organization but also it is less easy to justify as a contribution to national power; it deals rather with the improved health and life of individuals.

The idea of scientific service to society is reflected in a whole series of activities often undertaken with government support. During World War II, for example, the distinguished social psychologist Kurt Lewin, supported by other social scientists like the anthropologist Margaret Mead, set out on a government-sponsored campaign to change American dietary habits according to the latest scientific knowledge. Thus throughout the period science and social science joined together to find a way to improve the way of life. Such a commitment to science (which was to create deep and significant moral problems for the brilliant team of scientists whose work on atomic energy was to result in the building and detonating of an atomic bomb, the symbolic end of the period itself) was one characteristic response.

So, too, was the dedication not only to continued technological development and utilization, but to an even more important voice for planning, organization, and designing of the future. From the Technocrats of Howard Scott at the beginning of the 1930's, through the neo-Veblenians like Rexford Tugwell in the New Deal administration itself, to the new industrial designers and the older but even more vigorous city, regional, and even national planners, the whole of the period stressed the need to design and reorder the world according to a more rational scheme of things. The great World's Fair of 1939 was a brilliant symbolic cultural act demonstrating this commitment. By the 1930's the trained, professional, expert human designer had in a sense replaced the eighteenth-century vision of God as a god of design. In a world increasingly out of order, increasingly on the verge or in the midst of apocalyptic disruptions, man as designer was called upon to find some new order in the world.

There were other kinds of commitments as well: to a tradition, within the American experience like the Southern Agrarians or a Classical one propounded by the New Humanists; to the Left as an intense political, cultural, and even psychological experience wherein people might find themselves, might especially establish some kind of identity by working closely with others for the creation of a better world, sentimentally, perhaps; to the myth of the "people" as expressed in Carl Sandburg's long poem—part of a larger search for mythic and symbolic sources of identity discussed later in this introduction, to the New Deal itself because as a political movement (and through the keen sense Roosevelt and his administration had of the need of creating not only economic solutions to problems but of meeting psychological needs as well), it tried to establish a sense of personal identification by involvement of vast numbers of citizens, many of whom had never been involved before. Saul Alinsky, the professional social activist, recalls the lesson of the 1930's in Terkel's oral history: "In the Thirties, I learned . . . the big idea: providing people with a sense of power. Not just the poor. There is nothing especially noble about the poor. Everybody. That time may have been our most creative period. It was a decade of involvement. It's a cold world now. It was a hot world then."

Such a search for involvement and commitment had still further cultural consequences. It led on the one hand to a determined struggle for the attainment of the identity of an American Way of Life, a definition of culture in America and for Americans with an increased emphasis on strengthening basic cultural institutions seriously threatened by newer cultural forms (especially associated with the machine age), and the profound experiences of depression and war. At the same time it sponsored a redefinition of the role of the individual, especially in reference to such primary institutions, in ways which stressed the idea of *adjustment*. If the cultural historian can be permitted the use of metaphor, it might be helpful to think of the period as the Age of Alfred Adler. This is not to suggest that the writings themselves of that distinguished psychologist were a vital influence (although his *Understanding Human Nature* (1927) and *Social Interest* [an English translation of his *The Meaning of Life*, original 1933 and translation 1938] appear in this period). But the temper and direction of Adler's thought seems strikingly to fit the mood and response of the period in American culture generally.

The problem is not the more traditional Freudian one of strengthening the ego itself. Rather, the effort appears to be—both in popular psychology and even in rising schools of professional analysis—to find some way for individual adjustment, for overcoming shame and fear—perhaps Adler's "inferiority complex"—by adopting a life-style that enables one to "fit in," to belong, to identify. Since man always finds himself in positions of inferiority it is up to him to discover ways to overcome this. By finding and playing satisfactory roles in society man can find his identity and lose his sense of inferiority.

The whole definition of success which that best seller of 1936, Dale Carnegie's *How to Win Friends and Influence People*—certainly a key work in any attempt to understand the culture of the period—proposes, involves a view of individual personal achievement no longer simply measured by accumulation of wealth or even status or power. Success is measured by how well one fits in, how well one is liked by others, how well others respond to the roles he is playing. It is a strange kind of individualism for individualistic America. And what it often means is a stress on roles demanded by traditional and primary relationships. As the Adlerians would have it, "above all, it is the spontaneous acceptance to live in conformity to the natural and legitimate demands of the human community."

If we do think of this as an Adlerian Age, we can find a context in which we can begin to understand much of the search for a way of life and the reassertion of the role of popular religion, the family, the school, and the community of the kind that occurs in the period. Even—by admittedly an extraordinary and literary stretching of the more precise scientific definition of Adler—the political leader of the era, Franklin Roosevelt, becomes an Adlerian hero: a man with an "organ inferiority" who "compensates" for that inferiority.

In 1927 Andre Siegfried found the American family already under the threat of destruction, "its field of action greatly restricted; for in the eyes of the apostles of efficiency, the family is regarded as a barrier impeding the current." Yet by the early 1930's all the devices of the media, the energies of psychology and social science, were enlisted in a major effort to revitalize and reassert the primary importance of the family. Scientific marriage counseling was born as a profession. The importance of child-rearing in a strong family setting was reemphasized; the role of women was again to be found in the home primarily and not outside it.

Counseling by scientific experts, in fact, became a characteristic part of the American Way: to save the individual, the family, the worker as worker, even the community. Professional counseling was even now to be extended to the consumer to teach him how to be an effective consumer. In almost every area we can see the emergence of the professional counselor to help Americans *play those roles* they were having such great difficulty playing, *adjusting* to those situations and circumstances to enable them to overcome their own sense of fear and shame, their sense of their own ability to perform satisfactorily. By the time of World War II the word "morale" had become commonly used and the problem of how to maintain such morale the concern of a growing number of experts. Thus social science and design joined hands with an Adlerian vision to reshape man and his culture in America as Americans themselves sought help in finding their culture and playing their required roles in it. Education joined the struggle. In the state of Montana, as one of many examples, a Rockefeller grant supported a study to provide "a workable play of education for enriching the life of small communities."

In 1942 Florence C. Bingham edited for the National Congress of Parents and Teachers a volume of essays prepared by leading social scientists and educators, *Community Life in a Democracy.* In it the Depression and the war were seen as rich opportunities to help create a true collective democracy in the United States. "Perhaps," wrote the Chicago sociologist Louis Worth, "the war, like other crises in the collective life, may bring to light further sources of community solidarity, mutual aid, and strength, which in the postwar period may be used for the building of a more genuine democratic order than we have known since the days of the American frontier." The entire volume stresses the role of community, family, school, church—the whole culture—in providing for a stable order for the future with clear, well-defined roles for all to play, in which children can be trained and in which such basic institutions can be reevaluated and reshaped by experts to produce the kind of children who will indeed know their roles and know how to play them. "When we think of the American way of life," an expert on child welfare reported, "we think of a pattern of community functions, each of which contributes in some fashion to the well-being of all who reside within the community. Thus, good schools, good clinical facilities, good social services tend to develop together."

From the agonized beginnings in dreadful fear and embarrassing shame there could emerge a new American. This was the ultimate myth of the combining of machine-age expertise and the characteristic vision of man in an Adlerian age. It is no better expressed than by the president of the National Congress of Parents and Teachers in *Community Life in a Democracy:*

America has awakened to a new conception of community life. From coast to coast and from border to border there has sprung up a sense of unity and solidarity that binds citizens together in their communities and our communities together in the larger life of the nation to an extent, that, with all our national reputation for neighborliness, we have never experienced before. Today we are keenly aware of each other as human beings and each other's children as potential leaders and saviors of humanity. There is a breakdown of the old rigid conception of "mine" and "thine," especially where children and youth are concerned. The extension of the parent's affection and the parent's concern beyond the limits of the family to children on the outside, wherever they and their needs are to be found and regardless of race, creed, or social status, is unmistakable, and it is an epic development.

Yet at the very time this work appeared Gunnar Myrdal and his colleagues were preparing *An American Dilemma* (published in 1944), one of many examples of basic social problems, in this case race relations, that by no means had been "solved" in the great era of adjustment. But Americans had begun to believe they had found The American Way of Life and had created a culture and that it was good. Believing so had become part of the culture itself, a response in finding roles to play, and learning— often through the help of "counselors"—how to play them which re-emphasized basic institutions and values and reinforced them in a wide variety of forms in the culture.

V

It was, then, an Adlerian age of adjustment, and consciously so, an age when men and women sought to find a place and play a role and turned increasingly to a whole set of newly institutionalized agencies designed explicitly to provide such adjustment, when new professions arose to meet these needs and older ones increasingly assumed these functions. Science —and most especially the social sciences and various schools of psychiatry—joined with popular religion and popular self-help movements. Strong efforts were made to strengthen basic institutions. Counselors like Dr. Paul Popenoe could point with great pride to their success in keeping families together; social scientists like Prof. Elton Mayo could stress the role of proper "personnel management" making industrial operations function more happily with less sense of worker alienation; and Dr. Karen Horney could show the way through meaningful adjustment to overcome the "neurotic personality of our time."

The popular arts, meanwhile, developed an extraordinary skill in providing a kind of comedy that stressed for its audiences a vicarious recovery from humiliation, shame, and fear, while the great political movement of the period, the New Deal, brilliantly used the new media (especially the radio with the President's Fireside Addresses) and a set of significant symbols to give more Americans a sense of belonging and role. It was an era in which participation or at least a sense of participation became crucial, whether that participation was in sports, in block parties in urban communities, or in politics itself.

Even the Communist Party by 1935 was ready to play its role in an era of adjustment. The Popular Front was no doubt dictated by international as well as national political developments. But in the United States the enthusiastic effort to link Communism and "Americanism" created a firmer sense of belonging and involvement. The Party linked its movement to historic American tradition; it rewrote our history to find a place for itself so that the socialist movement would no longer be alienated from American life, meanwhile providing for its members a sense of participation in important work and roles that could be meaningfully played. It put ideological conditions to one side and stressed its relationship to the American Way of Life. Witness the dangerous radicalism of the Young Communist League at the University of Wisconsin during the height of the "Red Decade":

Some people have the idea that the YCLer is politically minded, that nothing outside of politics means anything. Gosh no. They have a few simple problems. There is the problem of getting good men on the baseball team this spring, of opposition from ping-pong teams, of dating girls, etc. We go to shows, parties, dances and all that. In short, the YCL and its members are no different from other people except that we believe in dialectical materialism as the solution to all problems.

Yet the very culture produced in some measure by the Popular Front itself, and by other forces struggling to provide a sense of belonging and belief in an era of shame and fear, led finally beyond the Adlerian age of adjustment to a search for metaphysical certainty, a search for a sense of transcendent being, a collective identity deeply responding to deeply felt needs and aspirations. Especially for the period after the mid-1930's up to and through the war years, it is perhaps permissible to use another psychological metaphor and think of the age as Jungian as well. Once again, few perhaps were consciously reading or following the work of Carl Jung himself (although Philip Wylie specifically claims to base his critique of America, *Generation of Vipers*, (1942) on his reading of Jung's analysis of human instincts revealed in myths and archetypes). It was an age which consciously sought new heroes, new symbols, even new myths; an age which rediscovered the "folk" and their work and deliberately sought to identify with this culture. It was an age that sought in established and regularized holidays and a host of new patriotic songs to return ritual to its proper place in American life.

A consumer culture in which advertising had become a crucial element of the economic life soon saw not only a series of clever advertising campaigns creating product identification, but also saw the advertising men behind these campaigns often turn their talents to the uses of the government to create symbolic means of citizen identification with their national administration and its objectives. Others, too, saw the importance of the manipulation of symbols—even words like "the people"—to create a sense of national morale, a national community properly directed toward proper ends. The importance of symbols for the builders of the World's Fair of 1939 and of the famous "Blue Eagle," the slogans, and the parades of the N.R.A. is obvious.

An age of heroes: how important, especially perhaps for the young. "Doc Savage," in the pulps, "The Shadow" on the radio, "Superman" in the new comic books—these are but a few examples of the type that by the end of the 1930's began to dominate much of the media. Archetypes in a kind of boyhood fantasy world, these heroic figures joined others like the hard-boiled detective of Dashiell Hammett and Raymond Chandler, or the tough-guy heroes of the films. They tended to be men without attachments to any family (although often closely associated with a small group of trusted fellow workers or followers). They seldom obeyed any rules, whether those were laws of nature or requirements proscribed by any existing institutions. Their commitment was always to themselves (with a firm and strong belief in themselves, without fear, shame, or doubt about their role or identity). Such commitment, however, almost always involved a strong sense of personal moral code that led them to "do good" and devote themselves to overcome the forces of evil. They triumphed precisely when and where traditional men and institutions could not. They worked for traditional American values and ends, but often—in a period that witnessed failures in the natural as well as the moral order to act "properly"—imposed their own order by themselves on a disordered world. And like the "Lone Ranger," one of the earlier of such heroes in the world of radio, they rode off, after establishing such order, asking no thanks, going as mysteriously as they had come. Many such heroes, further, when not in their heroic disguises and regarded as ordinary citizens found themselves either humiliated or treated with some contempt by their fellows. Only in their hidden identities did they find praise and admiration.

Often such heroic figures merged into a special kind of myth becoming increasingly important, for example, in the films of the era: the new westerns of John Ford and a whole new range of urban westerns, the gangster films whose emergence as a significant genre can be traced to Von Sternberg's brilliant *Underworld* (1927). A whole new epic vision of the American past and present was being created with a mythic sense of involvement and fulfillment created by the unfolding of the tale itself in which the very form of the presentation—a kind of ritualized performance in which all expectations are satisfied in due and proper course —provided a sense of order and continuity.

A fascination with the folk and its culture, past and present, aided many to find a kind of collective identification with all of America and its people. There were, at the same time, efforts made to collect and preserve folk material from the past and an interest in the songs being created by singers in the present out of their own real experiences—not songs from Tin Pan Alley, but songs that came from the farms and mines, from the men on the road and the workers on strike. These songs, the expression of special experiences of special people, became widely adopted by many middle-class Americans as part of their own culture in spite of the fact that the experiences they spoke of were often alien to the middle-class citizens who now enjoyed singing and listening to them. Such vicarious experiencing often became a political as well as a cultural act. By 1939, in the heyday of Popular Front culture in America, two Left-leaning writers, John La Touche (lyricist) and Earl Robinson (composer) produced a special kind of pseudo-folk ballad for a W.P.A. revue. That work, later popularized by Paul Robeson, became enormously popular—a "hit" as song and record that was even performed at the Republican National Convention in 1940. "Ballad for Americans" represents the kind of new "folk" material being created in the Jungian age. It was about America and its history and those who made it. It was about the role of belief, about the "nobody who was anybody" and the "anybody who was everybody," about ultimate identification: "You know who I am: the people!" The ballad was a testament—as sentimental as Norman Rockwell's *Saturday Evening Post* covers—to the unity in a way of life that involved all ethnic groups, creeds, colors.

This search for some transcendent identification with a mythic America led Americans in a few short years from the deep concern for the Okies of the Dust Bowl as a profound social and human problem to the joyous "Oh! What a Beautiful Morning" with the "corn as high as an elephant's eye" of Rodgers and Hammerstein's *Oklahoma!* (1943), a hugely successful if sentimental effort to recapture the innocent vitality of the historic American folk. Sometimes, however, the efforts were of more interest and greater significance. In 1935 George Gershwin tried to make the daring fusion of pop and art, Broadway musical and grand opera, jazz, folk, and popular music, folk and mythic materials, and modern theater. Working from material supplied by the black author DuBose Hayward which itself relies on material out of the folk, Gershwin's opera, *Porgy and Bess,* is set in a slum in what once had been a colonial palace. His theme, according to Wilfrid Mellers, is "the impact of the world of commerce on those who had once led, and would like to have led, may still lead, the 'good life,'" based on a close relationship between man and nature. Basic human relationships—mother and child, the rituals of a tight-knit community (like the picnic and prayer meetings), love—are contrasted with a world out of order, the violence and lure of gambling and the vices of the big city, the alienation of "that lonesome road," the brutality of the fighting, the deformities of nature (Porgy's legs, the devastation of the hurricane).

The drama pits the longing for a return to an Eden before history or man, before consciousness ("I ain't got no shame"). And while there is a longing for the "reestablishment of the tribal innocence" and a return to Eden, the opera ends with Porgy's symbolic gesture: toward New York and his Bess, the recognition, again as Mellers suggests, that "the

Promised Land *is* New York, where the new life can grow only when he and Bess can meet, accepting the city as a home." Thus in Gershwin's hands the folk material is not used to justify a refusal to accept the new order of things but to help us to understand what we must ultimately come to grips with, while his very use of collective dreams and hopes, basic instincts, and illusions provides a sense of identity for those who find themselves aliens in an alien world.

The great American dancer, Martha Graham, was also drawn to a vision of theater as ritual in an almost classic sense. She early turned to a private world of myth as the basis of her best work, as in her highly personal *Primitive Mysteries* (1931) where she was the poetic Virgin, woman inviolate of the Christian myth. By 1934 she was ready to explore America and her own Protestant background. As Leroy Leatherman suggests:

In *Letter to the World* (1940) . . . she confronted those dark inhuman forces. But the end was bleak. Then, in 1944, she was able to do *Appalachian Spring*. The doomful Ancestress of *Letter to the World,* a distillation of Cotton Mather and an archetypal figure of the past that drags one down to death, had undergone a marvellous transformation: In *Appalachian Spring* she is the Pioneer Woman, dominant, strong but loving and dedicated to the future. The Bride is joyous and will not be put down by a hell-fire-and-brimstone sermon.

Danced to a score by the American composer Aaron Copland, it was to prove one of her most popular and enduring works. In no sense is the work or even the music of the score "folk" nor does it pretend to be. But it does present itself as a special kind of American rite or series of rites—the sermon, the courtship, the marriage, the house-raising—which celebrates the American past and the American character (especially the American woman) with humor, joy, and tenderness. Copland's score, while it uses only one folk tune, makes an effort to relate to a body of characteristically American music, again uniquely in the composer's own gifted way. It was part of a body of music during the time demanded by the new media (radio and the movies) as well as by the development of the lyrical theatrical arts in America. Much of his music and much of Miss Graham's work of the period indicates a shift in mood, a desire to find a special collective relationship in which all Americans might share— not only in terms of a past but also in terms of a future. Composers, Copland himself tells us, felt "needed as never before"; this was combined with a "wave of sympathy for and identification with the plight of the common man." But at its very best the new lyric theater (and it was here that so many of the major cultural achievements of the period are, interestingly enough, to be found) strove to provide a new sense of common belief, common ritual observance, common emotional sharing that the psychological conditions of the era seemed to demand. Heroes, symbols, myths, and rituals: a Jungian Age in America.

VI

All ages demand, in Ezra Pound's words, a symbol: none more self-consciously than the age we speak of here. We began with one symbol, the reconstruction of historic Williamsburg as a hedge against the new rising industrial order. We end with another, thought of at the time of its construction as the fitting monument to the new era itself: ". . . The most interesting and efficiently designed mass office building. . . . The biggest in the world." Built of reinforced concrete, its designers and builders (who immediately formed a Society of the Pentagon to perpetuate themselves and their achievement) prophesied it would be as "lasting as the Republic." It was a "modern miracle of construction" built in a remarkably short time (in fourteen months; in traditional and not war time it would have taken seven years) and provided a "stimulus to the wartime imagination." A complete world unto itself, it contained some 16 miles of corridors, 600,000 square feet of office space, room initially for 32,000 workers. It was to be the gigantic brain cell of the army and one critic called it a "World's Fair gone to war." Within those enormous corridors—painted in various shades of pastel to help one find his way—there were food services, medical facilities, even a private printing press. Its roads were patrolled by military police and one author, visiting it while the approaches were being landscaped, commented on the picture presented: "The work (of landscaping) is being done almost entirely by squads of Negro women who all wear straw hats, cotton blouses, and blue trousers, giving the countryside something of a plantation aspect."

Yet a little different from the plantations of Colonial Virginia, one might suppose. The Pentagon, a final symbol of the great new world of industrial order and power, was made necessary by the venture into war. Perhaps, its defenders suggested, it would be unnecessary for the army after the war. In that case it could easily be converted into an archive storage building. But such exigencies did not come to pass and the Pentagon is still with us. What its symbolic value is today, however, is far different from that it presented when erected in 1942. Or perhaps there were some even then who might have seen in its design another image, that of the Castle that the Austrian author Franz Kafka had written about so chillingly back in 1927.

For the fact remains that by the early 1940's that culture often so self-consciously cultivated in response to the fear and shame which dominated so much of the early part of the period, and which gave way to a final celebration of the American Way of Life and strong sense of commitment to it, was under restudy and even attack. Many had begun to doubt that a rational or scientific order was enough; some had in fact allowed their commitments to wander to the idea of commitment itself

—a whole new interest in the existential mode, in neo-orthodoxy in religion, in neo-Thomism in philosophy, challenging not only the dominant American pragmatism in schools of philosophy but in the whole philosophy of education itself (as at the University of Chicago under Robert M. Hutchins). Sidney Hook set off a lively debate in 1943 when he attacked this attack on pragmatism and science, on rationality and social engineering as a new "Failure of Nerve." But already Philip Wylie had issued his best-selling blast at American myths, heroes, and values. The whole vision of a new order emerging out of a war was challenged by Carl Becker in 1942 in *How New Will the Better World Be* and in 1943 Ayn Rand produced a blockbuster of a novel, *The Fountainhead*, which was to gain a wide readership especially on college campuses. It preached a new individualism—exalting, in fact, selfishness as a virtue —in the face of the collectivism, often happy, that provided "identity." The following year Hayek's *Road to Serfdom* reinforced Miss Rand's individualism from the point of view of economic and social theory. The technological triumphs, even ultimate victory in war and the establishment of a total governmental structure after the war to put the finishing touches to the engineered welfare state did not hold; the critics found neither meaningful culture nor a civilization perhaps worth keeping: "Civilization—Take It Away," a postwar song would have it.

An age of shame and fear had passed into history; it was somehow to be followed by an age that frankly thought of itself as an age of anxiety. An age of Adler and Jung, one might propose, gave way to an Age of Wilhelm Reich:

Now there are times when a whole generation is caught . . . between two ages, between two modes of life and thus loses the feeling for itself, for the self-evident, for all morals, for being safe and innocent.

So Hesse's Harry Haller continues in a passage after the one quoted previously. And somehow this fits almost too perfectly the age which followed the technological achievements that built the Pentagon and the A-Bomb. The age of culture and commitment, the age of adjustment, provided respite: fear and shame drove it back into a series of conservative postures, provided the use and strength of cultural forms that worked as temporary responses to the problems the experiences of the period demanded. But by 1945 these appeared exhausted and perhaps even detested forms that could and would no longer serve.

Thus it is that the Pentagon can be viewed as a two-faced symbol: for the age it climaxed indeed the triumph of order, science, reason; the achievement of unity, purpose, morale; the establishment of identity and role. And yet, for the age being born it was the home (spiritual, at least, in the most ironic sense) of the atom bomb and a frightening bureaucratic structure, the beginning of a brave new world of anxiety.

PART ONE

THE PROBLEM STATED

1. America in Search of Culture

Since most discussions of the period after the Crash assume that the issues of those years were best defined in liberal or radical circles, it must seem perverse to begin the present volume with an article by a writer who is generally regarded as a conservative. The title of this opening section, moreover, is lifted from a book by another conservative, William Aylott Orton—a book that advances a similar point of view. Nevertheless, in striking ways both writers early presented—early in the period—the clash of issues that was to keynote much of the cultural, intellectual, and social work and analysis of the period.

Herbert Agar, born (1897) and educated in the industrial northeastern United States, was often associated with the so-called Southern Agrarians who, in 1929, published their manifesto *I'll Take My Stand.* In 1936 he was joint editor with Allen Tate of the group's second symposium, *Who Owns America?* Although he began his career as a poet and critic, he soon turned to historical, political, and economic studies, winning the Pulitzer Prize for history in 1933. Orton (1889–1952) (whose quite appropriate title I have borrowed) almost reversed Agar's experience. Born and educated as an economist in England, he had had considerable experience in industrial relations before he came to the United States in 1922 to fill a post as professor of economics at Smith College. Both men were fascinated by the potential—and the problems—of the development of an American culture in the machine age.

Culture Versus Colonialism in America

HERBERT AGAR

Having been told many times that the future must be a strife between communism and fascism, a number of Americans are beginning to believe it. But their hearts are not given to either side; so the belief leads to pes-

Herbert Agar, "Culture Versus Colonialism in America," *The Southern Review,* (July 1935), pp. 1–19.

simism, to the conviction that America is sold out and that there is nothing left to do but complain cleverly.

Such an attitude has the merit of completeness. It satisfies the part of the human mind that cries for an answer at any cost, even at the cost of suicide. But there is no excuse, as yet, for Americans to seek this shoddy comfort. We have a harder task and a more exciting. It is our job to save a corner of the world from the twin despotisms that encroach on Europe. If we do this we shall take a proud place in history. If we fail to do it we shall take no place at all; we shall just be a colony: a huge but awkward copy of the parent civilization.

If we are to seize our chance for greatness we must fight both the defeatism of the pessimists and the greedy optimism of those whose picture of a pretty future is a return to 1928. Our hope lies in the fact that we once had a political tradition which could give an answer in terms of freedom to this false fascist-or-communist dilemma. We have weakened that tradition shamefully, by taking its name in vain. We have betrayed it item by item while assuring each other that we were merely adapting it to the modern progress. It will not be easily revived today. Yet there is our job. All over the United States men are waking to that knowledge at last.

The first step toward reviving native America is to define it. And before it can be defined it has to be isolated. The "real" America, from which a native culture can grow, has to be distinguished from colonial America which seeks only to copy Europe. The present essay tries to make this distinction even at the risk of overstating the differences.

During six years of living in England I learned one basic fact about my own country. I learned that the best traits in American life are not the traits we have copied faithfully from Europe but the traits we have freely adapted, or else originated—the traits which are our own. I learned that in so far as America is an imitation of Europe, she is not so good as the original. This merely means that in so far as we are a colonial race we share the usual shortcomings of colonialism. "Society" life in the big cities of America is an example. "Society" has of course become ridiculous all over the Western world. The bourgeois revolution of the nineteenth century, the rise of stock-market wealth to a power and prestige overshadowing landed wealth, doomed urban "society" to a comic-section end. But granting that it is absurd everywhere, "society" in New York or Chicago is more absurd than in London. In London, something that once had dignity and purpose has grown sick and silly; in Chicago something sick and silly has been carefully improvised. A colonial status is a poor one at best; it becomes abject in a period when the model is not worth copying.

Modern American art offers a similar example. In so far as our art is a copy of French Modernism, it is colonial and inferior. As Mr. Thomas Craven writes:

Those who regard art as modish decoration, as inarticulate embellishment, have every reason to favor French Modernism, and every incentive to buy it. And it is more sensible to buy the original manufactures than the American imitations. Truly, they order these material things better in France. In the exhibition at the Chicago Fair, the French painters of the modern School of Paris made the American painters attached to that school look seedy and second-rate.

But there is another American art, such as that of Mr. Thomas Hart Benton, which has nothing to do with French Modernism, with Bohemia's abstract aloofness from Europe's passion and despair. This other art deals with American life; for side by side with our colonialism there is an America which makes an original contribution to the culture of Christendom. . . .

The town of Sheridan,* in the Middle West, illustrates the two Americas, and also the half-conscious fight taking place between them—a fight that will determine our future.

Sheridan is a suburb of one of our giant cities. Its population increased from thirty-seven thousand in 1920 to sixty-three thousand in 1930. But Sheridan is not yet "suburban." Having a strong local pride it has thus far kept its own identity. It has not become merely another dormitory to the giant city. It still has the character of a Middle Western small town. But it will not have this character for long, if recent tendencies continue unchecked into the future. For Sheridan is living on its spiritual capital. It is using the virtues that are left over from the past rather than tending the soil from which these virtues grew. Native America will not win its fight unless it grows more conscious of the danger, more vigilant in defence.

The most striking feature of life in Sheridan is that a feeling of equality is still almost universal, at least among the whites. It is an unforced equality, which is so widely accepted that it does not need to call attention to itself. A delivery-boy will meet the wife of a college professor on the street, and will wave his hand at her and call out, "Hello there, Mrs. Holt, you're looking just fine today." The clerk at the grocery store will say, "Good morning, Mrs. Holt. Why, you've washed your hair." And the ice-man will find Mrs. Holt digging in her garden, and will stop to tell her, "Don't plant your tulips there—it's too shady. Plant them over by that wall, where they'll have a chance to grow."

Social democracy of this sort is of course widespread in rural America. But there are few towns, and fewer suburbs to great cities, where it still is dominant. And in the big cities themselves it is giving way more and more to a nasty caricature of equality: a defensive smartness that has none of the virtues of equality and none of the virtues of a class system.

* This is a real town, which I am calling by a made-up name because I am using the town for what is typical in it, not for what is individual.

Relations between people of different incomes, backgrounds, and education can be made smooth either by the institution of equality or by the institution of social classes. Either will work agreeably; either will promote human dignity. The one thing that will not work agreeably is a mixture of the two, which often occurs in American big cities. When you get into a New York taxicab wearing a top hat your driver may be a friendly soul who assumes that in spite of your clothes you are human. In that case he will give you a trial, and at the next red light will start on murder, politics, or the strange habits of the taxi-riding public. On the other hand, your driver is quite likely to be a man who not only believes in classes but who believes, reasonably enough, that his own class is unenviable. The sight of your top hat will not soothe him. He will make it clear that he thinks you neither useful nor pretty. For with the exception of the small group of trained domestic servants, the American who is class conscious has become so in order to vent a grievance, commonly a just grievance, against society. He therefore gets no comfort from the American system of equality, and no comfort from the foreign system of classes. . . .

It is heartening to find Sheridan preserving its social democracy on the doorstep of a giant city where "equality" has no meaning at all, where a landless, toolless Marxian proletariat faces a Marxian bourgeoisie. There are several reasons why Sheridan has been able to do this. In the first place, it has kept a high standard in its public schools. Practically all the children of the town, therefore, are sent to these schools, so that the boy who grows up to be an ice-man and the girl who grows up to be the wife of a college professor may have sat side by side in class. This is often said to be customary in America; but it has long been quite uncustomary among people who, like many citizens of Sheridan, could afford to send their children to private school.

In the second place, there is no class of very rich people in Sheridan, and hardly any very poor. Though there is a wide range of income, there is no fantastic gulf of the sort that makes "equality" a joke. In the third place, the sense of civic pride among the citizens has been so strong that the town provides a number of amenities for all—not only cultural amenities, but abundant tennis courts, swimming beaches, and the like. These are well kept, with the result that the rich feel no need of having their own tennis courts, their own bathhouses and strips of beach. And not being over-rich they feel no need of advertising their pride. So they all use the communal facilities. In the fourth place there is a university in Sheridan, and the university has a large group of students from Middle Western farms where social democracy is as natural as breathing.

This equality which still lingers in Sheridan, making the half-hour drive from the huge neighboring city seem a bridge between two worlds, is a vital part of American culture. But what of the city, the antithesis to Sheridan? If the giant city grows and flourishes, Sheridan will die. And the city, with its skyscrapers, millionaires, gangsters, and polyglot proletariat—is it not the city typical of America, too? Yes: but it is not typical of American culture. It is my thesis that the city stands for the other America—big, loud, and unself-confident as a new boy at school, but not half so native as Sheridan, not half so well rooted, and in the end not half so strong.

Since Sheridan survived 1929, it may never be engulfed. It is still threatened, but its old character is not yet gone. Perhaps Sheridan will turn back and save the institutions which gave it that character, instead of accepting its metropolitan doom. If it does, the moment when the tide turns, the moment when the city stops encroaching on its tiny neighbor, will be an important moment in the story of American culture, and an important moment in world history. In order to show how I can hope for such an event, I must explain what I mean by the phrase, "American culture." In common speech the phrase has little meaning, or else a meaning that is clear but trivial.

In the advertising columns of the *American Magazine* for November 1934 there is a sample of the popular use of the word *culture*. "At Palm Beach and Nassau, California and Cannes," reads the caption under a picture, "every year they flock by scores—those smart cultured women with enough money to indulge the slightest whim. And the number of them who use Listerine Tooth Paste is amazing."

And in the *Saturday Evening Post* for December 1, 1934, in an article called "An Industrial Design for Living," the following sentences occur: "Our nation has been on the receiving end of a cultural movement the like of which would be hard to imagine. All the colleges, all the magazines, the newspapers and the movies, have been indoctrinating people with the idea of beauty in person, in clothing and in background, until they have developed an appetite for such things beyond ordinary comprehension."

Here we have two of the commonest uses of the word: culture as female wealth and smartness, and culture as a consumer's demand for beauty, a demand that has been whipped up by "all the colleges, all the magazines, the newspapers and the movies." The first use of the word is silly enough to be harmless. People are in no danger of believing that a cultured nation is a nation composed chiefly of beautiful bare young women "with enough money to indulge the slightest whim." But the second use is evil, for it leads to misunderstanding. It is a form of the heresy that culture is a thing which can be stored in libraries and museums. Culture, in this sense, is not a way of life but something you learn at school, like plane geometry, or something you catch, like measles. If you have learned it or caught it, if you have "been on the receiving end of a cultural movement," then you will know about beauty and will want some of it. And if you want beauty you will go to the shops where it is for sale and buy as much as you can afford, or as much as you have room for at home.

This is the industrial-commercial view of culture, as is made clear in the *Saturday Evening Post* article, which continues as follows: "The old-time pioneers who pushed beyond the Alleghenies felt that they had a continent to explore, and, if your mind runs that way, to exploit. But we who came after them, or rather, out of them, have lived into a time when the pioneering has come into something richer than a green continent. It is a fertile region that lies somewhere between the human intelligence and the human soul. Developing it will provide plenty of work for all the machines that can be contrived and all the labor that exists."

The last sentence is perfect. The "pioneers" are done with exploring North America, and they find themselves with quite a lot of redundant machinery on their hands. So they decide to "develop" the "fertile region that lies somewhere between the human intelligence and the human soul." By "developing" it they mean making it "beauty-conscious"; they mean teaching it to want goods and gadgets that have "eye-appeal." If you are in the market for goods with "eye-appeal," you have culture. Your "fertile region" has been developed. Of course, as the inventors turn out more and more machines, we shall have to get more and more cultured. In time, even our tooth paste and our telephones will have "eye-appeal." Everything we buy will be beautiful, and we'll buy an astonishing lot (for yesterday's eye-appeal can always be made into today's eyesore). In this way America should become the most cultured nation in the world's history.

This industrial-commercial view of culture, which sees it as the next field for industry "to explore, and, if your mind runs that way, to exploit," flourished during the years when Big Business was glorified. During the 1920's there were people who thought that as soon as Mr. Hoover finished solving the problem of poverty, Americans would apply sound business principles to the Higher Life and would shortly be delivering large packages of beauty and truth to every taxpayer. Today such people, though less hopeful about Mr. Hoover, still think that culture can be "laid on" like gas or water. They believe that if only a group of technocrats, or bureaucrats, or commissars, would organize things so that the whole working population would have mechanical jobs for four hours a day and freedom for twenty, the national demand for Higher Life would be too surprising for words. They may be right, for what they mean by higher life is reading "good books," going to concerts and picture galleries, and listening to lectures. None of these pastimes has any necessary connection with culture. The American public, for example, might spend its time reading Greek and Roman literature, looking at Italian and Dutch paintings, hearing German and Russian music, and attending lectures by visiting playwrights from Vienna and Budapest. The result would probably be a nation of prigs. I see no reason to think it would be a nation with culture. "If I read as many books as that man," said Hobbes, "I'd be as big a fool as he." "Beware of the man who would rather read than write," warns Bernard Shaw. Beware of the nation whose culture means admiring the creativeness of other people.

The Pittsburgh *Sun-Telegraph* for February 25, 1935, ran the following editorial:

Andrew W. Mellon, former Secretary of the Treasury, spent more than $4,000,000 to buy six famous paintings, five of them from Soviet Russia. He planned to build a great art museum in Washington to house his famous collection of pictures, worth about $19,000,000.

One by one he bought at huge prices great works of art from European collections in order to realize his dream of making Washington the art capital of the world.

Mr. Mellon is proof of the utter falsity of the conception, once so widespread abroad, of American millionaires as ruthless money-grubbing materialists.

In no other nation on earth, at no other time in history, have great individual fortunes so generously served the permanent scientific and artistic interests of mankind as here.

This is the perfect expression of false, colonial, imitative culture. The thought that Washington could become "the art capital of the world" by becoming the storehouse for a lot of Italian and Flemish and Byzantine paintings is a thought that does no honor to the human mind. Just as a city is a place where people live, not a place where they are buried, so an art capital is a place where art is produced, not a place where it is put away.

If the industrial-commercial concept of culture is dismissed to its proper home in the advertising columns, how can the word be redefined so that it can throw light on American life? As a prelude to trying such a redefinition, American life must be placed in a scheme of world history.

Until quite recently, the prevailing theory of history was the one devised to fit the nineteenth-century theory of progress. It showed man as advancing, in the course of a few thousand years, from a shocking and brutal-looking ancestor with long hair and a club to something quite commendable, like Mr. H. G. Wells. The advance was usually shown in two parts: first the advance from cave-man to classical civilization; then, after a brief relapse during the Dark Ages, a further advance to the mechanical triumphs of the modern world. The picture is a perfect example of false conclusions drawn from facts which are true but inadequate.

It is true that man was once a primitive nomad, possessing none of the arts of civilization. It is true that man, in certain parts of the world, has now become something which may fairly be symbolized by Mr. Wells. It is true that from our point of view Mr. Wells is more engaging than the cave man, which means that there has been progress. But what is quite untrue is the assumption underlying so much progressive thought, that this advance has been along one fairly constant line, that millennium by millennium the progress has continued, and that it can be described in some such terms as a steadily increasing power to control the physical environment, or a steadily increasing store of real and final knowledge, or a steadily increasing friendliness toward larger and larger groups of people—a friendliness that began with the family unit and is destined to end by embracing the world state. This outmoded nineteenth-century view of progress was summarized by Woodrow Wilson when he told an audience that "all through the centuries there has been this slow painful struggle forward, forward, up, up, a little at a time, along the entire incline, the interminable way."

It is a comforting view, for it suggests that if man refrains from committing suicide he will grow better and better until the time comes when he will have every reason for self-satisfaction. Such a theory of history transplants the Garden of Eden from the past, where it provoked nostalgia, into the future, where it provokes a lively hope. Heaven is transplanted out of space, where it was unattainable except by the grace of God, into time, where it becomes merely a question of patience, like waiting for the next train. But for all its soothing qualities the theory is now dying. It has been mortally hurt by the work done during the last thirty years in archeology, anthropology, comparative religion, and literature. Its place is being taken by a more complicated and less flattering view, which has at least the merit that it can be reconciled to the known facts.

The old division of history into Ancient, Medieval, and Modern is being scrapped. It was a division which cut straight across the facts, separating events that belonged together and joining others that had nothing in common. Instead of one long gratifying advance, with ourselves as the latest and most improved model of humanity, what history really shows is a series of high cultures passing through similar stages of growth and decay. In China, in Mexico, in India, in Mesopotamia, in Egypt, and now at last in our own West, we can trace this pattern. Out of a group of farming settlements a new culture is born, no one knows why. The challenge of life is suddenly met by a new affirmation.

A new statement is made of man's old faith that life has a meaning and that the meaning is good. In our case, in the years between 500 and 1000 A.D. this birth took place in western Europe. The Christian affirmation defined itself; it permeated the spirit of Western man; it began to find expression in social institutions which were to form the thought and manners of a continent.

The new culture, of course, may be much influenced by the remains of a previous civilization which occupied the same, or neighboring, lands —just as the emerging Western culture was influenced by the Classical. But the basic affirmation of the new culture, though it may be built on many foreign contributions, will be its own, will be characteristic. The Christianity of the West clearly rests on Hebrew, Classical, and Arabian foundations. Yet the religion of Western man is not just a version of a religion from Asia Minor, or from any other part of the dying Roman world. It is a new thing, born with Western culture and unlikely to survive it.

No historian can say why this new thing came to birth during those centuries, and in just that part of the world. But once the thing is born (and assuming that it is given a chance to grow, that it is not wiped out by force), the historian can predict certain stages through which it is likely to pass. He can predict, in the first place, that the life-drama of the new culture will take the form of a conflict between the deep instinctive faith which is the essence of the culture and an abstractly rationalizing self-destructive element which is a feature of man's mind. He can predict that religion (the expression of this deep faith) will dominate in the early period of the culture, that art and abstract thought will for a time be religion's servant. (For Western man, this is the period from the birth of his culture to about the end of the thirteenth century.)

The historian can predict that a little later there will be a second stage, where a more even balance is attained. The inquiring, self-probing mind becomes steadily more confident. Art and thought are secularized, though they are still for the most part in harmony with religion. They have not yet begun their final task of tearing up their own roots. (This is the period corresponding, roughly, to the years 1300–1700 in western Europe.)

The historian could also predict the character of the third period— which has proved the last great period of every previous culture. In this period the perilous balance between faith and critical thought slowly breaks down. The questioning, nihilistic mind, which in the beginning was religion's servant, and in the second period its ally, becomes its master. The instinctive faith weakens; the critical and analytical power is left undirected. In its new freedom it knows a burst of energy. The ardor of the human spirit, which was once shared between heaven and earth, is now lavished solely on practical ends. The results are impressive. In every culture this is the time of imperial expansion, of great world cities, of mechanical triumphs: the giant buildings of Luxor, the Great Wall of China, the straight proud Roman roads across the body of Europe, the straight proud steel belittling the American sky. This is the time when man learns to do so many striking things that his brain is warped with his own grandeur and he makes the mistake of thinking he understands the forces he is using. This is the period reached by Western man in the nineteenth and twentieth centuries.

The historian could go still further. On the basis of the same analogy with other cultures he could predict what is likely to be the mood and meaning of Western man's next stage. There is clearly no proof to these predictions; they are not a doom imposed upon us; but they are a useful warning, for hitherto none of the many cultures of which we have knowledge has escaped this final stage. Seeing what happened in the period comparable to our twentieth century in the Classical world, in the cultures of Egypt, Mesopotamia, India and China, the historian can say that instead of being on the verge of a final triumph Western man is probably on the verge of despair. For the crowning work of man's criticism, having discredited the thought and religion of the past, is to discredit the mind that criticizes. At the moment when intelligence dreams it is about to reach out and explain all things, it wakes to the annihilating theory that explanations are relative, that one is often as good—or as bad—as another. The mind which has dissolved the basic faith on which the whole culture rested, ends by dissolving itself, ends in Classical skepticism, ends in Eastern despair, ends in European nihilism and relativity. For the rootless intellect means nothing, leads nowhere, and cannot even sustain the will to struggle. At the highest point of the Civilization's physical achievement, this poisonous doubt strikes it, and it falls.

When a people have reached this stage of disillusionment, the rest of their story can be imagined. They can still do all their mechanical tricks, but the heart has gone out of such tricks except for the silly few who can enjoy themselves doing nothing but making money. The old faith in religion has faded under the attacks of the critical mind; the new faith in reason has proved a fraud under the self-slaughtering honesty of the same mind. And then appears one of the strangest but most often repeated facts of history. Man is stricken with sterility. In his giant cities he finds himself too bored or too unzestful even to breed normally. Rome was weak with depopulation long before the barbarians pulled her down. Just as the birth of every culture-cycle is marked by a new affirmation of life, the end is marked by a hospitality to death. Man lies down tired in the midst of his marvels. His numbers dwindle, his cities stand half empty, and once again the beasts of the wilderness prowl among ruined buildings.

Spengler reminds us that "Samarra was abandoned by the tenth century; Pataliputra, Asoka's capital, was an immense and completely uninhabited waste of houses when the Chinese traveler, Hsinan-tang, visited it about A.D. 635." And he cites a whole group of late Classical writers—Polybius, Strabo, Pausanias, Dio Chrysostom, Avienus—who tell "of old, renowned cities in which the streets have become lines of empty crumbling shells, where the cattle browse in forum and gymnasium, and the amphitheatre is a sown field, dotted wit hemergent statues and herms." And Mr. Charles Francis Atkinson adds that in the days of the Roman decline, "the amphitheatres of Nîmes and Arles were filled up by mean townlets that used the outer wall as their fortifications." The turn of the population tide in the Western world is clearly foreshadowed today.

In succeeding ages, after such a decline has run its course, the dwindled population takes refuge in the countryside, where, if not attacked from without, it multiplies until it pushes on the limits of subsistence, until it reaches the state of the teeming agricultural East.

A civilization, therefore, may simply fall into inner desuetude, enduring for millenniums as the booty of successive conquerors, like Egypt, or China, or India. But a civilization may also die suddenly, not merely looted but murdered, as happened to Mexico at the hands of the Spaniards. Here was one of the most dramatic confrontations in history: an old civilization where doubt and relativity had clearly done their corrosive work, and a group of energetic bandits from a world that still had trust in itself.

Tenochtitlan was an imperial city, on a scale that Western man was not to create for centuries. "We were amazed," wrote Bernal Diaz del Castillo, who fought with Cortez, "and said that it was like the enchantment they tell of in the legend of Amadis, on account of the great towers and *cues* and buildings rising from the water, and all built of masonry. And some of our soldiers asked whether the things that we saw were not a dream . . . I do not know how to describe it, seeing things as we did that had never been heard of or seen before, not even dreamed about." But the simple Spaniard was wrong. Such things had been seen and heard of many times before: in Imperial Rome, in Baghdad and Tell-el-Amarna, in the world-cities of the last years of every civilization. They were to be seen in the Western world after another four hundred years, by which time London and Paris and New York had taken on shapes that would have startled Cortez's soldiers quite as much as did Tenochtitlan— and by which time, in certain deep and decisive matters, the point of view of London and Paris and New York was closer to that of the Aztec city than to anything that Cortez's men could have understood.

Montezuma, for example, said to Cortez, "Throughout all time we have worshipped our own gods, and thought they were good, as no doubt yours are." Diaz tells us the Spaniards were amazed at such a remark; but a New York literary critic, in 1935, quotes Montezuma with approval, just after calling Spanish Catholicism "a provincial religion." And the critic represents his age faithfully. It is right that he should approve of Montezuma's relativism: world-city is talking to world-city, and they speak the same language. Montezuma was a "civilized" man. He knew that all truths are relative, that all the high eternal gods have ruled over comparatively small areas in space and time. He knew, therefore, that it would be banal to fight over religion. But the fierce and greedy Spaniards knew nothing of the sort. They knew that their religion was *true*—not true for them or true for the sixteenth century, but true for all men forever. So they fell on the tired cosmopolitans of that aging city, and a handful of men abolished one of the world's marvels. . . .

But why should a "civilized" man stir himself to a lot of vulgar fighting?

This cyclical view of history need not breed pessimism. Spengler, the great popularizer of the view, has used it to vent a pathological despair. As if driven to expiate some enormous guilt he offers the whole Western world as sacrifice to Fate, and he knows no words too impolite for the victim who demurs. With a scream of italics and exclamation marks, Spengler falls upon him: This is what *has* to be! History cannot be interfered with! Bare your throats and *don't argue!*

I should think, however, that a sincere Christian would be bound to argue, would be bound to insist that a pattern may have repeated itself eight or ten times and still be only a pattern, not a doom. For instance, it is reasonable to predict a sorry end for a man who has become a steady, sodden drunkard; but it would be stupid to say the man was doomed to such an end. He might have a religious conversion and become a saint. The only safe prediction we can make is that if nothing unusual happens the man will die a sot. Similarly, the only safe prediction about our cosmopolitan civilization is that if nothing unusual happens it will not turn out to be the start of a splendid new era, but the start of another dreary decline. In Europe, the unusual happening might be a revival of Christianity; in America it might be a strengthening of our native, as opposed to our colonial tradition.

While taking this hopeful view it would be wrong to ignore the warnings implicit in the new theory of history. It is right to reject determinism; it is right to insist that if we have the moral energy we can still save our Christian civilization from the fate which struck all the great civilizations that have gone down to the grave; but it is wrong to let ourselves be soothed by the silly dream that good must somehow triumph in the end since man has already progressed all the way from the mud to Mr. Henry Ford. Man has certainly progressed; but the point of the story told by modern archeology and history is that man has also declined, and with sinister regularity. He has not pushed steadily on, with a few temporary setbacks. On the contrary, he has risen again and again to what has seemed the top of his powers, and fallen again and again to a level not far above where he began. There are signs today that he may be preparing to fall once more, and though my own view of America's future is a hopeful one, it would be stupid not to take these signs into account, not to present my hope against the background of a real danger.

The great dividing line in the history of a high culture (such as the Classical, the Egyptian, or that of Western man) is the line between the second and third periods. On the one side of that line there is still a fruitful tension between instinct and intellect; on the other side the balance has been destroyed and the nihilistic mind has silenced the faith on which the whole culture rested. Spengler uses the word *culture* for the period before that fatal division, and the word *civilization* for the period that follows. The use of the words in this sense is arbitrary; but the distinction he makes is useful for an understanding of America today.

In these terms, Sheridan stands for American Culture, the giant city for Civilization. According to the pessimists, who have seized on the cyclical theory of history to justify their best fears, the giant city must win. And it is true that in the past, once the period of civilization has been reached, the clock has never turned back. The giant world-city, with its cosmopolitanism, its skepticism, its falling birthrate, its lack of morals, its imitative and then its decadent art—in the past each time this recurring prodigy has appeared, the stage has been set for an age of Caesars, of wars and dictatorships and aimless crowds kept quiet by doles, or by bread and circuses. In every characteristic detail, we seem to be giving our own Western version of the dejecting picture. Where our religious life, for example, has not been killed by skepticism, it shows signs of decaying into an eclectic superstition. Like the Romans who brought Isis and Ariman to the Tiber, many Westerners today flirt with Buddhism, or follow Hindu fakirs, or make strange mixtures of their own, adding a dash of neo-platonism to a smattering of Lao-tse.

There are good reasons for pessimism. And I agree with the most despairing that if civilization (the point of view of the world-city) became dominant in America, if the judgments, the ambitions, the interests, the conditions and habits of life, represented by Chicago and New York became the standard of the country, we would be old without ever having been young. We would be as old as Europe, but ours would be a graceless old age. No maturity, no serene memories, no wisdom—only decrepitude and loss of purpose. We should not be a rich culture drawing to an end with dignity; we should be just another colonial nation going down hill with (or perhaps before) the parent stock, without ever having been anything on our own. We should deserve the jibe flung at us by

Mr. Belloc in a magnificent passage where he gives the European Christian's answer to the pessimism that assails Europe:

Our Europe cannot perish. Her religion—which is also mine—has in it those victorious energies of defense which neither merchants nor philosophers can understand, and which are yet the prime condition of establishment. Europe, though she must always repel attacks from within and from without, is always secure; the soul of her is a certain spirit, at once reasonable and chivalric. And the gates of hell shall not prevail against her. . . .

Her component peoples have merged and remerged. Her particular famous cities have fallen down. Her soldiers have believed the world to have lost all, because a battle turned against them, Hittin or Leipzig. Her best has at times grown poor and her worst rich. Her colonies have seemed dangerous for a moment from the insolence of their power, and then again (for a moment) from the contamination of their decline. . . . She will certainly remain.

It is a proud boast. And even the attack on America is not unworthy. An American who has lived long abroad knows too well why foreigners take this view. They hear nothing about us except news from our world-cities, plays, and books about our world-cities (or else plays and books and news about our countryside from the point of view of our world-cities). They know America as a civilization; America as an attempt at a culture they do not know at all. And how should they? After six years in London I began to wonder, myself, whether there was such an America, or whether I had made it up and called it memory.

Why should Europe respect us as a big-city civilization? As a civilization we are derivative and second-hand; we have the instability of people who are not themselves. As a civilization we are somebody else's culture grown old. But we, the people, are not old. And the combination, though surprising, does not breed confidence. In art, in talk, in lack of morals, in cosmopolitan nihilism, New York is old. As old as Vienna, yet as vital as a gold-rush camp. The vitality would be attractive if it were lavished on something young; it is bizarre when it is lavished on decay.

There is no capital in Europe where cynicism and defeatism are more constant than in New York. But in Europe they are negative qualities, as fits their nature. In Europe they are a mood of tired disdain. In New York they are boyish and positive as battlecries. In New York men announce their ironies with a kind of hopeful ardor. The cartoonist James Thurber is an illustration. In Europe men are puzzled by Mr. Thurber. Not because they are strangers to his withering view of humanity. Thurber's men and women—small, misshapen, and malignant, sub-human because they have no trace of purpose, no memory of hope; sub-bestial because they have none of the dignity of beasts—Europe is accustomed to this view of human nature. From the early Huysmans to Anatole France to Aldous Huxley, half the cleverest minds have been perfecting it for seventy years. But what perplexes Europe is to find this scornful picture combined with such gaiety. Through all these deadly libels there runs a nursery touch. Enormous rabbits, fantastic misplaced seals, huge comforting dogs—if the men and women could be expunged, these drawings would be decorations for a child's bedroom. The mixture, to someone born in Mr. Thurber's world, is telling. But to many Europeans the mixture is merely distressful. They have their own picture of what age and disillusion should resemble. They do not like to know there can be such things as ancient, contemptuous children.

The mixture of moods that is found in a Thurber drawing is characteristic of New York. These boisterous pessimists, these hearty drunkards, these perverts who declare their barrenness with a happy grin—they make New York an exciting place, a puzzling place. I can see why Europeans should enjoy it, why they should marvel at it. But I cannot see why they should think well of it. I cannot blame them for predicting, like Mr. Belloc, a swift decline.

In Europe, if the soul is growing old, if hope and faith are dying, there is something to fall back on: the eternal tradition of the land, a religion that still makes the lives of millions, a memory of many disasters weathered. But to be old unnaturally, without these memories, without this background, is to be unstable. And Europe, knowing only those spots in America that suffer from abnormal, derivative old age, rightly judges us unstable. Civilization, in America, is derivative. It is colonial, and hence rootless. New York is colonial and rootless. But our provinces are not colonial. American culture, so far as there has been one, is not colonial. Sheridan is a new thing in the world, a product of American soil. But in all essentials, Chicago and New York are as old as Luxor— and just about as important to the future.

These generalizations on culture and the modern world cannot be proved. They are not offered as revelations. They are offered to suggest the following thoughts about our own culture: in America we have the beginning of a culture. It is derived from Europe, of course, and has the same ancestors as the culture of Europe; but it has been here long enough to take on a native character. If it were let alone we might hope for an American contribution to history. It has not been left alone. It has been overlaid, and hampered increasingly, by an alien imitative old age, a colonial-minded old age. The story of America today is the story of the struggle between these two forces. And there are reasons for hoping that the native America may win.

If these generalizations are true, then it is a primary duty for Americans today to be nationally self-conscious, to seek an answer to the question, What is America? If we cannot answer that, we cannot hope to make the real America come true. And if we do nothing, if we drift with the tide of modern history, our country might as well never have been founded. For the tide of modern history, at least in Europe, is not a pretty tide.

PART TWO

THE NATURAL
ORDER

2. The New Landscape

In 1933 the short-lived satiric magazine *Americana* established a feature called "Town and Country," consisting of a page of two juxtaposed photographs: a crowded New York City cemetery contrasted with the beach at Coney Island almost obliterated by the swarm of would-be bathers; an urban shantytown countered by a lovely rolling hillside barely visible because of the billboards that cover it. Traditional landscapes were disappearing and in their place what was emerging was a new landscape, the product largely of the increasingly mobile American and the advanced state of technology that abetted that mobility.

One of the key facts of this period is the vast increase in internal migration. While almost all commentators stress the movement of the "Okies" out of the Dust Bowl in search of a new life, or the increase in unemployed vagrants or tramps—even boy and girl tramps—in the Depression, many fail to report that other Americans were also on the move, often for purposes of sport and recreation, for leisure and tourism as well as for economic and social reasons. This was not only the era of the automobile; it was also the era of the streamlined train and most especially the newly designed Greyhound bus. It was the period that witnessed wide-scale development of the trailer (often significantly called the "mobile home") and with it the trailer camp. It was, indeed, the age of the camp: camps for migrant workers, C.C.C. camps, Hooverville camps of homeless and unemployed, organized camping facilities in public parks, trailer camps, tourist camps with cabins—along with the development of that new institution, the motel—and finally the army camps of World War II.

Americans were on the move and most especially along the new roads and over the new bridges of the era. Since their beginnings in the 1920's, vast federal and local highway systems had become increasingly a fact of the new landscape and with them came other transformations by man-made additions designed to help (and exploit) the traveler on his way. The American painter Edward Hopper (1882–1967) had realized as early as 1928 in his article on Charles Burchfield what he called "the chaos of ugliness" that was the United States and had insisted that man-made transformations of the environment must be included in any effort to paint the American landscape. As early as 1934 *Fortune* saw in the development of

"The Great American Roadside" a phenomenon of such economic and social consequence that it commissioned a major report on the subject for its readers, complete with photographs and paintings by John Steuart Curry. For the tourist cabin and the motel, the trailer and the trailer "park," the hot-dog stand and other short-order food operations for the traveler, had not only become big business but were in the process of transforming the nature of our cultural and social life.

By 1938 tourism was the third largest industry in the United States, next only to steel and to automobile production. Some 4,000,000 Americans traveled every year (four out of five of them by car) and spent some $5,000,000 a year doing so. While many sought lovely and unspoiled land, the beaches and the parks, the sentimental and historical landmarks, by 1938 the biggest single tourist attraction was the recently completed man-made addition to the urban landscape, Rockefeller Center in New York City, which welcomed over 20,000 out-of-towners a day. Even those who went to nature were to discover that designers and planners had often gotten there before them. There was an increasing sense in the 1920's and 1930's that only through the application of planning, design, and management could nature be made most useful for enjoyment and recreation by increased millions. The work of Robert Moses (born 1888) in New York is character-istic; his monument the Jones Beach State Park, with its 2400 acres of choice beach front on Long Island's South Shore, linked to the mainland by thirty-two miles of modern parkway, and only thirty-five miles from New York.

E. B. White (born 1899), the humorist and essayist long associated with the *New Yorker* magazine, had moved in the late 1930's from New York to Maine to escape the social difficulties in urban living and to bring himself reasonably close to natural phenomena. His visit to the site which produced a classic account of another man's effort to come to grips with the natural order provides us with an amusing and ironic disclosure of the transfor-mation that has taken place, largely by those who sought in this century to pay nostalgic respects to the vision of nature of that nineteenth-century writer.

The Great American Roadside

FORTUNE

The characters in our story are five: this American continent; this American people; the automobile; the Great American Road, and—the

From "The Great American Roadside," *Fortune*, 10 (September 1934), pp. 53–56.

Great American Roadside. To understand the American roadside you must see it as a vital and inseparable part of the whole organism, the ultimate expression of the conspiracy that produced it.

As an American, of course, you know these characters. This continent, an open palm spread frank before the sky against the bulk of the world. This curious people. The automobile you know as well as you know the slouch of the accustomed body at the wheel and the small stench of gas and hot metal. You know the sweat and the steady throes of the motor and the copious and thoughtless silence and the almost lack of hunger and the spreaded swell and swim of the hard highway toward and beneath and behind and gone and the parted roadside swarming past. This great road, too; you know that well. How it is scraggled and twisted along the coast of Maine, high-crowned and weak-shouldered in honor of long winter. How in Florida the detours are bright with the sealime of rolled shells. How the stiff wide stream of hard unbroken roadstead spends the mileage between Mexicali and Vancouver. How the road degrades into a rigorous lattice of country dirt athwart Kansas through the smell of hot wheat (and this summer a blindness and a strangulation of lifted dust). How like a blacksnake in the sun it takes the ridges, the green and dim ravines which are the Cumberlands, and lolls loose into the hot Alabama valleys. How in the spectral heat of the Southwest, and the wide sweeps of sage toward the Northwest, it means spare fuel strapped to the running board . . . oh yes, you know this road; and you know this roadside. You know this roadside as well as you know the formulas of talk at the gas station, the welcome taste of a Bar B-Q sandwich, in midafternoon, the oddly excellent feel of a weak-springed bed in a clapboard transient shack, and the early start in the cold bright lonesome air, the dustless and dewy road and the stammering birds, and the day's first hitchhiker brushing the damp hay out of his shirt.

All such things you know. But it may never have sharply occurred to you, for instance, that the 900,000 miles of hard-fleshed highway that this people has built—not just for transportation but to express something not well defined—is by very considerable odds the greatest road the human race has ever built. It may never have occurred to you that upon this continent and along this road this people casually moves in numbers and by distances which make the ancient and the grave migrations of the Celt and the Goth look like a smooth crossing on the Hoboken Ferry. And it may never have occurred to you that the Great American Roadside, where this people pauses to trade, is incomparably the most hugely extensive market the human race has ever set up to tease and tempt and take money from the human race. For only just now are people beginning to realize that these five characters, as they function in relation to one another, combine in simple fact to mean a new way of life, a new but powerfully established American institution. And that the roadside, the most vivid part of this institution, is a young but great industry which will gross, in this, the fifth year of the great world depression, something like $3,000,000,000.

And even if you're aware of these things as they are, it isn't likely that you know just why they grew so fast, just why they are as they are. Because few Americans are really wise to themselves.

When we say point-blank that this institution, this industry, is founded upon just one thing, the restlessness of the American people, it still won't be clear. Because too many sentimental tourists have written of the joys of going "a-gipsying," have talked too much and too loosely of the American pioneer spirit.

The truth is, it isn't at all easy to say right.

God and the conjunction of confused bloods, history, and the bullying of this tough continent to heel, did something to the American people— worked up in their blood a species of restiveness unlike any that any race before has known, a restiveness describable only in negatives. Not to eat, not for love, nor even for money, nor for fear, nor really for adventure, nor truly out of any known necessity is this desire to move upon even the most docile of us. We are restive entirely for the sake of restiveness. Whatever we may think, we move for no better reason than for the plain unvarnished hell of it. And there is no better reason.

So God made the American restive. The American in turn and in due time got into the automobile and found it good. The War exasperated his restiveness and the twenties made him rich and more restive still and he found the automobile not merely good but better and better. It was good because continually it satisfied and at the same time greatly sharpened his hunger for movement: which is very probably the profoundest and most compelling of American racial hungers. The fact is that the automobile became a hypnosis. The automobile became the opium of the American people.

After the autoist had driven round and round for awhile, it became high time that people should catch on to the fact that as he rides there are a thousand and ten thousand little ways you can cash in on him en route. Within the past few years, the time ripened and burst. And along the Great American Road, the Great American Roadside sprang up prodigally as morning mushrooms, and completed a circle which will whirl for pleasure and for profit as long as the American blood and the American car are so happily married.

If you wish to assure yourself, consider Exhibit A: the tourist cabin camp. Like the automobile, it is here to stay.

Much has been written about the auto cabin camp and most of it has been poking fun—at these curious little broods of frame and log and adobe shacks which dot the roadside with their Mother Goose and their Chic Sale architecture, their geranium landscaping, their squeaky beds, and their community showers. Most of the writing has been of the ancient Mencken school. Only in the unornamented pages of a hotel association's annual report has the truth about them been approached. For only hotelmen, viewing them with alarm, have seen them for what they are, both a sound invention and a new way of life. The geraniums and the architecture are inconsequential; what matters is that they offer pure functionalist shelter and that they work. Just as surely as the great Greyhound bus company grew out of the jitney, an industry is growing out of the tourist cabin. Just because it works. And here is how.

It is six in the afternoon and you are still on the road, worn and weary from three hundred miles of driving. Past you flashes a sign DE LUXE CABINS ONE MILE. Over the next hill you catch the vista of a city, smack in your path, sprawling with all its ten thousand impediments to motion—its unmarked routes, its trolley cars, its stop and go signs, its No Parking markers. Somewhere in the middle of it is a second-class commercial hotel, whose drab lobby and whose cheerless rooms you can see with your eyes closed. Beyond, around the corner, eyes still closed, you see the local Ritz with its doormen and its bellboys stretching away in one unbroken greedy grin. You see the unloading of your car as you stand tired and cross, wondering where you can find the nearest garage. Your wife is in a rage because she has an aversion to appearing in public with her face smudged, her hair disarranged and her dress crumpled. All these things and more you see with your eyes closed in two seconds flat. Then you open them. And around the next bend, set back amid a grove of cool trees you see the little semicircle of cabins which the sign warned you of. You pull in by a farmhouse—or a filling station, or a garage—which registers instantly as the mother hen to this brood.

If you are a novice the routine is so simple as to take your breath away. The farmer or the filling-station proprietor or either's daughter appears, puts a casual foot upon the running board, and opens the negotiation with a silent nod. You say "How much are your cabins?" He or she says "Dollar a head. Drive in by No. 7." He or she accompanies you, riding with the ease of habit on the side of your car. You make your inspection. You do not commit yourself—as you do in a hotel—until you see your room. If you don't like it, you drive on—to the next cabin camp.

In this one you find a small, clean room, perhaps ten by twelve. Typically, its furniture is a double bed—a sign may have told you it is a Simmons, with Beautyrest mattress—a table, two kitchen chairs, a small mirror, a row of hooks. In one corner a washbasin with cold running water; in another, the half-opened door to a toilet. There is a bit of chintz curtaining over the screened windows, through which a breeze is blowing. You think once more of the crowded streets ahead, you nod "O.K." and give the proprietor two dollars. He may, but probably won't, give you a card or a register in which to sign a name. He doesn't care what name you write because in case you seriously misbehave he has your car license number, noted as part of his professional routine. So he pockets the two dollars and walks away. That's all. You swing your car in between your cabin and the next. You unload what luggage you need; you have but a few feet to carry it. Inside you have just what you need for a night's rest, neither more nor less. And you have it with a privacy your hotel could not furnish—for this night this house is your own. And in the morning you will leave without ceremony, resume the motion you left off the day before without delay.

The point the satirist misses when he lampoons American folkways is that most folkways make sense. The American people have created the cabin camp because the hotel failed them in their new objective—motion with the least possible interruption. They have money to spend but not on the marble foyers of their forefathers. Their money is dedicated to motion; the cars in cabin camps are not cheap cars. So they have found the cabin camp good because it gives them just exactly what they want, simply and efficiently. And they made it multiply and they called it all kinds of names from the Wee Hame to Sevenoaks Farm, Mo-Tel to Auto Court.

Walden

E. B. WHITE

[*June 1939*]

Miss Nims, take a letter to Henry David Thoreau. Dear Henry: I thought of you the other afternoon as I was approaching Concord doing fifty on Route 62. That is a high speed at which to hold a philosopher in one's mind, but in this century we are a nimble bunch.

On one of the lawns in the outskirts of the village a woman was cutting the grass with a motorized lawn mower. What made me think of

E. B. White, "Walden," in his *One Man's Meat* (New York, 1944), pp. 80–87.

you was that the machine had rather got away from her, although she was game enough, and in the brief glimpse I had of the scene it appeared to me that the lawn was mowing the lady. She kept a tight grip on the handles, which throbbed violently with every explosion of the one-cylinder motor, and as she sheered around bushes and lurched along at a reluctant trot behind her impetuous servant, she looked like a puppy who had grabbed something that was too much for him. Concord hasn't changed much, Henry; the farm implements and the animals still have the upper hand.

I may as well admit that I was journeying to Concord with the deliberate intention of visiting your woods; for although I have never knelt at the grave of a philosopher nor placed wreaths on moldy poets, and have often gone a mile out of my way to avoid some place of historical interest, I have always wanted to see Walden Pond. The account which you left of your sojourn there is, you will be amused to learn, a document of increasing pertinence; each year it seems to gain a little headway, as the world loses ground. We may all be transcendental yet, whether we like it or not. As our common complexities increase, any tale of individual simplicity (and yours is the best written and the cockiest) acquires a new fascination; as our goods accumulate, but not our well-being, your report of an existence without material adornment takes on a certain awkward credibility.

My purpose in going to Walden Pond, like yours, was not to live cheaply or to live dearly there, but to transact some private business with the fewest obstacles. Approaching Concord, doing forty, doing forty-five, doing fifty, the steering wheel held snug in my palms, the highway held grimly in my vision, the crown of the road now serving me (on the righthand curves), now defeating me (on the lefthand curves), I began to rouse myself from the stupefaction which a day's motor journey induces. It was a delicious evening, Henry, when the whole body is one sense, and imbibes delight through every pore, if I may coin a phrase. Fields were richly brown where the harrow, drawn by the stripped Ford, had lately sunk its teeth; pastures were green; and overhead the sky had that same everlasting great look which you will find on page 144 of the Oxford pocket edition. I could feel the road entering me, through tire, wheel, spring, and cushion; shall I not have intelligence with earth too? Am I not partly leaves and vegetable mold myself?—a man of infinite horsepower, yet partly leaves.

Stay with me on 62 and it will take you into Concord. As I say, it was a delicious evening. The snake had come forth to die in a bloody S on the highway, the wheel upon its head, its bowels flat now and exposed. The turtle had come up too to cross the road and die in the attempt, its hard shell smashed under the rubber blow, its intestinal yearning (for the other side of the road) forever squashed. There was a sign by the wayside which announced that the road had a "cotton surface." You wouldn't know what that is, but neither, for that matter, did I. There is a cryptic ingredient in many of our modern improvements—we are awed and pleased without knowing quite what we are enjoying. It is something to be traveling on a road with a cotton surface.

The civilization round Concord today is an odd distillation of city, village, farm, and manor. The houses, yards, fields look not quite suburban, not quite rural. Under the bronze beech and the blue spruce of the departed baron grazes the milch goat of the heirs. Under the porte-cochère stands the reconditioned station wagon; under the grape arbor sit the puppies for sale. (But why do men degenerate ever? What makes families run out?)

It was June and everywhere June was publishing her immemorial stanza; in the lilacs, in the syringa, in the freshly edged paths and the sweetness of moist beloved gardens, and the little wire wickets that preserve the tulips' front. Farmers were already moving the fruits of their toil into their yards, arranging the rhubarb, the asparagus, the strictly fresh eggs on the painted stands under the little shed roofs with the patent shingles. And though it was almost a hundred years since you had taken your ax and started cutting out your home on Walden Pond, I was interested to observe that the philosophical spirit was still alive in Massachusetts: in the center of a vacant lot some boys were assembling the framework of the rude shelter, their whole mind and skill concentrated in the rather inauspicious helter-skeleton of studs and rafters. They too were escaping from town, to live naturally, in a rich blend of savagery and philosophy.

That evening, after supper at the inn, I strolled out into the twilight to dream my shapeless transcendental dreams and see that the car was locked up for the night (first open the right front door, then reach over, straining, and pull up the handles of the left rear and the left front till you hear the click, then the handle of the right rear, then shut the right front but open it again, remembering that the key is still in the ignition switch, remove the key, shut the right front again with a bang, push the tiny keyhole cover to one side, insert key, turn, and withdraw). It is what we all do, Henry. It is called locking the car. It is said to confuse thieves and keep them from making off with the laprobe. Four doors to lock behind one robe. The driver himself never uses a laprobe, the free movement of his legs being vital to the operation of the vehicle; so that when he locks the car it is a pure and unselfish act. I have in my life gained very little essential heat from laprobes, yet I have ever been at pains to lock them up.

The evening was full of sounds, some of which would have stirred your memory. The robins still love the elms of New England villages at sundown. There is enough of the thrush in them to make song inevitable at the end of day, and enough of the tramp to make them hang round the dwellings of men. A robin, like many another American, dearly loves a white house with green blinds. Concord is still full of them.

Your fellow-townsmen were stirring abroad—not many afoot, most of them in their cars; and the sound which they made in Concord at evening was a rustling and a whispering. The sound lacks steadfastness and is wholly unlike that of a train. A train, as you know who lived too near the Fitchburg line, whistles once or twice sadly and is gone, trailing a memory in smoke, soothing to ear and mind. Automobiles, skirting a village green, are like flies that have gained the inner ear—they buzz, cease, pause, start, shift, stop, halt, brake, and the whole effect is a nervous polytone curiously disturbing.

As I wandered along the toc toc of ping pong balls drifted from an attic window. In front of the Reuben Brown house a Buick was drawn up. At the wheel, motionless, his hat upon his head, a man sat, listening to Amos and Andy on the radio (it is a drama of many scenes and without an end). The deep voice of Andrew Brown, emerging from the car, although it originated more than two hundred miles away, was unstrained by distance. When you used to sit on the shore of your pond on Sunday morning, listening to the church bells of Acton and Concord, you were aware of the excellent filter of the intervening atmosphere. Science has attended to that, and sound now maintains its intensity without regard for distance. Properly sponsored, it goes on forever.

A fire engine, out for a trial spin, roared past Emerson's house, hot with readiness for public duty. Over the barn roofs the martins dipped and chittered. A swarthy daughter of an asparagus grower, in culottes, shirt, and bandanna, pedaled past on her bicycle. It was indeed a delicious evening, and I returned to the inn (I believe it was your house once) to rock with the old ladies on the concrete veranda.

Next morning early I started afoot for Walden, out Main Street and down Thoreau, past the depot and the Minuteman Chevrolet Company. The morning was fresh, and in a bean field along the way I flushed an agriculturalist, quietly studying his beans. Thoreau Street soon joined Number 126, an artery of the State. We number our highways nowadays, our speed being so great we can remember little of their quality or character and are lucky to remember their number. (Men have an indistinct notion that if they keep up this activity long enough all will at length ride somewhere, in next to no time.) Your pond is on 126.

I knew I must be nearing your woodland retreat when the Golden Pheasant lunchroom came into view—Sealtest ice cream, toasted sandwiches, hot frankfurters, waffles, tonics, and lunches. Were I the proprietor, I should add rice, Indian meal, and molasses—just for old time's sake. The Pheasant, incidentally, is for sale: a chance for some nature lover who wishes to set himself up beside a pond in the Concord atmosphere and live deliberately, fronting only the essential facts of life on Number 126. Beyond the Pheasant was a place called Walden Breezes, an oasis whose porch pillars were made of old green shutters sawed into lengths. On the porch was a distorting mirror, to give the traveler a comical image of himself, who had miraculously learned to gaze in an ordinary glass without smiling. Behind the Breezes, in a sun-parched clearing, dwelt your philosophical descendants in their trailers, each trailer the size of your hut, but all grouped together for the sake of congeniality. Trailer people leave the city, as you did, to discover solitude and in any weather, at any hour of the day or night, to improve the nick of time; but they soon collect in villages and get bogged deeper in the mud than ever. The camp behind Walden Breezes was just rousing itself to the morning. The ground was packed hard under the heel, and the sun came through the clearing to bake the soil and enlarge the wry smell of cramped house-keeping. Cushman's bakery truck had stopped to deliver an early basket of rolls. A camp dog, seeing me in the road, barked petulantly. A man emerged from one of the trailers and set forth with a bucket to draw water from some forest tap.

Leaving the highway I turned off into the woods toward the pond, which was apparent through the foliage. The floor of the forest was strewn with dried old oak leaves and *Transcripts*. From beneath the flattened popcorn wrapper (*granum explosum*) peeped the frail violet. I followed a footpath and descended to the water's edge. The pond lay clear and blue in the morning light, as you have seen it so many times. In the shallows a man's waterlogged shirt undulated gently. A few flies came out to greet me and convoy me to your cove, past the No Bathing signs on which the fellows and the girls had scrawled their names. I felt strangely excited suddenly to be snooping around your premises, tiptoe-ing along watchfully, as though not to tread by mistake upon the inter-vening century. Before I got to the cove I heard something which seemed to me quite wonderful: I heard your frog, a full, clear *troonk*, guiding me, still hoarse and solemn, bridging the years as the robins had bridged them in the sweetness of the village evening. But he soon quit, and I came on a couple of young boys throwing stones at him.

Your front yard is marked by a bronze tablet set in a stone. Four small granite posts, a few feet away, show where the house was. On top of the tablet was a pair of faded blue bathing trunks with a white stripe. Back of it is a pile of stones, a sort of cairn, left by your visitors as a tribute I suppose. It is a rather ugly little heap of stones, Henry. In fact the hillside itself seems faded, browbeaten; a few tall skinny pines, bare of lower limbs, a smattering of young maples in suitable green, some birches and oaks, and a number of trees felled by the last big wind. It was from the bole of one of these fallen pines, torn up by the roots, that I extracted the stone which I added to the cairn—a sentimental act in which I was interrupted by a small terrier from a nearby picnic group, who confronted me and wanted to know about the stone.

I sat down for a while on one of the posts of your house to listen to the bluebottles and the dragonflies. The invaded glade sprawled shabby and mean at my feet, but the flies were tuned to the old vibration. There were the remains of a fire in your ruins, but I doubt that it was yours; also two beer bottles trodden into the soil and become part of earth. A young oak had taken root in your house, and two or three ferns, unrolling like the ticklers at a banquet. The only other furnishings were a DuBarry pattern sheet, a page torn from a picture magazine, and some crusts in wax paper.

Before I quit I walked clear round the pond and found the place where you used to sit on the northeast side to get the sun in the fall, and the beach where you got sand for scrubbing your floor. On the eastern side of the pond, where the highway borders it, the State has built dressing rooms for swimmers, a float with diving towers, drinking fountains of porcelain, and rowboats for hire. The pond is in fact a State Preserve, and carries a twenty-dollar fine for picking wild flowers, a decree signed in all solemnity by your fellow-citizens Walter C. Wardwell, Erson B. Barlow, and Nathaniel I. Bowditch. There was a smell of creosote where they had been building a wide wooden stairway to the road and the parking area. Swimmers and boaters were arriving; bodies plunged vigorously into the water and emerged wet and beautiful in the bright air. As I left, a boatload of town boys were splashing about in mid-pond, kidding and fooling, the young fellows singing at the tops of their lungs in a wild chorus:

> *Amer-ica, Amer-ica, God shed his grace on thee,*
> *And crown thy good with brotherhood*
> *From sea to shi-ning sea!*

I walked back to town along the railroad, following your custom. The rails were expanding noisily in the hot sun, and on the slope of the roadbed the wild grape and the blackberry sent up their creepers to the track.

The expense of my brief sojourn in Concord was:

Canvas shoes	$1.95	
Baseball bat	.25	gifts to take
Left-handed fielder's glove	1.25	back to a boy
Hotel and meals	4.25	
In all	$7.70	

As you see, this amount was almost what you spent for food for eight months. I cannot defend the shoes or the expenditure for shelter and food: they reveal a meanness and grossness in my nature which you would find contemptible. The baseball equipment, however, is the kind of impediment with which you were never on even terms. You must remember that the house where you practiced the sort of economy which I respect was haunted only by mice and squirrels. You never had to cope with a shortstop.

PART THREE

THE MORAL
ORDER

3. A Definition
of Success

There is certainly nothing surprising in discovering an American commitment to success. We all know about Horatio Alger and have quoted William
James (in his 1906 letter to H. G. Wells) on the great American vice, "the
moral flabbiness born of exclusive worship of the bitch-goddess SUCCESS.
That—with the squalid cash interpretation put upon the word success—is
our national disease." But Dale Carnegie's *How to Win Friends and Influence
People* is nevertheless an extraordinary book. Published first in 1936, it
has since sold over 7,000,000 copies and is believed to be the most widely
circulated book in the history of American writing. It is a key American
document—perhaps *the* key to understanding the emerging culture of America
in the 1930's. Stressing the vital importance of interpersonal relations,
Carnegie rarely linked success with any ultimate material achievement.
Rather, to be successful is to be valued by others and one achieves that by
making others feel important as well. He showed no interest in the grave
social and economic maladjustments so obvious in the world around him.
Yet he managed to hit a fundamental and responsive note in the large
middle-class audience for which he wrote because, for most of them, the
Depression had not necessarily meant economic deprivation; it had, however,
often meant humiliation, shame, loss of status and prestige.

It is striking how certain scientific jargon quickly and easily enters the
regular language of society. No term was perhaps ever so readily adopted
as Alfred Adler's "inferiority complex." Adler's very definition of man—
"To be a man means to suffer from an inferiority feeling which constantly
drives him to overcome it"—somehow seemed most appropriate to the times.
And Carnegie in fact offered his readers a way to overcome their own sense
of inferiority by recognizing this same need in others. Few Americans had
read Adler but many knew and understood what an "inferiority complex" was;
Carnegie hit instinctively at the core of middle-class American fear that had
been heightened by the Depression, a new technological and scientific world
not quite understood, a complex political and social arrangement not so
easily mastered. That fear, that sense of inadequacy, that knowledge that
one might not any more be able to live up to expected standards, that
resultant sense of shame—here was the ground for the acceptance of his
immensely popular book.

The Feeling of Importance

DALE CARNEGIE

There is only one way under high Heaven to get anybody to do anything. Did you ever stop to think of that? Yes, just one way. And that is by making the other person want to do it.

Remember, there is no other way.

Of course, you can make a man want to give you his watch by sticking a revolver in his ribs. You can make an employee give you co-operation —until your back is turned—by threatening to fire him. You can make a child do what you want it to do by a whip or a threat. But these crude methods have sharply undesirable repercussions.

The only way I can get you to do anything is by giving you what you want.

What do you want?

The famous Dr. Sigmund Freud of Vienna, one of the most distinguished psychologists of the twentieth century, says that everything you and I do springs from two motives: the sex urge and the desire to be great.

Professor John Dewey, America's most profound philosopher, phrases it a bit differently. Dr. Dewey says the deepest urge in human nature is "the desire to be important." Remember that phrase: "the desire to be important." It is significant. You are going to hear a lot about it in this book.

What do you want? Not many things, but the few things that you do wish, you crave with an insistence that will not be denied. Almost every normal adult wants—

1. Health and the preservation of life.
2. Food.
3. Sleep.
4. Money and the things money will buy.
5. Life in the hereafter.
6. Sexual gratification.
7. The well-being of our children.
8. A feeling of importance.

Dale Carnegie, *How to Win Friends and Influence People* (New York, 1936). Selection from 92nd Printing of Pocket Book Edition, first published July 1940, pp. 30–40, 98–109.

Almost all these wants are gratified—all except one. But there is one longing almost as deep, almost as imperious, as the desire for food or sleep which is seldom gratified. It is what Freud calls "the desire to be great." It is what Dewey calls the "desire to be important."

Lincoln once began a letter by saying: "Everybody likes a compliment." William James said: "The deepest principle in human nature is the craving to be appreciated." He didn't speak, mind you, of the "wish" or the "desire" or the "longing" to be appreciated. He said the *"craving"* to be appreciated.

Here is a gnawing and unfaltering human hunger; and the rare individual who honestly satisfies this heart-hunger will hold people in the palm of his hand and "even the undertaker will be sorry when he dies."

The desire for a feeling of importance is one of the chief distinguishing differences between mankind and the animals. To illustrate: When I was a farm boy out in Missouri, my father bred fine Duroc-Jersey hogs and pedigreed white-faced cattle. We used to exhibit our hogs and white-faced cattle at the county fairs and livestock shows throughout the Middle West. We won first prizes by the score. My father pinned his blue ribbons on a sheet of white muslin, and when friends or visitors came to the house, he would get out the long sheet of muslin. He would hold one end and I would hold the other while he exhibited the blue ribbons.

The hogs didn't care about the ribbons they had won. But Father did. These prizes gave him a feeling of importance.

If our ancestors hadn't had this flaming urge for a feeling of importance, civilization would have been impossible. Without it, we should have been just about like the animals.

It was this desire for a feeling of importance that led an uneducated, poverty-stricken grocery clerk to study some law books that he found in the bottom of a barrel of household plunder that he had bought for fifty cents. You have probably heard of this grocery clerk. His name was Lincoln.

It was this desire for a feeling of importance that inspired Dickens to write his immortal novels. This desire inspired Sir Christopher Wren to design his symphonies in stone. This desire made Rockefeller amass millions that he never spent! And this same desire made the richest man in your town build a house far too large for his requirements.

This desire makes you want to wear the latest styles, drive the latest car, and talk about your brilliant children.

It is this desire which lures many boys into becoming gangsters and gunmen. "The average young criminal of today," says E. P. Mulrooney, former Police Commissioner of New York, "is filled with ego, and his first request after arrest is for those lurid newspapers that make him out a hero. The disagreeable prospect of taking a 'hot squat' in the electric chair seems remote, so long as he can gloat over his likeness sharing space with pictures of Babe Ruth, La Guardia, Einstein, Lindbergh, Toscanini, or Roosevelt."

If you tell me how you get your feeling of importance, I'll tell you what you are. That determines your character. That is the most significant thing about you. For example, John D. Rockefeller got his feeling of importance by giving money to erect a modern hospital in Peking, China, to care for millions of poor people whom he had never seen and never would see. Dillinger, on the other hand, got his feeling of importance by being a bandit, a bank robber and killer. When the G-men were hunting him, he dashed into a farmhouse up in Minnesota and said, "I'm Dillinger!" He was proud of the fact that he was Public Enemy Number One. "I'm not going to hurt you, but I'm Dillinger!" he said.

Yes, the one significant difference between Dillinger and Rockefeller is how they got their feeling of importance.

History sparkles with amusing examples of famous people struggling for a feeling of importance. Even George Washington wanted to be called "His Mightiness, the President of the United States"; and Columbus pleaded for the title, "Admiral of the Ocean and Viceroy of India." Catherine the Great refused to open letters that were not addressed to "Her Imperial Majesty"; and Mrs. Lincoln, in the White House, turned upon Mrs. Grant like a tigress and shouted, "How dare you be seated in my presence until I invite you!"

Our millionaires helped finance Admiral Byrd's expedition to the Antarctic with the understanding that ranges of icy mountains would be named after them; and Victor Hugo aspired to have nothing less than the city of Paris renamed in his honor. Even Shakespeare, mightiest of the mighty, tried to add luster to his name by procuring a coat of arms for his family.

People sometimes become invalids in order to win sympathy and attention, and get a feeling of importance. For example, take Mrs. Mc-Kinley. She got a feeling of importance by forcing her husband, the President of the United States, to neglect important affairs of state while he reclined on the bed beside her for hours at a time, his arms about her, soothing her to sleep. She fed her gnawing desire for attention by insisting that he remain with her while she was having her teeth fixed, and once created a stormy scene when he had to leave her alone with the dentist while he kept an appointment with John Hay.

Mary Roberts Rinehart once told me of a bright, vigorous young woman who became an invalid in order to get a feeling of importance. "One day," said Mrs. Rinehart, "this woman had been obliged to face something, her age perhaps, and the fact that she would never be married. The lonely years were stretching ahead and there was little left for her to anticipate.

"She took to her bed; and for ten years her old mother traveled to the third floor and back, carrying trays, nursing her. Then one day the old mother, weary with service, lay down and died. For some weeks, the invalid languished; then she got up, put on her clothing and resumed living again.

Some authorities declare that people may actually go insane in order to find, in the dreamland of insanity, the feeling of importance that has been denied them in the harsh world of reality. There are more patients suffering from mental diseases in the hospitals in the United States than from all other diseases combined. If you are over fifteen years of age and residing in New York State, the chances are one out of twenty that you will be confined to an asylum for seven years of your life.

What is the cause of insanity?

Nobody can answer such a sweeping question as that, but we know that certain diseases, such as syphilis, break down and destroy the brain cells and result in insanity. In fact, about one-half of all mental diseases can be attributed to such physical causes as brain lesions, alcohol, toxins, and injuries. But the other half—and this is the appalling part of the story—the other half of the people who go insane apparently have nothing organically wrong with their brain cells. In post-mortem examinations, when their brain tissues are studied under the highest-powered microscopes, they are found to be apparently just as healthy as yours and mine.

Why do these people go insane?

I recently put that question to the head physician of one of our most important hospitals for the insane. This doctor, who has received the highest honors and the most coveted awards for his knowledge of insanity, told me frankly that he didn't know why people went insane. Nobody knows for sure. But he did say that many people who go insane find in insanity a feeling of importance that they were unable to achieve in the world of reality. Then he told me this story:

"I have a patient right now whose marriage proved to be a tragedy. She wanted love, sexual gratification, children, and social prestige; but life blasted all her hopes. Her husband didn't love her. He refused even to eat with her, and forced her to serve his meals in his room upstairs. She had no children, no social standing. She went insane; and, in her imagination, she divorced her husband and resumed her maiden name. She now believes she has married into the English aristocracy, and she insists on being called Lady Smith.

"And as for children, she imagines now that she has a new child every night. Each time I call on her she says: 'Doctor, I had a baby last night.'"

Life once wrecked all her dream ships on the sharp rocks of reality; but in the sunny, fantastic isles of insanity, all her barkentines race into port with canvas billowing and with winds singing through the masts.

Tragic? Oh, I don't know. Her physician said to me: "If I could stretch out my hand and restore her sanity, I wouldn't do it. She's much happier as she is."

As a group, insane people are happier than you and I. Many enjoy being insane. Why shouldn't they? They have solved their problems. They will write you a check for a million dollars, or give you a letter of introduction to the Aga Khan. They have found in a dream world of their own creation the feeling of importance which they so deeply desired.

If some people are so hungry for a feeling of importance that they actually go insane to get it, imagine what miracles you and I can achieve by giving people honest appreciation this side of insanity.

There have been, so far as I know, only two people in history who were paid a salary of a million dollars a year: Walter Chrysler and Charles Schwab.

Why did Andrew Carnegie pay Schwab a million dollars a year or more than three thousand dollars a day? Why?

Because Schwab is a genius? No. Because he knew more about the manufacture of steel than other people? Nonsense. Charles Schwab told me himself that he had many men working for him who knew more about the manufacture of steel than he did.

Schwab says that he was paid this salary largely because of his ability to deal with people. I asked him how he did it. Here is his secret set down in his own words—words that ought to be cast in eternal bronze and hung in every home and school, every shop and office in the land—words that children ought to memorize instead of wasting their time memorizing the conjugation of Latin verbs or the amount of the annual rainfall in Brazil—words that will all but transform your life and mine if we will only live them:

I consider my ability to arouse enthusiasm among the men, said Schwab, the greatest asset I possess, and the way to develop the best that is in a man is by appreciation and encouragement.

There is nothing else that so kills the ambitions of a man as criticisms from his superiors. I never criticize anyone. I believe in giving a man incentive to work. So I am anxious to praise but loath to find fault. If I like anything, I am hearty in my approbation and lavish in my praise.

That is what Schwab does. But what does the average man do? The exact opposite. If he doesn't like a thing, he raises the Old Harry; if he does like it, he says nothing.

"In my wide association in life, meeting with many and great men in various parts of the world," Schwab declared, "I have yet to find the man, however great or exalted his station, who did not do better work and put forth greater effort under a spirit of approval than he would ever do under a spirit of criticism."

That, he said frankly, was one of the outstanding reasons for the phenomenal success of Andrew Carnegie. Carnegie praised his associates publicly as well as privately.

Carnegie wanted to praise his assistants even on his tombstone. He wrote an epitaph for himself which read: "Here lies one who knew how to get around him men who were cleverer than himself."

Sincere appreciation was one of the secrets of Rockefeller's success in handling men. For example, when one of his partners, Edward T. Bedford, pulled a boner and lost the firm a million dollars by a bad buy in South America, John D. might have criticized; but he knew Bedford had done his best—and the incident was closed. So Rockefeller found something to praise; he congratulated Bedford because he had been able to save sixty per cent of the money he had invested. "That's splendid," said Rockefeller. "We don't always do as well as that upstairs."

Ziegfeld, the most spectacular *entrepreneur* who ever dazzled Broadway, gained his reputation by his subtle ability to "glorify the American girl." He repeatedly took some drab little creature that no one ever looked at twice and transformed her on the stage into a glamorous vision of mystery and seduction. Knowing the value of appreciation and confidence, he made women *feel* beautiful by the sheer power of his gallantry and consideration. He was practical: he raised the salary of chorus girls from thirty dollars a week to as high as one hundred and seventy-five. And he was also chivalrous: on opening night at the Follies, he sent a telegram to the stars in the cast, and he deluged every chorus girl in the show with American Beauty roses.

I once succumbed to the fad of fasting and went for six days and nights without eating. It wasn't difficult. I was less hungry at the end of the sixth day than I was at the end of the second. Yet I know, and you know, people who would think they had committed a crime if they let their families or employees go for six days without food; but they will let them go for six days, and six weeks, and sometimes sixty years without giving them the hearty appreciation that they crave almost as much as they crave food.

When Alfred Lunt played the stellar role in *Reunion in Vienna*, he said, "There is nothing I need so much as nourishment for my self-esteem."

We nourish the bodies of our children and friends and employees; but how seldom do we nourish their self-esteem. We provide them with roast beef and potatoes to build energy; but we neglect to give them kind words of appreciation that would sing in their memories for years like the music of the morning stars.

Some readers are saying right now as they read these lines: "Old stuff! Soft soap! Bear oil! Flattery! I've tried that stuff. It doesn't work—not with intelligent people."

Of course, flattery seldom works with discerning people. It is shallow, selfish, and insincere. It ought to fail and it usually does. True, some people are so hungry, so thirsty, for appreciation that they will swallow anything, just as a starving man will eat grass and fish worms.

Why, for example, were the much-married Mdivani brothers such flaming successes in the matrimonial market? Why were these so-called "princes" able to marry two beautiful and famous screen stars and a world-famous prima donna and Barbara Hutton with her five-and-ten-cent-store millions? Why? How did they do it?

"The Mdivani charm for women," said Adela Rogers St. John, in an article in the magazine *Liberty*, ". . . has been among the mysteries of the ages to many.

"Pola Negri, a woman of the world, a connoisseur of men, and a great artist, once explained it to me. She said, 'They understand the art of flattery as do no other men I have ever met. And the art of flattery is almost a lost one in this realistic and humorless age. That, I assure you, is the secret of the Mdivani charm for women, I know.'"

Even Queen Victoria was susceptible to flattery. Disraeli confessed that he put it on thick in dealing with the Queen. To use his exact words, he said he "spread it on with a trowel." But Disraeli was one of the most polished, deft, and adroit men who ever ruled the far-flung British Empire. He was a genius in his line. What would work for him wouldn't necessarily work for you and me. In the long run, flattery will do you more harm than good. Flattery is counterfeit, and like counterfeit money, it will eventually get you into trouble if you try to pass it.

The difference between appreciation and flattery? That is simple. One is sincere and the other insincere. One comes from the heart out; the other from the teeth out. One is unselfish; the other selfish. One is universally admired; the other is universally condemned.

I recently saw a bust of General Obregon in the Chapultepec palace in Mexico City. Below the bust are carved these wise words from

General Obregon's philosophy: "Don't be afraid of the enemies who attack you. Be afraid of the friends who flatter you."

No! No! No! I am not suggesting flattery! Far from it. I'm talking about a new way of life. Let me repeat. *I am talking about a new way of life.*

King George V had a set of six maxims displayed on the walls of his study at Buckingham Palace. One of these maxims said: "Teach me neither to proffer nor receive cheap praise." That's all flattery is: cheap praise. I once read a definition of flattery that may be worth repeating: "Flattery is telling the other man precisely what he thinks about himself."

"Use what language you will," said Ralph Waldo Emerson, "you can never say anything but what you are."

If all we had to do was to use flattery, everybody would catch on to it and we should all be experts in human relations.

When we are not engaged in thinking about some definite problem, we usually spend about 95 per cent of our time thinking about ourselves. Now, if we stop thinking about ourselves for awhile and begin to think of the other man's good points, we won't have to resort to flattery so cheap and false that it can be spotted almost before it is out of the mouth.

Emerson said: "Every man I meet is my superior in some way. In that, I learn of him."

If that was true of Emerson, isn't it likely to be a thousand times more true of you and me? Let's cease thinking of our accomplishments, our wants. Let's try to figure out the other man's good points. Then forget flattery. Give honest, sincere appreciation. Be "hearty in your approbation and lavish in your praise," and people will cherish your words and treasure them and repeat them over a lifetime—repeat them years after you have forgotten them.

4. Not Such Nice Work If You Can Get It

Since the turn of the century we have accumulated a vast literature on what has come to be called the Protestant Ethic; we have learned how vital an ethic that stressed the powerful value of work was to the social, economic, and religious order of the modern era. The belief in that value persisted in the period after 1929; it was reinforced by our popular songs and by popular religion.

But at least two factors had already begun sorely to test the attachment to the work ethic both before and immediately after the Crash. First, the increased mechanization of the processes of industry—creating as it did early in the century the assembly line—led increasingly to the worker's boredom, fatigue, low morale and discontent. He increasingly questioned the value, not of his employment, but of the work he did and the value of his doing it. Fiction and films (witness, for example, Charlie Chaplin's *Modern Times* of 1936), sociological, psychological, and journalistic studies proposed serious questions and provided significant data about life on the assembly line. Secondly, the problem of work was further complicated by the fact of vast unemployment. The development of programs of welfare and social security raised only more questions for a society committed to the ethic of work. What happened to those who had to make a living but could no longer work —in terms of the traditional definition of and value placed upon "working" for a living rather than simply "making" a living?

In 1932 the Institute of Human Relations at Yale University began an important series of studies which resulted, in 1940, in the publication of two volumes by the economist E. Wight Bakke (born 1903), the director of the unemployment studies: *The Unemployed Worker* and *Citizens Without Work*. These volumes constitute a major effort to see the workers as members of a community striving toward certain goals within a particular cultural environment, using whatever personal equipment they might have in terms of practices—familial, recreational, religious, political, economic—to adjust to life without a job. Finally, these studies attempt to assess the effect of this experience not only on workers' life-styles but also upon their basic values.

Gene Richards, at the time he wrote his article, "On the Assembly Lines," was an automobile worker in his twenties. His editors at *Atlantic Monthly* said of him: "He is probably more sensitive to the strain of routine operations than the average automobile worker; before entering the factory he had some slight experience as a professional musician. Again, he is not typical because he is more articulate in expression than most of his mates, few of whom could identify and express the tensions which harass them." The attitudes of the editors need no special comment but they belong in the record of the American search for culture.

On the Assembly Line

GENE RICHARDS (Time Clock No. 1135284)

As I walk down the steps with many others, I am disturbed by the thought that the day is only beginning. I suddenly realize in one sensation that there is no escape. It is all unavoidably real and painful. How much energy I must expend today has been predetermined by my employer. I try to disregard the thought that is causing this nervous tension which will be with me throughout the hours. Around me I sense a similar reaction. It expresses itself in silence. Men are laughing insincerely. They are ashamed of their emotion. They would rather feel that they were at peace and not a part of this herd who can hide nothing of their day from each other.

The men wander quietly into their places. The shop is beautiful. Machines, blue steel, huge piles of stock. Interesting patterns of windows are darkened by the early hour. This is the impression one gets before he becomes a part of the thing. The beauty is perceivable then. The unbiased observer cannot relate it to the subjective outlook he later acquires.

There is a shrill note. It is impersonal, commanding, and it expresses the entire power which orders the wheels set in motion. The conveyor begins to move immediately. Mysteriously the men are in their places and at work. A man near me grasps the two handles of the air wrench he holds all day long. This is the extent of his operation. He leans forward to each nut as the machine does its work. One nut—two nuts—one motor. It is not necessary for him to change his position. The conveyor brings the next motor to him. One position, one job all day.

Noise is deafening: a roar of machines and the groaning and moaning of hoists; the constant *pssffft-pssffft* of the air hoses. One must shout to be heard. After a time the noise becomes a part of what is natural

Gene Richards, "On the Assembly Line," *Atlantic Monthly*, 159 (April 1937), pp. 424–428.

and goes unnoticed. It merely dulls for the time the particular sense of hearing.

Truss works next to me. We are breaking a man in. There is a lot of experimenting to find out how to divide the jobs so as to achieve the maximum of group efficiency. The job is new to me, too. We are putting fuel connections on the carburetor. Between Truss and me we do three men's work. We cannot keep up. Luckily we know enough not to take it out on each other. We cuss and work in a fit of nervousness. The nut which is supposed to be previously tightened for me won't screw down because it is a bit undersized. I try to tighten it with my fingers, but I keep slipping behind. I am losing my temper. The foreman and relief man have been filling in occasionally for the man who should be there. We just can't do it. Truss snaps out, "Hell with 'em! Let their damn motors go by if we can't get 'em!" We work and mumble curses. I finally discover how to put my wrench in the hole in such a way as to bite it into the soft brass and twist the lock nut down to where I can get a wrench on it. My ingenuity works out to save my fingers, but to my disgust is merely adding to the possibility of Truss and me doing the job without help.

"Watch your quality today, men," says Sammy, the squat line foreman. We are working so fast I don't see how anyone can think of quality. The old fellow next to me seems to be having trouble keeping up. He is supposed to run in a bolt on a clamp that I straighten and tighten with a hand wrench. When he gets behind I get behind, too. I take his ratchet wrench and do the added operation myself. I do this to two or three motors and give it back. Finally I just keep the wrench and do the added operation myself. I'll get sore each time I'm put behind anyway, so, to guarantee my own peace, I assume the extra work. He looks at me with mild appreciation and I go on feeling that I have big enough shoulders to make it easier for him. At least I'm younger and he's probably quite tired.

Up in the lavatory I usually lean out the window for a breath of fresh air. The out-of-doors smells fresh and free and reminds me how different it was when I could be outside and away from all this overwhelming noise and steel structure. But I can't take more than two or three breaths, for I must hurry back to the call of my stimulated conscience.

Men about me are constantly cursing and talking filth. Something about the monotonous routine breaks down all restraint. The men in most cases have little in common, but they must talk. The work will not absorb the mind of the normal man, so they must think. The feeling of isolation here leads one to the assurance that his confidences will never escape. Truss, without a trace of conscience, speaks of his more intimate relations with his wife. We work on and on with spurts of conversation. Suddenly a man breaks forth with a mighty howl. Others follow. We set up a howling all over the shop. It is a relief, this howling.

As the long-anticipated whistle blows for lunch the men burst into the aisles. There is a rule: "No running." Some of the men have developed a lunch-hour walk which is hard to distinguish from a run.

I am sitting on the greasy floor of the lunchroom leaning my back against the rail at the head of the stairs. The lunchroom is a great hall with many tables for the men to eat on. At the top of the stairs is a series of cages wide enough for a man to pass through when he rings his clock card. Twenty or thirty clocks are ringing, *ding-dong, ding-dong,* steadily for half an hour before the men go down to work. The floor is black from the dirty shoes. Some men's shoes are so soaked with oil that the surfaces shine and ooze at each step. The general manner of dress is not neat. The average worker probably wears a pair of work pants or old pants and a blue, brown, or black work shirt. Some wear vests. An old vest will protect the shirt and make a man feel dressed. In the cooler weather the whole costume can be covered when leaving the shop. In many cases it is done in such a manner as to create the illusion that the man is dressed much better than he really is. He usually has an old hat which, although it has become worn and dirty from handling, still retains form. An old topcoat then serves to disguise the rest.

In spite of the poorly regulated lives of these men, many gain weight. There are a great number of big massive hulks. This creates the impression of power. But I seldom see a man with a well-proportioned body. Some have a high left shoulder while the right droops. Some have large gnarled hands, the fingers of which fail to respond readily. Many hands lack a finger here and there. Most of the older men have a larger amount of beef in the region of the buttocks than they need. A protruding belly is almost the rule with the men who have been here long. The stomach muscles become relaxed and deformed from standing long hours in one position. I wonder if these men can be healthy. I suspect that they all have some nature of illness. The prevalence of halitosis might be accounted for some way.

Some of these men develop a surprisingly self-important air as though they were not a part of the group. They flaunt their independence. It has had me fooled since I've been here. Their attitude is effective, yet I sense there is something in it that is off color. The place has robbed these men of their true capacities and denied them a life of growth; but it cannot force them to be humble. Their outward front expresses an ownership of all those things they haven't got. They do even the most menial jobs with an air of great responsibility.

The shrill whistle blows. Some men start. It works as well as a whip. There is a rustling of clothing, a dropping of feet, and a prayerlike flow of voices as we go down the stairs.

This afternoon I am transferred to the rod department. My job is to weigh one end of the rod and stripe it with paint according to the colors indicated on the scale. There are usually a few piles of rods beside each man. The men figure it looks better to work this way. I take a rod off the pile and throw it on the scale, which is so made that the rod will sit on two pegs. The color is posted on the indicator instead of the weight, so all the operator needs to know is one color from another. I then pick up another rod, and as I take the first one off I put the next one on. While the scale is coming to a rest I paint the small end of the rod in my hand with a stripe corresponding to its weight. No time is lost. One soon gets so he can take a rod off the scale before it comes to a rest and predict where it will stop. As a matter of fact, to paint 5000 rods a day this is almost necessary.

As I am painting the small end of the rod I realize that I am not conscious of what I am doing. My accuracy surprises me. I seldom make a mistake, yet I never have my mind on my work. Perhaps this is why I am able to obtain accuracy, because my subconscious is more capable of this monotony than my personality.

It is soon after lunch. Someone has heard someone who heard someone else say the line was going home at two-thirty. Gradually it becomes a subject of discussion. Karl says to the bearer of the news, "You wouldn't kid me, would ya? 'Cause that's a dirty trick." "Well, I heard a guy ask a foreman," he said. We all know a foreman doesn't usually know any more than anyone else, yet we wishfully take stock in the rumor. The spirit of some men rises. Two o'clock finally arrives and there is no word yet. Karl curses the fellow who started the rumor. We still have hope, however, because we hate to abandon any chance of such a pleasant anticipation. After two o'clock we lose spirit.

Sometimes my thoughts will not hold me down. I think about all the mean things I have done, and all the things about myself I disrespect. Or I grow angry at some person out of my past. My thoughts go on and torture me. They are thoughts which I am sure are not sane. I try to stop thinking them and find that I don't really want to. I want to think them through until they satisfy me, and hope they will not come back. They do—and the process begins all over again. I cannot think them through to any finality because my work is constantly bringing me back to consciousness. These days and hours are bad. Sometimes I can lick my anxieties and think more objective thoughts. When I have contact with outside interests I can live them through the long hours of the day.

Some days I have two or three good topics for thought. Then I am at peace and will postpone each pleasant thought smugly with anticipation. As a beginner, I would try to think how fast each period of the day would go. This is a hard thing to get any satisfaction from. The day is just so long, and one gets to be as good a time reckoner as a clock.

I find now that I can put my mind to use. I have gained one thing from this hell. I have learned discipline. I can concentrate for an hour on one subject. But my efforts are fast losing direction. I have lost contact with anything to think about.

Today I am thinking, as usual, depressed thoughts. I have heard these thoughts, some of them, expressed before, but now I am feeling them from dire reality. I have worked long hours this week. Each day I go to work in the dark and leave in the dark. I have not seen daylight since Sunday, and it is Saturday afternoon. I feel strangely unimportant and insignificant. The experiences of the day have exposed my mode of existence in such a way that I see my relative position here too plainly and deeply for my own comfort. I realize how unimportant is personal worth here. When I come in the gate in the morning I throw off my personality and assume a personality which expresses the institution of which I am a part. The only personality expressed here is the personality of the employer, through those authorized to represent him. There is no market for one's personal quality. Any expression of my own individual self beyond the scope of my work is in bad taste.

When a man insinuates here by any action that he is an individual, he is made to feel that he is not only out of place but doing something dishonorable. One feels that even the time he spends in the lavatory is not a privilege but an imposition. He must hurry back because there are no men to spare. After hours on one operation I realize that the only personal thing required of me is just enough consciousness to operate my body as a machine. Any consciousness beyond that is a contribution to my discomfort and maladjustment. I am a unit of labor, and labor is cheap. There is no market or appreciation of my worth except my self-respect. I struggle to keep it. My mood is perhaps a result of a discussion over the bench with Glen. He says, "No matter whatcha do, they gotcha licked." It makes me depressed to see him take himself so cheaply. He is convinced of his lack of value here. I feel a sudden wave of fear that I might some day feel exactly as he does.

Some of the men are taking to horseplay. Horseplay among bench workers has less limitation than among line workers. The bosses are not intolerant of horseplay. It is a noticeable fact that they will tolerate it where they will deal severely with serious loafing. As we are working we are unexpectedly interrupted by the foreman. He steps up between

Karl and me. While we stop work and look around, he starts slowly to pave the way for what is to be a bawling out. His Swedish accent drawls out:

Now listen, fellas. I don't know whether anybody ever tolja this before or whether ya know how it looks from the outside [glides his fingers over the bench in pattern of self-justification], but I'm gonna tell ya now. Now I ain't kickin' on how much work yer gittin' out er how well yer doin' it. Yer gittin' out enough perductchin and yer work's fine; but whatcher doin' is shovin' a whole buncha rods down the bench in a hurry and then gangin' up an talkin'. Now if any one a those big shots come down 'ere an' see one guy leanin' on the bench like this, another guy over here standin' around, some guys bunched up here, an' everything all goin' ta hell, they wonder what kinda buncha guys they got down here and a hellova man runnin' it. Now I been takin' a lot up there lately an' I ain't been sayin' nothin'. Now I don't want to be a —— ——, but if I hafta I will. Those guys been comin' down here lately an' I been hearin' about it. They're kickin' an' they got a kick comin'. So —— damn it; you fellas work with me an' —— damn it I'll work with you, 'cause—well—ya see how it is, doncha? I ain't kickin' about yer work, but what I wancha ta do is—work a little slower if ya hafta and a little steadier.

We start back to work in silence. It leaves a bad taste and we feel as though we really had been falling down on the job. Later we see him making the rounds, so we feel at least it wasn't meant just for us. We slip into some pretty childish ruts sometimes. We are so completely dulled by our work that trivial and boyish pranks amuse us. We cuss and talk filth.

When four-thirty finally arrives we get word that we are working until six. We have all settled into sullen moods. No one has a thing to say. We are grieved at this regular policy of detaining us without consulting us. Karl is working seriously for some time and finally drops back on one foot and bellows: "—— damn it I'm gettin' sick of this stuff. I guess we never will get out of here before daylight." He grabs the nearest rod and slams it down on the bench. I am mad too, so I egg him on. We take it out on the most faithful man in the department. Later we take to hollering to build up a morale which will help us lick the last hour. Finally we are walking out, punching our cards. Laughter is now sincere but weary. It is still dark on the outside. I am so dulled that I have gotten here without realizing it. I stop—ponder. I can't think where I parked my car: the morning was so long ago.

The Meaning of the Job

E. WIGHT BAKKE

High on the list of circumstances which set boundaries to the worker's field of activity and achievement is income. There are few subjects about which there is more talk, less understanding, and more feeling than this. Few workers in New Haven *make* a living. Each *buys* a living with money received primarily from wages. The fact is an important clue to what they do and think and hope for. The pay envelope or the salary check gives to each an individual claim upon what all in cooperation have produced. But wages are more than that—they set standards of prestige, they give a measure of a man's worth, they make spending habits a measure of character, and they furnish us with a whole set of practices which make our culture distinctive. In an earlier day when money was not the key to most of life, money did not drive men on to exceptional effort, nor the lack of it to drink.

In New Haven in the twentieth century, if one were to take away the making and the spending of money, most societal arrangements would collapse. We should be confused about who was successful and why. Society bluebooks would have to be revised. The development of enterprises involving billions of dollars would no longer startle the imagination and we should have to get our vicarious thrills from thinking about those who went looking for a sacred cup. We should be forced to find another set of qualifications for some (not all) of our directors of nonprofit agencies. The "upper" classes would have to find some way other than spending money to make them different from the "lower" classes. We should not be considering wages as one of the major facts in the lives of New Haven workers.

For it is the fact that we have arranged in our society to give a man a pay envelope for doing his work and then leave him to live or not, to save or not, to spend or not, to marry or not, to have children or not, to work or not—it is just that fact that makes the amount and the steadiness of the wage, and the arrangements we make to fill in the gap when there is no envelope, so important.

Now the fact that wages and the buying of a living with wages and

Selections from E. Wight Bakke, *The Unemployed Worker: A Study of the Task of Making a Living without a Job* (New Haven, 1940), pp. 63–67, 80–82, 87–91; and *Citizens Without Work: A Study of the Effects of Unemployment upon Workers' Social Relations and Practices* (New Haven, 1940), pp. 247–251.

the determining of a social status by wages are all part of the folk-ways is in itself no more a distinctive problem of labor than its being customary for men to wear low-heeled shoes is. It is the fact that those wages do not buy the kind of living men would like to have, possibly that they will have to have if our present organization of industry sur-vives—that is what makes the wages of men a labor problem. Mr. Dooley once put a part of the issue this way—"Wan iv the strangest things about life is that th' poor, who need the money th' most, ar-re the viry wans that niver have it."

Very few of our informants earned more than $1000 a year. Only six of our informants had had family incomes of over $1500 when employed. In 1932–33 over two-fifths of the families in New Haven reported incomes below $1000, and three-fifths, incomes of less than $1500.* The propor-tions would be much larger, of course, if only the working classes were considered. . . .

It is not surprising under such circumstances that workers whose incomes hover around $1000 to $1500 a year feel underpaid. They need no union organizer to tell them that. The feeling is a product of the inade-quacy of the wages they receive to meet their problems of living com-fortably. It is not a product of comparison of their wage with the value they give to their employer nor of a comparison with what *he* has. Ideas of the relationship of wages to work may be seen from a very typical response. "What is a fair wage? Now you've got me; but it would be enough to live on without worry and it would come regular. I guess really what I mean when I say fair wages is more wages."

Very few coupled the cost of living with wages in judging the ade-quacy of the latter. Wives are more likely to consider the prices of goods in their judgment of the adequacy of wages than were the actual bread-winners. To most of the latter, high earnings meant high money wages. As one man put it—"You get satisfaction out of handling larger sums of money, even if it doesn't buy you as much." . . .

Second only in importance to the amount of wages is their regularity. Since the adjustment to the major irregularity caused by unemployment is to be the main theme of our discussion, it will be unnecessary to do more than record this fact now. The difficulties in, and indeed the im-possibility of, undertaking any systematic plan for accomplishing results must be evident if the income so necessary to implementing those plans is irregular. The importance of this factor in the life of a worker's family is clearly evident from the response to our question as to whether on the whole they would prefer high but irregular wages or lower but regular

* Thelma A. Dreis, A *Handbook of Social Statistics of New Haven, Con-necticut*, p. 124.

wages. Out of every hundred, ninety voted unhesitatingly for the latter, three (one American, two Italians) preferred the high but irregular wages, and seven couldn't make up their minds. Our informants were of course unemployed, or had recently been unemployed, and this fact undoubtedly influenced their judgment. It is no longer possible, however, to consider the reactions of the unemployed as a minority opinion to be discounted in favor of the reactions of employed men. The condition of irregularity of work may vary in degree, but it is ever present in some degree as a problem demanding adjustment from all workers. Only one-fourth of the two hundred unemployed we interviewed in 1933 had had no previous major spell of unemployment.

A few of the workers' own comments will make more clear what is meant by "getting ahead." "What was the chief satisfaction which you derived from work?" we asked. In view of the several noneconomic goals for which these same men were striving, in view of the changes they would have made in their work, opportunities, and environments in order the better to achieve these noneconomic goals, the realized satisfactions of actual experience are an interesting commentary on the degree to which employment for wages makes it possible for men to realize their ambitions.

One type of response made by about 15 per cent of our informants emphasized the value of work as "keeping a man normal."

That's what we're made for, work is. If you don't work you ain't human.

Work is necessary to keep a man's mind at ease.

Work is necessary to keep from going crazy.

What is life without a job? You are nobody.

Work is a necessary discipline. It's tough discipline but so was the army. But we got a job done, didn't we—or did we?

Work keeps you from feeling like a damn fool.

It's natural instinct I tell you. Why even rich people work. It *must* be an instinct.

Work is necessary to keep healthy. You get old quick if you don't work.

Work makes a man feel like he amounted to something. He's got to occupy his mind with something. And with what if it ain't work? You can't sleep more than eight of the twenty-four hours—and when you've no job you can't even sleep that long.

Work is a man's best friend, not because you enjoy him so much, but because you're somebody when you're in his company and he has lots of drag.

Work gives you a sense of belonging.

The only other response which recurred frequently enough to make it a dominant indication of what a lifetime of work has to offer workers is contained in the words of an Italian cabinetmaker:

I've been able to give a few comforts to my family, pay the doctor bills for my crippled son and send my daughter to high school.

Exactly half of our informants stressed the provision of "a decent life for the family" as the major satisfaction of their working life. In practically every case this was the response of Italians and Italian-Americans.

To this 50 per cent might be added the 10 per cent who claimed "the pay check is the only real kick you get out of a job"—and many added "that ain't much."

Said an Italian baker's assistant:

I don't make bread for people because I love to but because I get paid for it. I'd work I suppose even if I had money. But I'd do pleasant work. That's the difference in me and the man with dough. He can choose what he wants and wait and fit himself to do it. I can't and never could.

The miscellaneous answers other than these three and comprising about 25 per cent of all answers stressed a variety of satisfactions, no one of which seems to dominate. A few took pride in their superiority in being able to do a job which few could do, carry on processes or operate machines others did not understand, or undertake dangerous tasks others were afraid to do. A very few experienced a mastery of tools or machines that increased their self-esteem. A minority emphasized the realization of what most of them said they would have liked to experience, the importance and usefulness of their job.

A munitions worker put it this way:

You like to work even if you're dead tired at night if you know what you've done is some use. I got a big kick out of making shells during the war. Then when the Kaiser ran into Holland they used our machines to make pencil holders. My God what a comedown! Same job but there was no kick in it now.

The pride men took in explaining the products upon which they worked, the claims of having participated in erecting important buildings, the attempts to justify themselves as producers are indicative of the greater importance of this satisfaction than would be inferred from the small number who emphasized it as the *chief* satisfaction of their working lives.

When the goals men work for, the environment of work which surrounds them, and the actually realized satisfactions of work are placed side by side, the inference is clear. Among the rewards of work men would like to have, only the minimum of economic security is extensively realized. Even this is precarious. Prestige and other indications of successfully playing a socially respected role, independence and self-determination, understanding, these are doled out to them in very scanty parcels, and for a large number not at all. Chiefly among the American-born skilled workers were those who had realized such noneconomic rewards. We know the desire for these noneconomic rewards is strong—so strong that men in suggesting changes in their work environment stressed chiefly the factors that kept them from these rewards. Even if a minimum of economic security were provided, it is probable that the lure of these other rewards would continue to operate, even gain strength to attract men because their realization had become a little less impossible with bread and butter more nearly assured. Anyone fearful that economic security would remove all incentive to work can well ponder these numerous stimuli to such effort which resides in the desire of all younger workers to see themselves functioning in roles admired by their fellows, to gain a degree of freedom and independence so that their decisions count for something, and to understand the forces and circumstances in the midst of which they live. . . .

Not all workers enter a period of unemployment with the same amount of incentive to self-reliance. The first three of the goals we have indicated workers strive to reach furnish stimuli toward the achievement of that status, for self-reliance is an essential part of the definition of these goals. The majority of *socially respected* roles assume a job and self-support. *Economic security* does not involve maintenance guaranteed by others, but that won by one's own efforts. A minimum requirement for an *increasing degree of control* over one's own affairs is a job and an income which one may spend as he chooses. The general character of the goals which workers seek to reach is similar. All want to perform in a *socially respected* role: to be a producer, the holder of a "swell" job, a fellow his mates look to, a thrifty man, a good provider, a man who never lets his family down, the good father of successful kids. *Economic security* means to all a successful achievement of the standard of living customary among one's associates, some hope of lifting that standard to the level of those just beyond one in economic fortune, regularity of income, a comfortable margin of resources beyond mere maintenance, evidence of some progress from the point at which one started, and a sufficient "gearing in" to community relations and institutions so that one is assured of the friendly concern of others in meeting his economic problems. Obtaining *an increasing measure of control* over one's own affairs meant to all an enlarging of the area of life in which one's own decisions determined the outcome of one's efforts and a decreasing of the area in which others had a controlling voice.

But the strength of these goals as incentives to self-reliance varied in accordance with the objective content given them by the experience out of which the worker came to the company of the unemployed. The goals were built out of the actual possibilities available to the workers. They represented no utopian hopes. They were visible on the horizon of the workers' world, and the distance to that horizon was closely related to the nature of the terrain over which the worker must travel in pursuit of them. That terrain was not the same for all workers and each was inclined so to define his objectives that they would not be impossible of achievement *for him.*

True, there are similarities in the problems with which all workers must deal and these similar problems have set general limits to what workers as a group can hope to achieve. The roles in which a worker can perform are limited to those available to wage earners, and to those the trappings for which can be purchased with a wage earner's income. A few may qualify for other roles by getting out of the working class, but the great majority must find their satisfaction in the activities, relationships, and institutions customary among workers. Satisfaction is possible. Work itself keeps a man "normal"; many have kept their families fairly comfortable; a few gain distinction as skillful workers among their associates and as leaders in activities of interest to their own group; many are proud of their connection with particular firms; some are aware of the social usefulness of their work; all are producers. But rewards are doled out in small parcels and satisfaction is extensively possible only by modification of goals so that they are consistent with the possible achievements within a working-class world.

Work-for-another-for-wages is the worker's lot, and who can deny that he who sells his labor for a price must ultimately depend upon the decision of a buyer? Almost at the beginning of their working careers a large number of workers learned that their choice was not the primary determinant of the work they were to do. The most interesting fact revealed by questions about ambitions was that both those who had and those who had not any real occupational goal were eventually distributed in about equal proportions over all the occupations. There was little relation between wanting a particular job at the beginning of one's working life and getting that job later on. That the demand for labor, the accident of fathers' or friends' occupations, rather than personal choice, determines the job channel into which these workers' energies flowed is clear. Very few actually chose their jobs with a planned future in mind. Those who did stood less than an even chance of following where their plans led. Even in this important matter of the selection of an occupation, the worker's decision was not the controlling factor, unless the decision to take what was available, rather than do nothing, may be considered a controlling one. How is one to believe that his own decisions are important during his working years in the face of examples of "pull" and "luck," and in the presence of little understood but powerful impersonal economic events that sweep upon him almost without warning and rob him of his job?

The response to this practical control "from another world," as one of them put it, has an important bearing on the sort of attitude with which the worker approaches the adjustments to unemployment. He has already had some practice in rationalizing personal failure and frustration by reference to the causal factors he does not control. "Good luck" or "bad luck" has long since actively entered his explanatory vocabulary. The usefulness of personal planning has already been seriously questioned on many occasions. He has become accustomed to watching for evidence that he has satisfied or displeased someone whose decision as to his fate *does* count.

The degree of economic security he can hope to have is also limited by the problems peculiar to working-class life. Wages earned roughly in proportion to his usefulness to someone else are designated in our culture as the proper and acceptable means for buying as much of a "living" as possible. His usefulness to another bears little necessary relation, however, to his "living" needs. After meeting the basic physical necessities, the margin left for "bettering" himself and his family is small. He has modified that goal to fit the possibilities of reaching it. The "living" he has been able to buy is in many cases uncomfortably close to the minimum of sustenance which the community feels obligated to supply if the worker can find no job. The latter situation is frequent; irregular earnings present him with a constant problem.

Hanging over every day's satisfactions in meeting a hard problem successfully are many other clouds which at any moment may turn into black storm clouds containing the power to destroy what economic security he has been able to gain for himself and his family. The possibilities that machines or women may get his job; that the pace of work may prove him unqualified; that an accident may decrease his earning power; that old age, as industry counts age, may creep on him before his time, are ever present. What workers mean by "getting ahead," is made real by the possibilities remaining after these obstacles are overcome. It is not surprising that something lower than the sky is the limit of their ambitions: enough to keep the family on the standard familiar to workers; enough to keep out of debt; enough to provide for a rainy day and, if possible, to remain semi-independent when working days are over; enough to make contacts with friends and institutions which one can count on in time of difficulty.

The need for constantly revising goals in the presence of such factors is thoroughly damaging to one of the basic assumptions in American culture that a person "gets ahead" in proportion to his skill and effort and foresight.

The struggle with such forces does not develop an enthusiastic desire for work, nor an intense loyalty to the dispensers of work, nor an exceptional concern for the preservation of all the economic and political arrangements in the midst of which work is carried on. But it does produce a dogged determination to hold on to what one has and a persistent desire to make the best of what is, and, if possible, to do a little better than that. Whatever desire to work hard and to be self-reliant may exist, does not for the majority grow out of any stimulating exceptional success in making progress toward these goals. It grows out of the fact that if any progress at all is to be made or even if present gains are to be held, a job and self-support are necessary.

Financial resources are necessary in order to achieve all these goals, however modified. But the fact that one *works* for those resources is equally necessary. It is to be noted that even if cash equivalent to the standard of living customary among one's associates were guaranteed to a man, the achievement of his limited goals is premised on the holding of a job. If the goals men work for could remain unmodified during the entire period of unemployment, the danger that income without work would appear a satisfactory basis for adjustment would be meager indeed even for the lowest paid unskilled workers. For those whose wages and skill had made possible success at a higher level, still further removed from adjustment to life on a minimum of resources, the danger is of course even more remote.

5. Fun and Games: The Problem of Leisure

Leisure has existed since the birth of civilization, but leisure as a *problem,* a special problematic condition within culture is something new. The sense of the problematic quality of leisure in the modern world is no more effec- tively dramatized than in the enormous growth of the literature on the sub- ject. The leading bibliography lists, roughly, 20 items published in the period of 1900–1909. The decade between 1910 and 1919 produced almost 50 new titles; that between 1920 and 1929 about 200. But the period be- tween 1930 and 1939 witnessed the publication of some 450 titles—with almost 100 more added between 1940 and 1945. (The war decade in fact saw a significant decrease in the number of titles produced.)

On the most obvious level, there simply existed more free time, whether the consequence of increased technological mastery and the limitation therefore on necessary hours of labor or whether enforced because of the breakdown of opportunity for work. Yet the existence of such leisure time created special problems in the very nature of the social order and for its stability. A whole new set of professionals developed, equipped to deal with the problem. Deep concern and serious attention was turned on how leisure time was spent—new and often "scientific" attention to the role of movies and radio in the life of adults and children, the consequence of children reading the new comic books of the late 1930's and early 1940's, for example. Social investigators were often shocked to discover that among the very poor,, the extreme marginal elements not always quite *in* our society, children often had no sense of what it meant to "play." High value was increasingly placed on play and the growth of the idea of "teaching" people how to play, or of organizing and monitoring ways of play, of finding and fostering socially acceptable recreation was itself an important factor in the development of the idea of culture.

Yet the very stress on the importance of leisure and the significance of play in human and social growth contained within it a challenge to social order it often sought to reinforce. The stress on the importance of play posed a threat to the value placed on work; the concern for development of individual potential often seriously challenged the belief in uniform effort for the community. The very new forms of play surely reinforced the values of the existing order: "Monopoly," "Bingo," and other forms of gambling, the complicated bidding of "Contract Bridge," the unrestrained dances of the period actually encouraged by a major corporate leader who urged "dancing our way out of the Depression," the use of a wide variety of machines— those basic instruments of the new technological order—like the jukebox, pinball machine, and the radio. Yet at the same time such reinforcement was challenged by what might appear to be a subtle mocking of that order as well. Lenny Bruce, the sardonic commentator on American life in the 1950's and 1960's, recalls in his autobiography his own enthralldom upon discovering the jukebox, "a machine that didn't sew, drill, boil or kill; a machine solely for fun."

Thus by the close of the period the new stress on the importance of leisure and the significance of play coupled with new knowledge about man and the many other challenges to the traditional moral order had created a whole new vision of a "fun morality," something quite new under the American sun.

Dr. Martha Wolfenstein (born 1911) is an associate clinical professor of psychiatry who has devoted much of her study to how children grow up in various cultures.

Fun Morality

MARTHA WOLFENSTEIN

A recent development in American culture is the emergence of what we may call "fun morality." Here fun, from having been suspect, if not taboo, has tended to become obligatory. Instead of feeling guilty for having too much fun, one is inclined to feel ashamed if one does not have enough. Boundaries formerly maintained between play and work break down. Amusements infiltrate into the sphere of work, while, in play, self-estimates of achievement become prominent. This development appears to be at marked variance with an older, Puritan ethic, although, as we shall see, the two are related.

The emergence of fun morality may be observed in the ideas about child training of the last forty years. In these one finds a changing conception of human impulses and an altered evaluation of play and fun which express the transformation of moral outlook. These changing ideas

Martha Wolfenstein, "Fun Morality: An Analysis of Recent American Child-training Literature," as reprinted in Margaret Mead and Martha Wolfenstein, eds., *Childhood in Contemporary Cultures* (Chicago, 1955), pp. 168–176. [Footnotes in original omitted.—Ed.]

about child training may be regarded as part of a larger set of adult attitudes current in contemporary American culture. Thus I shall interpret the development which appears in the child-training literature as exemplifying a significant moral trend of our times. . . .

The innovations in child-training ideas of the past few decades may readily be related to developments in psychological research and theory (notably behaviorism, Gesell's norms of motor development, and psychoanalysis). However, the occurrence and particularly the diffusion of certain psychological ideas at certain periods are probably related to the larger cultural context. A careful study of the ways in which psychological theories have been adapted for parent guidance and other pedagogical purposes would show that a decided selection is made from among the range of available theories, some points being overstressed, others omitted, and so on. . . .

As the infant embodies unmodified impulses, the concept of his nature is a useful index of the way in which the impulsive side of human nature generally is regarded. The conception of the child's basic impulses has undergone an extreme transformation from 1914 to the 1940's. At the earlier date, the infant appeared to be endowed with strong and dangerous impulses. These were notably autoerotic, masturbatory, and thumb-sucking. The child is described as "rebelling fiercely" if these impulses are interfered with. The impulses "easily grow beyond control" and are harmful in the extreme: "children are sometimes wrecked for life." The baby may achieve the dangerous pleasures to which his nature disposes him by his own movements or may be seduced into them by being given pacifiers to suck or having his genitals stroked by the nurse. The mother must be ceaselessly vigilant; she must wage a relentless battle against the child's sinful nature. She is told that masturbation "must be eradicated . . . treatment consists in mechanical restraints." The child should have his feet tied to opposite sides of the crib so that he cannot rub his thighs together; his nightgown sleeves should be pinned to the bed so that he cannot touch himself. Similarly for thumb-sucking, "the sleeve may be pinned or sewed down over the fingers of the offending hand for several days and nights," or a patent cuff may be used which holds the elbow stiff. The mother's zeal against thumb-sucking is assumed to be so great that she is reminded to allow the child to have his hands free some of the time so that he may develop legitimate manual skills; "but with the approach of sleeping time the hand must be covered." The image of the child at this period is that he is centripetal, tending to get pleasure from his own body. Thus he must be bound down with arms and legs spread out to prevent self-stimulation.

In contrast to this we find in 1942–1945 that the baby has been transformed into almost complete harmlessness. The intense and concentrated impulses of the past have disappeared. Drives toward erotic pleasure (and also toward domination, which was stressed in 1929–1938) have become weak and incidental. Instead, we find impulses of a much more diffuse and moderate character. The baby is interested in exploring his world. If he happens to put his thumb in his mouth or to touch his genitals, these are merely incidents, and unimportant ones at that, in his overall exploratory progress. The erogenous zones do not have the focal attraction which they did in 1914, and the baby easily passes beyond them to other areas of presumably equal interest. "The baby will not spend much time handling his genitals if he has other interesting things to do." This infant explorer is centrifugal as the earlier erotic infant was centripetal. Everything amuses him, nothing is excessively exciting.

The mother in this recent period is told how to regard autoerotic incidents: "Babies want to handle and investigate everything that they can see and reach. When a baby discovers his genital organs he will play with them. . . . A wise mother will not be concerned about this." As against the older method of tying the child hand and foot, the mother is now told: "See that he has a toy to play with and he will not need to use his body as a plaything." The genitals are merely a resource which the child is thrown back on if he does not have a toy. Similarly with thumb-sucking: "A baby explores everything within his reach. He looks at a new object, feels it, squeezes it, and almost always puts in in his mouth." Thus again what was formerly a "fierce" pleasure has become an unimportant incident in the exploration of the world. Where formerly the mother was to exercise a ceaseless vigilance, removing the thumb from the child's mouth as often as he put it in, now she is told not to make a fuss. "As he grows older, other interests will take the place of sucking." (Incidentally, this unconcerned attitude toward thumb-sucking is a relatively late development. The 1938 edition still had an illustration of a stiff cuff which could be put on the infant at night to prevent his bending his elbow to get his fingers to his mouth. The attitude toward masturbation relaxed earlier, diversion having already been substituted for mechanical restraints in 1929).

This changing conception of the nature of impulses bears on the question: Is what the baby likes good for him? The opposition between the pleasant and the good is deeply grounded in older American morals (as in many other ascetic moral codes). There are strong doubts as to whether what is enjoyable is not wicked or deleterious. In recent years, however, there has been a marked effort to overcome this dichotomy, to say that what is pleasant is also good for you. The writers on child training reflect the changing ideas on this issue.

In the early period there is a clear-cut distinction between what the baby "needs," his legitimate requirements, whatever is essential to his health and well-being, on the one hand, and what the baby "wants," his illegitimate pleasure strivings, on the other. This is illustrated, for instance, in the question of whether to pick the baby up when he cries. In 1914 it was essential to determine whether he really needed something or whether he only wanted something. Crying is listed as a bad habit. This is qualified with the remark that the baby has no other way of expressing his "needs"; if he is expressing a need, the mother should respond. "But when the baby cries simply because he has learned from experience that this brings him what he wants, it is one of the worst habits he can learn." If the baby cries, "the mother may suspect illness, pain, hunger or thirst." These represent needs. If checking on all these shows they are not present, "the baby probably wants to be taken up, walked with, played with," etc. "After the baby's needs have been fully satisfied, he should be put down and allowed to cry." (This position remained substantially unchanged up to 1942.)

In 1942–1945, wants and needs are explicitly equated. "A baby some-times cries because he wants a little more attention. He probably needs a little extra attention under some circumstances just as he sometimes needs a little extra food and water. Babies want attention; they probably need plenty of it." What the baby wants for pleasure has thus become as legitimate a demand as what he needs for his physical well-being and is to be treated in the same way.

The question of whether the baby wants things which are not good for him also occurs in connection with feeding. The baby's appetite was very little relied on to regulate the quantity of food he took in the early period. Overfeeding was regarded as a constant danger; the baby would never know when he had enough. This is in keeping with the general image of the baby at this time as a creature of insatiable impulses. In contrast to this, we find in the recent period that "the baby's appetite usually regulates successfully the amount of food he takes." Thus again impulses appear as benevolent rather than dangerous.

Formerly, giving in to impulse was the way to encourage its growing beyond control. The baby who was picked up when he cried, held and rocked when he wanted it, soon grew into a tyrant. This has now been strikingly reversed. Adequate early indulgence is seen as the way to make the baby less demanding as he grows older. Thus we get the opposite of the old maxim, "Give the devil the little finger, and he'll take the whole hand." It is now "Give him the whole hand, and he'll take only the little finger."

The attitude toward play is related to the conception of impulses and the belief about the good and the pleasant. Where impulses are danger-ous and the good and pleasant are opposed, play is suspect. Thus in 1914, playing with the baby was regarded as dangerous; it produced unwholesome pleasure and ruined the baby's nerves. Any playful handling of the baby was titillating, excessively exciting, deleterious. Play carried the overtones of feared erotic excitement. As we noted, this was the period of an intensive masturbation taboo, and there were explicit apprehensions that the baby might be seduced into masturbation by an immoral nurse who might play with his genitals. . . .

The mother of 1914 was told: "The rule that parents should not play with the baby may seem hard, but it is without doubt a safe one. A young, delicate and nervous baby needs rest and quiet, and however robust the child much of the play that is indulged in is more or less harmful. It is a great pleasure to hear the baby laugh and crow in apparent delight, but often the means used to produce the laughter, such as tickling, punching, or tossing, makes him irritable and restless. It is a regrettable fact that the few minutes' play that the father has when he gets home at night . . . may result in nervous disturbance of the baby and upset his regular habits." It is relevant to note that at this time "playthings . . . such as rocking horses, swings, teeter boards, and the like" are cited in connection with masturbation, as means by which "this habit is learned." The dangerousness of play is related to that of the ever present sensual impulses which must be constantly guarded against. (In 1929–1938, play becomes less taboo, but must be strictly confined to certain times of the day. In this period the impulse to dominate replaces erotic impulses as the main hazard in the child's nature, and the corresponding danger in that he may get the mother to play with him whenever he likes.)

In the recent period, play becomes associated with harmless and healthful motor and exploratory activities. It assumes the aspect of diffuse innocuousness which the child's impulse life now presents. Play is derived from the baby's developing motor activities, which are now increasingly stressed. "A baby needs to be able to move all parts of his body. He needs to exercise. . . . At a very early age the baby moves his arms and legs aimlessly. . . . As he gets older and stronger and his movements become more vigorous and he is better able to control them he begins to play." Thus play has been successfully dissociated from unhealthy excitement and nervous debilitation and has become associated with muscular development, necessary exercise, strength, and control. This is in keeping with the changed conception of the baby, in which motor activities rather than libidinal urges are stressed. For the baby who is concerned with exploring his world rather than with sucking and masturbating, play becomes safe and good.

Play is now to be fused with all the activities of life. "Play and singing make both mother and baby enjoy the routine of life." This mingling of play with necessary routines is consonant with the view that the good and pleasant coincide. Also, as the mother is urged to make play an aspect of every activity, play assumes a new obligatory quality. Mothers are told that "a mother usually enjoys entering into her baby's play. Both of them enjoy the little games that mothers and babies have always played from time immemorial." (This harking back to time immemorial is a way of skipping over the more recent past.) "Daily tasks can be done with a little play and singing thrown in." Thus it is now not adequate for the mother to perform efficiently the necessary routines for her baby; she must also see that these are fun for both of them. It seems difficult here for anything to become permissible without becoming compulsory. Play, having ceased to be wicked, having become harmless and good, now becomes a new duty.

In keeping with the changed evaluation of impulses and play, the conception of parenthood has altered. In the earlier period the mother's character was one of strong moral devotion. There were frequent references to her "self-control," "wisdom," "strength," "persistence," and "unlimited patience." The mothers who read these bulletins might either take pride in having such virtues or feel called upon to aspire to them. The writers supposed that some mothers might even go to excess in their devoted self-denial. Thus the mothers were told that, for their own health and thus for the baby's good, they should not stay bound to the crib-side without respite, but should have some pleasant, although not too exhausting, recreation. The mother at this time is pictured as denying her own impulses just as severely as she does those of her child. Just as she had to be told to let the baby's hands free occasionally (not to overdo the fight against thumb-sucking), so she must be counseled to allow herself an intermission from duty. (In the 1929–1938 period parenthood became predominantly a matter of knowhow. The parents had to use the right technique to impose routines and to keep the child from dominating them.)

In the most recent period parenthood becomes a major source of enjoyment for both parents (the father having come much more into the picture than he was earlier). The parents are promised that having children will keep them together, keep them young, and give them fun and happiness. As we have seen, enjoyment, fun, and play now permeate all activities with the child. "Babies—and usually their mothers—enjoy breast feeding"; nursing brings "joy and happiness" to the mother. At bath time the baby "delights" his parents, and so on.

The characterization of parenthood in terms of fun and enjoyment may be intended as an inducement to parents in whose scheme of values these are presumed to be priorities. But also it may express a new imperative: You ought to enjoy your child. When a mother is told that most mothers enjoy nursing, she may wonder what is wrong with her in case she does not. Her self-evaluation can no longer be based entirely on whether she is doing the right and necessary things but becomes involved with nuances of feeling which are not under voluntary control. Fun has become not only permissible but required, and this requirement has a special quality different from the obligations of the older morality.

I should now like to speculate on the connection between the attitudes revealed in this child-training literature and a wider range of attitudes in American culture today. The extent of diffusion with respect to class, region, etc., of the attitudes I shall discuss would be a topic for further research.

The changing attitudes toward impulse and restraint, the changing treatment of play, the changing evaluation of fun which we have found in the child-training literature, would seem to have many counterparts in other areas of adult life. Play, amusement, fun, have become increasingly divested of puritanical associations of wickedness. Where formerly there was felt to be the danger that, in seeking fun, one might be carried away into the depths of wickedness, today there is a recognizable fear that one may not be able to let go sufficiently, that one may not have enough fun. In the recent past there has been an increased tendency to attempt by drinking to reduce constraint sufficiently so that we can have fun. Harold Lasswell has defined the superego as that part of the personality which is soluble in alcohol. From having dreaded impulses and being worried about whether conscience was adequate to cope with them, we have come round to finding conscience a nuisance and worrying about the adequacy of our impulses.

Not having fun is not merely an occasion for regret but involves a loss of self-esteem. I ask myself: What is wrong with me that I am not having fun? To admit that one did not have fun when one was expected to arouses feelings of shame. Where formerly it might have been thought that a young woman who went out a great deal might be doing wrong, currently we would wonder what is wrong with a girl who is not going out. Fun and play have assumed a new obligatory aspect. While gratification of forbidden impulses traditionally aroused guilt, failure to have fun currently occasions lowered self-esteem. One is likely to feel inadequate, impotent, and also unwanted. One fears the pity of one's contemporaries rather than, as formerly, possible condemnation by moral authorities. In our book, *Movies: A Psychological Study*, Nathan Leites and I referred to this new obligatoriness of pleasure as "fun morality" as distinguished from the older "goodness morality," which stressed interference with impulses. We noted a particular type of current American film heroine, the masculine-feminine girl, whose major merit consists in making the achievement of fun not too effortful. She initiates the flirtation, keeps it casual, makes it clear that she does not require excessive intensity from the man. At the same time she supports his self-esteem by implying that she never doubts his resources for having fun, however cool or abstracted he may seem. She affords a relief from the pressures of fun morality.

David Riesman, in *The Lonely Crowd,* has observed how extensively work and play have become fused in business and professional life. Activities formerly sharply isolated from work, such as entertainment, have become part of business relations. Aspects of the personality, such as pleasingness or likability, formerly regarded as irrelevant to work efficiency, have been increasingly called into play in working life. Relations with work associates have become less and less sharply distinguishable from relations outside working hours. Thus there has been a mutual penetration of work and play. Work tends to be permeated with behavior formerly confined to after work hours. Play, conversely, tends to be measured by standards of achievement previously applicable only to work. One asks one's self not only in personal relations but now also at work: Did they like me? Did I make a good impression? And at play, no less than at work, one asks: Am I doing as well as I should?

In the past when work and play were more sharply isolated, virtue was associated with the one and the danger of sin with the other. Impulse gratification presented possibilities of intense excitement as well as of wickedness. Today we have attained a high degree of tolerance of impulses, which at the same time no longer seem capable of producing such intense excitement as formerly. Is it because we have come to realize that the devil does not exist that we are able to fuse play and fun with business, child care, and so on? Or have we developed (without conscious calculation) a new kind of defense against impulses? This defense would consist in diffusion, ceasing to keep gratification deep, intense, and isolated, but allowing it to permeate thinly through all activities to achieve by a mixture a further mitigation. Thus we would have preserved unacknowledged and unrecognized the tradition of puritanism. We do not pride ourselves on being good, and we secretly worry about not having enough fun. But the submerged superego works better than we know, interspersing play in small doses with work and applying a norm of achievement to play. Instead of the image of the baby who has fierce pleasures of autoeroticism and the dangerous titillation of rare moments of play, we get the infant who explores his world, every part of whose extent is interesting but none intensely exciting, and who may have a bit of harmless play thrown in with every phase of the day's routine. We get the adult whose work is permeated with personal relations and entertainment requirements, the impact of which is far from intensely pleasurable, and whose playtime is haunted by self-doubts about his capacity for having as much fun as he should.

6. Love as a National Problem

In 1931 the American composer George Gershwin and the comedy writer George S. Kaufman created the Pulitzer-Prize winning musical *Of Thee I Sing*. It was a satire on the American scene, most especially the political scene. In order to elect John P. Wintergreen to the Presidency, his campaign managers decide that he must marry the winner of an Atlantic City beauty contest. One of the show's most memorable songs announced that "Love is Sweeping the Country." Few Americans would disagree. The high value placed on romantic love was nothing new; the post-Depression world seemed merely to intensify the attachment to the dream of the modern Cinderella story. We find it over and over in the pulps, the special "true romance" magazines, the popular novels in the movie-magazine versions of the life of the Hollywood star, and in the films themselves. No one—no matter of what wealth or status or power—could count himself successful without love: even Orson Welles' *Citizen Kane* in the film of 1941 insists that all he ever really wanted was love and that his whole life was in fact a failing search for love.

Yet at the same time, in spite of popular mistrust of overinterest in and the "frivolous" or "pornographic" treatment of sex and sexual love, the movement toward greater understanding of the sexual side of man's nature continued. With the more tolerant attitudes of the courts, expressed in a series of important decisions in the early 1930's, the dissemination of professional medical literature about sexual matters, "scientific" sex manuals, and the growth generally of sex education was encouraged. Americans were showing a marked interest in the "science of love." However, such advancements were made within stricter and more conservative bounds than they had been in the 1920's. Here the talk was not about "free love" or even "companionate marriage." The justification for the more scientific study of sex was often the effort to sustain marriage and the family structure.

One of the most widely discussed articles on this subject was written by the French journalist Raoul de Roussy de Sales (born 1896) long-time resident in the United States as American correspondent for several Parisian newspapers. Dr. Alexis Carrel (1873–1944), a world-famed scientist on the staff of the Rockefeller Institute for Medical Research, won the Nobel Prize in 1912 for his work in organ and blood vessel transplants and his research in keeping isolated living matter alive. In 1936 he wrote the best-selling

Man, the Unknown, one of those curious works of combined science and mysticism that were so extremely popular in the period. In the late 1930's he wrote a series of articles for *Reader's Digest* (the first advocated a return to breast feeding) which found much favor among readers.

Love in America

RAOUL de ROUSSY de SALES

I

America appears to be the only country in the world where love is a national problem.

Nowhere else can one find a people devoting so much time and so much study to the question of the relationship between men and women. Nowhere else is there such concern about the fact that this relationship does not always make for perfect happiness. The great majority of the Americans of both sexes seem to be in a state of chronic bewilderment in the face of a problem which they are certainly not the first to confront, but which—unlike other people—they still refuse to accept as one of those gifts of the gods which one might just as well take as it is: a mixed blessing at times, and at other times a curse or merely a nuisance.

The prevailing conception of love, in America, is similar to the idea of democracy. It is fine in theory. It is the grandest system ever evolved by man to differentiate him from his ancestors, the poor brutes who lived in caverns, or from the apes. Love is perfect, in fact, and there is nothing better. But, like democracy, it does not work, and the Americans feel that something should be done about it. President Roosevelt is intent on making democracy work. Everybody is trying to make love work, too.

In either case the result is not very satisfactory. The probable reason is that democracy and love are products of a long and complicated series of compromises between the desires of the heart and the exactions of reason. They have a peculiar way of crumbling into ashes as soon as one tries too hard to organize them too well.

The secret of making a success out of democracy and love in their practical applications is to allow for a fairly wide margin of errors, and not to forget that human beings are absolutely unable to submit to a

Raoul de Roussy de Sales, "Love in America," *Atlantic Monthly,* 161 (May 1938), pp. 645–651.

uniform rule for any length of time. But this does not satisfy a nation that, in spite of its devotion to pragmatism, also believes in perfection.

For a foreigner to speak of the difficulties that the Americans encounter in such an intimate aspect of their mutual relationship may appear as an impertinence. But the truth is that no foreigner would ever think of bringing up such a subject of his own accord. In fact, foreigners who come to these shores are quite unsuspecting of the existence of such a national problem. It is their initial observation that the percentage of good-looking women and handsome men is high on this continent, that they are youthful and healthy in mind and body, and that their outlook on life is rather optimistic.

If the newcomers have seen enough American moving pictures before landing here—and they usually have—they must have gathered the impression that love in America is normally triumphant, and that, in spite of many unfortunate accidents, a love story cannot but end very well indeed. They will have noticed that the love stories which are acted in Hollywood may portray quite regrettable situations at times and that blissful unions get wrecked by all sorts of misfortunes. But they never remain wrecked: even when the happy couple is compelled to divorce, this is not the end of everything. In most cases it is only the beginning. Very soon they will remarry, sometimes with one another, and always—without ever an exception—for love.

The observant foreigner knows, of course, that he cannot trust the movies to give him a really reliable picture of the American attitude toward love, marriage, divorce, and remarriage. But they nevertheless indicate that in such matters the popular mind likes to be entertained by the idea (1) that love is the only reason why a man and a woman should get married; (2) that love is always wholesome, genuine, uplifting, and fresh, like a glass of Grade A milk; (3) that when, for some reason or other, it fails to keep you uplifted, wholesome, and fresh, the only thing to do is to begin all over again with another partner.

Thus forewarned, the foreigner who lands on these shores would be very tactless indeed if he started questioning the validity of these premises. Besides, it is much more likely that he himself will feel thoroughly transformed the moment he takes his first stroll in the streets of New York. His European skepticism will evaporate a little more at each step, and if he considers himself not very young any more he will be immensely gratified to find that maturity and even old age are merely European habits of thought, and that he might just as well adopt the American method, which is to be young and act young for the rest of his life—or at least until the expiration of his visa.

If his hotel room is equipped with a radio, his impression that he has at last reached the land of eternal youth and perfect love will be confirmed at any hour of the day and on any point of the dial. No country in the world consumes such a fabulous amount of love songs. Whether the song is gay or nostalgic, the tune catchy or banal, the verses clever or silly, the theme is always love and nothing but love. . . .

In America the idea seems to be that love, like so much else, should be sold to the public, because it is a good thing. The very word, when heard indefinitely, becomes an obsession. It penetrates one's subconsciousness like the name of some unguent to cure heartaches or athlete's foot. It fits in with the other advertisements, and one feels tempted to write to the broadcasting station for a free sample of his thing called Love.

Thus the visitor from Europe is rapidly permeated with a delightful atmosphere of romanticism and sweetness. He wonders why Italy and Spain ever acquired their reputation of being the lands of romance. This, he says to himself, is the home of poetry and passion. The Americans are the real heirs of the troubadours, and station WXZQ is their love court.

To discover that all this ballyhoo about love (which is not confined to the radio or the movies) is nothing but an aspect of the national optimistic outlook on life does not take very long. It usually becomes evident when the foreign visitor receives the confidences of one or more of the charming American women he will chance to meet. This normally happens after the first or second cocktail party to which he has been invited.

II

I wish at this point to enter a plea in defense of the foreign visitor, against whom a great many accusations are often made either in print or in conversation. These accusations fall under two heads. If the foreigner seems to have no definite objective in visiting America, he is strongly suspected of trying to marry an heiress. If for any reason he cannot be suspected of this intention, then his alleged motives are considerably more sinister. Many American men, and quite a few women, believe that the art of wrecking a happy home is not indigenous to this continent, and that in Europe it has been perfected to such a point that to practice it has become a reflex with the visitors from abroad.

It is very true that some foreign visitors come over here to marry for money in exchange for a title or for some sort of glamour. But there are many more foreigners who marry American women for other reasons besides money, and I know quite a few who have become so Americanized that they actually have married for love and for nothing else.

As for the charge that the Europeans are more expert than the Americans in spoiling someone else's marital happiness, it seems to me an unfair accusation. In most cases the initiative of spoiling whatever it is that remains to be spoiled in a shaky marriage is normally taken by one of the married pair, and the wrecker of happiness does not need any special talent to finish the job.

What is quite true, however, is that the American woman entertains the delightful illusion that there *must* be some man on this earth who can understand her. It seems incredible to her that love, within legal bonds or outside of them, should not work out as advertised. From her earliest years she has been told that success is the ultimate aim of life. Her father and mother made an obvious success of their lives by creating her. Her husband is, or wants to be, a successful business man. Every day 130,000,000 people are panting and sweating to make a success of something or other. Success—the constant effort to make thinks work perfectly and the conviction that they can be made to—is the great national preoccupation.

And what does one do to make a success?

Well, the answer is very simple: one learns how, or one consults an expert.

That is what her husband does when he wants to invest his money or improve the efficiency of his business. That is what she did herself when she decided to "decorate" her house. In the American way of life there are no insoluble problems. You may not know the answer yourself, but nobody doubts that the answer exists—that there is some method or perhaps some trick by which all riddles can be solved and success achieved.

And so the European visitor is put to the task on the presumption that the accumulation of experience which he brings with him may qualify him as an expert in questions of sentiment.

The American woman does not want to be understood for the mere fun of it. What she actually wishes is to be helped to solve certain difficulties which, in her judgment, impede the successful development of her inner self. She seldom accepts the idea that maladjustments and misunderstandings are not only normal but bearable once you have made up your mind that, whatever may be the ultimate aim of our earthly existence, perfect happiness through love or any other form of expression is not part of the program.

III

One of the greatest moral revolutions that ever happened in America was the popularization of Freud's works.

Up to the time that occurred, as far as I am able to judge, America lived in a blissful state of puritanical repression. Love, as a sentiment, was glorified and sanctified by marriage. There was a general impression that some sort of connection existed between the sexual impulses and the vagaries of the heart, but this connection was not emphasized, and the consensus of opinion was that the less said about it the better. The way certain nations, and particularly the French, correlated the physical manifestations of love and its more spiritual aspects was considered particularly objectionable. Love, in other words—and that was not very long ago—had not changed since the contrary efforts of the puritanically minded and the romantic had finally stabilized it midway between the sublime and the parlor game.

The important point is that up to then (and ever since the first Pilgrims set foot on this continent) love had been set aside in the general scheme of American life as the one thing which could not be made to work better than it did. Each one had to cope with his own difficulties in his own way and solve them as privately as he could. It was not a national problem.

Whether or not people were happier under that system is beside the point. It probably does not matter very much whether we live and die with or without a full set of childish complexes and repressions. My own view is that most people are neither complex nor repressed enough as a rule; I wish sometimes for the coming of the Anti-Freud who will complicate and obscure everything again.

But the fact is that the revelations of psychoanalysis were greeted in America as the one missing link in the general program of universal improvement.

Here was a system, at last, that explained fully why love remained so imperfect. It reduced the whole dilemma of happiness to sexual mal-adjustments, which in turn were only the result of the mistakes made by one's father, mother, or nurse, at an age when one could certainly not be expected to foresee the consequences. Psychoanalysis integrated human emotions into a set of mechanistic formulas. One learned with great relief that the failure to find happiness was not irreparable. Love, as a sublime communion of souls and bodies, was not a legend, nor the mere fancy of the poets. It was real, and—more important still—practically attainable. Anybody could have it, merely by removing a few obstructions which had been growing within himself since childhood like mushrooms in a dark cellar. Love could be made to work like anything else.

It is true that not many people are interested in psychoanalysis any more. As a fad or a parlor game, it is dead. Modern débutantes will not know what you are talking about if you mention the Oedipus complex or refer to the symbolic meaning of umbrellas and top hats in dreams. Traditions die young these days. But the profound effect of the Freudian revelation has lasted. From its materialistic interpretation of sexual impulses, coupled with the American longing for moral perfection, a new science has been born: the dialectics of love; and also a new urge for the American people—they want to turn out, eventually, a perfect product. They want to get out of love as much enjoyment, comfort, safety, and general sense of satisfaction, as one gets out of a well-balanced diet or a good plumbing installation.

IV

Curiously enough, this fairly new point of view which implies that human relationships are governed by scientific laws has not destroyed the romantic ideal of love. Quite the contrary. Maladjustments, now that they are supposed to be scientifically determined, have become much more unbearable than in the horse-and-buggy age of love. Husbands and wives and lovers have no patience with their troubles. They want to be cured, and when they think they are incurable they become very intolerant. Reformers always are.

Usually, however, various attempts at readjustment are made with devastating candor. Married couples seem to spend many precious hours of the day and night discussing what is wrong with their relationship. The general idea is that—according to the teachings of most modern psychologists and pedagogues—one should face the truth fearlessly. Husbands and wives should be absolutely frank with one another, on the assumption that if love between them is real it will be made stronger and more real still if submitted, at frequent intervals, to the test of complete sincerity on both sides.

This is a fine theory, but it has seldom been practiced without disastrous results. There are several reasons why this should be so. First of all, truth is an explosive, and it should be handled with care, especially in marital life. It is not necessary to lie, but there is little profit in juggling with hand grenades just to show how brave one is. Secondly, the theory of absolute sincerity presupposes that, if love cannot withstand continuous blasting, then it is not worth saving anyway. Some people want their love life to be a permanent battle of Verdun. When the system of defense is destroyed beyond repair, then the clause of hopeless maladjustment is invoked by one side, or by both. The next thing to do is to divorce and find someone else to be recklessly frank with for a season.

Another reason why the method of adjustment through truthtelling is not always wise is that it develops fiendish traits of character which might otherwise remain dormant.

I know a woman whose eyes glitter with virtuous self-satisfaction every time she has had a "real heart-to-heart talk" with her husband, which means that she has spent several hours torturing him, or at best boring him to distraction, with a ruthless exposure of the deplorable status of their mutual relationship to date. She is usually so pleased with herself after these periodical inquests that she tells most of her friends, and also her coiffeur, about it. "Dick and I had such a wonderful time last evening. We made a real effort to find out the real truth about each other— or, at least, I certainly did. I honestly believe we have found a new basis of adjustment for ourselves. What a marvelous feeling that is—don't you think so?"

Dick, of course, if he happens to be present, looks rather nervous or glum, but that is not the point. The point is that Dick's wife feels all aglow because she has done her bit in the general campaign for the improvement of marital happiness through truth. She has been a good girl scout.

A man of my acquaintance, who believes in experimenting outside of wedlock, is unable to understand why his wife would rather ignore his experiments. "If I did not love her and if she did not love me," he argues, "I could accept her point of view. But why can't she see that the very fact that I want her to know everything I do is a proof that I love her? If I have to deceive her or conceal things from her, what is the use of being married to her?"

Be it said, in passing, that this unfortunate husband believes that these extramarital "experiments" are absolutely necessary to prevent him from developing a sense of inferiority, which, if allowed to grow, would destroy not only the love he has for his wife, but also his general ability in his dealings with the outside world.

V

The difference between an American cookbook and a French one is that the former is very accurate and the second exceedingly vague. A French recipe seldom tells you how many ounces of butter to use to make *crêpes Suzette*, or how many spoonfuls of oil should go into a salad dressing. French cookbooks are full of esoteric measurements such as a *pinch* of pepper, a *suspicion* of garlic, or a *generous sprinkling* of brandy. There are constant references to seasoning *to taste*, as if the recipe were merely intended to give a general direction, relying on the experience and innate art of the cook to make the dish turn out right.

American recipes look like doctors' prescriptions. Perfect cooking seems to depend on perfect dosage. Some of these books give you a table of calories and vitamins—as if that had anything to do with the problem of eating well!

In the same way, there is now flourishing in America a great crop of books which offer precise recipes for the things you should do, or avoid doing, in order to achieve happiness and keep the fires of love at a constant temperature. In a recent issue of *Time* magazine, four such books were reviewed together. Their titles are descriptive enough of the purpose of the authors as well as the state of mind of the readers: *Love and Happiness, So You're Going to Get Married, Marriages Are Made at Home, Getting Along Together.*

I have not read all these books, but, according to the reviewer, they all tend to give practical answers to the same mysterious problem of living with someone of the opposite sex. They try to establish sets of little rules and little tricks which will guarantee marital bliss if carefully followed, in the same way that cookbooks guarantee that you will obtain pumpkin pie if you use the proper ingredients properly measured. . . .

Time's review of these books is very gloomy in its conclusion: "Despite their optimistic tone," it says, "the four volumes give a troubled picture of United States domestic life—a world in which husbands are amorous when wives are not, and vice versa; where conflicts spring up over reading in bed or rumpling the evening paper . . . the whole grim panorama giving the impression that Americans are irritable, aggravated, dissatisfied people for whom marriage is an ordeal that only heroes and heroines can bear."

But I believe that the editors of *Time* would be just as dejected if they were reviewing four volumes about American cooking, and for the same reasons. You cannot possibly feel cheerful when you see the art of love or the art of eating thus reduced to such automatic formulas, even if the experts in these matters are themselves cheerful and optimistic. Good food, the pleasures of love, and those of marriage depend on imponderables, individual taste, and no small amount of luck.

VI

Thus the problem of love in America seems to be the result of conflicting and rather unrealistic ways of approaching it. Too many songs, too many stories, too many pictures, and too much romance on the one hand and too much practical advice on the other. It is as if the experience of being in love could only be one of two things: a superhuman ecstasy, the way of reaching heaven on earth and in pairs; or a psychopathic condition to be treated by specialists.

Between these two extremes there is little room for compromise. That the relationship between men and women offers a wide scale of variations seldom occurs to the experts. It is not necessarily true that there is but one form of love worth bothering about, and that if you cannot get the de luxe model, with a life guarantee of perfect functioning, nothing else is worthwhile. It is not true either that you can indefinitely pursue the same quest for perfection, or that if a man and a woman have not found ideal happiness together they will certainly find it with somebody else. Life unfortunately does not begin at forty, and when you reach that age, in America or anywhere else, to go on complaining about your sentimental or physiological maladjustments becomes slightly farcical.

It is not easy, nor perhaps of any use, to draw any conclusion from all this, especially for a European who has lost the fresh point of view of the visitor because he lives here, and who is not quite sure of what it means to be a European any more. I sometimes wonder if there is any real difference between the way men and women get along—or do not get along—together on this side of the Atlantic and on the other. There are probably no more real troubles here than anywhere else. Human nature being quite remarkably stable, why should there be? But there is no doubt that the revolt against this type of human inadequacy is very strong indeed here, especially among the women who imagine that the Europeans have found better ways of managing their hearts and their senses than the Americans.

If this is at all true, I believe the reason is to be found in a more philosophical attitude on the part of the Europeans toward such matters. There are no theories about marital bliss, no recipes to teach you how to solve difficulties which, in the Old World, are accepted as part of the common inheritance.

Men and women naturally want to be happy over there, and, if possible, with the help of one another; but they learn very young that compromise is not synonymous with defeat. Even in school (I am speaking more particularly of France now) they are taught, through the literature of centuries, that love is a phenomenon susceptible of innumerable variations, but that—even under the best circumstances—it is so intertwined with the other experiences of each individual life that to be overromantic or too dogmatic about it is of little practical use. *La vérité est dans les nuances,* wrote Benjamin Constant, who knew a good deal about such matters.

And, speaking of the truly practical and realistic nature of love, it is a very strange thing that American literature contains no work of any note, not even essays, on love as a psychological phenomenon. I know of no good study of the process of falling in and out of love, no analytical description of jealousy, coquettishness, or the development of tediousness. No classification of the various brands of love such as La Rochefoucauld, Pascal, Stendhal, Proust, and many others have elaborated has been attempted from the American angle. The interesting combinations of such passions as ambition, jealousy, religious fervor, and so forth, with love are only dimly perceived by most people and even by the novelists, who, with very few exceptions, seem to ignore or scorn these complicated patterns. These fine studies have been left to the psychiatrists, the charlatans, or the manufacturers of naive recipes.

The reason for this neglect on the part of real thinkers and essayists may be that for a long time the standards imposed by the puritanical point of view made the whole study more or less taboo with respectable authors. And then the Freudian wave came along and carried the whole problem out of reach of the amateur observer and the artist. In other words, conditions have been such that there has been no occasion to fill this curious gap in American literature.

Of course, nothing is lost. The field remains open, and there is no reason to suppose that love in America will not cease to be a national problem, a hunting ground for the reformer, and that it will not become, as everywhere else, a personal affair very much worth the effort it takes to examine it as such. All that is necessary is for someone to forget for a while love as Hollywood—or the professor—sees it, and sit down and think about it as an eternally fascinating subject for purely human observation.

Married Love
ALEXIS CARREL

Love is a mysterious thing. Invisible, immaterial, yet as real as steel. As elusive as smoke in the wind—and stronger than death. From wild passion, it may grow into this selfless, indissoluble affection, whose presence in the house even a stranger can easily detect. If carefully nurtured, it will, in spite of the progress of age and the extinction of reproductive life, continue to expand with the full strength of its beauty.

The origin of love is both organic and mental. The substances set free in the blood stream by the testicle or the ovary have a powerful influence on affective and intellectual activities. They permeate the whole organism with sexual desire. They inspire selfless love and dedication. They illuminate the world of lovers with the eternal joy of spring. In other terms, they supply the physiological requisites for the loftiest activities of the mind. Whether conscious or unconscious, the reproductive urge is the source of love. Man is unity and multiplicity. He has to create, love, and pray with all his organs.

Today, as in the remotest past, youth entertains the charming and dangerous illusion of its innate ability at lovemaking. In consequence, lovemaking, especially in marriage, is frequently not an enduring success. For married love is no easy enterprise. Unfortunately, the science of marriage has remained rudimentary, although its development is essential both to the happiness of man and to the greatness of civilization.

The immediate purpose of marriage is the gratification of the sexual urge, and fecundation. This urge is an inexorable law of nature. And it is more than a romantic glow. It is the biologic source of aspiration and achievement. It *can* be kept fresh and vital if intelligence and imagina-

Alexis Carrel, "Married Love," *Reader's Digest*, 35 (July 1939), pp. 12–16.

tion are given creative scope. Such richly shared sex life is a cornerstone of marital stability and happiness.

Married love is a creative enterprise. It is not achieved by accident or instinct. Perfunctory coitus is a confession of lack of intelligence and character. There is profound beauty and even holiness in the act of fecundation. We should not forget that the Church blesses the sexual union of man and woman by a sacrament. Mothers sometimes inflict grave injury by instilling in their daughters contempt of sex. "You will have to tolerate sex. Often you can escape by pleading tiredness." All the resources of science and technique must be used in order to make of marital relations an ever-flowing source of *mutual* joy.

The problem of marriage is to transform mating into an enduring union. Male and female are attracted by their opposite characteristics. The more masculine the man, the more feminine the woman, the more passionate the mating. But sexuality permeates both mind and body. Man and woman are profoundly different. While intimately united, they are separated by an abyss.

An enduring union is thus rendered difficult by the physiological and mental disparities that are the essence of femaleness and maleness. Man is active, hard, logical. Woman, passive, sentimental, and intuitive. Her nervous system, her temperament, prepare her for maternity. Marriage is an association of two different but complementary individuals. These characteristics of the partners are responsible for both the efficiency and the difficulties of the association.

Not only are husband and wife separated by organic and mental differences, but these differences vary from week to week, according to sexual rhythms. Sexual rhythms are incomparably more marked in woman than in man. During the whole menstrual cycle, fluctuations take place in activity, courage, temper, sex desire. Man also manifests oscillations of temper and activity. This knowledge should allow mutual understanding of various moods, and may prevent tragedies.

Success in marriage requires continence as well as potency. In other words, character is indispensable in well-ordered sexual life. Certain periods, including illness and pregnancy, impose continence. To refrain from sexual intercourse during married life demands nervous equilibrium and moral strength. For many individuals, it is true heroism. Before marriage, the ideal state is chastity. Chastity requires early moral training. It is the highest expression of self-discipline. Voluntary restraint from the sex act during youth, more than any other moral and physical effort, enhances the quality of life. The use of prostitutes is injurious. For paid lovemaking is a degradation of the real sex act. It lacks the essential quality of profound mutuality. It is without the benison of beauty.

Even true love may not protect husband and wife against certain dangers of sexual relations. Early excesses prevent the full development of body and mind. Late excesses accelerate the rate of aging and decay. When exhausted or worried, the husband should not be induced by an oversexed wife to perform the sex act. Reciprocally, the untimely ardor of an ignorant husband may tire or exasperate his undersexed wife. Love is incompatible with ignorance and selfishness. Also with disease. Since chastity in girls, as well as in boys, is far from being the habitual rule, lovers must ascertain before marriage whether they are free of gonorrhea and syphilis.

There is no apparent natural rule for sexual relations. The frequency of the sex act varies widely. There are sexual athletes as well as weaklings. Copulation can be performed at any time, while in other mammals it takes place only during the heat period. Therefore, intelligence and self-control must replace instinct in the management of sexual life. The enormous variations in individual constitution have rendered impossible the elaboration of precise rules. Each couple must take into consideration their physical and mental peculiarities. For the failure of married life often comes from technical ignorance.

Lovers are seldom perfectly mated. Often the husband has a stronger sexual appetite than the wife. Sex indifference may be induced by the ignorance or brutality of the husband. As in the animal kingdom, the female has to be enticed by the male.

In married life, sexual intercourse has a tendency to become a monotonous performance. On the contrary, it must retain its profound meaning. All senses, especially the sense of beauty, should participate in it. It is the capacity, through mind and spirit, to exalt the symbolism of the act that differentiates man from the animals. Affection must bestow a benediction upon emotional manifestations.

There are abundant resources in the field of sensory and psychologic stimulation. All the little arts of lovemaking should be brought into play. The expected, taken-for-granted attitude is to be avoided by both partners. An infinite variety of expressions can be given to sex love.

Small attentions kindle conjugal affection. Endearing words and expressions of appreciation should be liberally mingled with everyday matters not necessarily connected with sex. How can a woman accept the love addresses of a man who at all other times ignores or criticizes her? In the actual lovemaking ritual, words are as desirable as caresses.

In woman, sexual excitation rises slowly. She needs to be prepared for the act. Generally, the masculine orgasm occurs before her senses are totally roused. Thus, she is left unsatisfied, nervous, perhaps disgusted. In order that she may really consummate the sex act, her husband must learn self-control and enlightened technique. It will augur well for the future of the race when women demand a higher intelligence quotient of men as lovers.

Marriage should provide a proper environment for the offspring. The slow development of children, the necessity of their organic and spiritual formation, require permanency in human mating. In other terms, monogamy and indissolubility of marriage. Since the quality of the children depends on the hereditary endowment of the parents, the wise selection of a mate is of the utmost importance. Only in this manner can eugenics be realized.

Between husband and wife, intellectual union is highly desirable. Feminine intelligence, although differing from masculine intelligence, is not inferior to it. Girls should receive as advanced an intellectual education as boys do. In order to play their specific part in life, they need extensive knowledge. It is folly to confine their interests to the details of housekeeping, or to the so-called duties of society. Love becomes anemic if not helped by intellectual activity. Both the happiness of married life and the future of society depend on intelligence in love. The main enemy of love is the innate selfishness that modern education develops to its maximum in each boy and girl.

The sex act has been deprived of its natural consequences by the technical progress of contraception. However, the biological law of reproduction remains imperative. And transgressors are punished in a subtle manner. It is a disastrous mistake to believe we can live according to our fancy. Being parts of nature, we are submitted to its inexorable laws. Sterile love may sink into monotonous dreariness or selfish folly. Generally, the old age of those without children resembles a barren desert.

Insufficient fecundity is also dangerous. For the only child is deprived of the companionship, formative influence, and help that his potential brothers and sisters would have given him. In large families, there is more cheerfulness and mutual aid than in small ones. It is probable that three children are the indispensable minimum for the harmony of the family and the survival of the race. The true social unit is not the isolated individual, but the functional group constituted by husband, wife, and offspring. Curiously enough, democracy gives more importance to the individual than to the family.

We have not yet fully understood that love is a necessity, not a luxury. It is the only ingredient capable of welding together husband, wife, and children. The only cement strong enough to unite into a nation the poor and rich, the strong and the weak, the employer and the employe. If we do not have love within the home, we shall not have it elsewhere. Love is as essential as intelligence, thyroid secretion, or gastric juice. No human relationships will ever be satisfying if not inspired by love.

The moral command, "Love one another," is probably a fundamental law of nature, a law as inexorable as the first law of thermodynamics.

Those who achieve greatness in business, in art, in science, are strongly sexed. There are no sexual weaklings among the heroes, the conquerors, the truly great leaders of nations. But sublimated love does not need material consummation. Inspiration may come from the repression of sexual appetite. "If Beatrice had been the mistress of Dante, there would be perhaps no *Divine Comedy*."

To conclude: Man and woman have no innate knowledge of the physical, mental, and social requisites of married love. But they are capable of learning the indispensable principles and technique of this complex relation. Prospective husbands and wives will be wise in applying their sense of material and spiritual values to the selection of a mate, and to preparation for the great adventure. Those who are married, and perhaps already disappointed, should realize that failure is avoidable, that success can still be achieved. For intelligence, which has given man mastery over the material world, also possesses the power to usher him into the realm of love.

7. Sex: The Case Against Mae West

All Americans, then, loved a lover but at the same time—and this was increasingly the case after 1933—there seemed to be a growing demand that the lover, at least finally, be a married lover. In spite of the liberalization of sexual behavior generally associated with the 1920's and even the gradual growth of systematic studies of sexuality and sexual education, the 1930's witness a return to what has been regarded as a Puritan fundamentalism in reference to sexual conduct. Censorship was of course not new and many of the battles against censorship in the arts—witness Judge Woolsey's important 1937 decision in the case of the long-banned *Ulysses* of James Joyce—were won in the period. But the fact remains that there was a striking increase in general concern for high standards of sexual conduct and especially an outpouring of criticism against any deviations from the supposed norm in ways that most seriously affected the popular media.

Hollywood, for example, had called in former Postmaster General Will Hays in 1922 to help it when threatened by a series of scandals among the film stars. By 1933 the Episcopal Church had established its Committee on Motion Pictures, denouncing the movies as tending to promote immorality. The Catholic Bishops took action as well by establishing their own National Legion of Decency. The Hays Office responded in 1934 with a new and revised Code to govern the making of films—and this one had teeth in it. Hays was finally able to achieve the "dictatorship of virtue" he had been striving for during his twelve years in Hollywood. Many critics have commented on the absurd lengths to which such censorship went, what an unreal world it forced the motion pictures to portray. But it suggests the nature of the strict moral code organized religious groups and leaders of the social order generally tried to enforce, in theory if not always in practice.

It is perhaps suggestive that the Episcopal Committee on Motion Pictures was formed exactly six months after the release of Mae West's first film and that the new code forced changes even in the titles of some of her later films as well as the omission of such double entendres as "I wouldn't lift my veil for that guy," and "I wouldn't let him touch me with a ten-foot pole." But the most memorable episode involving Miss West—an episode which caused her to be barred from radio—actually led to Congressional discussion and debate. The selection from the *Congressional Record* incorporates editorial and private opinion indicating the due seriousness with which many middle-class Americans took the matter. Robert Forsythe was the pseudonym used by Kyle Crichton (1896–1960), one of the wittiest of American writers on the Left. His biting collection of pieces originally published in *The New Masses* provide, in addition to their humor, a significant left-wing commentary on American culture and morals. *Redder Than the Rose* is, in its own way, a significant study of American popular culture as seen from an American Marxist perspective.

The Issue in The Congress
CONGRESSIONAL RECORD

Mr. CONNERY. Mr. Chairman, I have listened with a great deal of interest during the past 2 weeks to the gentleman from Texas [Mr. McFarlane] and to my colleague from Massachusetts [Mr. Wigglesworth] and their statements calling the attention of the Members of the House to conditions which today exist in the radio industry.

Yesterday morning I found on my desk a communication from the Federal Radio Commission which contained a mimeographed copy of a press release issued on December 27 with reference to the so-called Mae West program.

The press release reads as follows:

Chairman Frank R. McNinch announced today that the Commission has received, in response to its request, a letter from Mr. Lenox R. Lohr, president of the National Broadcasting Co., Inc., transmitting an exact copy of the transcript of the Adam and Eve feature, the electrical transcription of the skit, a copy of the contract between Chase & Sanborn (sponsors of the program) and the National Broadcasting Co. covering this broadcast, and a list of the stations over which this feature was broadcast.

The Commission will give further consideration to this matter after considering the script and the electrical transcription.

This, as I have said, was dated December 27, and here it is January 14. I know a large number of the Members of the House are joining with me in wondering if this incident is going to be whitewashed. The American people are clean of mind, and naturally they resent the intrusion into their homes of any blasphemous, sensuous, indecent, obscene,

From the *Congressional Record*, 83, pt. 1, 75th Congress, 3rd Session, January 14, 1938, pp. 560–563.

or profane utterance, printed matter, or radio broadcast, and that is exactly what this particular broadcast was.

It is claimed by radio officials that some 40,000,000 homes in this country have radio receivers. The people who buy these radio receivers and listen to them do so in the belief and with the thought that such receivers will not be a medium of receiving into their homes any salacious radio broadcast. While the American family can protect its home from the intrusion of salacious and indecent printed matter, radio broadcasts are an entirely different proposition. You simply turn the switch on your radio receiver and you have to take what comes out of it, without having the least idea what the program will contain. It is true you probably have some knowledge of who is sponsoring the program and who are the principals—the artists who are to be presented—and you place your confidence in the reputations of the sponsor and the artists. You certainly do not expect to hear a program that is offensive. . . .

This is not the first time that an incident such as this has happened. This is not the first time we have had such an intrusion into American homes of salacious, indecent, and blasphemous programs. There have been several occasions in the past where similar conditions have existed and my late brother, Congressman Connery, called the conditions prevailing at that time to the attention of the Federal Communications Commission. The usual whitewash was the result.

I am here today wondering if we are going to see a whitewash of this particular incident. Three weeks have elapsed since the electrical transcription of the skit, the script, and the list of stations using the broadcast have been received by the Federal Communications Commission, and it is about time that we received a report on the matter. . . .

The American people rightfully look to the Congress for protection. The Congress has delegated the regulation and supervision of radio broadcasting to a Federal commission. The Congress, realizing, as it must, that such regulation and supervision has proven to be faulty, has but one recourse and that is the removal from office of those who failed to carry out the law and the enactment of laws which will, in reality, protect the millions of American homes equipped with radio sets from the intrusion therein of foul, sensuous, or blasphemous radio programs. The Congress cannot and should not dodge its responsibility.

During the past few weeks the American people, following the wholly unexpected but actual intrusion into their homes of a foul, sensuous, indecent, and blasphemous radio program, indicated their abhorrence by protesting against this type of radio broadcast.

Indicating the character of the radio broadcast complained of, I desire to quote excerpts from just two of the many letters which I have received, as well as some editorial excerpts:

To have this filthy and lewd take-off on the Bible Adam and Eve story was a disgrace. I heard the program and thought it a shock even to our tougher brethren.

Here is another:

I have never listened to anything over the radio coming into my home or elsewhere that I consider so debasing and outrageous as that broadcast. Today I took luncheon with 10 business and professional men. The subject was brought up without my taking any part in it. The unanimous opinion condemned the broadcast. The way it was presented over the radio reduced the Garden of Eden episode to the very lowest level of bawdy-house stuff. Young folks listening to the same would have been led to believe by the broadcast that the Garden of Eden episode was on a level with the lowest courses and cheapest immorality. Among those who have expressed themselves upon the subject, there is the unanimous view that the broadcast was not fit to be used on the air.

Some of the editorial comments I have clipped from newspapers from throughout the country are as follows:

We were shocked last Sunday evening, when Mae West, the very personification of sex in its lowest connotation, appeared on a very popular radio program.

The radio has brought to many a fuller life, carrying the culture of the world into the homes of America. The home is our last bulwark against the modern overemphasis on sensuality, and we cannot see why Miss West and others of her ilk should be permitted to pollute its sacred precincts with shady stories, foul obscenity, smutty suggestiveness, and horrible blasphemy.

It was the most indecent, scurrilous and irreverent program that it has been my misfortune to hear. In her peculiarly indecent style, Miss West introduced her own sexual philosophy into the Biblical incident of the fall of man.

The radio is a piece of machinery as common to the household as electric lights. If programs such as Mae West's burlesque Sunday night are allowed, it can become a very dangerous instrument. The dial is always within easy access of the children.

In thousands of homes where families are wont to seek a little innocent relaxation and amusement on Sunday evenings at the radio, the most barefaced insult was inflicted upon them until some member of the family had the presence of mind to relieve the embarrassment by quickly switching the dial. Some people who listened in have since said that they waited with bated breath, expecting momentarily that a studio censor might step in with some improvised alibi and kill the program.

Those responsible for the intrusion into millions of American homes of this foul and indecent radio broadcast, fearing the wrath of the American people, and possibly fearing some action on the part of Washington authorities, or the Congress, made haste to try to overcome the indignation of the American people by having the Chairman of the Federal Communications Commission issue a public statement calling upon the National Broadcasting Co. for a copy of this foul and sensuous radio program. . . .

Naturally, Members of the Congress . . . advised their constituents that the radio broadcast complained of was under official consideration on the part of the Federal Communications Commission. Believing, as they had a right to, from the tenor of the letter sent to the National Broadcasting Co., that the Chairman of the Federal Communications Commission, the "Charley McCarthy" of the radio monopolists, was sincere, they expected some definite and disciplinary action.

It is common knowledge that these radio programs are well rehearsed days before they are broadcast. It is understood that officials of the National Broadcasting Co. are present at these rehearsals. The many thousands of clean-minded Americans who protested did not know, presumably, but the officials of the National Broadcasting Co. did know, that protests were made at the time of the rehearsals by those participating who realized the sensuousness and the indecency of this particular program.

However, the Congress, as well as many others, who believed in the sincerity of the Chairman of the Federal Communications Commission, I am afraid, will soon awaken to learn that they might as well have sent their protests to the party responsible for the intrusion into millions of American homes of this foul and sensuous radio broadcast so far as securing any action other than a faint apology.

Mae West: Treatise on Decay
ROBERT FORSYTHE

When you consider Madame Du Barry and Nell Gwynne, it is evident that Mae West has made a mistake in confining her immorality to stage and screen. Granted that a woman of her intelligence could be prevailed upon to favor a Congressman or a Secretary of War, the spectacle of

Robert Forsythe, "Mae West: Treatise on Decay," reprinted in *Redder Than a Rose* (New York, 1935), pp. 105–110. Originally appeared in *The New Masses*, October 9, 1934.

Miss West affecting state policy as well as private temperatures is something which no future historian could afford to overlook. It is plain that on any basis of comparison she belongs to the great line.

There are so many indications of the breakdown of capitalist civilization that we are inclined to become tender and sympathetic in the midst of the debacle, much in the manner of "don't cheer, boys; the poor devils are dying," but it is obvious that Miss West, more than any of her associates, symbolizes the end of an epoch. Her stage plays, *Sex* and *The Drag,* uncovered such a horrifying picture of homosexuals, lesbians and ordinary degenerates that Miss West was sentenced to the work house for ten days as a way of restoring the faith of the populace in the great city. Her motives in presenting the plays were undoubtedly mercenary, but her attorneys overlooked a great opportunity of establishing her as a sociologist and humanitarian, moved solely by her concern for reform.

The movies were more astute in their management of her films. They retained the spiciness, the lustiness and bawdiness, but they carefully confined them to the past. In a sense it may be said that the golden era of Chuck Conners and the Bowery was bourgeois vigor at its peak. With all its dirt and squalor the Bowery managed to maintain an Elizabethan rowdiness and crudity which could pass as strength. The Puritan was at last defeated; men were again honest animals. They killed, they whored and they flaunted the broken bits of Methodist morality in the faces of the nice people who came down to look with fascinated horror at these mad barbarians.

The Christian fathers are quite correct in worrying about Miss West. Whether the success of her bawdiness is a sign that we have conquered Puritanism and are a mature people at last or whether it represents a complete collapse of morality, it is evident that it reveals the lack of authority of religion. The Catholic campaign for clean films succeeded in changing the title of the latest West film from *It Ain't No Sin* to *Belle of the Nineties,* but it is still Mae West in *It Ain't No Sin.*

But it is in her stage plays that her significance lies. If we judged alone from her screen comedies we should be tempted to say that she represented sexual honesty in a world given over much too completely to the antics of the fairy. I refer to the world of the theater and to the race of people known as perverts. Without seeking to alarm you with a sensational exposé of vice conditions in the green room, I may say merely that the condition within the profession is notorious. The facts of the matter are plain enough, but I may not be able to convince you that they have historical importance, and I am not even going to attempt to prove that the bitterly reactionary character of the stage, with the few exceptions you recognize so well, are the result in some small part of this disease. We know quite well that the reasons for reaction are class reactions and if I make any point at all in this respect it would be to indicate that introversion is essentially a class ailment and the direct result of a sybaritic life which finally results in profound boredom for lack of any further possible stimulation or titillation. It is invariably associated with those twin elements of perversion, sadism and masochism, and generally reveals itself among the thinned-out representatives of a decaying class. The sadistic cruelty of Hitlerism is no accident. It is the unmistakable symptom of an incurable malady.

I am not a psychologist and what I have to say about the coincidences of history in this regard are not to be taken as gospel from the scientific archangels, but three widely separated incidents prior to the world war have always struck me as being significant. There was first the Oscar Wilde case in England. The divorce suit of Sir Charles Dilke with its resultant exposure of the hypocrisy and moral laxness of the aristocracy had been the first break in the dike of British class superiority. It showed that not only were the nobles human but they were something less than admirably human. Even this, however, was outshadowed by the revelations of the Wilde affair. The wave of indignation swept Wilde to jail, but it also revealed the fact that sexual debauchery was so common among the nobility that Frank Harris could report, without legal action being taken against him, that seventy-five members of the House of Lords were notorious perverts.

Not long after Germany was stirred by the revelations that Prince Philip Eulenberg, intimate friend of the Kaiser, had been accused by Maximilian Harden of indulging in unnatural vice. Harden had attacked Eulenberg publicly in his paper *Zukunft*, trying to force a charge of libel. Eulenberg refused and was disgraced. Evidence later produced in another trial at Munich proved conclusively that he was guilty. What was even more damning was the knowledge that others besides Eulenberg of the Imperial court were involved and that conditions were generally bad in high circles. The war came along several years later to place the world's attention on other forms of perversion such as mass slaughter and it was only with the advent of the *Fuehrer* that homosexuality was raised to the rank of statesmanship.

There was a third case in Russia which practically coincided with the outbreak of the war. By a coincidence France at the same time was so stirred by the sensational trial arising out of the killing of Calmette, editor of *Figaro*, by Madame Caillaux that the death of the Archduke at Sarajevo was almost overlooked by the smartly gowned crowds who gathered in court each day for the details. In the same way the nobility of Russia could scarcely take their fascinated gazes away from the St. Petersburg scandal long enough to watch the troops marching to the front.

What Mae West did in the plays I have mentioned and what she does in her motion pictures is to show in her frank, cynical way the depths to which capitalistic morality has come. There is an honesty in her playing which is even more devastating. It is not the bouncing lechery of Ben Jonson but the mean piddling lewdness of the middle classes getting their little hour of sin before the end. Miss West has a marvelous capacity for the theater and she acts in what might be termed the grand manner, but I can never hear her "C'm up and see me some time" without thinking of Ruth Snyder carrying on her cheap pathetic romance with Judd Gray. Because she epitomizes so completely the middle-class matron in her hour of license I feel that Miss West has never been properly appreciated as the First Artist of the Republic. It is palpable nonsense to be concerned about such children as Katherine Hepburn, who will be as forgotten as Mary Miles Minter in a few years' time, when we possess a lady who could assume her position now as the Statue of Liberty and who so obviously represents bourgeois culture at its apex that she will enter history as a complete treatise on decay.

8. Christ: Genteel and Robust

No account of the development of American culture in any period can be complete without some effort to suggest the relationship of popular religion to that culture. This has been a fact since the outset of the American experience; it is as significant in our period of depression and war as in any other. While leading intellectuals found much to interest them in the Neo-Orthodox theology of men like Reinhold Niebuhr and the drive toward a new political realism by a reformed social-gospel vision, there remained the vital continuation of a tradition expressed in many popular inspirational books that reflected a vision of a Christian culture—often shared, too, by non-Christians—widely held by middle-class Americans. Two sociologists, Louis Schneider and Sanford M. Dornbusch, have seriously studied that literature from 1875 to 1950. A summary of their conclusions based on a careful analysis of the content of those books follows. The authors examined whose works were widely read in the period of this volume include Harry Emerson Fosdick, Emmet Fox, E. Stanley Jones, Henry C. Link, Glenn Clark, and Elton Trueblood.

But the most important of all such inspirational writers of the period may well have been a practicing Protestant minister turned novelist, and one of the best-selling novelists of the period, Lloyd C. Douglas. His first novel, *Magnificent Obsession* (1929), sold more than a million copies in this country alone. A series of similar novels—all successful—was to follow. Unabashedly sentimental, they all suggested that "forgiveness and unquestioning self-sacrifice in the face of the multitudinous tribulations of modern life" are vital and that "patience, courage, and service to humanity is conducive not only to spiritual serenity but to material comfort as well." Douglas climaxed his career of preaching—in novel form—a robust, practicing Christianity by producing an historical novel, *The Robe* (1942), which sold over two million copies and became, as did most of Douglas's other works, the basis of a major motion picture.

Popular Religious Themes

LOUIS SCHNEIDER and
SANFORD M. DORNBUSCH

SUMMARY OF THEMES AND TRENDS

The following synoptic view, though not designed to constitute an exhaustive summary, covers main findings and marks significant elements in the literature.

A. *Constant Elements*

1. The writers of the literature hold to the view that religion gives life meaning by providing a feeling of individual worth or significance.

2. Religious faith is said to ease the making of decisions: one needs only to surrender to God and the right decision will be forthcoming.

3. The writers insist that religion gives power to live by.

4. Religion promotes success, successful living, life-mastery.

5. It is true both that religious faith is asserted to bring happiness and satisfaction in this world and that man is said to be able to *expect* happiness in this world. It is further claimed that religion brings emotional security.

6. Religious faith is viewed as likely to bring *either* wealth or (emotional or physical) health.

7. The individual can make changes beneficial to himself by religious means.

8. There is small eschatological concern among Protestant writers. The notion of punishment in the next life is nearly absent among them, and they refer to a next life at all less than do the Catholics. A powerful stress on salvation in this life rather than the next prevails, and there is correspondingly slight preoccupation with the agencies of salvation in the next life.

9. God is averred to exist objectively in his own right, although an important undercurrent sustains the view that he exists since belief in him "works." (Note item 26, below.)

10. God is a God of good will toward man, liberal with rewards in this life, averse to punishments in the next. The conception of him as judge is given little attention.

11. The divinity of Christ is generally assumed.

Louis Schneider and Sanford M. Dornbusch, *Popular Religion: Inspirational Books in America* (Chicago, 1958), pp. 38–92.

12. The literature consistently sees man as inherently good.

13. Teleological or anthropomorphic views of nature are weak and subdued.

14. Although man in the literature is involved in *interpersonal* relations, within the family, on the job, and so on, he lives remarkably unaffected by institutional realities, in a world where his destiny is ostensibly largely remote from social, political, or economic circumstance.

15. The association of poverty with virtue is nearly absent.

16. Of some prominence in the literature is a technology of affirming positive thoughts, denying negative thoughts, denying the negative by affirming the positive. A corresponding stress on thought control is quite evident, and rather frequent emphasis is given to the view of the metaphysical primacy of the mental over the material. (Note item 27, below.)

17. Favorable mention of subjective religious experience is a strong general feature of the literature.

18. The literature has a pronounced antidogmatic strain (mitigated in recent years).

B. Variable Elements

19. After 1940 there is sharply increased stress on religion as performing the function of reconciling to the inevitable.

20. The view of religion as promoting a better world hits its stride about 1940. Correlative findings which combine into a pattern with this are the recent emphases on religion's providing a moral basis or vindication for action (after 1946) and functioning to link one to one's fellow man and to make one more fully a member of a solidary community (after 1936).

21. During World War II and the postwar anti-Communist crusade religion is often linked to national aspirations, and this stress had begun to appear in 1940.

22. Beginning about 1940, the view that religion specifically promotes optimism shows decline. The writers of the literature do not indorse a pessimistic view of the world, but they are not so markedly optimistic about it as before.

23. Until about the time of World War I, except in the sense indicated in 1, above, there is no great concern with religion in connection with the "meaning" of existence. Each of the two world wars appears to evoke or reinforce such concern.

24. Beginning about 1930, there is an increase in emphasis that "the world can be changed by religious means," in contrast with previous emphasis on the salvation of the individual alone. But this should definitely not be construed to mean that the literature has taken on Social Gospel characteristics since the onset of the Depression.

25. Since 1946 there has been some attention to the theme that the world can be changed by institutional means (through taking account of major political and economic structures, etc.), alone or in some combination with religious or psychological means, but the actual stress on this has been very slight.

26. The pragmatic view that God exists because belief in him produces positive results ("it works") evidently finds most favor in the Depression.

27. The view that thought is the highest reality and matter subservient thereto, or illusory, seems also to have been most favored during the Depression, although the evidence on the point is not conclusive.

28. The use of testimonials from scientists for the value of religion does not begin until the end of the 1920's. The somewhat aberrant *identification* of religion and science (to which writers like Fox and Peale are partial) begins at about the same time.

29. Psychological and psychiatric orientations, previously of small significance, enter the literature in the 1930's and remain important.

30. The stress that religion brings wealth is present in the earlier period and comes to a peak during the Depression. Since then it is dropped, with the exceptions of Fox and Peale. The echoes of the Calvinist connection of riches with personal worth and of poverty with lack of personal worth show the same pattern, ceasing with the Depression and thereafter found in Fox and Peale alone.

31. The view of religion as alleviating suffering and promoting health is more pronounced in recent years, with the shift occurring about 1932. The shift is perhaps clearer for mental than physical ills, but the change is present for both.

32. The early period finds more emphasis on faith, and on faith as more important than reason. The later period has greater weight on the interdependence and cooperation of faith and reason, with faith no longer viewed as standing on its own feet and requiring no support from reason. The approximate time of the shift is the mid-1930's.

33. Although subjective religious experience is more important in the literature than either dogma or ritual, there is a clear trend in recent years toward a more favorable evaluation of the latter two components of religion. Stress on overemphasis of dogma as a source of doubt about religious truth lapses after the mid-1930's.

34. Emphases on attending and participating in church, reading the scriptures, and consulting a spiritual counselor all increase in very recent years. The greatest increase has come in the post-World War II period. The last two trends noted (33 and 34) are probably not unrelated to the so-called religious revival, and the shift noted in 32, above, may also be interpreted in the same sense.

35. Trends toward secularization are present in the literature. After about 1930 the specific stress that religion functions to "promote spirituality" is rather clearly less marked than it was before that year. There is a hint of Protestant decline of stress since about 1900 on the theme that suffering has divine significance (yet the evidence is tenuous and not entirely consistent). After the mid-thirties the theme that suffering means disharmony with the divine virtually disappears, although the "meaning" of this theme is not unambiguous. While it is true that Christ's divinity is generally accepted, after about 1930 the stress on *love* of Christ seems to be less heavy.

We're Getting Along
LLOYD C. DOUGLAS

The world is in a muddle. This is no new sensation. The world has always been in a muddle. The muddle is simply more apparent than ever before. We know more about it. Improved processes of communication have multiplied a thousandfold, for every man, the sins and shames of all humanity. At present there is no grief, no greed, no guile anywhere on earth that we do not know about—hour by hour. . . . *The world is doomed! Stay tuned to this station!*

Much of our purposeless worry may be explained by our desire for a world that never was. Some of us have constructed an ideal civilization that has had no existence in fact. We are shocked to learn of crimes we thought had been outlawed, outgrown. And, having been blasted out of our comfortable but ill-founded optimism, we are inclined to stampede in the other direction and conclude that civilization has suddenly come to "the brink of an abyss," to "the crossroads," to "the parting of the ways." This is nonsense. It is jargon.

If civilization is a long march of humanity across the ages toward some bright fulfillment of intelligent purpose—as all religions teach—this procession is not following a highway. It is *making* a highway, and all talk of its having arrived at a crossroads or at the parting of the ways merely makes a mess of a metaphor.

We simply wanted too much too soon. We thought we had a contract

Lloyd C. Douglas, "We're Getting Along," *The Rotarian*, 64 (June 1944), pp. 8–9.

with evolution which provided that it was annually to furnish the whole human race with better impulses and was to sweep us eventually and irresistibly to some great luminous dawn.

That was a mistake. We wanted evolution to work too fast. We wanted to hear the clock tick. How absurd that in a little life's span of 70 years I should hope to hear the hour strike in evolution's clock. Knowing that we are not going to be here very long, we build up a resistance to the idea of the passage of time until we know nothing about time. In a world full of precise knowledge, no one has any arbitrary concept of time at all.

An hour at a circus and an hour waiting outside the door of an operating room at a hospital are not the same thing. The four years between 16 and 20 and the four between 58 and 62 bear no resemblance. Why, even so little a piece of time as three minutes depends for its meaning on whether you are on the long-distance telephone talking to your best friend, or boiling an egg, or in a boxing ring with Joe Louis.

Yet knowing nothing about time we hoped it would do something, would pull us forward, while we watched. That is where we erred. Evolution does not inevitably pull things up into a better state of life. If we do not look out, evolution will "throw" us—as it did the mastodon.

Time was when the mastodons were breeding for tusks, and that was all that mattered. They wanted heavier tusks for defensive purposes. And they went on year after year, era after era, and cycle after cycle, thinking of nothing but tusks, teaching their children to avoid any other young mastodons that did not have big tusks. There came a time, then, when their tusks had grown so heavy they could not keep their rear feet on the ground—and the mastodons went out of business.

My point is that what has long been the right direction for mastodons or men to move in may eventually become the wrong direction.

We have essayed, at times, to determine that direction ourselves; we tried to help evolution. And, of course, we can do it—within limits. We can switch the machinery from "automatic" to "manual." We can breed the horns off cattle and the tails off cats. Some time ago the animal-husbandry department of the University of Illinois came out with a cus-tom-built hog. He was bred for thicker hams and thinner legs, and his offspring were given still thicker hams and still thinner legs. The trend continued until this new-model hog could not stand up any more, and the farm scientists had to put his old legs back on again.

A few years ago some inventive and inspired gentlemen developed an airplane. To it they gradually added speed and strength, and, at length, the ability to fly across neighbor countries with a bellyful of bombs. We are always going to have the airplane. The question is: are we going to be able to breed the bombs out of it? *There* is a postwar job for us!

You cannot simplify the story of humanity to a precise table of causes and effects, as in a chemical laboratory where, if elements are combined in certain proportions, you get a food or a medicine; or if you combine them in some other relationship, you go out through the skylight.

Great leaders are not a product of what they eat. Their environment may have but little to do with their aspirations or capacities. Galvani, brought up in the scenic splendor of the Alps, did not become a renowned sculptor or architect. He invented the electric battery. You cannot explain Galileo or Pasteur by their background; nor Edison, who had three months' education in an ungraded school. Environment does not account for Lincoln. There was nothing in Nazareth that inspired the Sermon on the Mount.

There's no accounting for what a people will produce, either for the world's weal or for its woe. Backward old China, content to stay at home and hoe in the garden and mind her own business, gave the world the mariner's compass. Allergic to new thought, she built a wall 30 feet high, 15 feet thick, and 1400 miles long, to insure herself against any interchange of ideas with other people—and then invented printing. Devoted to peace, she discovered gun powder.

If the story of civilization made any sense, the older and more experienced nations would be leading the way for all the others, pointing out the pitfalls, and inspiring the pioneers. For current examples of such leadership, see Syria, Egypt, India.

The world was always bewildered; always restless. All the standard theologies begin with the proposition of "a lost and ruined world." This is foggy thinking. If you are going to have a lost world, you have to presuppose a world that once knew where it was. If you've never known where you were, you can't get lost. You can't have a ruined world without hypothecating a world that once was a sound and solvent institution. Our world has never been sound and solvent.

You say, "Why can't the unhappy people over there on the other side of the earth settle down and live normal lives of peace and brotherhood?" Well—when was peace normal? When was brotherhood popular? The world has always been in confusion. It seems likely to be that kind of world for a long time. But it is the only world we have. We are part of it and we have to live in it. We must accept the risks that belong to our generation.

Do you think you would have had any more fun, you readers in Wisconsin and Ontario and New South Wales, if you had lived a century or two ago—without roads, lights, books, and doctors, and with the woods full of angry animals and aborigines; your whole life spent in the dark and the danger? Perhaps you readers in Massachusetts would have enjoyed coming over in the *Mayflower*. A lot of people did come over in the

Mayflower. Would you folks there in Kentucky have found life more pleasant if you had lived during the War Between the States?

Every era has its own pains and perplexities. That's the kind of world we're in. And yet, this world has its good points. Many days are fair. Many families are happy. Many friends are true. Some employers are considerate. Some employees are loyal. Some parents are kind and understanding. Some children are obedient and affectionate. Most people—if given a chance—would live in peace with their neighbors, at home and abroad.

Let's not be routed by the current frets and frights. Civilization is moving on. Sometimes it goes up by sharp grades, and then levels off on a plane on which a half-dozen generations will settle down to something like a cohesive, organized life. Just about the time "stability" seems won at last, civilization takes another grade.

That is what it is doing now, and we must recognize the motion for what it is. Eventually we shall get on top of events and shall tie up our loose ends, write off our losses, shake things down, and carry on.

That is the way it has always been and that is the way it is always going to be.

Despair, you know, is contagious. If you and I can't help defend our countries by bearing arms, we can at least sustain their morale. I don't want to be a despair carrier.

If any acquaintance of mine comes down with an acute attack of dismay, I don't want him to say that he caught it at my house.

PART FOUR

ARTS AND VALUES

9. The Nation Sings

Some of the more popular songs of the era indicate how readily such commercial works reflect and reinforce the moods and values of the large American middle class in the period, from Harold Arlen's mournful metaphor—"Stormy Weather"—in 1933 to the utopian optimism of the song he wrote at the close of the 1930's for the movie fantasy *The Wizard of Oz*. Here is the stress on the value of work and the ease with which it can be accomplished if one only learns to whistle, the abolition of fear and sense of inferiority, the importance of personal grooming and of making oneself liked, the value of money and love—and their interrelationship, the "irrelevancy" of higher education in the practical world, the intense nationalism and isolationist sentiment on the eve of European war.

There were other Americans singing and they were singing other songs, songs that came from different experience and reflected different life-styles, values and goals. Yet no history of the search for an American culture is complete without them for the experiences, the institutions (notably the more militant unions), the dreams were central in defining the life of millions of citizens during the period and the effort to express what all of this meant became an important heritage for those who followed. That is in fact why the Federal Government encouraged, through the Archives of American Folk Song at the Library of Congress, the accumulation and recording of this kind of important American artifact, whether the product of this period or of earlier ones.

The leading figure in the movement to collect these songs was Alan Lomax (born 1915). His father, John Lomax (1867–1948) had grown up along the old Chisholm trail and developed a special interest in the cowboys and their traditional ballads; his book on the cowboy ballads in 1910 is thought by many to mark a significant beginning of the serious study of American folk literature. Lomax helped establish the Archives at the Library of Congress; his son Alan was director from 1937 to 1942. He realized the importance not only of the traditional songs but that the current period was itself producing a remarkable body of comparable songs based on contemporary experience. One of the best—and best-known—writers and performers of these new (and old) "folk" songs was Woody Guthrie (1912–1967), who wrote more than a thousand songs. He also published his highly regarded autobiography *Bound for Glory* in 1943. Just before the outbreak of World War II, Guthrie joined Lomax—with an assist from another major singer-composer, Pete Seeger (born 1919) in providing special arrangements —to compile a brilliant collection of these songs, most of them composed during the Depression era and reflecting the distinct fears, values, goals and even experiences of those often outside the traditional bounds of American middle-class culture. The book was finally made available only in 1967, effectively illustrated with many of the great photographs from the Farm Security Administration's massive effort to document every aspect of American life. It was called *Hard-Hitting Songs for Hard-Hit People*. Woody Guthrie's Introduction to this book follows.

Hard-Hitting Songs for Hard-Hit People
WOODY GUTHRIE

Howdy Friend:

Here's a book of songs that's going to last a mighty long time, because these are the kind of songs that folks make up when they're a-singing about their hard luck, and hard luck is one thing that you sing louder about than you do about boots and saddles, or moons on the river, or cigarettes a shining in the dark.

There's a heap of people in the country that's a having the hardest time of their life right this minute; and songs are just like having babies. You can take either, but you can't fake it, and if you try to fake it, you don't fool anybody except yourself.

For the last eight years I've been a rambling man, from Oklahoma to California and back three times by freight train, highway, and thumb, and I've been stranded, and disbanded, busted, disgusted with people of all sorts, sizes, shapes, and calibers—folks that wandered around over the country looking for work, down and out, and hungry half of the time. I've slept on and with them, with their feet in my face and my feet in theirs—in bed rolls with Canadian Lumberjacks, in greasy rotten shacks and tents with the Okies and Arkies that are grazing today over the states of California and Arizona like a herd of lost buffalo with the hot hoof and empty mouth disease.

Then to New York in the month of February, the thumb route, in the snow that blanketed from Big Springs, Texas, north to New York, and south again into even Florida . . . Walking down the big road, no job, no

From *Hard-Hitting Songs for Hard-Hit People* (New York, 1967).

money, no home . . . no nothing. Nights I slept in jails, and the cells were piled high with young boys, strong men, and old men; and they talked and they sung, and they told you the story of their life, how it used to be, how it got to be, how the home went to pieces, how the young wife died or left, how the mother died in the insane asylum, how Dad tried twice to kill himself, and lay flat on his back for 18 months—and then crops got to where they wouldn't bring nothing, work in the factories would kill a dog, work on the belt line killed your soul, work in the cement and limestone quarries withered your lungs, work in the cotton mills shot your feet and legs all to hell, work in the steel mills burned your system up like a gnat that lit in the melting pot, and—always, always had to fight and argue and cuss and swear, and shoot and slaughter and wade mud and sling blood—to try to get a nickel more out of the rich bosses. But out of all of this mixing bowl of hell and high waters by George, the hard-working folks have done something that the bosses, his sons, his wives, his whores, and his daughters have failed to do—the working folks have walked bare handed against clubs, gas bombs, billys, blackjacks, saps, knucks, machine guns, and log chains—and they sang their way through the whole dirty mess. And that's why I say the songs in this book will be sung coast to coast acrost the country a hundred years after all nickel phonographs have turned back into dust.

I ain't a writer, I want that understood, I'm just a little one-cylinder guitar picker. But I don't get no kick out of these here songs that are imitation and made up by guys that's paid by the week to write 'em up— that reminds me of a crow a settin on a fence post a singing when some guy is a sawing his leg off at the same time. I like the song the old hen sings just before she flogs hell out of you for pestering her young chicks.

This book is a song book of that kind. It's a song book that come from the lungs of the workin' folks—and every little song was easy and simple, but mighty pretty, and it caught on like a whirlwind—it didn't need sheet music, it didn't need nickel phonographs, and it didn't take nothing but a little fanning from the bosses, the landlords, the deputies, and the cops, and the big shots, and the bankers, and the business men to flare up like an oil field on fire, and the big cloud of black smoke turn into a cyclone—and cut a swath straight to the door of the man that started the whole thing, the greedy rich people.

You'll find the songs the hungry farmers sing as they bend their backs and drag their sacks, and split their fingers to pieces grabbing your shirts and dresses out of the thorns on a cotton boll. You'll find the blues. The blues are my favorite, because the blues are the saddest and lonesomest, and say the right thing in a way that most preachers ought to pattern after. All honky tonk and dance hall blues had parents, and those parents were the blues that come from the workers in the factories, mills, mines, crops, orchards, and oil fields—but by the time a blues reaches a honky tonk music box, it is changed from chains to kisses, and from a cold prison cell to a warm bed with a hot mama, and from a sunstroke on a chain gang, to a chock house song, or a brand new baby and a bottle of gin.

You'll find a bunch of songs made up by folks back in the hills of old Kentucky. The hills was full of coal. The men was full of pep and wanted to work. But houses wasn't no good, and wages was next to nothing. Kids died like flies. The mothers couldn't pay the doctor, so the doctor didn't come. It was the midwives, the women like old Aunt Molly Jackson, that rolled up her sleeves, spit out the window, grabbed a wash pan in one hand and a armful of old pads and rags, and old newspapers, and dived under the covers and old rotten blankets—to come up with a brand new human being in one hand and a hungry mother in the other. Aunt Molly was just a coal miner's wife, and a coal miner's daughter, but she took the place of the doctor in 850 cases, because the coal miners didn't have the money.

You'll find the songs that were scribbled down on the margins of almanacs with a penny pencil, and sung to the rhythms of splinters and rocks that the Winchester rifles kicked up in your face as you sang them. I still wonder who was on the tail end of the rifles. Also in the Kentucky Coal Miner Songs, you'll sing the two wrote by Jim Garland, "Greenback Dollar" and "Harry Simms"—a couple of ringtail tooters you're bound to like.

Sarah Ogan, she's the half sister of Aunt Molly, about half as old, and a mighty good worker and singer—she keeps up the spirit of the men that dig for a hamburger in a big black hole in the ground, and are promised pie in the sky when they die and get to heaven, provided they go deep enough in the hole, and stay down there long enough.

Then the next batch of wrong colored eggs to hatch—out pops the New Deal songs—the songs that the people sung when they heard the mighty good sounding promises of a reshuffle, a honest deck, and a brand new deal from the big shots. A Straight flush, the Ace for One Big Union, the King for One Happy Family, the Queen for a happy mother with a full cupboard, the Jack for a hard working young man with money enough in his pockets to show his gal a good time, and the ten spot for the ten commandments that are overlooked too damn much by the big boys.

Next you'll run across some songs called "Songs of the One Big Union" —which is the same Big Union that Abe Lincoln lived for and fought for and died for. Something has happened to that Big Union since Abe Lincoln was here. It has been raped. The Banking men has got their Big Union, and the Land Lords has got their Big Union, and the Merchants has got their Kiwanis and Lions Club, and the Finance Men has got their

Big Union, and the Associated Farmers has got their Big Union, but down south and out west, on the cotton farms, and working in the orchards and fruit crops it is a jail house offence for a few common everyday workers to form them a Union, and get together for higher wages and honest pay and fair treatment. It's damn funny how all of the big boys are in Big Unions, but they cuss and raise old billy hell when us poor damn working guys try to get together and make us a Working Man's Union. This Book is full of songs that the working folks made up about the beatings and the sluggings and the cheatings and the killings that they got when they said they was a going to form them a Working Man's Union. It is a jail house crime for a poor damn working man to even hold a meeting with other working men. They call you a red or a radical or something, and throw you and your family off of the farm and let you starve to death. . . . These songs will echo that song of starvation till the world looks level—till the world is level—and there ain't no rich men, and there ain't no poor men, and every man on earth is at work and his family is living as human beings instead of like a nest of rats.

A last section of this book is called Mulligan Stew which are songs that you make up when you're a trying to speak something that's on your mind . . . telling your troubles to the blue sky, or a walkin' down the road with your 2 little kids by the hand, thinking of your wife that's just died with her third one—and you get to speaking your mind—maybe to yourself the first time, then when you get it a little better fixed in your head, and you squeeze out all of the words you don't need, and you boil it down to just a few that tell the whole story of your hard luck. Then you talk it or sing it to somebody you meet in the hobo jungle or stranded high and dry in the skid row section of a big town, or just fresh kicked off a Georgia farm, and a going nowhere, just a walkin' along, and a draggin' your feet along in the deep sand, and—then you hear him sing you his song or tell you his tale, and you think, That's a mighty funny thing. His song is just like mine. And my tale is just like his. And everywhere you ramble, under California R.R. bridges, or the mosquito swamps of Louisiana, or the dustbowl deserts of the Texas plains—it's a different man, a different woman, a different kid a speaking his mind, but it's the same old tale, and the same old song. Maybe different words. Maybe different tune. But it's hard times, and the same hard times. The same big song. This book is that song.

You'll find a section in this book about Prison & Outlaw songs. I know how it is in the states I've rambled through. In the prisons the boys sing about the long, lonesome days in the cold old cell, and the dark nights in the old steel tank and a lot of the best songs you ever heard come from these boys and women that sweat all day in the pea patch, chain gang, a makin' big ones out of little ones, and new roads out of cow trails—

new paved roads for a big black limousine to roll over with a lady in a fur coat and a screwball poodle dog a sniffing at her mouth. Prisoners ain't shooting the bull when they sing a mournful song, it's the real stuff. And they sing about the "man that took them by the arm," and about the "man with the law in his hand," and about the "man a settin' up in the jury box," and the "man on th' judges bench," and the "guard come a walkin' down that graveyard hall," and about the "man with th' jail house key," and the "guard a walkin' by my door," and about the "sweethearts that walk past the window," and the old mother that wept and tore her hair, and the father that pleaded at the bar, and the little girl that sets in the moonlight alone, and waits for the sentence to roll by. These outlaws may be using the wrong system when they rob banks and hijack the rich traveler, and shoot their way out of a gamblin' game, and shoot down a man in a jewelry store, or blow down the pawn shop owner, but I think I know what's on these old boys minds. Something like this: "Two little children a layin' in the bed, both of them so hungry that they cain't lift up their head . . ."

I know how it was with me, there's been a many a time that I set around with my head hanging down, broke, clothes no good, old slouchy shoes, and no place to go to have a good time, and no money to spend on the women, and a sleeping in cattle cars like a whiteface steer, and a starving for days at a time up and down the railroad tracks and then a seeing other people all fixed up with a good high rolling car, and good suits of clothes, and high priced whiskey, and more pretty gals than one. Even had money to blow on damn fool rings and necklaces and bracelets around their necks and arms—and I would just set there by the side of the road and think . . . Just one of them diamonds would buy a little farm with a nice little house and a water well and a gourd dipper, and forty acres of good bottom land to raise a crop on, and a good rich garden spot up next to the house, and a couple of jersey cows with nice big tits, and some chickens to wake me up of a morning, and . . . the whole picture of the little house and piece of land would go through my head every time I seen a drunk man with three drunk women a driving a big Lincoln Zephyr down the road—with money to burn, and they didn't even know where the money was coming from . . . yes, siree, it's a mighty tempting thing, mighty tempting.

Now, I might be a little haywired, but I ain't no big hand to like a song because it's pretty, or because it's fancy, or done up with a big smile and a pink ribbon, I'm a man to like songs that ain't sung too good. Big hand to sing songs that ain't really much account. I mean, you know, talking about good music, and fancy runs, and expert music. I like songs, by george, that's sung by folks that ain't musicians, and ain't able to read music, don't know one note from another'n, and—say something that amounts to something. That a way you can say what you got to say just singing it and if you use the same dern tune, or change it around twice, and turn it upside down, why that still don't amount to a dern, you have spoke what you had to speak, and if folks don't like the music, well, you can still pass better than some political speakers.

But it just so happens that these songs here, they're pretty, they're easy, they got something to say, and they say it in a way you can understand, and if you go off somewhere and change'em around a little bit, well, that don't hurt nothin'. Maybe you got a new song. You have, if you said what you really had to say—about how the old world looks to you, or how it ought to be fixed.

Hells bells, I'm a going to fool around here and make a song writer out of you. No, I couldn't do that—wouldn't do it if I could. I ruther have you just like you are. You are a songbird right this minute. Today you're a better songbird than you was yesterday, 'cause you know a little bit more, you seen a little bit more, and all you got to do is just park yourself under a shade tree, or maybe at a desk, if you still got a desk, and haul off and write down some way you think this old world could be fixed so's it would be twice as level and half as steep, and take the knocks out of it, and grind the valves, and tighten the rods, and take up the bearings, and put a boot in the casing, and make the whole trip a little bit smoother, and a little bit more like a trip instead of a trap.

It wouldn't have to be fancy words. It wouldn't have to be a fancy tune. The fancier it is the worse it is. The plainer it is the easier it is, and the easier it is, the better it is—and the words don't even have to be spelt right.

You can write it down with the stub of a burnt match, or with an old chewed up penny pencil, on the back of a sack, or on the edge of a almanac, or you could pitch in and write your walls full or your own songs. They don't even have to rhyme to suit me. If they don't rhyme a tall, well, then it's prose, and all of the college boys will study on it for a couple of hundred years, and because they cain't make heads nor tails of it, they'll swear you're a natural born song writer, maybe call you a natural born genius. . . .

10. The Fine Art of Advertising

During the 1920's and 1930's advertising in America became a fine art aided in its practice by the best available skills from the science of psychology. A most significant trend in the advertising of the period was the strong sense of individual improvement repeatedly stressed: if the consumer would buy and use the product he might find himself better off physically or mentally, or more successful in the world of competition for love, money, or power. Customers were made conscious of a wide range of "diseases" (some real and some invented by the advertising agencies)—and a wide range of new scientific properties in products (again some real and some concocted by the advertisers). No doubt these diseases were holding some consumers back from full achievement; little doubt, new scientific properties in products would cure the condition. The appeal to science was especially effective; the term vitamin had, for example, become a household word around 1920; by 1940 ten such food factors had been discovered; by 1936 ways had been found to synthesize vitamin B complex so that it could be manufactured in large quantities.

The news of all of this not only changed American dietary patterns but the pitch of much of American advertising as well. Not only health but also mental well-being was offered; all sorts of products might improve your "nerves," obviously a key complaint in the period. In 1931 the manufacturers of Lucky Strike cigarettes spent $19,000,000 on advertising, trying (successfully) to convince women that smoking was a vital aid in dieting. All such advertising frequently resorted to the use of endorsement from people in admired social positions, achievers in the business or professional world, athletes, movie stars—a wide range of celebrities from a rather new social world called Café Society.

Edward L. Bernays (born 1891) has had a brilliant career in the public relations field as a counsel to a wide variety of clients, in government as well as in private industry, who wished somehow to persuade the public to believe or to do certain things. In the process Bernays, often relying on expert help in psychology and psychiatry, has not only carried through campaigns that have effectively altered behavior patterns of Americans but has become one of the leading experts himself on the whole vital issue of public opinion. In the early 1930's he served George Washington Hill and his American Tobacco Company in the attempt to attract women smokers. Part of that story is reprinted below.

Techniques of the Advertising Trade
EDWARD L. BERNAYS

[George W.] Hill thought the time had arrived for a direct, vigorous campaign to induce women to smoke in public places. In 1929 it was acceptable for women to smoke at home, but a woman seen smoking in public was labeled a hussy or worse.

Hill called me in. "How can we get women to smoke on the street? They're smoking indoors. But, damn it, if they spend half the time out-doors and we can get 'em to smoke outdoors, we'll damn near double our female market. Do something. Act!"

"There's a taboo against such smoking," I said. "Let me consult an expert, Dr. A. A. Brill, the psychoanalyst. He might give me the psychological basis for a woman's desire to smoke, and maybe this will help me."

"What will it cost?"

"I suppose just a consultation fee."

"Shoot," said Hill.

Brill explained to me: "Some women regard cigarettes as symbols of freedom," he told me: "Smoking is a sublimation of oral eroticism; holding a cigarette in the mouth excites the oral zone. It is perfectly normal for women to want to smoke cigarettes. Further, the first woman who smoked probably had an excess of masculine components and adopted the habit as a masculine act. But today the emancipation of women has suppressed many of their feminine desires. More women now do the same work as men do. Many women bear no children; those who do bear have fewer children. Feminine traits are masked. Cigarettes, which are equated with men, become torches of freedom."

In this last statement I found a way to help break the taboo against women smoking in public. Why not a parade of women lighting torches of freedom—smoking cigarettes?

The Easter Sunday Parade on Fifth Avenue seemed a natural occasion on which to launch the idea. One of my friends who worked for *Vogue* gave us a list of thirty debutantes. We sent each the following telegram signed by my secretary, Bertha Hunt, from our office:

IN THE INTERESTS OF EQUALITY OF THE SEXES AND TO FIGHT ANOTHER SEX TABOO I AND OTHER YOUNG WOMEN WILL LIGHT ANOTHER TORCH OF FREE-

Edward L. Bernays, *Biography of an Idea: Memoirs of Public Relations Counsel Edward L. Bernays* (New York, 1965), pp. 386–395.

DOM BY SMOKING CIGARETTES WHILE STROLLING ON FIFTH AVENUE EASTER SUNDAY. WE ARE DOING THIS TO COMBAT THE SILLY PREJUDICE THAT THE CIGARETTE IS SUITABLE FOR THE HOME, THE RESTAURANT, THE TAXICAB, THE THEATER LOBBY BUT NEVER NO NEVER FOR THE SIDEWALK. WOMEN SMOKERS AND THEIR ESCORTS WILL STROLL FROM FORTY-EIGHTH STREET TO FIFTY-FOURTH STREET ON FIFTH AVENUE BETWEEN ELEVEN-THIRTY AND ONE O'CLOCK.

We expressed similar sentiments in an advertisement in the New York newspapers that was signed by Ruth Hale, a leading feminist, who was glad to find a platform for her views, which happened to coincide with American's. Ten young debutantes agreed to march.

Our parade of ten young women lighting "torches of freedom" on Fifth Avenue on Easter Sunday as a protest against woman's inequality caused a national stir. Front-page stories in newspapers reported the freedom march in words and pictures. For weeks after the event editorials praised or condemned the young women who had paraded against the smoking taboo.

The demonstration became almost a national issue. E. H. Gauvreau, editor of the New York *Graphic,* wanted us to reassemble the girls for a special photograph; another, the editor of the Ventura, California, *Star,* in a headline—"SWATS ANOTHER TABOO"—acknowledged that the parade had accomplished its purpose. Women's clubs throughout the country expressed grief that women would smoke in public, papers in Boston, Detroit, Wheeling, West Virginia, and San Francisco reported women smoking on the streets as a result of the New York parade. Age-old customs, I learned, could be broken down by a dramatic appeal, disseminated by the network of media. Of course the taboo was not destroyed completely. But a beginning had been made, one I regret today.

Hill squeezed each advertising theme he used until he thought it had run dry, then he looked for a new one. Ultraviolet rays were first hailed as an elixir of life in 1931. Factories and nurseries installed ultraviolet glass; Northerners obtained healthful-looking Florida tans with sunlamps. We bought a sunlamp and had ultraviolet window panes installed in our Washington Square home to improve our health and that of our children. Hill recognized the impact of the fad and was eager to exploit it. He decided to toast the tobacco that went into Lucky Strikes with ultraviolet ray lamps during its processing. He built a huge nationwide advertising campaign around the theme of this new achievement of science: "Lucky Strikes—they're toasted with ultraviolet rays."

By then the public was getting increasingly skeptical about the testimonials of opera stars and society figures, so Hill introduced a new category of leader to the testimonial brotherhood. He began to run huge, signed photographs of top American business leaders with their testimonials praising the toasting process.

Big businessmen permitted the use of their names, pictures and signatures as endorsements. The novelty of the approach made these testimonials effective. No money was paid for the endorsements. Alfred A. Knopf, among others, joined our parade. I suppose it flattered his huge vanity to see a Knopf face looking at him in the morning *Times*. In 1931 business was reeling under the stock-market crash and the Depression. Businessmen whose heads were above water were glad to see their oversize photographs in newspapers around the country at no cost to their companies or to them.

Hill also gave serious personal attention to the publicity of the Lucky Strike radio hour, which he had masterminded. The program featured the B. A. Rolfe orchestra and reached hundreds of thousands of dancing enthusiasts on a national NBC hookup. Hill spent hours at rehearsal in the broadcasting studio. In keeping with his personality, Hill insisted that the dance music have strongly marked rhythms, rapid tempos, and crashing noise. Such music gave people confidence, he said. It was an antidote to the Depression.

After the program's popularity had been established, Hill called me in and asked, "How do we hold on to that popularity? I can start a trend, but how do I keep it up?"

I suggested that we should have Rolfe write to group leaders, prominent musicians, personnel directors (in relation to music for the working man), the clergy (in relation to family unity), dance teachers and professors of music studies—all people who might influence the public's listening and dancing habits—explaining that the music of the Lucky Strike orchestra put most of America on its dancing feet and asking if, in this time of Depression, it hadn't given them confidence. Hill agreed to my proposal and Rolfe signed the letter we sent out. The Lucky Strike Dance Orchestra and its social significance soon became the subject of extensive nation-wide discussion. The replies to Rolfe's letter ran the gamut of the Pareto curve, from praise to disdain, but we didn't mind whether people talked for or against the thesis as long as they talked.

A year after our Rolfe campaign Hill hired Walter Winchell for Lucky Strike news broadcasts, capitalizing on a new trend in journalism—the telling of the inside story about people and events. Hill wanted me to help build a radio audience for Winchell, who was unknown except to readers of his syndicated newspaper column. I had never met the columnist, although he worked on the *Graphic* when I was public relations counsel for Bernarr MacFadden, but I recognized the great appeal he had to the public. I planned to build him as if he were an institution.

I engaged a photographer to trail him during his midnight rounds and distributed pictures of his night-life activity to newspapers throughout the country to increase his glamour. I made Winchell's penchant for coining new words the basis of a letter to philologists, calling attention to him as a creator of new Americanisms.

Hill watched the Winchell campaign closely. He posted 45,000 billboards in 18,886 communities. The poster carried Winchell's picture and the phrase he used in his broadcast, "Okay, America." Hill never whispered.

Soon Winchell became a national institution; when he went on the air, all America placed its ear to the keyhole.

Hill never stopped thinking about the huge potential Luckies market —the women of America. New surveys showed him that women were now smoking in and out of the house; they also disclosed that many women objected to Luckies because the green package with its red bulls-eye clashed with the colors of the clothes they wore. Some time in the spring of 1934 Hill called me.

"Women aren't buying Luckies as they should. What do you suggest, Mr. Bernays?" he asked.

"Change the Lucky package to a neutral color that will match anything they wear," I replied.

This was a logical suggestion, but Hill became emotional at the idea of changing the color of his package. "I've spent millions of dollars advertising the package. Now you ask me to change it. That's lousy advice."

My experience with Cheney [the American industrial designer] suggested my next thought: "If you won't change the color of the package, change the color of fashion—to green."

"Change the fashion—that's a good idea. Do it," Hill shouted enthusiastically, adding as an afterthought, "What will it cost?"

I knew that money alone couldn't change a fashion. Such a change depended on setting forces in motion that would influence other forces, and these in turn might change the fashionable color. I had no idea of the money necessary for mechanics, so I plucked a round figure out of the air.

"Twenty-five thousand."

"Spend it!" yelled Hill.

That was the beginning of a fascinating six-month activity for me— to make green *the* fashionable color. My work with Cheney had shown me that fashions seldom happen fortuitously; they follow trends. A planned event of importance can play a part in affecting these trends. The costumes and décor of the Bal de l'Opéra in Paris, held annually by French textile manufacturers and the *haute couture* of Paris, with the cooperation of the *haut monde,* had influenced French fashion trends —so why not a Green Ball in New York? Why shouldn't an American ball planned along comparable lines influence fashion trends here, particularly if it was linked with Paris fashion influences?

Some years before I had asked Alfred Reeves, of the American Automobile Manufacturers Association, how he had developed a market for American automobiles in England, where roads were narrow and curved.

"I didn't try to sell automobiles," he answered. "I campaigned for wider and straighter roads. The sale of American cars followed."

This was an application of the general principle which I later termed the engineering of consent. Like an architect, I drew up a comprehensive blueprint, a complete procedural outline, detailing objectives, the necessary research, strategy, themes and timing of the planned activities. I wanted to be sure the money Hill had authorized was spent effectively.

Next, consistent with our usual policy, I researched the impact of green on society. The future always holds within it something of the past and present. I wanted to know the values embraced in the color green. Green had psychological, health and aesthetic values. Green was "the color of spring, an emblem of hope, victory and plenty," the springtime of life and recuperation"; it suggested calm, peace and serenity. Many universities used green as their school color; graduate students in physical education and pharmacy wore jade-green hoods. A statistical analysis disclosed that green was featured in 5 per cent to 50 per cent of the current lines of the great French fashion houses; the average was almost 20 per cent, an encouraging base on which to build. I also studied the part played by fashion magazines, socialites, top dress houses and manufacturers, newspapers and women's magazines in influencing the popular colors in the country.

Soon we were at work on two continents, making contact with a variety of social and economic groups.

First I talked to Mrs. Frank A. Vanderlip, a friend, chairman of the Women's Infirmary of New York, wife of the former chairman of the National City Bank. Mrs. Vanderlip's imaginative fund-raising efforts kept this voluntary hospital going. I suggested that a Green Ball be held in November under the Infirmary's auspices for the hospital's benefit. I explained that a nameless sponsor would defray the costs up to $25,000; our client would donate our services to promote the ball; the color green would be the ball's motif and the obligatory color of all the gowns worn at the ball.

I added, "I can assure you the cause is not Paris green, a poison."

I now approached Philip Vogelman, the enterprising president of the Onondaga Silk Company, and suggested his firm become the spearhead for color leadership in the United States. He listened to the program I outlined, and then agreed to bet on green. This was somewhat of a speculation on his part, but not financially, because green would have been in his line anyway. He was risking at most a wrong prediction. If he lost, it would not hurt much; such miscalculation was a part of the textile business. But if he was right—with our help—it would raise him to leadership.

Vogelman gave a "Green Fashions Fall" luncheon that spring for fashion editors and fashion trades at the Waldorf-Astoria to induce these industries to follow his lead in picking green and to stimulate public acceptance of the color. We printed the menus on green paper and served green food—green beans, asparagus-tip salad, pistachio mousse glacé, green mints, and crème de menthe. Joseph Cummings Chase, a portrait painter and the head of Hunter College's Art Department, discussed green in the work of great artists; Dr. Joseph Jastrow, the psychologist, discussed the psychological implications of green.

I had wondered at the alacrity with which scientists, academicians and professional men participated in events of this kind. I learned they welcomed the opportunity to discuss their favorite subject and enjoyed the resultant publicity. In an age of communication their own effectiveness often depended on public visibility.

Widespread publicity followed the lunch. The New York *Sun* headlined its story, "It Looks Like a Green Winter"; the *New York Post* stressed a "Green Autumn." One press service reported "Fall fashions stalking the forests for their color note, picking green as the modish fall wear."

Vogelman invited buyers to a showing of his new green fall silks. We supplied Onondaga with green letterheads and green sheets for press releases and organized a Color Fashion Bureau, which sent authentic fashion data from New York and Paris to editors of feature and women's pages. It alerted the fashion field to green's leadership in the whole women's clothing and accessories area. The bureau also promoted green in interior decoration. Nothing stands by itself. There is an interrelationship between the elements of fashion. House décors affect dress colors; if green dresses clashed with prevailing décors, women might not wear them. Costume accessories need to match the basic fabrics. In May, 1500 letters on the dominance of green were sent to interior decorators, home-furnishings buyers, art-in-industry groups and clubwomen; 5000 announcements were sent to department stores and merchandise managers.

Throughout the summer the bureau maintained its barrage. We were encouraged to note that green pencils and green writing paper followed the accelerating trend to that color. Without our nudging, other firms got on the green bandwagon. Peggy Sage announced a new emerald nail polish to be worn with green costumes; Lilly Daché designed a special green hat; Prosper McCallum introduced green stockings. McGibbon & Company arranged a green window display in their Fifth Avenue shop. The woman's-page editor of a Philadelphia newspaper wrote: "Let me know what you are plugging. It is so adroit that even I, hard-boiled old she-dragon, can't detect it. If, as I suspect, it is glazed chintz, I will add a description with place to buy, including prices. I have a lot of respect for the clever copywriter who is responsible for such readable material, and I am quite willing to play along in a helpful way." Our effort to make green the fashion color sold chintz as an unanticipated corollary.

Onondaga didn't make chintz, and I never asked them how much green silk they sold. That was of less concern to them than their style leadership. The retail buyer, who purchases his material from the manufacturer long before the consumer does, bets on the public acceptance of a color or weave when he buys. If he believes a manufacturer is right about future consumer demand, he is more likely to patronize him. Thousands now asked to be put on the Onondaga bulletin mailing list. Department stores, theatrical producers, radio fashion commentators, art editors, pattern companies and trade papers added to the spreading enthusiasm for green. The praise of green in newspapers rose in a crescendo through the summer.

An Infirmary Green Ball Committee of prominent social leaders sold Green Ball tickets. At Mrs. Vanderlip's request an invitation committee —Mrs. James Roosevelt, Mrs. Walter Chrysler, Mrs. Irving Berlin, and Mrs. Averell Harriman—invited the patronesses. The ball committee held a series of luncheons with representatives of the accessory trades to encourage them to make available green accessories for the green gowns the ball guests would wear. At my suggestion the committee started a news bulletin of its own about the ball. Emphasis by repetition gains acceptance for an idea, particularly if the repetition comes from different sources.

In 1934 high fashion in the United States still needed Paris backing. At my suggestion Mrs. Vanderlip sailed for France. We wanted the *haute couture* of Paris to supply the green dresses that would be modeled by American society women in the fashion show at the ball. We also wanted official approval and support of the Beaux Arts department of the French Government for our tableaux, based on the Barbizon paintings I had admired on my last visit to France.

In Paris our publicity woman arranged a tea for Mrs. Vanderlip. Forty French fashion VIP's—top figures at Worth, Lelong, Callot, Patou, Chanel and other members of the *haute couture*, plus Marian Taylor of

Vogue and Carmel Snow of *Harper's Bazaar*—attended and agreed to support the campaign. The *haute couture* people and the French Government agreed to co-operate. The *haute couture* was dependent economically on the purchasing power and good will of American women. Because of her husband's standing, Mrs. Vanderlip was recognized by the French as a formidable spokesman for the American women, their customers. The French Government, too, acted in recognition of the place luxury goods occupied in their international trade.

Next, the committee engaged a consultant to handle the mechanics of the ball. Debutantes flocked to her call; society editors followed her lead. As early as August the New York *Herald Tribune* carried a full page headlined "Charity Benefit to Stress Fashion Importance of Green" showing pictures of the costumes to be worn and the paintings that inspired them. Newspaper interest mounted. Meanwhile, we trod gingerly through the political mazes of the American fashion world. Experts had advised us to await the return of Edwin Goodman, of Bergdorf Goodman, from a trip abroad before we approached other New York high-fashion houses for cooperation. If he played along, they would too. We waited; Goodman liked the idea, and his competitors came along, as predicted.

In September, Altman's Fifth Avenue windows were filled with green dresses and suits. Women's magazines were featuring green fashions on their covers. The November issue of *Vogue* carried two pages of sketches of the green dresses to be brought from Paris to New York. We knew now that green had arrived.

The unsuspecting opposition gave us a boost: The November magazine advertisements for Camel cigarettes showed a girl wearing a green dress with red trimmings, the colors of the Lucky Strike package. The advertising agency had chosen green because it was now the fashionable color. . . .

Having succeeded in matching fashion's green with Luckies' package, Hill now thought the time was ripe to go after the women's market with a billboard campaign. He showed me a colored poster design featuring a picture of a woman offering a package of Luckies to two men. Up to then the idea of displaying pictures of women smoking had been too radical a departure from the mores, even for Hill.

"What do you think of it?" he asked.

"It makes me feel queasy," I said. "I think a psychoanalyst could help us analyze its impact. Let me go to Dr. A. A. Brill again and get his advice."

"O.K.," said Hill.

I took the layout to Dr. Brill. Instantly he pointed out that three people in the picture created a conflict in the mind of the observer. "No observer can identify himself with anyone in the illustration," he explained. "Two people should appear, one man and one woman. That is life. Nor should a woman offer two men a package of cigarettes. The cigarette is a phallic symbol, to be offered by a man to a woman. Every normal man or woman can identify with such a message."

Brill's lightning interpretation was, I thought, a brilliant piece of psychoanalytic thinking. The use of psychoanalysis as the basis of advertising is common today, but I believe this may have been the first instance of its application to advertising.

11. Consumerism, The Counterattack to Advertising

It would be a mistake—and a fundamental failure in understanding some of the forces operating in search of an American culture—to assume that there was no counterattack to the powerful assault launched by American advertising. Only an analysis of the nature of that response can provide certain additional essential clues to the nature of the culture itself. First, there was humor. The American search for health, wealth, beauty, and romance through the purchase of a wide variety of products was an effective butt for comedic talent in print and on radio as well. The piece reprinted below from *Americana,* the unusual magazine of humor and satire produced in 1932 and 1933 and edited by Alexander King and Gilbert Seldes (with assists from such figures as George Grosz, S. J. Perelman, and Nathanael West among others), not only represents the tone of that magazine's humor but reveals a good deal about "the enemy" as well as something about the nature of the genuine rise of a consumer opposition.

Perhaps the most obvious counter to false or misleading advertising in an era of the rise of a welfare state would have been increased governmental regulation. There were many efforts at strengthening already on-going government activities in this area and even new legislation. But such redress through law was often difficult to obtain; advertisers and manufacturers provided a powerful lobby against stringent codes. Increasingly, therefore, American consumers turned to other means characteristic, too, of trends developing within the cultural scene. There were the crusades of those like Ralph Borsodi's to go back to an older order of living, to rely less and less on the devices of industry and machine production and stress the home as a center of domestic production. This went hand-in-hand with the movement back to agrarian communities—most popular in the period—which also stressed natural living and natural products, an eschewing of the artificial, machine-made, mass-produced, *and* advertising-induced. Interest in cooperatives of all kinds had proceeded during the 1920's and blossomed even more fully in the postcrash period. Consumer cooperatives were especially attractive, and the literature about cooperatives grew rapidly.

But even more significant was the emergence of various research organizations and their services. In 1927 F. J. Schlink, an engineer and physicist who had spent six years in the U.S. Bureau of Standards, and

Stuart Chase, an economist and writer with some engineering background who had been a part of the Technical Alliance with Veblen, organized Consumers' Research, a testing bureau for consumers that made available to its members the results of its research and testing. It was joined in the field in 1936 by Consumer's Union which issued its own Consumer Reports. Such efforts were reinforced by a wide series of articles and books designed to enlighten the gullible consuming public. None was more successful—it went through thirteen printings in its first six months in print—than the volume Schlink co-authored with Arthur Kallet (also an engineer and one of the directors of Consumers' Research)—*100,000,000 Guinea Pigs: Dangers in Everyday Foods, Drugs, and Cosmetics* (1933).

Consumers, Arise!

DON LANGAN

No one was more surprised than the police on that memorable day. Who would have suspected an organization named The Consumers of being anything but orderly? And Mr. R. Thomas Uppercue, who applied for the parade permit, was such a quiet, polite gentleman according to the clerk at the City Hall.

Of course the police knew it was to be some kind of a protest demonstration. The night before the parade a mass meeting had been held in the park, and there had been speakers who used such phrases as "Are we mice or men?", "Our homes and families are being invaded," and "It is high time we act."

On the day of "The Consumers" parade close to two thousand people, men and women, gathered at the end of The Drive. They were to march on foot, and had secured permission to go across 72nd Street to Broadway, down Broadway to 42nd, and across 42nd to Madison. The line of march was to end at about that point, in the center of the "office section."

It was easy to see that military precision would play a small part in this parade. The people lined up in any old fashion, eager to dispense with formality and get started. Banners and placards were distributed through the ranks, and cries of encouragement greeted each one as it was held aloft.

In a few minutes the parade got under way. No one bothered much

Don Langan, "Consumers, Arise!", *Americana*, 2 (November 1933), p. 15.

about keeping step, or holding a straight line. This was the first parade Mr. Uppercue had ever led. As a matter of fact he didn't have the slightest idea what a Grand Marshal did . . . especially a Grand Marshal without benefit of a horse.

The banners and placards were interesting. One read, "They are pursuing our daughters with the specter HALITOSIS." Another said, "They tell our wives they have 'THAT HAGGARD LOOK.' " A third proclaimed "WASH DAY HANDS is just another sales insult . . . not a slogan." Some of the signs seemed quite defiant. For instance, one lady brandished a card which read "We've watched out for 'B.O.' long enough . . . now you watch out for us." Still another banner stated "Have *you* got Gigolo Hair? . . . Stand up and tell them NO!" As the parade progressed the onlookers seemed to catch the spirit of the thing. When a banner which said "We're going to kick with our ATHLETE'S FOOT" came along, a great shout went up, and at least a hundred bystanders joined the ranks right there. Another sign which provoked an outburst along the crowded curbs said, "AMERICAN STOMACH your grandmother . . . you'll have 'that tired feeling' when we get through with you."

As they started down Broadway the ranks of the marchers had swelled to triple its original size. Sympathizers joined them in every block. At about 50th Street they passed a drug store. Some one in the line of march noticed a display in the window. It advertised a new mouth wash; there was a large picture of a man in pajamas, hair awry, mouth open, tongue out, as though he had just swallowed a very bitter pill. Over his head ran the legend, "Don't start the day with that MORNING TASTE * * * Use William's Wonder Wash."

It was a very unfortunate window for that particular day. "There's one now," the marcher who spied it shouted. A piece of brick hurtled through the air. The window was shattered. A half-dozen of the men dashed from the line, reached the broken window and dragged the personification of MORNING TASTE into the street. "This is the way we look to them in the morning," one of the men shouted, as they tore the sign to bits.

Mr. Uppercue came running back in a state of great excitement. "Consumers, Consumers," he shouted, "we must keep order." But Mr. Uppercue was not a Grand Marshal, nor a leader of men. The marchers broke ranks and swelled down Broadway at a quickened pace. The drug store window incident was an appetizer. All semblance of order disappeared and the parade of The Consumers became a riot.

The police had been caught off guard. Hurry calls went in from panic-stricken merchants but before the sirens had shrieked their way to within two blocks of the angry mob a dozen more store windows had been smashed, and every sign board and poster in sight had been torn down.

After some minutes' frantic work the riot squad succeeded in quieting the crowd. Mr. Uppercue was located, and soon appeared in the second-floor window of an office building, determined to address the people and bring them to their senses.

"Fellow consumers," he began, "this is all wrong. It's tragic, I tell you. We'll never accomplish what we intended to by violent action. The way to stop the kind of advertising which prompted this parade is to get to those who are directly responsible. [Cheers, applause.] Now I said get *to* them, not get them. [Voice in the crowd, "We heard you the first time, 'Uppy' ol' boy."] If we are to end these brazen insinuations and prove to the world that the American people are not over-run with minor diseases and such things as Halitosis, B. O., Bad Skin, Daily Attacks of Indigestion, Weak Stomachs, and Unsightly Hair we must get the signatures of the advertisers on the code which we have drawn up. The police here have volunteered to accompany a committee of five to the office of the Eureka Soap Company, one of the leading offenders, located in this building. If you will agree to that action no charges will be placed against us for the unfortunate incidents that have just taken place." [Cheers.]

Mr. Uppercue was lucky. The violent temper of the crowd subsided about as quickly as it had flared up. It was not, however, Mr. Uppercue's oratorical powers that brought about the miraculous change. Almost before he had started to speak many of the consumers looked at each other in shame. They could hardly believe their own eyes and ears. Not one in a hundred of them had so much as raised a voice in public ever before. And when they realized that the police had been called, horror gripped their hearts.

Quietly and efficiently they went through the routine of selecting the committee members. Mr. Uppercue was chosen spokesman, and accompanied by three uniformed policemen the five consumers made their way to the office of the vice-president in charge of advertising of the Eureka Soap Co.

It was said later that the vice-president of the Eureka Soap Co. was astounded at the advertising code presented by the consumers. It cannot be quoted here in full because of lack of space. But it included, among other provisions, the following:

The product of the signing company would be advertised strictly on its intrinsic merits.

No social benefits would be claimed for the product.

No medicinal value would be claimed without a reputable physician's certificate.

Signature was at first flatly refused. But when it was declared that national boycott would be the retaliatory weapon of the consumers the Eureka Soap Co. capitulated. It was the first of many agreements to the Consumers Advertising Code, and the companies who signed up became prosperous and respected. The Consumers Parade went down in history as the most successful revolt of the people in a century.

The Great American Guinea Pig
ARTHUR KALLET and F. J. SCHLINK

In the magazines, in the newspapers, over the radio, a terrific verbal barrage has been laid down on a hundred million Americans, first, to set in motion a host of fears about their health, their stomachs, their bowels, their teeth, their throats, their looks; second, to persuade them that only by eating, drinking, gargling, brushing, or smearing with Smith's Whole Vitamin Breakfast Food, Jones' Yeast Cubes, Blue Giant Apples, Prussian Salts, Listroboris Mouthwash, Grandpa's Wonder Toothpaste, and a thousand and one other foods, drinks, gargles, and pastes, can they either postpone the onset of disease, of social ostracism, of business failure, or recover from ailments, physical or social, already contracted.

If these foods and medicines were—to most of the people who use them—merely worthless; if there were no other charge to be made than that the manufacturers', sales managers', and advertising agents' claims for them were false, this book would not have been written. But many of them, including some of the most widely advertised and sold, are not only worthless, but are actually dangerous. That All-Bran you eat every morning—do you know that it may cause serious and perhaps irreparable intestinal trouble? That big, juicy apple you have at lunch—do you know that indifferent Government officials let it come to your table coated with arsenic, one of the deadliest of poisons? The Pebeco Toothpaste with which you brush your teeth twice every day—do you know that a tube of it contains enough poison, if eaten, to kill three people; that, in fact, a German army officer committed suicide by eating a tubeful of this particular tooth paste? The Bromo-Seltzer that you take for headaches—do

Arthur Kallet and F. J. Schlink, *100,000,000 Guinea Pigs: Dangers in Everyday Foods, Drugs, and Cosmetics* (New York, 1933), pp. 3–7, 9–11, 14–15, 18.

you know that it contains a poisonous drug which has been responsible for many deaths and, the American Medical Association says, at least one case of sexual impotence?

Using the feeble and ineffective pure food and drug laws as a smoke screen, the food and drug industries have been systematically bombarding us with falsehoods about the purity, healthfulness, and safety of their products, while they have been making profits by experimenting on us with poisons, irritants, harmful chemical preservatives, and dangerous drugs.

Just how we consumers are being forced into the rôle of laboratory guinea pigs through huge loopholes in obviously weak and ineffective laws is described at length in the chapters that follow. A brief glance at a few cases that show our present helplessness will suffice here.

William J. A. Bailey, an ex-auto swindler, thought he could make money by dissolving radium salts in water and selling this water to rich men to cure their ills. Bailey's radium water has sent at least two men to horrible deaths, and a similar fate may be awaiting scores or hundreds of others who drank this deadly fluid.

Kora M. Lublin read or heard that thallium acetate had once been used by physicians in an ointment to remove hair in certain disease conditions. She did not bother to learn or did not care that this method of hair removal had been abandoned by physicians after several patients died; she marketed a depilatory cream containing a large percentage of thallium acetate. The medical journals have reported case after case of dreadful illness and suffering by women who used the cream, and the company exploiting it has gone bankrupt with $2,500,000 in damage suits as liabilities, and $5 assets; yet the cream continued to be sold.

A manufacturer seeking a cheap adulterant for Jamaica ginger came upon tri-ortho-cresyl phosphate. Jamaica ginger extract containing this chemical, sold in drug stores in many states, has caused terrible deformity and paralysis in from fifteen to twenty thousand victims, many of whom have died.

What, you may ask, has happened to these men and women who have killed and maimed? Nothing. William J. A. Bailey is now engaged in other ventures similar to his deadly radium water. Persons in the company that sold the thallium acetate depilatory are now manufacturing and selling another depilatory called Croxon. Nobody knows who supplied the chemical that was used to make Jamaica ginger into a deadly poison for which there is no known antidote, and nothing could be done to him if he were known.

These people violated no law. They were all carrying on "legitimate business," and the law gives them the right to experiment on the public whatever the consequences to the human beings involved. In the eyes of the law we are all guinea pigs, and any scoundrel who takes it into his head to enter the drug or food business can experiment on us. He may be uneducated, even feeble-minded. If he decides to become a manufacturer, it is his privilege to take down a dozen bottles from a shelf, mix their contents together, advertise the mixture as a remedy for indigestion, or asthma, or coughs, and persuade us to buy it. The mixture may contain strychnine, arsenic, carbolic acid, and other deadly poisons. But—in most States—he will have violated no law, indeed will not have offended the ethical sense of the average judge or legislator. (This statement is made advisedly, after a careful study of many cases in the courts and before legislative hearings.) When the experiment has failed and several of us have died, damage suits may make the business unprofitable and so for the time being end it. But its owner may again take down the same dozen bottles and start over with a new name.

The Federal Food and Drugs Act prohibits false labeling of drugs shipped across State lines; but if no claims are made *on the label,* if the ingredients are not stated *on the label,* the Act does not apply. The Act does prohibit the addition of poisonous substances to foods. Yet even with foods the public must be the guinea pig, since the manufacturer is not required to *prove* that the substances he adds are safe for human consumption; his customers by dying or by becoming ill in large numbers —and in such a way that the illness can be directly traced to the foodstuff involved and to no other cause—must first prove that it is harmful before any action will be considered under the Food and Drugs Act. If prohibition of the poison will not interfere with the business of any large and influential interest, the Government may then take action.

If the poison is such that it acts slowly and insidiously, perhaps over a long period of years (and several such will be considered in later chapters), then we poor consumers must be test animals all our lives; and when, in the end, the experiment kills us a year or ten years sooner than otherwise we would have died, no conclusions can be drawn and a hundred million others are available for further tests. . . . It will be helpful, in understanding how absurdly small are the amounts spent by the nation and the States on food and drug control, to make a rough estimate of the losses caused by the wholesale poisoning of the public. When industrial statisticians wish to evaluate the seriousness of an accident hazard, or of the industrial losses resulting from illness, they figure the total number of work days lost, and the amount this represents in wages. Let us try to make a similar approximation for the poison hazard to the American population.

It is exceedingly likely that the poisons legally and systematically fed to the American public will, by disturbing the bodily functions, overtaxing the kidneys and other organs, and upsetting the digestive processes, bring the onset of old age and functional weakness and infirmity earlier than it would otherwise have come; and in individual cases, by lowering the normal resistance, opening the way to such diseases as pneumonia, tuberculosis, arthritis, or colitis, will subtract several decades from a person's normal expectancy of life.

Such shortening of the average life can conservatively be estimated at from three to ten years. Our statistical score of time lost does not, however, end here. A large part of all disabling and partially disabling illness, such as headaches, obscure pains, indigestion, constipation, "nerves," general weariness, "laziness," and lethargy, arise from no known causes. They come, and we accept them as unavoidable. They may not incapacitate us completely, but they do decrease producing power, general health and vigor, and, even more, the joy of living. It is certain that many of these obscure types of illness are due to poisons in food and in drugs. In addition to these slight and passing ailments, much serious disease invited by lowered resistance must also be added to the score. A very conservative estimate of the average time lost from productive activities through both slight and serious illness and untimely death might be put at five years, or, for the total population, 625,000,000 years: a tremendous tribute of human life to the carelessness or avarice of the producers and to the indifference of legislatures and courts—the equivalent of the total life span of over ten million persons.

Is our crude, approximate figure too high? Divide it by two, or by ten. It still is intolerably high. Divided by ten, it is equivalent to the needless sacrifice of thousands upon thousands of lives each year.

Let us give each year of life the low cash value of $500, appropriate to the times in which we find ourselves. On this basis we estimate that the economic waste attributable to the slow poisoning of the public is over 300 billion dollars. This is equivalent to nearly 5 billion dollars annually, or, if you prefer to divide this by ten, 500 million dollars. As against this figure, we have a figure of approximately one million dollars, or one cent per capita per annum, spent by the United States Government for the enforcement of its feeble and obsolete Food and Drugs Act. . . .

There can be no doubt that the legal forms of consumer protection have failed. Can we look for aid outside the law—in the integrity of the manufacturer, in the watchfulness of the scientist, in the scrupulousness of publications carrying food and drug advertising?

All of the propaganda agencies of business have skillfully conditioned the public to believe that the only safeguard needed is the integrity of the manufacturer. There are rare cases where the public welfare is a major concern in small businesses owned and controlled by a few persons. The better manufacturers of jams, jellies, and preserves come very near to forming a trade operating in a way to produce pure and whole-some products prepared under sanitary conditions and honestly labeled and marketed. But, on the whole, this first link in the chain of consumer protection is the weakest. In case after case, the manufacturers have demonstrated that their chief and most consistent interest is in profits; and we speak here not only of the small herb compounder and cancer quack, but also of the largest and most reputable drug and food houses. Read, for example, in a later chapter, how dozens of shipments of anesthetic ether put out by great drug manufacturers have been so bad as to be destroyed by the Government; how the important firm of Hynson, Westcott and Dunning persuades the public to buy its danger-ously ineffective antiseptic; how the fruit packers send out apples coated with more lead and arsenic than even the tolerant Government officials permit. Case after case demonstrates only too well that the average manufacturer will resist to the end any interference with his business, any attempt to deprive him of his vested interest, even when it has been proved beyond doubt that his product is a menace to health and life.

This does not prove, however, that food and drug manufacturers are exceptional, or that their members have been drawn from a peculiarly ruthless class. On the contrary, it means only that they are the norm in a society which has sanctified the fastest acquisition of the greatest number of dollars as the standard for high achievement of the individual; in a society where misrepresentation and exploitation are the unfailing hand-maidens of success, in all business which deals with the ultimate consumer in the mass. . . .

12. Soapland

Few writers in this period of search for a culture and the related struggle for commitment understood middle-class American fears and fantasies as well as did James Thurber (1894–1961). He used them in his own brilliant fashion in a series of stories, cartoons, and essays. He is remembered as a humorist; by his own definition humor was "emotional chaos remembered in tranquility" and he dealt, both touchingly and cynically, with that emotional chaos of his own generation as it grew up to face the twentieth century in America. Since his business was American fears and fantasies it was not perhaps surprising that in the 1940's he took a year to study that great institution of American radio, the "soap opera," which itself was so heavily rooted in exploiting those very forces. The result was an exceptional and fully researched study, one of the most remarkable ever undertaken up to that time in the whole field of popular culture and certainly one of the best written. With knowledge, understanding, and his own humorous outlook it remains a classic account of one of the most important institutions of the era. What follows is a selection from that very long study.

The Soap Opera
JAMES THURBER

In the intolerable heat of last August, one Ezra Adams, of Clinton, Iowa, strode across his living room and smashed his radio with his fists, in the fond hope of silencing forever the plaintive and unendurable chatter of one of his wife's favorite afternoon programs. He was fined ten dollars for disturbing the peace, and Mrs. Adams later filed suit for divorce. I have no way of knowing how many similarly oppressed husbands may

James Thurber, "Soapland," in *The Beast in Me and Other Animals*, (New York, 1948), pp. 191–193, 208–222, 251–260.

have clapped him on the back or sent him greetings and cigars, but I do know that his gesture was as futile as it was colorful. He had taken a puny sock at a tormentor of great strength, a deeply rooted American institution of towering proportions. Radio daytime serials, known to the irreverent as soap opera, dishpan drama, washboard weepers, and cliff-hangers, have for years withstood an array of far more imposing attackers, headed by Dr. Louis I. Berg, a New York psychiatrist and soap opera's Enemy No. 1.

A soap opera is a kind of sandwich, whose recipe is simple enough, although it took years to compound. Between thick slices of advertising, spread twelve minutes of dialogue, add predicament, villainy, and female suffering in equal measure, throw in a dash of nobility, sprinkle with tears, season with organ music, cover with a rich announcer sauce, and serve five times a week. A soap opera may also contain a teaser ("Be sure to tune in next Monday for a special announcement"), a giveaway ("Send a box top and twenty-five cents for a gorgeous lovebird brooch"), a contest offer ("Complete this sentence and win a Bendix washer"), or a cowcatcher or hitchhike; that is, a brief commercial for another of the sponsor's products, such as a Kolynos plug on an Anacin program. It is the hope of every advertiser to habituate the housewife to an engrossing narrative whose optimum length is forever and at the same time to saturate all levels of her consciousness with the miracle of a given product, so that she will be aware of it all the days of her life and mutter its name in her sleep.

Beginning at ten-thirty in the morning and ending at six o'clock in the evening with the final organ strains of "Front Page Farrell," thirty-six soap operas are now being broadcast from New York stations Monday through Friday. Sixteen of NBC's run one after another, and CBS has a procession of thirteen. Eight or ten other serials, without New York outlets, bring the nation's present total to around forty-five. The average is closer to fifty, and at one time before the war sixty-five such programs overburdened the air waves and the human ear. Soap opera has an estimated audience of twenty million listeners, mainly women in the home, for whose attention the serials' sponsors—Procter & Gamble, Lever Brothers, General Mills, General Foods, and other big manufacturers of household products—pay a total of nearly thirty-five million dollars a year. The average serial costs about eighteen thousand dollars a week, of which three thousand is for talent and fifteen thousand for network time. The latter figure includes basic time costs, plus a 15 per cent cut for the advertising agency handling the show. Serials are variously owned, most of them by individuals or radio-production firms, some by sponsors, advertising agencies, networks, and local stations.

The headquarters of soap opera is now in New York and has been for a dozen years or so, but serials originated in Chicago. No other city has ever disputed Chicago's half-proud, half-sheepish claim to the invention of the story-coated advertising medium that either fascinates or distresses so many millions of people. Since soap opera is a form of merchandising rather than of art, the records of its beginnings are somewhat vague. It waited fifteen years for serious researchers, and it has had few competent critics. Almost none of the serial writers has saved his scripts. If the more than four thousand scripts (eight million words) of "Just Plain Bill," the oldest serial now on the air, had been saved, they would fill twenty trunks, and the entire wordage of soap opera to date, roughly two hundred and seventy-five million words, would fill a good-sized library.

The idea of a daytime radio program that would entertain the housewife and sell her a bill of goods at the same time was in the air in Chicago around 1928, "give or take a year," as one serial writer puts it. During the next four years, a dozen persons fiddled and tinkered with the ancient art of storytelling, trying to adapt it to the cramped limitations of radio, the young, obstreperous, and blind stepsister of entertainment. . . .

The last time I checked up on the locales of the thirty-six radio daytime serials, better known as soap operas, that are broadcast from New York five days a week to a mass audience of twenty million listeners, the score was Small Towns 24, Big Cities 12. I say "score" advisedly, for the heavy predominance of small towns in Soapland is a contrived and often-emphasized victory for good, clean little communities over cold, cruel metropolitan centers. Thus daytime radio perpetuates the ancient American myth of the small town, idealized in novels, comedies, and melodramas at the turn of the century and before, supported by Thornton Wilder in "Our Town," and undisturbed by the scandalous revelations of such irreverent gossips as Sherwood Anderson and Edgar Lee Masters. Soapland shares with the United States at least five actual cities—New York, Chicago, Boston, Washington, and Los Angeles—but its small towns are as misty and unreal as Brigadoon. They have such names as Hartville, Dickston, Simpsonville, Three Oaks, Great Falls, Beauregard, Elmwood, Oakdale, Rushville Center, and Homeville. "Our Gal Sunday" is set in Virginia, but no states are mentioned for the towns in the other serials.

The differences between small-town people and big-city people are exaggerated and oversimplified by most serial writers in the black-and-white tradition of Horatio Alger. It seems to be a basic concept of soap-opera authors that, for the benefit of the listening housewives, distinctions between good and evil can be most easily made in the old-fashioned terms of the moral town and the immoral city. Small-town Soaplanders occasionally visit, or flee to, one of the big cities, particularly New York, out of some desperation or other, and they are usually warned against this foolhardy venture by a sounder and stabler character in tones that remind me of such dramas of a simpler era as "York State Folks" and "The County Chairman." A few months ago, Starr, a young, selfish, and restless wife who ornamented "Ma Perkins" with her frets and tears, ran away to New York. She promptly met two typical Soapland New Yorkers, a young woman who talked like Miss Duffy in "Duffy's Tavern" and an underworld gent with a rough exterior and a heart of gold. This type of semi-gangster threads his way in and out of various serials, using such expressions as "on the up-and-up," "baby doll," and "lovey-dovey stuff," and, thanks to some of the women writers, the fellow has become a kind of extension of Editha's burglar. In "Rosemary," a conniving chap named Lefty actually conceived a fond and pure devotion for a little girl. But the Soaplanders do not have to come to New York, as we shall see, to become entangled with the Misses Duffy and the Lefties and all the rest.

A soap opera deals with the plights and problems brought about in the lives of its permanent principal characters by the advent and inter- ference of one group of individuals after another. Thus a soap opera is an endless sequence of narratives whose only cohesive element is the eternal presence of its bedeviled and beleaguered principal characters. A narrative, or story sequence, may run from eight weeks to several months. The ending of one plot is always hooked up with the beginning of the next, but the connection is unimportant and soon forgotten. Almost all the villains in the small-town daytime serials are émigrés from the cities—gangsters, white-collar criminals, designing women, unnatural mothers, cold wives, and selfish, ruthless, and just plain cussed rich men. They always come up against a shrewdness that outwits them or destroys them, or a kindness that wins them over to the good way of life.

The fact that there are only two or three citizens for the villains to get entangled with reduces the small town to a wood-and-canvas set with painted doors and windows. Many a soap town appears to have no policemen, mailmen, milkmen, storekeepers, lawyers, ministers, or even neighbors. The people live their continuously troubled lives within a socioeconomic structure that only faintly resembles our own. Since the problems of the characters are predominantly personal, emotional, and private, affecting the activities of only five or six persons at a time, the basic setting of soap opera is the living room. But even the living room lacks the pulse of life; rarely are heard the ticking of clocks, the tinkling of glasses, the squeaking of chairs, or the creaking of floor boards. Now and then, the listener does hear *about* a hospital, a courtroom, a confectionery, a drugstore, a bank, or a hotel in the town, or a roadhouse or a large, gloomy estate outside the town limits, but in most small-town serials there are no signs or sounds of community life—no footsteps of passersby, no traffic noises, no shouting of children, no barking of dogs, no calling of friend to friend, no newsboys to plump the evening papers against front doors. A few writers try from time to time to animate the streets of these silent towns, but in general Ivorytown and Rinsoville and Anacinburg are dead. This isolation of soap-opera characters was brought about by the interminability of daytime serials, some of which began as authentic stories of small-town life. The inventiveness of writers flagged under the strain of devising long plot sequences, one after another, year after year, involving a given family with the neighbors and other townsfolk. Furthermore, the producers and sponsors of soap opera and the alert advertising agencies set up a clamor for bigger and wider action and excitement. The original soap-opera characters are now often nothing more than shadowy and unnecessary *ficelles*, awkwardly held on to as confidants or advisers of the principal figures in the melodramas that come and go in chaotic regularity. Even "Mrs. Wiggs of the Cabbage Patch" followed the formula and degenerated into radio melodrama after six months. Its heroine spent her time dodging the bullets of gangsters and the tricks and traps of other scoundrels from the city.

If the towns in Soapland are not developed as realistic communities, neither are the characters—except in rare instances—developed as authentic human beings. The reason for this is that the listening housewives are believed to be interested only in problems similar to their own, and it is one of the basic tenets of soap opera that the women characters who solve these problems must be flawless projections of the housewife's ideal woman. It is assumed that the housewife identifies herself with the characters who are most put-upon, most noble, most righteous, and hence most dehumanized. Proceeding on this theory, serial producers oppose the creation of any three-dimensional character who shows signs of rising above this strange standard. Advertising agencies claim—and the record would appear to sustain them—that a realistically written leading woman would cause the audience rating of the show to drop. The housewife is also believed to be against humor in the daytime—in spite of the long success of the truly funny "Vic and Sade"—on the ground that comedy would interfere with her desire to lose herself in the trials and tribulations, the emotional agonies and soul searchings, of the good women in the serials. The only serial that deliberately goes in for comedy now is "Lorenzo Jones," whose narrator describes it as "a story with more smiles than tears." The lack of humor in most of the others is so complete as to reach the proportions of a miracle of craftsmanship.

The principal complaint of audience mail in the early days of the serials was that they moved so swiftly they were hard to follow. Surveys showed that the housewife listens, on an average, to not more than half the broadcasts of any given serial. Plot recapitulation, familiarly called "recap," was devised to slow down the progress of serials. "We told them what was going to happen, we told them it was happening, and we told them it had happened," says Robert D. Andrews. The listeners continued to complain, and action was retarded still further, with the result that time in a soap opera is now an amazing technique of slow motion. Compared to the swift flow of time in the real world, it is a glacier movement. It took one male character in a soap opera three days to get an answer to the simple question "Where have you been?" If, in "When a Girl Marries," you missed an automobile accident that occurred on a Monday broadcast, you could pick it up the following Thursday and find the leading woman character still unconscious and her husband still moaning over her beside the wrecked car. In one sequence of "Just Plain Bill," the barber of Hartville said, "It doesn't seem possible to me that Ralph Wilde arrived here only yesterday." It didn't seem possible to me, either, since Ralph Wilde had arrived, as mortal times goes, thirteen days before. Bill recently required four days to shave a man in the living room of the man's house. A basin of hot water Bill had placed on a table Monday (our time) was still hot on Thursday, when his customer stopped talking and the barber went to work.

Soap-opera time, by an easy miracle, always manages to coincide with mortal time in the case of holidays. Memorial Day in Hartville, for example, is Memorial Day in New York. Every year, on that day, Bill Davidson, Hartville's leading citizen, makes the Memorial Day address, a simple, cagy arrangement of words in praise of God and the Republic. One serial writer tells me that the word "republic" has been slyly suggested as preferable to "democracy," apparently because "democracy" has become a provocative, flaming torch of a word in our time. For Soapland, you see, is a peaceful world, a political and economic Utopia, free of international unrest, the menace of fission, the threat of inflation, depression, general unemployment, the infiltration of Communists, and the problems of racism. Except for a maid or two, there are no colored people in the World of Soap. Papa David, in "Life Can Be Beautiful," is the only Jew I have run into on the daytime air since "The Goldbergs" was discontinued. (Procter and Gamble sponsored "The Goldbergs" for many years, and the race question did not enter into its termination.) Lynn Stone and Addy Richton, who have written several serials, were once told by a sponsor's representative to eliminate a Jewish woman from one of their shows. "We don't want to antagonize the anti-Semites," the gentleman casually explained. They had to take out the character.

Proponents of soap opera are given to protesting, a little vehemently, that serials have always promoted in their dialogue an understanding of public welfare, child psychology, and modern psychiatric knowledge in general, and that this kind of writing is supervised by experts in the various fields. There was an effective lecture on the dangers of reckless driving in "The Guiding Light" one day, and I have heard a few shreds of psychiatric talk in a dozen serials, but I have found no instances of sustained instruction and uplift in soap opera. During the war, it is true, at the behest of government agencies, many writers worked into their serials incidents and dialogue of a worthy sociological nature. Charles Jackson, the author of *The Lost Weekend*, who wrote a serial called "Sweet River" for more than two years, brought to his mythical town factory workers from the outside and presented the case for tolerance and good will. Social consciousness practically disappeared from serials with the war's end, and Soapland is back to normalcy. Three weeks after Charles Luckman's food-conservation committee had begun its campaign, Ma Perkins invited a young man who had not been satisfied by a heavy breakfast to "fill up on toast and jam." It was just a slip. The script had been written before the committee started work. But, after all, there is plently of bread in Soapland, which never has scarcity of production.

A study of the social stratification of Soapland, if I may use so elegant a term, reveals about half a dozen highly specialized groups. There are the important homely philosophers, male and female. This stratum runs through "Just Plain Bill," "Ma Perkins," "David Harum," "Life Can Be Beautiful," and "Editor's Daughter," a soap opera not heard in the East but extremely popular in the Middle West, whose male protagonist enunciates a gem of friendly wisdom at the end of every program. ("Life Can Be Beautiful," by the way, is known to the trade as "Elsie Beebe." You figure it out. I had to.) Then, there are the Cinderellas, the beautiful or talented young women of lowly estate who have married or are about to marry into social circles far above those of their hard-working and usually illiterate mothers. (Their fathers, as a rule, are happily dead.) On this wide level are Nana, daughter of Hamburger Katie; Laurel, daughter of Stella Dallas; and my special pet, Sunday, of "Our Gal Sunday," who started life as a foundling dumped in the laps of two old Western miners and is now the proud and badgered wife of Lord Henry Brinthrop, "England's wealthiest and handsomest young nobleman." Christopher Morley's famous Cinderella, Kitty Foyle, also lived in Soapland for some years. Mr. Morley was charmed by the actors and actresses who played in "Kitty," but he says that he never quite gathered what the radio prolongation of the story was about. Kitty eventually packed up and moved out of Soapland. The late Laurette Taylor received many offers for the serial rights to "Peg o' My Heart," which was written by her husband, J. Hartley Manners, but it is said that she rejected them all with the agonized cry "Oh, God, no! Not that!" On a special and very broad social stratum of Soapland live scores of doctors and nurses. You find scarcely anyone else in "Woman in White," "Road of Life," and "Joyce Jordan, M.D." The heroes of "Young Dr. Malone," "Big Sister," and "Young Widder Brown" are doctors, and medical men flit in and out of all other serials. The predominance of doctors may be accounted for by the fact that radio surveys have frequently disclosed that the practice of medicine is at the top of the list of professions popular with the American housewife.

A fourth and highly important group, since it dominates large areas of Soapland, consists of young women, single, widowed, or divorced, whose purpose in life seems to be to avoid marriage by straight-arming their suitors year after year on one pretext or another. Among the most distinguished members of this group are Joyce Jordan, who is a doctor when she gets around to it; Helen Trent, a dress designer; Ellen Brown, who runs a tearoom; Ruth Wayne, a nurse; and a number of actresses and secretaries. For some years, Portia, the woman lawyer of "Portia Faces Life," belonged to this class, but several years ago she married Walter Manning, a journalist, and became an eminent figure in perhaps the most important group of all, the devoted and long-suffering wives whose marriages have, every hour of their lives, the immediacy of a toothache and the urgency of a telegram. The husbands of these women spend most of their time trying in vain to keep their brave, high-minded wives out of one plot entanglement after another.

All men in Soapland must be able to drop whatever they are doing and hurry to this living room or that at the plaint or command of a feminine voice on the phone. Bill Davidson's one-chair barbershop has not had a dozen customers in a dozen years, since the exigencies of his life keep him out of the shop most of every day. In eight months, by my official count, Kerry Donovan visited his law office only three times. He has no partners or assistants, but, like Bill, he somehow prospers. The rich men, bad and good, who descend on the small town for plot's sake never define the industries they leave behind them in New York or Chicago for months at a time. Their businesses miraculously run without the exertion of control or the need for contact. Now and then, a newspaper publisher, a factory owner, or a superintendent of schools, usually up to no good, appears briefly on the Soapland scene, but mayors, governors, and the like are almost never heard of. "The Story of Mary Marlin," just to be different, had a President of the United States, but, just to be the same, he was made heavily dependent on the intuitive political vision of his aged mother, who, in 1943, remained alive to baffle the doctors and preserve, by guiding her son's policies, the security of the Republic.

The people of Soapland, as Rudolf Arnheim, professor of psychology at Sarah Lawrence, has pointed out, consist of three moral types: the good, the bad, and the weak. Good women dominate most soap operas. They are conventional figures, turned out of a simple mold. Their invariably strong character, high fortitude, and unfailing capability must have been originally intended to present them as women of a warm, dedicated selflessness, but they emerge, instead, as ladies of frigid aggressiveness. The writers are not to blame for this metamorphosis, for they are hampered by several formidable inhibitions, including what is officially called "daytime morality," the strangest phenomenon in a world of phenomena. The good people, both men and women, cannot smoke cigarettes or touch alcoholic beverages, even beer or sherry. In a moment of tragedy or emotional tension, the good people turn to tea or coffee, iced or hot. It has been estimated that the three chief characters of "Just Plain Bill" have consumed several hundred gallons of iced tea since this program began, in 1932. Furthermore, the good women must float like maiden schoolteachers above what Evangeline Adams used to call "the slime"; that is, the passionate expression of sexual love. The ban against spirituous and amorous indulgence came into sharp focus once in "Just Plain Bill" when the plot called for one Graham Steele to be caught in a posture of apparent intimacy with the virtuous Nancy Donovan. He had carelessly upset a glass of iced tea into the lady's lap and was kneeling and dabbing at her dress with his handkerchief—a compromising situation indeed in Soapland—when her jealous husband arrived and suspected the worst.

The paternalistic Procter & Gamble, famous for their managerial policy of "We're just one big family of good, clean folks," do not permit the smoking of cigarettes at their plants during working hours except in the case of executives with private offices. This may have brought about the anticigarette phase of daytime morality, but I can adduce no evidence to support the theory. The supervision of Procter & Gamble's eleven soap operas is in the tolerant hands of the quiet, amiable William Ramsey, who smokes Marlboros. In daytime radio, the cigarette has come to be a sign and stigma of evil that ranks with the mark of the cloven hoof, the scarlet letter, and the brand of the fleur-de-lis. The married woman who smokes a cigarette proclaims herself a bad wife or an unnatural mother or an adventuress. The male cigarette smoker is either a gangster or a cold, calculating white-collar criminal. The good men may smoke pipes or cigars. A man who called on the hero of "Young Dr. Malone" brought him some excellent pipe tobacco and announced that he himself would smoke a fine cigar. As if to take the edge off this suggestion of wanton sensual abandon, a good woman hastily said to the caller, "Don't you want a nice, cold glass of ice water?" "Splendid!" cried the gentleman. "How many cubes?" she asked. "Two, thank you," said the visitor, and the virtue of the household was reestablished.

Clean-living, letter-writing busybodies are unquestionably to blame for prohibition in Soapland. When Mrs. Elaine Carrington, the author of

"Pepper Young's Family," had somebody serve beer on that serial one hot afternoon, she received twenty indignant complaints. It wasn't many, when you consider that "Pepper" has six million listeners, but it was enough. The latest violation of radio's liquor law I know of occurred in "Ma Perkins," when a bad woman was given a double Scotch-and-soda to loosen her tongue. Letters of protest flooded in. The bad people and the weak people are known to drink and to smoke cigarettes, but their vices in this regard are almost always just talked about, with proper disapproval, and not often actually depicted.

As for the sexual aspect of daytime morality, a man who had a lot to do with serials in the nineteen-thirties assures me that at that time there were "hot clinches" burning up and down the daytime dial. If this is so, there has been a profound cooling off, for my persistent eavesdropping has detected nothing but coy and impregnable chastity in the good women, nobly abetted by a kind of Freudian censor who knocks on doors or rings phones at crucial moments. Young Widder Brown has kept a doctor dangling for years without benefit of her embraces, on the ground that it would upset her children if she married again. Helen Trent, who found that she could recapture romance after the age of thirty-five, has been tantalizing a series of suitors since 1933. (She would be going on fifty if she were a mortal, but, owing to the molasses flow of soap-opera time, she is not yet forty.) Helen is soap opera's No. 1 tormentor of men, all in the virtuous name of indecision, provoked and prolonged by plot device. One suitor said to her, "After all, you have never been in my arms"—as daring an advance as any of her dejected swains has ever made in my presence. Helen thereupon went into a frosty routine about marriage being a working partnership, mental stimulation, and, last and least, "emotional understanding." "Emotional understanding," a term I have heard on serials several times, seems to be the official circumlocution for the awful word "sex." The chill Miss Trent has her men frustrated to a point at which a mortal male would smack her little mouth, so smooth, so firm, so free of nicotine, alcohol, and emotion. Suitors in Soapland are usually weak, and Helen's frustration of them is aimed to gratify the listening housewives, brought up in the great American tradition of female domination. Sniveled one of the cold lady's suitors, "I'm not strong, incorruptible, stalwart. I'm weak." Helen purred that she would help him find himself. The weak men continually confess their weakness to the good women, who usually manage to turn them into stable citizens by some vague and soapy magic. The weak men and the good men often confess to one another their dependence on the good women. In one serial, a weak man said to a good man, "My strength is in Irma now." To which the good man replied, "As mine is in Joan, Steve." As this exchange indicates, it is not always easy to tell the weak from the good, but on the whole the weak men are sadder but less stuffy than the good men. The bad men, God save us all, are likely to be the most endurable of the males in Soapland.

The people of Soapland are subject to a set of special ills. Temporary blindness, preceded by dizzy spells and headaches, is a common affliction of Soapland people. The condition usually clears up in six or eight weeks, but once in a while it develops into brain tumor and the patient dies. One script writer, apparently forgetting that General Mills was the sponsor of his serial, had one of his women characters go temporarily blind because of an allergy to chocolate cake. There was hell to pay, and the writer had to make the doctor in charge of the patient hastily change his diagnosis. Amnesia strikes almost as often in Soapland as the common cold in our world. There have been as many as eight or nine amnesia cases on the air at one time. The hero of "Rosemary" stumbled around in a daze for months last year. When he regained his memory, he found that in his wanderings he had been lucky enough to marry a true-blue sweetie. The third major disease is paralysis of the legs. This scourge usually attacks the good males. Like mysterious blindness, loss of the use of the legs may be either temporary or permanent. The hero of "Life Can Be Beautiful" was confined to a wheel chair until his death last March, but young Dr. Malone, who was stricken with paralysis a year ago, is up and around again. I came upon only one crippled villain in 1947: Spencer Hart rolled through a three-month sequence of "Just Plain Bill" in a wheel chair. When their men are stricken, the good women become nobler than ever. A disabled hero is likely to lament his fate and indulge in self-pity now and then, but his wife or sweetheart never complains. She is capable of twice as much work, sacrifice, fortitude, endurance, ingenuity, and love as before. Joyce Jordan, M.D., had no interest in a certain male until he lost the use of both legs and took to a wheel chair. Then love began to bloom in her heart. The man in the wheel chair has come to be the standard Soapland symbol of the American male's subordination to the female and his dependence on her greater strength of heart and soul.

The children of the soap towns are subject to pneumonia and strange fevers, during which their temperatures run to 105 or 106. Several youngsters are killed every year in automobile accidents or die of mysterious illnesses. Infantile paralysis and cancer are never mentioned in serials, but Starr, the fretful and errant wife in "Ma Perkins," died of tuberculosis in March as punishment for her sins. There are a number of Soapland ailments that are never named or are vaguely identified by the doctors as "island fever" or "mountain rash." A variety of special maladies affect the glands in curious ways. At least three Ivorytown and Rinsoville doctors are baffled for several months every year by strange seizures and unique symptoms.

Next to physical ills, the commonest misfortune in the world of soap is false accusation of murder. At least two-thirds of the good male characters have been indicted and tried for murder since soap opera began. Last year, the heroes of "Lone Journey," "Our Gal Sunday," and "Young Dr. Malone" all went through this ordeal. They were acquitted, as the good men always are. There were also murder trials involving subsidiary characters in "Portia Faces Life," "Right to Happiness," and "Life Can Be Beautiful." I had not listened to "Happiness" for several months when I tuned in one day just in time to hear one character say, "Do you know Mrs. Cramer?", and another reply, "Yes, we met on the day of the shooting." Dr. Jerry Malone, by the way, won my True Christian Martyr Award for 1947 by being tried for murder and confined to a wheel chair at the same time. In March of this year, the poor fellow came full Soapland circle by suffering an attack of amnesia.

The most awkward cog in the machinery of serial technique is the solemn, glib narrator. The more ingenious writers cut his intrusions down to a minimum, but the less skillful craftsmen lean upon him heavily. Most soap-opera broadcasts begin with the narrator's "lead-in," or summary of what has gone before, and end with his brief résumé of the situation and a few speculations on what may happen the following day. The voice of the narrator also breaks in from time to time to tell the listeners what the actors are doing, where they are going, where they have been, what they are thinking or planning, and, on the worst programs, what manner of men and women they are: "So the restless, intolerant, unneighborly Norma, left alone by the friendly, forgiving, but puzzled Joseph . . ."

Another clumsy expedient of soap opera is the soliloquy. The people of Soapland are constantly talking to themselves. I timed one lady's chat with herself in "Woman in White" at five minutes. The soap people also think aloud a great deal of the time, and this usually is distinguished from straight soliloquy by being spoken into a filter, a device that lends a hollow, resonant tone to the mental voice of the thinker.

In many soap operas, a permanent question is either implied or actually posed every day by the serial narrators. These questions are usually expressed in terms of doubt, indecision, or inner struggle. Which is more important, a woman's heart or a mother's duty? Could a woman be happy with a man fifteen years older than herself? Should a mother tell her daughter that the father of the rich man she loves ruined the fortunes of the daughter's father? Should a mother tell her son that his father, long believed dead, is alive, well, and a criminal? Can a good, clean

Iowa girl find happiness as the wife of New York's most famous matinée idol? Can a beautiful young stepmother, can a widow with two children, can a restless woman married to a preoccupied doctor, can a mountain girl in love with a millionaire, can a woman married to a hopeless cripple, can a girl who married an amnesia case—can they find soap-opera happiness and the good, soap-opera way of life? No, they can't—not, at least, in your time and mine. The characters in Soapland and their unsolvable perplexities will be marking time on the air long after you and I are gone, for we must grow old and die, whereas the people of Soapland have a magic immunity to age, like Peter Pan and the Katzenjammer Kids. When you and I are in Heaven with the angels, the troubled people of Ivorytown, Rinsoville, Anacinburg, and Crisco Corners, forever young or forever middle-aged, will still be up to their ears in inner struggle, soul searching, and everlasting frustration.

During the nineteen-thirties, radio daytime serials were occasionally sniped at by press and pulpit, and now and then women's clubs adopted halfhearted resolutions, usually unimplemented by research, disapproving of the "menace of soap opera." Husbands and fathers, exacerbated by what they regarded as meaningless yammering, raised their voices against the programs, and some of them, pushed too far, smashed their sets with their fists, like Mr. Ezra Adams, in Clinton, Iowa. But it wasn't until 1942 that the opponents of the daytime monster discovered in their midst a forceful and articulate crusader to lead the assault on the demon of the kilocycles. He was Dr. Louis I. Berg, of New York, psychiatrist and physician, author, and, according to *Who's Who*, medico-legal expert. In a report published in March 1942 and widely quoted in the press, Dr. Berg confessed that he had been unaware of the menace of the radio serial until late in 1941. His examination of several female patients undergoing change of life had convinced him that radio serials were a main cause of relapses in the women. He thereupon made a three-week study of two of the aggravations, "Woman in White" and "Right to Happiness." He found these serials guilty of purposefully inducing anxiety, dangerous emotional release, and almost everything else calculated to afflict the middle-aged woman, the adolescent, and the neurotic. "Pandering to perversity and playing out destructive conflicts," Dr. Berg wrote, "these serials furnish the same release for the emotionally distorted that is supplied to those who derive satisfaction from a lynching bee, who lick their lips at the salacious scandals of a *crime passionnel,* who in the unregretted past cried out in ecstasy at a witch burning." Hitting his stride, Dr. Berg referred to "the unwitting sadism of suppurating serials." The Doctor then admitted, "There are several excellent ones," and added, somewhat to my bewilderment, since he had set himself up as a critic, "Naturally, an analysis of them has no place in a study of this kind." In a later report, Dr. Berg set down such a list of serial-induced ailments, physiological and psychological, as would frighten the strongest listener away from the daytime air. It began with tachycardia and arrhythmia and ended with emotional instability and vertigo.

Dr. Berg's onslaught was not unlike the cry of "Fire!" in a crowded theater, and a comparable pandemonium resulted. The uneasy radio industry decided to call in experts to make a study of the entire field. Professors, doctors, psychologists, research statisticians, and network executives were all put to work on the problem. In the last five years, their findings have run to at least half a million words. This vast body of research covers all types of programs, and an explorer could wander for weeks just in the section devoted to soap opera. Among the outstanding investigators are Dr. Paul S. Lazarsfeld, of Columbia University, whose Bureau of Applied Social Research has the dignified backing of the Rockefeller Foundation, and Dr. Rudolf Arnheim, professor of psychology at Sarah Lawrence College, who, for *his* three-week study of serials, had the fascinated assistance of forty-seven students at Columbia University. CBS appointed Mrs. Frances Farmer Wilder, a former public-relations director in radio, as program consultant with special reference to the investigation of daytime serials. Both NBC and CBS, the only national networks that broadcast soap opera, appointed research committees, and were cheered up by their reports, which admitted that soap opera could be greatly improved, but decided that its effect on the listening woman was more likely to be benign than malignant. The cry of "whitewash" went up from the enemy camp, but the networks were able to prove that the data of their specialists agreed in general with studies made by independent researchers in the field. It is not always easy to distinguish between independent investigators and the ladies and gentlemen whose work is stimulated by the networks, and I am not even going to try.

In 1945, Mrs. Wilder summarized the findings of the CBS experts in a pamphlet called "Radio's Daytime Serial." If you have been worried about America's womanhood left home alone at the mercy of the daytime dial, you will be relieved to know that forty-six out of every hundred housewives did not listen to soap opera at all. This figure was approximately confirmed a year later by checkers working for the United States Department of Agriculture, which had presumably become worried about the effect the serials were having on the women in small towns and rural areas of the country. Estimates differ as to how many serials the average addict listens to each day. Mrs. Wilder puts the figure at 5.8. She also points out that a housewife listens to a given serial only about half the time, or five programs out of every ten. On the other hand, a survey by an advertising agency indicates that the ladies listen to only three broadcasts out of every ten.

There have been all kinds of measurements of the social stratification of the listening women, and all kinds of results. There is a popular notion that only ladies of a fairly low grade of intelligence tune in soap operas, but some of the surveys would have us believe that as many as 40 per cent of the women in the upper middle class, or the higher cultural level, listen to soap opera. The most interesting specimen that the scientists have examined in their laboratories is the habitual listener who has come to identify herself with the heroine of her favorite serial. Many examples of this bemused female have been tracked down by Dr. Arnheim and other workers, and a comprehensive analysis of the type was completed last year by Professor W. Lloyd Warner and Research Associate William E. Henry, both of the University of Chicago, at the instigation of the Columbia Broadcasting System. They made a study of a group of listeners to "Big Sister," using as subjects mostly women of the lower middle class, and found that almost all of them were "identifiers," if I may coin a pretty word. Let us take a look at the summary of their conclusions about the nature of the serial and its impact on its audience. "The 'Big Sister' program arouses normal and adaptive anxiety in the women who listen," wrote Warner and Henry. "The 'Big Sister' program directly and indirectly condemns neurotic and nonadaptive anxiety and thereby functions to curb such feelings in its audience. This program provides moral beliefs, values, and techniques for solving emotional and interpersonal problems for its audience and makes them feel they are learning while they listen (thus: 'I find the program is educational'). It directs the private reveries and fantasies of the listeners into socially approved channels of action. The 'Big Sister' program increases the women's sense of security in a world they feel is often threatening, by reaffirming the basic security of the marriage ties (John's and Ruth's); by accentuating the basic security of the position of the husband (Dr. John Wayne is a successful physician); by 'demonstrating' that those who behave properly and stay away from wrongdoing exercise moral control over those who do not; and by showing that wrong behavior is punished. The 'Big Sister' program, in dramatizing the significance of the wife's role in basic human affairs, increases the woman's feeling of importance by showing that the family is of the highest importance and that she has control over the vicissitudes of family life. It thereby decreases their feeling of futility and makes them feel essential and wanted. The women aspire to, and measure themselves by, identification with Ruth, the heroine; however, the identification is not with Ruth alone, but with the whole program and the other characters in the plot. This permits sublimated impulse satisfaction by the listeners', first, unconsciously identifying with the bad woman and, later, consciously punishing her through the action of the plot. Unregulated impulse life is condemned, since it is always connected with characters who are condemned and never related to those who are approved."

"Big Sister" is written by two men, Robert Newman and Julian Funt, and they have made it one of the most popular of all serials. For more than two years it has dealt with a moony triangle made up of Ruth Wayne, the big sister of the title, her estranged husband, Dr. John Wayne, and another doctor named Reed Bannister. The authors, I am told, plan to tinker with the popular old central situation, but they are aware that they must proceed with caution. The identifiers are strongly attached to the status quo of plot situation, and to what psychologists call the "symbols" in soap opera—serial authors call them "gimmicks"—and they do not want them tampered with. Thus, the soap-opera males who go blind or lose the use of both legs or wander around in amnesia are, as the psychologists put it, symbols that the listening women demand. As long as the symbols are kept in the proper balance and the woman is in charge and the man is under her control, it does not seem to make a great deal of difference to the female listeners whether the story is good or not.

We come next to that disturbing fringe of the soap-opera audience made up of listeners who confuse the actors with the characters they play. These naive folk believe that Bill Davidson, the kindly Hartville barber of "Just Plain Bill," is an actual person (he is, of course, an actor, named Arthur Hughes), and they deluge him with letters in the fond belief that he can solve their problems as successfully as he does those of the people in the serial. James Meighan and Ruth Russell, who play the husband and wife in "Just Plain Bill," have had to lead a curious extra-studio life as Mr. and Mrs. Kerry Donovan. When it became apparent to the listening audience, some thirteen years ago, that Mrs. Donovan was going to have her first child, the network and local stations received hundreds of gifts from the devoted admirers of the young couple—bonnets, dresses, bootees, porringers, and even complete layettes were sent by express to the mythical expectant mother—and when, several years later, the child was killed in an automobile accident, thousands of messages of sympathy came in. Such things as this had happened before, and they still happen, to the bewilderment and embarrassment of network executives. In 1940, when Dr. John Wayne married the heroine of "Big Sister," truckloads of wedding presents were received at the CBS Building on Madison Avenue. This flux of silver, cut glass, and odds and ends presented the exasperated broadcasting system with a considerable problem. Gifts for babies had always been disposed of by sending them to children's hospitals and orphanages, but the wedding gifts were another matter. Since network men are a little sheepish about the entire business, they are inclined to change the subject when the question of the misguided largess of listeners is brought up.

The quandary is enlarged when, in addition to gifts for the nursery, parlor, and dining room, checks, paper money, and even coins arrive for this serial hero or that who has let it out over the air that he is in financial difficulties. The money, like the presents, cannot very well be returned to the senders, for fear of breaking their naive hearts, and the sponsors have adopted the policy of giving it to the Red Cross and other charities. In addition to the newly married, the pregnant, and the broke, soap-opera characters who are single and in the best of health and circumstances receive tokens of esteem, in a constant, if somewhat more moderate, stream. One young actress who plays in a Procter and Gamble serial estimates that she is sent about three hundred pounds of soap every year, much of it the product of her sponsor's rivals. The year 1947 was the Big Year for live turtles and alligators, and radio listeners from all over the country bombarded the studios with gifts of hundreds of these inconvenient creatures.

Mrs. Carrington's "Pepper Young's Family" used to have a recurring scene in which a man and his wife were heard talking in bed—twin beds, naturally. When the man playing the husband quit and was replaced by another actor, indignant ladies wrote in, protesting against these immoral goings on. Equally outraged was the woman who detected that Kerry Donovan, the husband in "Just Plain Bill," and Larry Noble, the husband in "Backstage Wife," were one and the same man. This pixilated listener wrote Kerry Donovan a sharp letter revealing that she was on to his double life and threatening to expose the whole nasty mess unless the bigamous gentleman gave up one of his wives. The key to this particular scandal is simple. One actor, James Meighan, plays both husbands. A woman in the Middle West once wrote to NBC asserting that the wrong man was suspected of murder in her favorite serial. She said she was tuned in the day the murder took place and she knew who the real culprit was. She offered to come to New York and testify in court if the network would pay her expenses.

Even the listening women who are shrewd enough, God bless them, to realize that serial characters are not real people but are played by actors and actresses expect superhuman miracles of their idols. They never want them to take vacations, but usually the weary players manage to get away for a few weeks in the summer. Sometimes they are replaced by other performers, but often the characters they play are "written out" of the script for the periods of their absence. Thus the housewives who love Mary Noble, the heroine of "Backstage Wife," are not told that Claire Niesen, who plays that role, is taking her annual vacation. Instead, the script arranges for Mary Noble to visit her sick mother in San Diego for a while or travel to Bangkok to consult a swami who has the secret of the only known cure for that plaguey summer rash of hers. Now and then, a serial audience hears one of its favorite characters complain of a severe headache. This is almost always a symptom of brain tumor. It means that the part is going to be written out of the soap opera forever, perhaps because the player wants to go to Hollywood, or the author is bored with the character, or the producer has to cut the budget. In any case, the listeners become slowly adjusted to the inevitable, and when the character finally dies, many of them write letters of condolence, often bordered in black.

The gravest real crisis in years came a few months ago when Lucille Wall, who plays Portia in "Portia Faces Life," was critically hurt in a fall in her Sutton Place apartment. Until her accident, Miss Wall had taken only one vacation in eight years, and her devoted audience was alarmed when her replacement, Anne Seymour, went on playing Portia week after week. The news that Miss Wall was in the hospital in a serious condition spread swiftly among her followers, and letters, telegrams, flowers, and gifts poured in. Because of this evidence of her popularity, Miss Wall improved rapidly, to the amazement and delight of her doctors, who had told her that she could not go back to work for a year. When she got home from the hospital, Miss Wall spoke to her listeners at the end of a "Portia" broadcast one day over a special hookup at her bedside, thanking them for their kindness and promising to be back soon. She repeated this message on the Thursday before Mother's Day, and again, some time later, while she was still recuperating. On June 14th, after being away less than four months, she began to play Portia again.

This reporter is too tired, after more than a year of travel in Soapland, and too cautious in matters of prophecy, to make any predictions about the future of soap opera. One thing, though, seems certain. The audience of twenty million women has taken over control of the daytime serial. The producers must give them what they want and demand. The formula has been fixed. The few serious writers who have tried to improve on it are gradually giving up the unequal struggle. It is probable that superior serials, like "Against the Storm," winner of a Peabody Award for excellence, are gone from the air forever, and that only the old familiar symbols and tired plots will survive.

Your guess is as good as mine about the effect that television will have on the daytime serial. The creeping apparition called video has already made several experiments with continuous narratives. Two of them have been dropped, but one called "The Laytons," the story of a family, though off the air at the moment, will be back next month. It differs from soap opera in that it is a half-hour nighttime show once a week, but the agent I sent to watch a performance at the WABD studio at Wanamaker's reports that it has the basic stuff of the daytime serials, even if the producer is horrified at the mention of such a thing. Just how television could manage to put on a fifteen-minute program five times a week, I have no idea, but from what I know of American technological skill, I wouldn't bet that it can't be done. There is a problem, however, that the wizards of television may find insurmountable if they attempt to transpose any of the current radio serials to the screen. The researchers have discovered that the listening women have a strong tendency to visualize the serial heroine and her family. Some of them even go so far as to describe to their interviewers what the different women characters wear. If their favorites did not come out to their satisfaction on television (imagine their dismay if they find that the tall, handsome hero of their daydreams is really a mild little fellow, five feet four), the ladies might desert the video versions by the million. The way around that, of course, would be to invent entirely new soap operas for telecasting, and "The Laytons" may well be the first lasting adventure in this field.

It is hard for one who has understood the tight hold of "Just Plain Bill," "Big Sister," and some of the others to believe that their intense and far-flung audience would ever give them up easily. If soap opera did disappear from the air (and I see no signs of it), the wailing of the housewives would be heard in the land. I doubt that it could be drowned out even by the cheers and laughter of the househusbands dancing in the streets.

I took the train from Hartville one day last week, waving good-bye to Bill Davidson and his family, and vowing—I hope they will forgive me—to put my radio away in the attic and give myself up to the activities and apprehensions of the so-called real world. I have also put away the books and pamphlets dealing with the discoveries of the serial researchers. In closing, though, I think you ought to know that Benton & Bowles, an advertising agency, recently employed a system invented by Dr. Rudolph Flesch, of New York University, to determine mathematically the comparative understandability, clarity, and simplicity of various kinds of prose and poetry. The agency wanted to find out just how easy it was to understand that old and popular serial of Elaine Carrington's called "When a Girl Marries." The results of Dr. Flesch's formula showed that this soap opera is as easy to understand as the Twenty-third Psalm and a great deal clearer than what Abraham Lincoln was trying to say in the Gettysburg Address. I don't know about you, but when the final delirium descends upon my mind, it is my fervent hope that I will not trouble the loved ones gathered at my bedside by an endless and incoherent recital of the plot of "When a Girl Marries." It will be better for everyone if my consciousness selects that other clear and famous piece of English prose, and I babble of green fields.

13. The Movies as History

Much of the cultural history of the period appears inexorably interwoven with the rich parade of films that marched from Hollywood in this period. Thus far we have made repeated use of movie references to suggest a point or bolster an argument; it seemed not only logical but necessary, so central had movies become to any understanding of the culture. Yet so complex is the nature of that relationship between movies and history, between our movies and our culture, that the brief explorations offered below can only suggest the complexity of the problem.

Ruth Suckow (1892–1960) was a short-story writer and novelist whose special interest seemed to rest particularly with Middle Western Americans (often German-Americans) living out their lives in small Iowa towns. Her interest in the article excerpted below was in the images of the stars and the meaning of those images in understanding America, especially the America of 1936. The brief editorial from the liberal magazine *The Nation* bitterly points up the often contradictory meaning of Hollywood and the films: industry, glamour, probing analyst of social problems. The *Time* essay looks back on the films of the period from the perspective of the 1960's in an effort to see what those movies as cultural artifacts really have to tell us today.

Hollywood Gods and Goddesses
RUTH SUCKOW

The immense influence of Hollywood in our national life has lately passed the point where it was matter for comment (frequently for denunciation) and seems to be accepted as matter of fact. Manners, clothes, speech,

Ruth Suckow, "Hollywood Gods and Goddesses," *Harper's Magazine,* 173 (July 1936), pp. 189–200.

tastes, all are affected by the actors and actresses of the motion picture screen as they never were by the popular figures of the stage or by any of our popular idols.

Robert Edmond Jones, I believe, once wrote of the motion picture stars as a new race of gods and goddesses comparable in their symbolic nature and the worship accorded them to the pagan deities of Greece and Rome. The fan magazines frequently, and even matter of factly, refer to the feminine stars as "goddesses," while at the same time trying to prove that these shining ones are just like the rest of us.

Just why do the figures of the screen loom so large in our day? A few, a very few, of the great motion picture figures have also been great actors; but it is not through superlative excellence in their profession that they have been raised to mythical heights. It often works the other way. To be an artist is a drawback. It would seem at times that this nation, losing the stern Puritan orthodoxy which it brought with it to the new continent, yet still crude and young in the mass, has turned to the worship of these picture gods, real and yet unreal, common as life and yet larger than life, known in minuter detail than next-door neighbors and yet shiningly remote, because they have come to represent certain national ideals reduced to the lowest common denominator. For that is what the screen does—it reduces while it magnifies, grinds down what it exalts into the typical.

The stories of The Stars, told over and over in those curious Hollywood addenda, the fan magazines, follow the national fairy tale; the overnight rise to fame and material wealth, to social opulence, with Sex and Beauty in headline type, and all turned out in mass quantities with great technical smoothness and ingenuity by machinery. These stories—for the screen dramas and supposedly "real" biographies have been hopelessly mixed—reveal an amazing combination of small-town familiarities, front-page magnification, and "glamorous" remoteness. The present status of the motion picture art as an art—at least in Hollywood terms—is reflected in this naive mixing of the personal with the objective.

❋　　❋　　❋

In the idolization of the present great god of the screen ordinary American manhood has its innings. The story of the dimming of the Valentino image and the rising of the Gable star is very much on the order of a popular novel of the Graustarkian era in which the plain American six-foot hero wins in the end over the more romantic (but ah, how much less sterling!) foreign prince. There is nothing foreign or morbid about the "appeal" of Clark Gable. It is native American. It goes with popcorn, horseshoe games, and BVD's. No preliminary publicity campaign was required to put over this hero. The girls themselves picked him out of his obscurity as a minor screen "heavy." Producers, still blinded doubtless by the glory of Valentino, had popularized Gable at first as "a menace"—the term was a hang-over from the overwrought days of the Valentino craze—as a he-man cave-man lover, whose first great popular action on the screen was to give the heroine a sock on the jaw. But the girls were right when they discovered the handsome ice-man, or laundry man, or whatever the role was, and demanded that he be placed among The Stars. As a god in picture mythology Clark Gable has as much validity as Bill Hart.

For surely that face—ears, eyes, dimples, and all—is the face of the good-looking fellow in the next block. It is essentially a small-town face, although its owner has learned to slick back his hair and wear evening clothes. It bears the unmistakable look of the native good fellow—a Mason, an Elk, who might stand for a popular athletic coach, or be chosen as Scout Master to take the children on a camping trip. Although now groomed and made familiar with nightclubs, as the movies require, this is the same fellow who used to bring his girl a box of candy every Saturday night. And Clark Gable is almost as popular with masculine as with feminine fans; for in his person, or in his screen image, the ordinary American—whether business man or garage mechanic—long famous as a good husband and a poor lover, and a big child all his days, receives the accolade from the women.

✿   ✿   ✿

In picture mythology the goddesses have always outnumbered the gods. The very fact that their chances for stardom are greater, however, makes their artistic opportunities less. More even than handsome actors, they are forced into the strict mold of accepted charm. They must all seem worthy to be loved; each be a version of *As You Desire Me*. Even the most talented soon loses her appeal as an actress and becomes interesting chiefly for what she reveals and typifies. She appears as the embodiment of some ideal already loosely present in contemporary life and consciousness. . . .

Perhaps more influence has been exerted by the personality of Greta Garbo herself than by those of earlier stars—in some ways an individuality marked to the degree of bizarre eccentricity. Nevertheless, the picture image is a representative one. Nor is it truly adult. For this goddess' strange charm analyzed proves to be that of adolescence—not the precociously and voluptuously maturing childishness of Clara Bow, but adolescence all the same, strangely childlike, still more strangely mature. The tall figure has an awkwardness sometimes crudely coltish, sometimes divinely odd with its queer off-grace. The long swinging bob of soft light hair, a variation of which is still the favorite coiffure of youth in spite of the hairdressers' efforts to supersede it, is that of a girl just past childhood.

And even about the face—that face so purely marked in its character-istic outlines, with the high cheekbones, the extravagant lashes, the brows curved into a willful exaggeration of temperamental individuality—there is something immaturely overdone. Immaturity lies in its very enigma. For the peculiar charm and power of this beauty taken as the symbol of "allure" are not those of womanhood but of neurotic adolescence crystallized and held spellbound. This face holds intact the "mysterious" entity of emotional youth, mysterious because not yet yielded. It is a self-centered loveliness. . . .

But although she has compelling power and intensity, beauty and dis-tinction, it is still, I make bold to state, as a "personality" that Greta Garbo holds her place; and, in a more subtle way than that of the earlier screen goddesses, as a representation and a symbol. The image which she has created out of herself gives a mold to ideal feminine qualities of an era even more than it suggests a unique individual. The way in which girls everywhere have responded to this representation proves the point. The Greta Garbo image has caught their imaginations not so much because it was itself strange and new as because it embodied in thrilling and exquisite form that which they all desired to be.

It was altogether fitting that this more subtle quality of charm should have a foreign flavor; that America's Postwar Sweetheart should bring the conscious "allure" of the Old World. The image came into popularity along with the awareness of "civilized" sophistication which was so much an outgrowth of the mingling of the Old World and the New. It is easy of course to read too much into these symbols; and yet I think the comment holds. Feminine charms were no longer open, but artful—touched with the peculiar glow of decadence in which magic lies. The luminous goddess of this day was no longer a figure of bounding health, but anemic and almost emaciated, pale, introspective, at once adoles-cently boyish and ultrafemale. America's new sweethart was distinctly a neurotic girl.

Greta Garbo was the first great popular introvert heroine of a nation of blithe extroverts; and in that shift from earlier and simpler ideals lay the galvanizing shock of change, and perhaps of self-development. This image was the final reduction to the lowest common denominator—glorified of course for screen purposes—of a heroine who had appeared long ago in literature, disturbingly and variously, as the heroine of the Brontë novels, of Russian fiction, of the plays of Ibsen. She had come late to these shores but, arriving in lovely and distinguished form, had overturned the feminine ideal of the nation. The It Girl was popularly transformed into the Glamorous One.

Yet it must be repeated that Greta Garbo, although the quality of her acting is indubitably higher, is no more essentially an actress than the goddess who preceded her. An objective artistry is not at the source of her fascination or her power. The truth is that of all the feminine Narcissi who have gazed into the mirror of their own beauty on the silver screen she ranks first. Using the screen as a magic magnifying glass, she like the others, even more than the others, has been acting out her fairy story. For even those famous love scenes with which she won her first popularity had this queer unreality, this lack of human give and take, as if they were being played out alone in a dream. The companion of these scenes is only a shadow prince who never quite comes to life. The drama seems hers alone. She might have created it. . . .

Demi-goddesses have appeared meanwhile during the Garbo reign. They are important enough to offer cause for interesting speculation. . . .

Joan Crawford is probably the most widely popular of these demi-goddesses. But her own story is more representative than her image on the screen. It is as the heroine of this story, retold in almost every issue of the fan magazines, and not as an actress, not even as a movie star, that Joan Crawford appears as a genuinely significant figure of our times. The story might be called "The Rise of an American Girl." It is a Cinderella story of course, but put into modern terms, for its heroine is an active and not a passive figure. The frank story of a climber, yet it carries an intensity of burning ambition which gives a compelling and moving pathos to a half-shoddy tale.

The same story unrolls, even more clearly, in the pictures in which Miss Crawford appears first as a buxom hoofer with all the obvious charms of burlesque; then as the hungrily ambitious heroine, thin and big-eyed, of the shopgirl's drama; and last as a gorgeously gowned typical star of the screen. The dramas in which she has figured have not been tragic—success stories, rather, although beset with trials. Yet there is a tragic note in the representative history of Joan Crawford as its outline appears through the pictures and beneath the ballyhoo. It is the tragedy of a naive materialism. A self-made tragedy, it might almost be called. For in the intensity of the effort to Become Someone, to Develop a Personality, the personality itself has become almost wholly externalized. The face has been "groomed" until the earlier interesting and strongly human qualities have been almost entirely ironed out of it; and the image now presented on the screen has become a mask no longer capable of expressing any truly genuine emotion.

Yet the same pathos hovers about this image as about the dramas built round it—and about the movies themselves—that queer pathos of great promise and cheapened accomplishment, the promise nullified by too golden a success. The profile etched for a moment upon the screen gives an effect of nobility, never carried out by the character in the flashy play. A tragic sense of waste is hidden somewhere in the success story.

✿   ✿   ✿

How truly are these images, in spite of their worship, the gods of America? How much are they actually and literally "build-ups"? And do they, taken all over the world to represent America and "Americanization" in the deepest sense, represent it at all? How much of this mythology is real and how much is bogus, like any overadvertised commercial product?

Examine these images, and the bogus element becomes apparent at once. To create them Hollywood has misused rather than used the true power of photography. Look at the faces of the goddesses in the huge close-ups. Artificiality is so much taken for granted that it is almost accepted as a picture convention—the bleached hair, the painted eyebrows, the false eyelashes, the made-to-order mouth, the shining teeth— these are not faces, but masks, created to conceal rather than to reveal. The process can be seen in the history of almost any European star brought over and "glorified" for the American screen. Take only the unfortunate history of the Russian actress, Anna Sten. In *The Tempest,* a German film in which she appeared with Emil Jannings, Miss Sten looked the part which she portrayed, that of a rough-neck charmer of the slums; crudely dressed, tousle-haired, she had all the weakness and the power of the vixen she was meant to be. But in the ill-fated *Nana,* after a year or more of "grooming," with eyebrows penciled, hair coiffed, clothes by Somebody-or-Other, body attenuated, all the force inherent in that broad Slavic face was diminished to a conventionalized prettiness. To make over the actuality into predetermined types, set to stereotyped and mechanical notions of beauty, is a falsification at the start.

Having examined the images themselves, it is interesting next to try to find the actors and actresses behind the images—the "real" this one and that one.

First of all, let us look into the literature that has been built up round them; those curious contemporary documents, the fan magazines. These are all made to pattern. All are addressed to "the fans" in order to bring them into personal touch with their gods and goddesses. The personal note runs throughout—runs riot. It is in the editorials, intimate and flattering, addressed to "you and you and you," with a chummy air which says, this is *your* magazine, run only for *you,* to bring *you* news of your idols—for we, the writers, and you, the readers, are all common folk together basking in the light of these shining beings. They go into the homes of the deities, leading the readers by the hand, showing them the living rooms, the swimming pools, the playrooms, the kitchens, placing them at the tables (set for guests, menus included), almost in the beds of The Stars.

In all this mass of print, acting itself gets short shrift. The articles are a mixture of highly personal criticism and ballyhoo. The same thing happens over and over again, with nearly all the actors and actresses brought to Hollywood, until it becomes a routine. First the magazines bring out a big ballyhoo, devoted to the fresh charms of the new heart-throb, or menace, or sensation. Each is billed as an utter alien to the accepted rules of Hollywood. The actor is made one of us by being called at once by his first name. Even that is abbreviated if the name itself offers any chance. The Margarets become Maggies, the Constances Connies, the Jameses Jimmies; and even when Katherine Cornell got as close to Hollywood as a theater in Los Angeles, she at once became in the fan magazines·Kit Cornell. The glorifying process starts immediately, attempting to lift the actor into mythology through mechanical processes. There were never beings in the world like these; so exciting, so glamorous, so good to the poor, such householders, with such fine cooks, such good dressers on budgets, such parents, such lovers.

But right along with this glorification goes that jeering reduction to the bottom level which runs through American journalism. The fan articles present a curious mixture of adulation and a touchy sense that these deities are no better than the rest of us. The deities are examined first to see if they are "regular"—that is, if they are going to play ball according to Hollywood rules. The first rule is, of course—tell all. You are ours, so open up. A desire to stick to professional instead of personal issues becomes "high-hat," a sign that the actor thinks himself too good to tell. Thus one magazine spoke of the "vulgar taste" of an actress who refused to "come across" with the intimacies of her marriage. If actors hold out for the conditions under which they can do their best work they are damned with the other bludgeon adjective, "temperamental."

A quotation from a fan article with the subtitle: "Frank Knows All the Answers and Tells Them All." We will call the actor Frank Jones.

More than this, Frank is available to his fans. A lot of women have traveled across the country with the sole and intense purpose of meeting Frank Jones, and, almost unheard of in this town, these fans do meet him. Some of them even lunch and dine with him.

And this is offered seriously as evidence of the *realness* of Frank Jones. As an actor? Don't be silly. As a movie star and a popular god.

In all this grind of the mill, what wonder that the edge soon wears off the acting? Some few survive it. Not many. The waste is enormous. Sometimes an actor is brought to Hollywood to play the same role he has played on the stage. It is informing to observe the differences between that first part, with its finesse, its sinking of the actor in the part, and the succession of film roles as the same actor gradually comes to play them. The acting of Helen Hayes in her first motion picture was a revelation to film audiences; but her acting had become worn down to the ordinary when she left Hollywood. Charles Laughton is in danger of applying a formula for villainousness in those terribly wicked parts which he plays with a childlike enjoyment. Paul Muni, able and earnest actor, appears in dramas in which the original intention still shows through; but which, under screen manipulation into Hearstian ideals, tend to fall into the deteriorated compromise hash of *Black Fury*.

There is little criticism worth the name. This is true not only of the fan magazines. Critics not connected with Hollywood are still too grateful for any favor in the films; either that or they still take the position (fewer of them now) that no good can be expected to come out of Hollywood. In the fan magazines there is such a naive emphasis upon the personal that acting is called "natural" and "sincere" when it isn't acting at all; when an actor, met face to face, is exactly as he appears upon the screen. When will the producers throw away these siren roles, the complaint runs, and show us the real Marianna, natural, gay, and just a girl at heart?

The blame is by no means entirely on the side of the producers, however. Too many of the actors and actresses themselves very probably come to love the image in the magic looking glass. Motion pictures constitute the only art in which the players are actually able to see themselves. Nearly everybody prefers a flattering photograph.

Meanwhile, these images which Hollywood has presented have at least the raw value of revealing where the lowest reach of the lowest common denominator seems to lie. That is how they must be read—as a broad typification, half genuine and half imposed, creative only in the tremendous influence which they exert.

With the Hollywood setup as it is to-day, we cannot ask for very much else. The stories that Hollywood permits can only scrape the gaudy and tawdry surface of American life and legend. The images of its gods and goddesses are now magnified out of all proportion to their genuine value and significance. So far, American motion pictures, in spite of the skill that goes into their making, form an unconscious social document rather than an art.

Private Preview

MICHEL MOK

> Mine eyes have seen the glory of the coming of the Lord;
> He is trampling out the vintage where the grapes of wrath
>   are stored . . .
>   —"The Battle Hymn of the Republic."

Mine eyes have seen the glory of the coruscating assemblage that attended the private preview of Darryl F. Zanuck's film version of John Steinbeck's *The Grapes of Wrath* at the Normandie Theater in New York.

Mine eyes were dazzled by the diamonds, the sapphires and emeralds, the silks and satins, the sables, ermine, and fox of the lovely ladies who, on the arms of tailed-and-toppered escorts, swept into the lobby of the little picture house in East Fifty-third Street. Dressed in bibs and tuckers from the ateliers of Mainbocher and Molineux, the gals from Park Avenue came in gleaming limousines with their men-about-town to take a peek at the raggedy Joads and the miseries of their jalopy migration.

Among the freshly pressed and perfumed pilgrims there were such Blue Book, Broadway, and Beverly Hills magnificos as the W. Averell Harrimans, the Theodore Roosevelts, the Sonny Whitneys, the William Paleys, the Gilbert Millers, the Irving Berlins, and Miss Hedy Lamarr, the *Ecstasy* lass, fully clothed for this occasion in pink satin and three or four feet of diamond necklace. Many of the women, in addition to baubles that would buy sizable farms, wore bunches of orchids the cost of which might have kept the Joads' in sidemeat for a year; the plump torso of Miss Jane Darwell, the actress who plays Ma Joad in the picture, was covered with the blooms from chin to waist.

The preview was scheduled to start at 8:30. At 8:45 Mr. Zanuck himself arrived with Miss Dorothy Lamour, the whilom siren of the sarong. By that time the theater was filled with a swanky, glittering, noisily chattering, neck-craning, hand-waving crowd. Photographers dashed up and down the aisles, snapping the members of that small group of personages whose faces provide a never-failing treat for city editors' eyes. Only another dozen camera men and the strains of the Prelude to *Tristan und Isolde* would have been needed to turn the scene into a duplicate of a Metropolitan Opera opening.

Three rows in the parquet were occupied by officers and directors of the Chase National Bank and their ladies. The Chase National controls

Michel Mok, "Private Preview," *The Nation* 150 (February 3, 1940), pp. 137–138.

Twentieth Century-Fox, which produced the picture, and by an odd coincidence it is also one of the Eastern financial institutions, along with the Irving and Manufacturers' Trust companies and the National City and Central Hanover banks, which control the Western land companies that tractored the Joads, and thousands like them, off their farms.

The presence of the Chase National gentlemen and their resplendent women furnished a graphic and enlightening demonstration of the virtues of our system of free competition and individual enterprise without too much Government interference or regulation. Here they were; having added greatly to their wealth by taking possession of the lands of the Joads, and about to wax still richer from the profits of a dramatization of the agonies of those unfortunately stupid and shiftless people. The Chase National, its sleek officials seemed to say, can't lose; it gets 'em coming and going.

After a newsreel the Okie odyssey was finally unveiled. In the dark it was of course impossible to get a clue to the reactions of Mr. Zanuck's chichi guests, and that, perhaps, was just as well. Except for a smattering of applause from the balcony when the migrant farmers at the government camp foiled the deputies' scheme to break up their dance and a general polite round at the finish, the invited audience witnessed the picture in silence. The crowd on the lower floor returned to its limousines after Ma Joad had made her final speech: "Rich fellas come up an' they die, an' their kids ain't no good, an' they died out. But we keep a-comin'. We're the people that live. Can't nobody wipe us out. Can't nobody lick us. We'll go on forever. We're the people."

Well, maybe so. Meanwhile, the Park Avenue gals and their escorts drove to Fefe's Monte Carlo for a little champagne supper tossed by Mr. Zanuck. From the Dust Bowl to the flowing one—Glory, glory, hallelujah!

The Late Show as History

TIME

This week in the U.S. of 1968, a Negro waiter will shuffle off, mumbling: "Yassuh, I'se hurrin' fas' as I know how." An angry Indian will vow:

Essay, "The Late Show as History," *Time* (June 28, 1968), 91, pp. 32–33.

"Many white eyes will die!" A Marine sergeant will cry: "Come on, let's get the yellowbellies!"

Such quaint language endures in the movies from the 1930's and 1940's that unreel on television with the steady persistence of an arterial throb. Ranging back to the baby talkies, late-show films represent what Jean Cocteau called the "petrified fountain of thought." Ghosts of America's past, they evoke the naiveté, exuberance—and problems of a simpler society. To middle-aged Americans, they can also be embarrassments with commercials. Did the public truly love those painful Blondie pictures so much that Hollywood made 28 of them? How did Turhan Bey ever become a star? Did anyone really take Errol Flynn seriously in *Desperate Journey*, after he sabotaged German munitions plants, hijacked a Nazi bomber and shouted: "Now for Australia and a crack at those Japs!"?

Says Producer Billy Wilder: "A bad play folds, and is forgotten, but in pictures we don't bury our dead. When you think it's out of your system, your daughter sees it on television and says: 'My father is an idiot.'"

Most children are not related to film directors, however, and to them movies on TV are an integral part of their epoch; they are growing up with a borrowed nostalgia for a time they never knew. The once-irretrievable past has become as salable as a personality poster, as audible as a Fred Astaire LP. The late show is ransacked for trivia questions and recherché clichés. . . .

With more than 13,000 films waiting to be rerun on television, old movies have become America's National Museum of Pop Art, the biggest repository of cultural artifacts outside the Smithsonian Institution. On TV, of course, the movies are tiny, like warriors who have become trophies of a head-shrinking tribe. Despite this diminution—despite faded prints and commercials perforating climactic scenes—old flicks remain more compelling than most of the shows that surround them. Films may go in one era and out the other, but even the flattest Tarzan epic or the corniest war saga offers a series of clues to history. Like a paleontologist reconstructing a Brontosaurus from a vertebra and two teeth, the patient late-show viewer can reconstruct some of the main currents of American thought.

The old movies almost always portrayed U.S. dreams—and thus, indirectly, realities. Just as the peasant tales retold by the Grimm brothers spoke of common maidens who could spin gold from straw, Hollywood created its own folk stories from the yearnings of 1930's audiences. *If I Had a Million*, for example, tells of a quirky financier who sends million-dollar checks to strangers. A colorless clerk played by Charles Laughton receives his check in the mail, goes to the president of his company, sticks out his tongue and delivers a loud Bronx cheer. Blackout. In those precarious years, the vicarious thrill of giving a razz to the boss was irresistible—to say nothing of the complex moral that a nobody can suddenly acquire the money that can't buy happiness.

With a celebrated conscience that writhed with guilt beside the swimming pool, Hollywood writers sang a song of social significance. The loner of the 1930's film—Gary Cooper, Cary Grant, Jimmy Stewart—always triumphed against Big Money, amid settings of dreamlike luxury, cluttered with butlers, white pianos, and canopied beds. Like animated editorial cartoons, their opposition was always a vested—and usually watch-chained—interest on the order of Edward Arnold. The heroine—Barbara Stanwyck or Jean Arthur—spoke with a catch in her throat that accented her vulnerability. But she had a whim of iron, and when she urged John Doe or Mr. Smith to Washington, the nation's laws were rewritten on the spot. As the Girl Friday, she was the flip, half-emancipated helpmeet to the strong but bumbling American Male.

In those films, passion was expressed with a kiss or a cheek-to-cheek dance. Yet, in retrospect, they often seem sexier than some of today's celebrated shockers. What made Mae West's *double-entendres* titillating was that they really had double meanings; current cinematic sex jokes have but one unmistakable point.

Today, children constitute one of the most militant majorities in America. And since a threat cannot be cute, the late-show screen child seems like a kid who has stayed up past his bedtime. During the Depression parents somehow found their children easier to get along with —perhaps because they had a sense of sharing a common crisis. Children seemed comforting, or at least cheering. Hollywood fostered Jackie Cooper, Frankie Darro, Mickey Rooney, Our Gang and the apotheosis of innocence, Shirley Temple. "I class myself with Rin-Tin-Tin," she later said, referring to such films as *Bright Eyes* and *Curly Top*. "At the end of the Depression, people were perhaps looking for something to cheer them up. They fell in love with a dog and a little girl—it won't happen again."

That love was not universal. Only a changed America could drive the Temple from the money changers, but even in the 1930's a bulbous misanthrope named W. C. Fields declared that "no man who hates small dogs and children can be all bad." Fields had a following that identified with his constant character, the put-upon male who could neither support nor desert his yapping family. This original style of explosive comedy arose from humanity under pressure—a kind of pressure that affluence has released, perhaps forever. The Marx Brothers, for example, remain as inseparable from the 1930's and 1940's as F.D.R. More than any other stars, they bridge vaudeville, the silents, the talkies and TV itself. But Fields, who always blew his cool, exerts an appeal rivaled only by Bogart, who never blew his. Both men nurse a surly integrity and loathing for any Establishment except the neighborhood bar—attitudes that delight today's young cynical idealists.

If the late show has a single classic hero, it is the outlaw with the gun. *Bonnie and Clyde* has its obvious origins in the old gangster films— there were 50 in 1931 alone. *Little Caesar, Scarface* and *Smart Money* mirror the hostile hustle of Prohibition years and parody Horatio Alger by putting the happy ending in the middle, then massacring the criminal-hero in the end. The private eye too was a fixture of the time. Alone, armed only with a wisecrack and a .38, he faced the forces of evil and escaped intact. Today, the hero has joined the organization; like everyone else, 007 has an employee number.

Nor is that the only alteration. Today, the word anti precedes such terms as hero and war. In the 1940's, those words stood naked and unembarrassed as Hollywood took the entire American melting pot and put it into uniform: "Here are the volunteers, sir—Jorgenson, O'Brien, Goldberg, Van Jones, Milwitzski . . ." A generation of war heroes seemed to be Xeroxed from the recruiting posters: Alan Ladd, Gregory Peck, Van Johnson, William Holden. Not until the late 1950's were leading men, like Rod Steiger, allowed to act humanly scared again.

The war also simplified villains even more than heroes. Before Pearl Harbor, the heavy was a foxy seducer, a neurotic thug or a fastidious mastermind ("I despise violence, but my assistant Hugo . . ."). The wartime villain was a wicked, witless German or a Japanese with Coke-bottle lenses on his sinister glasses. All this continued through the cold-war 1950's, with their Slavic bad guys. Now the dominant heavies are a polyglot crew, their lunacy more important than their lineage.

Probably the most striking changes in American attitudes are reflected in the film progression of the teen-ager and the Negro. Before James Dean met Freud in *Rebel Without a Cause* (1955), adolescence in the movies was the period between acne and marriage. To modern teen-agers, Henry Aldrich seems as remote as Henry VIII. In a day when, in certain quarters at least, student is synonymous with riot, nothing is more anachronistic than a conference in Dad's study or the dutiful screech, "Coming, Mother!" It seems inconceivable that Louis B. Mayer's fondest memories were of the Andy Hardy films. "In one," he recalled, "Andy's mother was dying—and they showed him standing outside the door. Standing. I told them: 'Don't you know that an American boy like that will get down on his knees and pray?' They listened—the biggest thing in the picture."

Just about the only benefit today's Negroes can trace to the standard Hollywood product is the current Black Power slogan, "*Ungawa!*"—a fake African chant from a Tarzan picture. Even in 1950 reruns, Negroes are chuckle-headed or criminal. In mystery pictures, it is a Negro who discovers the corpse and scampers away shouting "Feets, do yo' stuff!"

Says the comic: "I don't want any dark innuendoes." Chirps the chauffeur: "Anybody call me?" Even such all-black musicals as *Stormy Weather* and *Cabin in the Sky* patronized as they provided employment. "It's been a long journey to this moment," said Sidney Poitier when he received his Oscar for *Lilies of the Field* in 1963. But his was only the last lap. The first million miles were traveled by Eddie Anderson, Stepin' Fetchit, Willie Best, Butterfly McQueen and other gifted actors whose long ride in the back of the bus can be seen again every week on television.

With the new liberalities of the current cinema, such antique prejudices seem laughable—almost as laughable as the 1960's movies will be to late-show fans of the 1970's and 1980's. Then as now, viewers equipped with 20/20 hindsight will perceive the depressed, desolated land that bled through the 1930's films, the hunger for absolutes and the shrill patriotism that surrounded the war and cold war of the 1940's. They will recognize the erosion of supposedly permanent mores and attitudes that character-ized the late 1950's and early 1960's. They will survey the clichés of this period—the alienation bit, the under-30 thing, the unromantic sex kick—and will realize that no matter how laughable, these stereotypes, too, reflect a troubled reality. The hippie scene and the identity crisis will no doubt someday assume an air of innocence and cherished worth along with the Front Porch, the Soda Fountain and the Family, which now warm the nostalgia of late-night retrospection. Hollywood, which liked to see itself as Everyman's Scheherazade, has also been his Cassandra—the two roles are inseparable.

PART FIVE

LIFE-STYLES FOR A MACHINE AGE

14. The Average American

Whatever history may have to tell us about the development of the science of statistics, there can be little doubt that Americans as a people rapidly became fascinated by what one can do with them. We wrote a census into our very constitutional structure; we compile volumes of statistics not only for knowledge but for entertainment; we recall to mind our athletic heroes not only because of individual achievements on individual occasions but because of statistical achievements over long-ranging careers; we like to know what risks we are taking on the basis of statistical calculations of chances, although our death, presumably, would be ours alone.

A culture that has enshrined "individualism" as a key virtue at the same time has an unusual interest in "the average." We are as interested in one outstanding school achievement as in the student's academic "average." We are not as interested in how Willy Mays did today as in what his baseball "average" is. We of course respect the opinions of great experts but read as eagerly what the "average man" feels as revealed by statistical accounts called "polls." We hesitate, often, to call ourselves "typical" and prefer instead the safety-in-numbers of being "average." The Common Man may or may not be a key figure in understanding the Jacksonian world in America; the Average Man is crucial to any understanding of the American culture as we moved toward the middle of the world of Franklin D. Roosevelt.

The great social and economic studies developed increasingly in the 1920's and 1930's by the government (like *Recent Economic Trends* and *Recent Social Trends,* both begun in the late 1920's and published in the early 1930's), the private studies done under the auspices of organizations like the Brookings Institution, foundations like the Carnegie and Rockefeller, university research (one thinks of the important studies by the Chicago sociologists and political scientists starting after the first world war)—all of these rested on a basis of empirical research involving at least in part the gathering of statistics. The establishment of the Bureau of Labor Statistics under Wesley Clair Mitchell in the Hoover Administration is a historic event of considerable importance and the New Deal itself might be viewed as resting in large part on the gathering of enormous statistical data.

But our interest here is in the cultural consequences of such "statistical" ways of thinking. By the 1930's the Average American and even the

Average American Family had become central to the vision of what that culture might be. No matter how strong the commitment to individualism in the announced value system, all during the period under review more and more attention was paid to the Average American. Even Frank Lloyd Wright, exemplar of individualism and noncomformity sometimes *in extremis,* designed mass housing for the Average American (Usonian, he called this house) and his Broadacre City was again built for some kind of roughly statistical model. In 1935 an Industrial Arts exposition at Rockefeller Center featured an Average American Home; The New York World's Fair of 1939 not only had as one of its ringing themes "unity without uniformity" while it featured again a vision of the American Home of the future, but one of the Fair's Committees engaged in a search to find the Average American Family presumably to live Average American lives *in* the Average American House so that other Americans could find out how the Average American did—or would—live.

It is against this background that the article on American life-style by Walter B. Pitkin is offered. Pitkin (1878–1953) was a professionally trained psychologist with a special interest in consumer psychology. Prolific writer on a wide range of subjects, he was especially successful with self-improvement books, and most significantly his best-selling *Life Begins at Forty* (1932). The essay reprinted below was written for a volume published in 1932 and edited by F. J. Ringel. Entitled *America as Americans See It,* it was one of those not untypical collections common especially in the 1920's and 1930's—a collection of assessments of all aspects of American life, thought, and culture written by experts in their respective fields.

The American: How He Lives
WALTER B. PITKIN

The American lives better than anybody else. His average income is $750 a year. He owns an average of $3300 worth of property. Outside of the largest cities, most families live in their own homes and have a sizable front- and backyard. No country in Europe has so many abominably built houses. It is estimated that Americans are swindled out of half a billion dollars a year by crooked building contractors. Unpretentious and ugly as such dwellings are, they preserve the unity of the family

Walter B. Pitkin, "The American: How He Lives," in Fred J. Ringel, *America as Americans See It* (New York, 1932), pp. 200–205.

group and a certain freedom of coming and going which the metropolitan folk have lost. And, in contrast to the typical home in Europe, they contain an amazing array of luxuries.

It is the rule rather than the exception that a cheap wooden house will contain, among other things, a $500 piano or automatic player piano, a $150 radio, a $50 talking machine, and a $50 icebox (the latter now rapidly being displaced by $200 electric refrigerators). There is usually a good bathroom, usually with a shower; and almost always there is central heating, with hot and cold water upstairs and down. All these are bought on installments which run from one to five years. A few years ago there was a dangerous amount of installment selling; but now it has been stabilized around $2,000,000,000 a year. This represents less than 5 per cent of the personal incomes of Americans—a fairly conservative fraction.

The home without electric light and gas is a freak, save in the remoter country districts. So too is the home without its own garage in the backyard or else a nearby rented garage for the family automobile. Rare the American family today which does not own a car! Carpenters go to work every morning in their own vehicles. And the middle-class man usually has a car for business purposes and another for his wife and children. It is only the poorest class of city workers and farmers who walk or use street cars nowadays.

The American eats more and eats better food than anybody else. Indeed the superiority of his diet probably accounts largely for his high output as a workingman and business executive. The growing and distributing of food are enterprises which work on a continental basis, and even on an international scale quite unknown elsewhere. It is an old jest, and strictly true too, that the Californian who wishes to eat the finest oranges must go to some big American city to get them; so too with the Brazilian who wishes fine coffee and the West Indian who seeks grapefruit or pineapples.

Fresh fruits and vegetables are available in every town save the very poorest, all the year around; and in abundance too. Canned goods of every sort have become so fine and cheap that the American workingman's wife sets a table which would seriously tax the financial resources of a European middle-class family (except in a few favored regions such as central France). The ordinary chain store carries, at low prices, fully fifty varieties of such canned goods; and a large city store may carry two or three hundred.

The American drinks incredible quantities of milk and coffee. He eats more sugar than three average men elsewhere. He consumes vast quantities of chocolate. But the most significant fact is that, on the whole, he tends to eat a scientifically well-balanced diet of proteins, carbohydrates, fats, and vitamins. This is improving the physique and general health of our people at a great rate.

How about work? Well, by and large, the American's days shorten, and so do his weeks and years. In many large industries the six-hour day has begun, and with it the five-day week. Vacations are lengthening, even for the ordinary worker; and the habit of knocking off for a long trip or rest spreads. This tendency is the result of many influences, among which the strongest are the automobile, good roads, cheap gasoline (about one-third as costly as in Europe), labor-saving devices in factories, organization technique in offices, and the relieving of the housewife's drudgery by central laundries, cleaning services, valet services, delicatessens, bakeries, and so on. The man's work is done in short order, and so is his wife's.

The ordinary American and his family travel more than 5000 miles every year, mostly on pleasure trips. They go off on long camping jaunts in summer and down South in winter. Steadily the weekend touring radius grows. And the farther people travel, the farther they crave to travel. The American is the greatest of all globe-trotters, and is becoming more so with every passing year. In one sense, he knows more about the world than anybody else—though in another he knows much less! When traveling in America, he sees little save huge, gaudy billboards advertising all the commonplace things he uses at home. An American highway is the ugliest spot on earth; and so low is the aesthetic taste of the average American that he does not even object to the defacement of his loveliest landscapes.

Next to the automobile, the motion picture fascinates the American most keenly. He sees a show on the average of about once a week, year in and year out; if more prosperous than the average, he goes twice a week, and so do all members of his family except the baby. The advent of the talking picture has drawn more adults and fewer children, for reasons into which we cannot go here.

But the radio is swiftly gaining on the motion picture and, in the opinion of some observers, may equal it in vogue within a few years. It offers wider variety at less cost; and, above all, it may be enjoyed at any hour of the day or night, without any more effort than the turning of a dial. In fact, the radio is even cutting in heavily on the automobile during these years of depression; and it would surprise nobody to see a radio in every American home by 1935 or thereabouts. If that happens, the attendance at the motion-picture houses will dwindle, and so too will automobile mileage.

The American man spends less and less on his clothes, while the American woman spends more and more. He buys a new suit only once in about fifteen months. He wears fewer and fewer shoes, while the woman wears more. He prefers spending money on travel and other pleasures; and in this his children side with him more often than with their mother.

His pettiest vices are cigarettes, of which he consumes between 1000 and 1200 a year; or, if an addict, as many as 10,000; the average American family spends $70 a year for cigarettes! Next to cigarettes, coffee, of which he drinks about four cups a day, year in and year out; then candy and chewing gum; and, last but far from least, soft drinks of incredible bulk, mostly nothing more than sweetened water well chilled.

Although his country has the largest and cheapest periodicals in the world and a host of excellent book publishers, he reads little, particularly of a serious sort, outside of his vocational interests. He buys about four books every five years—not counting school texts for his children. He draws a book from his public library not oftener than twice a year. And he rents or borrows two more books annually. At the highest estimate, he uses five or six books a year; and this does not mean that he peruses each from cover to cover. As for periodicals, he gets less than one a week, aside from his newspaper. And he reads perhaps one-fifth of its contents. Furthermore, he is a poor reader, being less skillful than he himself was in boyhood. In America the reading habit is dying fast.

Perhaps the most striking, if not the most bewildering way of American life, from the European point of view, is the brief time spent at home. The ordinary citizen and his children are never home except when they have to be; they seem to feel out of place there. They eat and sleep within its walls, then rush off to work, to school, to the movies. In the larger cities, the union laborer spends more of his non-working hours in his lodge room than at home; but this would not be true of the small villages and open countryside. There the home remains more or less the center of family and social life. The lack of a genuine social life is one of the most startling features of the American scene. Life is a routine of work, sleep, and a few highly standardized pleasures.

The American saves more money than anybody else, in spite of the high cost of living. Bank deposits prove it. He leaves nearly all of the family spending to his wife and older children; with the result that the center of selling and advertising policy has shifted to the feminine and infantile appeals. No European can understand the tone and manner of American advertisements unless he understands that women and children control the purse strings. More and more women are coming to own stocks and bonds, partly as a result of inheritance and partly through their own business acumen. It is not at all beyond possibility that, in another generation, women and older children will own more securities than men.

"How rich the average American must be!" exclaims the European. That's a mistake! Most of the good things which the American enjoys are not bought outright but paid for over a long period on the installment plan. At least nine out of every ten of the ordinary American homes are being purchased out of weekly savings and become the property, free and clear, of the residents only after seven to twelve years of steady toil and thrift. Automobiles are paid for within one to two years. Radios and electric household appliances are acquired with a small down payment and a note for the balance that often runs two full years.

So popular has this long-term purchase plan become that the working-man of good local reputation is now able to buy almost anything in that manner: even doctors allow installments for medical services, and many stores have followed the lead of the huge mail-order concerns in granting a year or longer for the buying of tables, chairs, rugs, and children's clothing.

Real wages are measured in terms of their buying power. It will amaze the European to know that the American's real wages have increased by only 1.5 per cent in the past forty years. What then explains his tremendously high standard of living? First of all, the immense variety of things he can buy with his money; and secondly, the amount of service that is given by sellers along with goods. Were there some reliable method of converting variety and service values into dollars and cents, we should find that, for all practical purposes, the American has prospered much more than strict economic theory would allow. While he is by no means so prosperous as the foreign observer fancies, he is considerably more so than men of his same status in other lands.

15. The Study of
the Community

Herbert Agar said it at the outset: culture is linked to the community, civilization to the city. Sufficient work has been done by our historians and sociologists to make us well aware how important the idea of the community was in America since at least the days of the Progressives. The community became the central core of social study and concern as early as the Chicago School of sociology. A long series of community studies in the 1920's and 1930's reached a kind of culmination in the general popular reception of the Lynds' two volumes, in 1929 and 1937. Many of the men and women active at least as early as the 1920's in the movement we call town or urban planning—men like American planning genius Henry Wright (1878–1936) who was to execute often unfilled plans for the New Deal Resettlement Administration—were really thinking in terms of "model communities," some of which were developed with private means during the 1920's.

All of this found reinforcement during the American search for culture in the 1930's. Out of the South the Agrarians, with their intellectual center at Vanderbilt, made community central to their thought. In the Northeast socialists and radicals of various kinds fled from cities to organize their own communities. And out of the Middle West Sherwood Anderson, long a writer about communities, wrote a text to be neatly entwined around a collection of some of the best Farm Security Administration photographs and called it *Home Town* (1940), a volume in *The Face of America* series. The Federal Writers' Project with its *Guides* also put stress on American communities. But this is better discussed by Robert Cantwell (born 1908) in the article reprinted below. Cantwell, himself a writer of some distinction, served as well on the editorial staff of several important publications: *New Republic, Time,* and *Fortune.*

Yet there remains no study of an American community as memorable and classic an American document as the photo-essay Margaret Bourke-White did of Muncie, Indiana, the "real 'Middletown,' " for *Life* Magazine in 1937 (the same year she published with her husband Erskine Caldwell one of the first successful combinations of journalism and photography, *You Have Seen Their Faces*). Miss Bourke-White (1906–1970) had been doing industrial and news photography since 1927. She served on both *Fortune* and *Life* in editorial capacities as well as a photographer. But her development of the extended photo-essay remains one of her outstanding achievements. It helped redefine what was news; it marshaled the machine—the camera and the presses—to provide a series of related images. The one on Muncie provides the kind of insight into what Americans mean when they talk of a community that no amount of research or statistics could, for a community means space, juxtaposition of man and things in nature, details of artifacts that make understandable life-styles not otherwise comprehensible. Since the design and layout of this photo-essay are important parts of the whole, instead of attempting to make it fit these pages we refer the reader to the issue of *Life* for May 10, 1937.

America and the Writers' Project
ROBERT CANTWELL

The America that is beginning to emerge from the books of the Writers' Project is a land to be taken seriously: nothing quite like it has ever appeared in our literature. It is a country of odd contraptions and strange careers, where all the big houses have secret rooms and where, in the 1840's, innumerable towns withered and died because the railroad passed three miles to the east. Nothing in our academic histories prepares you for it, and very little in our imaginative writing; none of the common generalizations about America and the American temperament seem to fit it, least of all those attributing to Americans qualities of thrift, sobriety, calculation, or commercial acumen. On the contrary, it is doubtful if there has ever been assembled anywhere such a portrait, so laboriously and carefully documented, of such a fanciful, impulsive, childlike, absent-minded, capricious and ingenious people, or of a land in which so many prominent citizens built big houses (usually called somebody's folly) that promptly fell into ruins when the owner backed inventions that didn't work.

It is a slightly alarming picture, largely because of the impression it gives that carelessness and accident bulk so large in American history. Whitman was its only poet, but even Whitman's Americans lacked some amiable, yawning, sardonic quality that shows through these histories of towns, roads, and houses. These Americans have their creepy side, as

Robert Cantwell, "America and the Writers' Project," *New Republic* 98 (April 26, 1939), pp. 323–325.

witness their love of secret rooms—the *Guides* probably contain more concrete information on this strange quirk of the American temperament than has ever before been assembled. In the old Betsy Thompson House on Dividing Creek Road, Maryland; at Beverly Farms not far away; in Patty Cannon's Tavern; in the old Cooper House in Camden; in Bowman's Folly in Virginia, in the old Wharton Place near Mappsville, in the Old Brick House near Sough Mills, South Carolina—America is so full of secret rooms, invisible closets, hidden stairways and false halls that they seem once to have been as essential to a well-planned house as a kitchen. It is difficult to think of our New England ancestors as thrifty, practical folk when you discover them equipping their homes with trap doors and sliding panels.

There was unquestionably something secretive and mysterious about them, but it was counteracted by an odd, clownish, lunatic sense of humor—they composed irreverent jingles for their tombstones, made up jocular names for their villages and farms—the land grant in Maryland legally named Aha the Cow Pasture being typical—and were continually deciding boundary lines, the locations of county seats and the ownership of plantations by flipping a coin. They were the greatest coin-flippers ever known, all the way back to the time Stephen Girard won his boss's boats, business and home, only to have the boss's daughters drive away the new owner with a goose gun. In the same way that the *Guides* are a vast catalogue of secret rooms, they are a catalogue of remarkable instances of Americans' ability to take extraordinary happenings in their stride, of their unwillingness to admit surprise, even if they felt it—like Ann Whitall of Red Bank, who was spinning quietly in her attic when a cannon ball crashed through the wall, whereupon she simply moved the spinning wheel to the cellar and went on spinning. Even their wars, as they pop in and out of the *Guides*, seem to have no more relation to military strategy than darebase: when the Tories killed Daniel P. Schenck of Pleasant Valley, Mrs. Schenck got his gun, followed them and shot the Tory who had killed him; and when the British captured John Burrowes of Matawan, his neighbors rowed over to Flatbush to capture the mayor of New York. They were secretive and sometimes violent, but they had an almost childlike awe of people more romantic and eccentric than themselves: in each village they kept alive the legends associated with the cliffs and crags from which unhappy lovers jumped, a practice which, if preserved now, would result in most big hotels being known as somebody's Leap.

They were great builders of spite fences, spite churches, spite towns—their captains of industry even built spite railroads. After you read the *Guides* you see that the New Jersey voter who started to chop down his own trees because he couldn't stand Mayor Hague was running true to a national pattern of exasperation. The four hundred citizens of Ilo, Idaho, moved their whole town a mile and a half to set it up across the railroad tracks from another town and for thirty years refused to incorporate with it; the Quakers of Odessa, Maryland, splitting in 1828, remained split until the last insurgent died in 1880, after having worshiped alone in the rival church for years. None of the generalizations about Americans seems to fit the people described in the *Guides;* about the best is that of the anonymous writer in "The Ocean Highway" who says that the Sussex County farmer is composed, stubborn, independent, has an evident feeling of equality, "may politely defer to someone he thinks knows more about something than he does, and above all respects a smart lawyer."

But that characterization gives no impression of their fantastic careers. Scattered through these two hundred-odd books are brief biographies of prominent, notorious or merely eccentric individuals who once swung weight in their own communities and whose marks—whether they be the Shot Tower of old Dubuque, or the addresses of prominent prostitutes scratched on the transoms of New Orleans—still remain. The careers that are traced in the *Dictionary of National Biography* have always seemed to me interesting reading, provided you do not take them too seriously; but they lack variety, and they generally deal with successful people—stuffed shirts, bureaucrats, vice-presidents, bankers, editors, generals, railroad presidents—whose prominence in history seems somehow directly connected with the lack of excitement in their lives. But the biographies in the *Guides* have no such rigorous standard to determine inclusion: people are mentioned whether they succeeded or failed, whether their inventions worked or not, whether they won or lost their duels, made money inside or outside the law: the only test seems to be that some living evidence of their presence, if only a legend or the name of a street, still persists in their own towns. So you get a wide range—gamblers, storekeepers, cranks, innkeepers, spies, murderers, Indians, surveyors, people who planted orchards, or people who built fish ponds on the roofs of their houses, or contrived machines to capture power from the sun, or like the Presbyterians of Squabbletown, became memorable only because of the ferocity of their struggle with the Baptists. There is space for David Brinkman, the young evangelist from Erskine Caldwell's country, whose mark on the national life consists in the many disconcerting signs he has lately been placing on the highways reading "Prepare to meet thy God," as well as for Nordica, the musician of Backus Corner, Maine. I do not know how Nordica's career stands in relation to the history of American music, but it seems almost typical, in its offhand acceptance of incongruities, in relation to the life of the country as the *Guides* record it. Turn right at Backus Corner, says the Maine *Guide,* go down a dirt road, turn right again, and you come to a one-and-a-half story cottage where, in 1859, Lillian Norton was born. Her high voice was light and sweet, the *Guide* says, and she had a varied matrimonial career; she assumed the name of Gigli Nordica; her first husband sailed off in a balloon and was never seen again, and she herself died in Java after being shipwrecked off Thursday Island.

How has it happened that nobody ever thought before to trace the careers of the vast majority who guessed wrong—the leading bankers who put their money in canals in 1840 and in Maine shipyards in 1856, who plunged on slaves in 1859, and bet that Florence, in Baboon Gulch, Idaho, would be the leading city of the state? What a fine group of far-sighted financiers have really turned up in the *Guides!* They bought lots in Indianola, Texas, and refused to let the railroad enter Cantwell's Bridge, Delaware; they invested in river steamers, stage-coach companies, pony expresses, whale fishing, cannonball foundries, or like Captain Hauser of South Dakota shot foul gases into the air to bring on rain. But not only the commercial failures loom large in the *Guides*—they record notable Americans who were wrong in all fields, who announced that the world was coming to an end on a certain date, or made plans to get Napoleon off St. Helena—but the project failed, the boom collapsed, the railroad went the other way, the authorities got wind of the plot, the current shifted, the bay filled in, new deposits were discovered in Africa or, after Yanktown had been chosen as the capital, the legislature moved it to Pierre.

But they left their traces all over the country. Some of their marks are gigantic ones, calling to mind those footprints of dinosaurs that are found in South Dakota—big buildings, unused canals, tumbledown factories. More often they are elusive, like the legend of Kelly of Kelly's Bluff, who shot a man under the delusion that he was being followed. They are of all kinds: the unearthly house constructed by the Holy Ghost and Us Society in Shiloh, Maine; the pile of bricks marking the spot where there was once a munitions works at Gombo Falls; the broken trestle that supported the water tower in the once flourishing town of Medbury, Idaho. Or, as the New Orleans *Guide* soliloquizes on the redlight district of the city:

Where can one find the equals of former celebrated procuresses? Countess Willie Piazza, under whose roof a Central American revolution was hatched, is dead . . . her gilded mirrors and green plush chairs sold at auction, the piano, badly in need of tuning, going for $1.25. Josie Arlington was buried in and later removed from Metaire Cemetery, but a bronze maiden, representative of the virgins whom Josie never allowed in her house, still knocks in vain on the door of her tomb. . . . Tom Anderson's name is in tile on the corner of Iberville and Saratoga Streets, and Lulu White's name may still be seen cut in the glass transom of her palace on Basin Street; but the palace is now a warehouse.

It is a grand, melancholy, formless, democratic anthology of frustration and idiosyncrasy, a majestic roll call of national failure, a terrible and yet engaging corrective to the success stories that dominate our literature. These financiers and prostitutes who went broke, these prophets whose positive predictions were so badly mistaken, these skilled engineers and technicians whose machines never worked, these miners who never found any gold and these birthplaces of people who never accomplished anything—all of these combine in the American *Guides* to make the country's past seem simpler than we could have imagined it, and to make some of the horrors of its present less difficult to endure. Even Martin Dies seems all right in this company, with Lulu White and Tom Anderson and Joseph Keeney and Tom Kelly and David Weems, with Patty Cannon and Willie Piazza, with Frank Sandford, who thought the world was coming to an end, and with Nehemiah King, who busily built a sloop for the rescue of Napoleon, not knowing that Napoleon was dead.

Now that the Federal Writers' Project is in danger of being abandoned, the value of the work it has done stands out sharply: the least publicized of the three art projects, it may emerge as the most influential and valuable of them all. The shortcomings of its books are obvious. They are cast in a cumbersome and unattractive form, with essays on history, geology, weather and the arts inserted with tours through the states and towns; the result is that they are often too comprehensive for tourists and too superficial for scholars. They are extraordinarily meaty volumes, yielding twice as many unfamiliar facts to the page as most encyclopedias, but their material is scattered; some of the information on a man's life may appear in the historical section, some in connection with his birthplace, some when the tours pass scenes of his exploits. The indexes are so bad they prevent the books having their full value as works of reference. The *Guides* are full of contributions to Indian history that are, generally speaking, excellent; they are civilized and humane, and they combine to give a tragic picture of the suppression of the race, but even so, there seems to be too much about the Indians.

When the *Guides* attempt current history, they do it without much art: you get an impression that the editors fought so hard for the inclusion of controversial episodes, such as strikes, that they ignored important sociological material which could have been included—the ownership of the land through which the tours pass, for instance, or of the factories that are described on both sides of the road. There are inaccuracies, but they are unimportant compared with the omissions: it seems incredible that the Homestake Mine could be described in the South Dakota *Guide* without reference to Hearst's ownership of it. But the biggest limitation seems to result from the bohemianism that afflicts some writers on the Project. It is especially noticeable in the book of creative writing, "American Stuff," and in "New York Panorama." The New York book contains a long and quite interesting piece on jazz, placing practically every trumpet player in town, but has no history of the financial district; it lists all the publishers, playwrights and poets, but does not mention such local weight-swingers as Sidney Hillman and David Dubinsky. And I cannot see why, when factories, railroads and mines are placed and described, a line could not be added saying that they are owned by so-and-so; local politics might be clarified, as well as the line taken by Congressmen—including the line taken by Dies on the Federal Art Projects.

But the *Guides* are getting better; there is no comparison between the weighty, dutiful guide to Washington, D. C., and the suave and consistently entertaining guide to New Orleans. The books on Idaho—the Idaho *Guide* and the Idaho *Encyclopedia*—are one of them early and the other more recent, but they both belong with the best of the books that have come out the West. The Mississippi *Guide*, granted the limitations imposed on it by its form, is a better contribution to an understanding of Southern life than most Southern novelists and Southern Congressmen have given us. When the Project was launched, all emphasis was placed on the state *Guides,* and the city *Guides* that appeared were merely by-products; lately these have become more important, and promise in the long run to be the Project's most fertile field.

For American history has never before been written in terms of communities—it has been written in terms of its leading actors, and of its dominant economic movements, but never in terms of the ups and downs of the towns from which the actors emerged and in which the economic movements had their play. It is one kind of experience to read, in Beard or in Turner, of the opening of the West, but it is another kind of experience to read of the rise and fall of Chillicothe in relation to the railroads, or of Galena in relation to the world market for lead. Everybody knows in a general way what happened when the railroads supplanted the canals, but nobody knew until the *Guides* dramatized it how many careers were deflected in the process or how many towns disappeared. Everybody knows in a general way that the rise of the Delta as the world's leading cotton producer exercised an enormous influence on pre-Civil War politics; but that rise has never been made as concrete as in the Mississippi *Guide*.

History in relation to place also has the effect of transforming the roles of the leading actors. You can read a dozen biographies of Grant and get less insight into his early career than is supplied by a history of Galena—no biography communicates the sense of the boom environment in which he functioned, or pits him so clearly against the hard-drinking, violent, amoral, get-rich-quick world that formed his character.

When you read Grant's biography in relation to his own development, you wonder why he lent himself to the schemes of speculators; when you consider it in relation to the history of Galena, you wonder how he could have been expected to do otherwise.

The project is still unfinished, and there is a chance that it may never be permitted to complete the work it has started. Thus far it has merely outlined its task; the books that have appeared have the same relationship to its full potential influence that a negative has to the final print of a picture. If it continues—if the state *Guides* can be completed and organized nationally, if the state *Encyclopedias* can be brought out in consistent forms, and if the material in the files can be segregated and indexed for historians—there can be no question of the Project's value. It will revolutionize the writing of American history and enormously influence the direction and character of our imaginative literature.

16. The Home, the Family, the Child

The intense interest in "the community" and the organized efforts to revitalize it occupy a crucial place in any history of the cultural strivings of the period. But perhaps even more noteworthy was the sustained attention given to the family. Fully aware of at least some of the vital changes that had affected the role and function of the family in a machine age and the problems these created in maintaining the family as an institution, Americans tried as never before to keep the family functioning and even to revitalize it. Even issues of public policy, for instance those involving housing, raised major questions in connection with family structure: Should home ownership be encouraged (the assumption often that a house was in fact necessary if there was to be a home); Could apartment living provide the proper setting to enable family stability? The family was a center of controversy and discussion.

The early 1930's witnessed the rapid development of a movement that at least one expert calls "indigenous to American culture": professional marriage counseling. Dr. Paul Popenoe became famous for his success in keeping families together through his American Institute of Family Relations; he was widely known through his writings, perhaps especially his column in *Ladies Home Journal*. John J. Anthony resorted to radio to provide needed help. Books like *The Good Housekeeping Marriage Book: Twelve Ways to a Happy Marriage* (1939) could be found in great numbers and even Dale Carnegie included a chapter on successful marriage in his best-selling book. Courses in marriage and the family could be found on many college campuses; they had proliferated and attracted many students since Ernest R. Grove first offered his famous course at the University of North Carolina in the late 1920's. Science—so often accused of creating the conditions which helped lead to the decline of the family—was called upon to develop the skills to maintain it.

Magazines were filled with stories making marriage sound attractive (even romantic) and articles proposing programs like government subsidies to assure the stability of the family as well as praise for the rediscovered virtues of home. Even the comics played a role with a strong series of family-centered strips, notably Frank King's "Gasoline Alley," which gave its readers "through the mirror of the comics, one of the most faithful and cheering pictures of the ordinary business family we have to show." The movies did their part as well—for example, the whole series of Hardy family films, fifteen between 1937 and 1945. So enormously popular, sentimental in defense of the basic structure of the American family, were most especially Judge Hardy, the understanding and all-wise Father and his son Andy, basically sound but always in a little trouble, that the whole series was awarded a special Oscar by the Motion Picture Academy in 1942 for "furthering the American Way of Life."

Such sentiment was reinforced by the nostalgia for family life in days gone by. Even Eugene O'Neill, who had previously seen in family relationships a basic source of neurosis and human misery (and would again) could provide 1933 Broadway audiences with the sweet recollections of *Ah, Wilderness*. Clarence Day's *Life with Father* (1935) and *Life with Mother* (published posthumously in 1936) became classics almost overnight.

It is of course not surprising that the central reason for the effort to reinvigorate family life was the development of the child; children continued to be a central American concern and the problem of the family was largely thought of in terms of the potential development of the child. In the following pages Lawrence K. Frank (born 1890), who has been associated with some of the more significant private foundations and governmental agencies in the field of child development and mental health, writes of "The Family in the Machine Age."

Floyd Dell (1887–1969), a writer out of the American Middle West associated with the so-called Chicago Renaissance, came to New York in 1914 in time to involve himself with some aspects of Greenwich Village bohemianism. His first novel, the autobiographical *Moon Calf* (1920), is often regarded as a kind of key cultural document of the period. During the 1920's he developed an interest in psychoanalysis and child training which finally led to the writing of his remarkable study in history, sociology, and psychology he called *Love in a Machine Age*. It is not only a defense of the family; it is an explicit attack on notions of Platonic overthrow of the familial structure, free love, and many of the child-rearing patterns achieving popularity in the 1920's. Dell hopes to see a radical transformation of society, but he still sees the need to strengthen the kind of family emerging in the modern capitalist machine age freed of remnants of older patriarchal forms.

The Family in the Machine Age
LAWRENCE K. FRANK

Perhaps the most direct evidence of the effect of the changing social-economic situation upon the individual is to be seen in earning a living. At the outset it is well to remind ourselves that today it is largely a question of *earning* a living, while a few generations ago it was a question of *making* a living. Then, the individual man and woman was for the most part engaged in agriculture or handicrafts in which strength, skill, patience, and endurance bulked large. Money, as income and as expenditure, played a relatively small rôle, as the following extract from the diary of a New England farmer clearly shows:

My farm gave me and my whole family a good living on the produce of it and left me, one year with another, one hundred and fifty silver dollars, for I never spent more than ten dollars a year, which was for salt, nails and the like. Nothing to eat, drink or wear was bought, as my farm produced it all.

The family was the industrial and economic unit, and to make a living a man had before him the example of his father and his neighbors, with a body of lore and custom to guide him in growing food and raw materials and fabricating them into needed articles. The young woman also had her guides and teachers in her mother and other older women, who taught her the arts and crafts needed in her activities as a housewife or a spinster.

Today the situation has changed completely, and even in the rural sections, few farmers are engaged in *making* a living; for the most part they are occupied in raising cash crops to sell in order to *earn* a living. Moreover, where formerly only the most enterprising and courageous (and perhaps also the black sheep) went out to seek new occupations and livings, today, with the decline of the rural population and the growth of the urban, almost everyone is being forced out to seek a job and to face new and unfamiliar conditions. Thus we see how, for the majority of persons, no longer are there safe and comfortable refuges of

Excerpts from Lawrence K. Frank, "Social Change and the Family" in *The Annals of the American Academy of Political and Social Science*, 160 (March, 1932), pp. 95–99, as reprinted in Bernhard Stern, ed., *The Family: Past and Present* (New York, 1938) pp. 251–255; and Lawrence K. Frank, "Life Values for the Machine Age," in Dorothy Canfield Fisher and Sedonie M. Gurenberg, *Our Children: A Handbook for Parents* (New York, 1933), pp. 303–306.

traditional occupations and ways of life; all are faced with uncertainty, often anxiety, and are called upon to exert themselves in strange surroundings with few guideposts and traditions. How much this has to do with the current mood of anxiety and restless uneasiness, we can only speculate.

Money income is the focus of endeavor and the only means to a livelihood, in earning which not only men but increasingly women, unmarried and married, are engaged. The conditions affecting gainful occupations are therefore of prime significance for the family life and the home, since the individual man and woman are subject to their governance.

The helplessness of the individual is perhaps the outstanding characteristic of these conditions. . . .

When we turn to the question of what is this living for which an income must be earned, we again see a large shift in process. The functions of the home upon which the family life was focused are being transferred to other agencies and organizations. Food, as we know, is to be found increasingly in restaurants and cafeterias, and that which is consumed in the home is prepared by canning factories, bakeries, ice cream factories, and so on.

The care of the sick and the maintenance of health has become institutionalized in hospitals, sanatoria, and clinics, aided by visiting nurses and related personnel who render the care formerly given by members of the family.

Childbirth is increasingly taking place in hospitals, and the care and nurture of the child is likewise moving outside of the home to clinic, nursery school, kindergarten, school, summer camp, playground and youth organization. The young adult who formerly lived at home is now living in dormitories and bachelor hotels, thus leaving the family group as soon as wage earning begins, instead of waiting until marriage. With the prolongation of schooling, however, the economic dependence of the child is continuing into the years when the maintenance of the child is probably most costly.

The making of clothes for men and now for women is being industrialized, as is their cleaning and laundering, which marks another transfer of home functions. . . .

In the religious sphere, the home and the family are becoming an increasing object of concern on the part of the church leaders, while the old-time intimate religious life of the family appears to be fading out or losing much of its former importance and significance.

These transfers and losses of home functions are being met by changes in housing. We are rapidly becoming residents of congregate dwellings, or apartment houses as we call them, where we live as tenants, paying rent. The home as a secure haven and as a symbol of solid achievement and status, is passing, so that we may in truth refer to the homeless millions, who occupy a house or an apartment only so long as the rent is forthcoming. This homelessness is reflected in the frequent moving from one apartment to another, since our complete lack of responsibility or concern, save for the rent, prevents the formation of ties to the particular dwelling we inhabit. In this connection it should be remembered that by paying rent we are provided with all the services which members of the family once performed, such as maintaining the heating and hot water, removal of garbage and trash, cleaning the premises, repairing equipment, and the like, not forgetting the use of gas for cooking and electric power for lighting, and the innumerable household chores they have wiped out.

Thus stripped of its functions and responsibilities, the home no longer is a focus of human endeavor and interest, but is becoming rather a place at which various services are rendered, for which the payment of a money income is necessary. Home ownership is ceasing to be the goal of striving it once formed for the family; houses are purchased or built for financial reasons, and mortgages are not reduced except when required.

Other goals are being relinquished in this shift of home functions. To own property, especially land and a house, was once the chief aim of a family and the mark of its solid worth in the community. Various furnishings also occupied a special position in the family aspirations and were objects to be sought through thrifty saving. But installment purchasing has changed that, and as the automobile and the radio have superseded the piano and other prized items of furniture, the need for waiting and saving has passed. The care and the radio are not goals, they are necessities and are purchased as such, to be paid for "on time."

Status in the community has long been the goal of endeavor, but today has a limited appeal. The restrictions upon small enterprise and industry have closed the door to the usual route to respectable competence and a dignified position in the community, and the frequency of moving about in large cities has rendered the neighborhood of little account except to the children. The prestige of the competent housekeeper and mother of a family has diminished with the simpler function of the household and the decrease in number of children.

Children have been both a goal and the focus of family endeavor; but with the declining birth rate they are playing a somewhat altered role in the family. Today economic insecurity and conditions of urban life unfavorable to child care are both to be considered before child-bearing is undertaken. When and if a couple has children, the number is less frequently four or five, as formerly, and more often one or two. The multiplication of child-caring techniques, each calling for additional expenditures of energy and money, has enhanced the cost of child rearing for the conscientious parents who are anxious to provide the best available care and treatment for their children.

While we rapidly note the passing of these different goals and enumerate the loss of home and family functions, we cannot too much emphasize that the disappearance of these various activities and strivings marks the passing of a *way of life*. To marry, have children, acquire property, gain a position of respect and dignity in the community, share in the common body of beliefs and affirmations about the universe and man's place therein—these made up a way of life to which the teachings of family, school, and church and the sanction of government and religion were all directed. Young people grew up in a society where the patterns appropriate to this way of life were ready-made, and, while they often criticized their stodgy parents and revolted against their demands, middle age found them more or less settled into the ruts of conformity, since there were no socially sanctioned alternatives.

The patterns for this older way of life remain, but the social-economic situation to which they were addressed has altered. Young men and women face either frustration in their efforts to conform to the older patterns, or confusion and anxiety as they explore for new patterns of conduct. These frustrations and anxieties are the dominant aspect of home and family life today.

❊   ❊   ❊

On one side is the force of the family patterns and standards, and on the other, the call of the contemporary life as expressed by the boys and girls of the same age whose acceptance and approval are essential. It must never be forgotten that youth must follow its own group, for it is within this group that mating, social life, and economic status must be achieved. When this is blocked or prevented by parental control, devastating conflicts are often set up.

Here the issue is not between parent and child, but rather between the parent's values and the world's standards, since the conduct of the child will, in the long run, be colored by the intrinsic merits of his parent's standards. Parental confidence is justified when it is placed not on its own power of discipline and control, but on the sheer force of the child's own personality. In no relation of life is the real impress of the parent's life upon that of his child so clearly shown as in the manner of the child's reaction to the conduct of his or her own age and sex group. But the issue is not to be judged in a day or month. It is a question of years of experiment and "muddling through" before the outcome is made clear.

No young person can or should be asked or compelled to flout his contemporaries. When a boy or girl shows no interest in his age companions, no concern for their judgment, there is indeed reason to be worried lest he or she is failing to make the social adjustments necessary to a sane, wholesome maturity. But the importance of conformity to contemporary life does not imply any necessity for slavish obedience to the standards of the gang. Whether a young person apes the dress, manners, and conduct of the neighborhood, high school, or college group, depends in large measure upon his need of reassurance and approval.

Here we catch a glimpse of values in the process of formation and begin to see again how the ideals of the individual emerge from his own inner life and its fate under the impact of both family and friends. While generalizations may be premature, there is good evidence for the view that the individual is driven, often against his own desires and liking, to conduct that he hates, because the feeling of insecurity, of doubt of his status or standing has compelled conformity. What part in causing this insecurity and uncertainty the parents play thus becomes an all-important question. If the parents of a boy or girl have tampered with his self-confidence, destroyed his feeling of security as a well-liked, approved member of the family and, thereby, driven him to seek excessive approbation from age and sex mates, they cannot be held blameless when the youth seems to have lost his bearing and his grip on the helm. Indeed the self-defeating treatment of adolescents by parents is probably one of the most frequent causes for the familiar teen age steering without a course or goal.

We must not forget for a moment that what the individual does in most situations is a response to his personality needs, especially his need of security and of intimacy to be fulfilled only by reassurance and affection from those he considers important. If a boy or girl pursues a path disapproved by the parents, the first question to ask is, "In what way have the parents failed him in reassurance and affection?"

This is no light responsibility, in a world where even the adults cannot always be secure. Parents are no less human than their children, and oftentimes hardly less confused by complexities for which their own early training had not prepared them. They, too, have their lives outside the home with which they must come to terms. Frequently we hear the expression that something has gone out of life, some of the zest, some of the incentive, and parents are prone to sigh for the good old days when the whole duty of a man and woman was fairly clearly and unequivocally established. There are many indeed who are convinced that we must go back to the good old days. They are sure that if only we can persuade our sons and daughters to dedicate themselves anew to the standards which our parents cherished, an effective answer will be found to our present questionings. It must be clear, however, that not only do the changed social and economic conditions around us render such a return impracticable, but, what is perhaps more important, that once we have begun to question the standards and the sanctions of life, it is impossible to revive a feeling of conviction, of surety that alone gives those standards any vitality and effectiveness.

If we were to take each item in this traditional code of behavior that we still hold up to our young men and women as standards and against it note the actual living conditions to which they will have to conform, I think we would begin to see rather clearly how impossible it is for them to look forward to accepting these as their own standards— and if we are fair-minded, how undesirable it would be if they did. A much more difficult task would be to inventory the new responsibilities and duties. This would call for a high order of imagination and insight, because we may assume that the fundamental needs of men and women for intimacy, for affection, for mating, their desire for reassurance and security, for the personality satisfactions that come from the bearing and rearing of children are continuing—and will continue for our children. The trouble is that opportunities for their satisfaction are not being adequately provided, either in present-day living conditions or the code of behavior brought down from yesterday for their guidance. No one has pointed out for most of them just where they are likely to go astray in terms of these present-day conditions, while most of the warnings and admonitions addressed to them are so obviously outmoded and inappropriate, as to excite either amusement or contempt.

Yet honest parents may well ask, "Must I surrender all my own standards and values and watch my son and daughter pursue a path which violates all I hold dear? What *can* I do to give them the values, the goals and the security that will carry them through the confusing, high speed life pressing in upon them today?"

Probably the most important contribution we can make to their preparation for meeting that life is the conviction that "values" are few and profoundly simple but that the means of expressing and achieving them are as changing and as varied as social living itself. Can we contrive to make our sons and daughters realize that whatever is valuable and worthy in life must be interpreted anew by each generation in its own terms? Out of our own experience we shall then be able to assure them in their human relations of mating, of parenthood, of friendship, they will discover the one means to security which is effective, because it gives them ideals and goals within their power to achieve. Just that realization—that upon *them,* not upon their parents, rests this responsibility—would create the attitude needed so sorely today by youth, confused and baffled by parental admonitions, contemporary fashions, and an inner feeling of frustration. That which endures is never changeless. Our present necessity to re-examine these values which the human race, through the long slow growth of years, has found worthy of preservation, is the measure of their continued validity.

Love in the Machine Age

FLOYD DELL

The aim of this book is to make people modern-minded, by explaining in sufficient detail exactly what are the differences between the psychological requirements of modern life and those of the patriarchal regime. It is believed by the writer that people want to know just that. But they are put off by vague generalities which teach them nothing, or by false prophecies which merely reassure and confirm them in their neurotic compromises.

Thus, for example, it is often said that the mechanization of our modern world is inevitably destroying romantic love and family life. This book will undertake to show that modern machinery and the modern economic system in general are destroying the last remnants of the *patriarchal* family, and with that destruction removing the ancient social uses and justifications of such patriarchal compromises with our biological instincts as are presented in the institutions of homosexuality, prostitution, arranged marriage, polite adultery, and sacred celibacy. It will be shown that by the destruction of the patriarchal family and its accompanying social-sexual institutions, *modern machinery has laid the basis for a more biologically normal family life than has existed throughout the whole of the historical period, or indeed in the whole life of mankind.* As for romantic love, it will be shown that modern life puts it back where it biologically belongs, as a part of the normal love pattern which leads through courtship and love-choice to mating and family life—instead of, as in the patriarchal era, leaving it outside, as an illusion to be pursued in homosexuality, prostitution-patronage, and polite adultery, serving thereby as a safety-valve to ensure the stability of the loveless arranged marriages characteristic of the patriarchal system. In brief, modernity reestablishes family life on the basis of romantic love. Only people trained to live modern lives can live them successfully in love and work. To train young people for adjustments to the patriarchal system is to train them for homosexuality, prostitution, and prostitution patronage, polite adultery, or sacred celibacy; and insofar as they cannot with social approval and inward satisfaction nowadays lead such careers, they are doomed to neurotic maladjustments to the actualities of life.

These statements imply a social and historical basis for modern

Floyd Dell, *Love in the Machine Age, A Psychological Study of the Transition from Patriarchal Society* (New York, 1930), pp. 6–12, 42–47, 67–69, 403–405.

neurotic maladjustments. They imply that modern neuroses occur because we are in a transition stage between our patriarchal past and our non-patriarchal future. Exactly how *ways of life which in the past were useful and socially acceptable mores have become mischievous and socially inacceptable neuroses* will be explained in this book. And that explanation rests upon a modern conception of psychic development. We find a natural and biologically determined growth in emotion from the self-centered stage of infancy to the adult capacities for responsible social and sexual relationships. We find, however, that this emotional growth is controlled always by social education, which dictates how much development in love and usefulness shall be permitted to or required of the individual. And what we find historically is that the patriarchal period was one in which this emotional growth was halted, with regard to both love and work, in an infantile or childish stage—*that it was necessary, in order for the patriarchal system to exist, that nobody should ever grow up to complete adulthood.* If this seems an extravagance, or a mere paradox, the book is here to justify it; and its apparently extravagant or paradoxical character is one reason why so many pages are given to a discussion of the past. It is necessary that we should understand the nature of our break with the past, if we are to understand the precepts for happiness and success in modern life.

The present time appears to be the second great break with tradition in our human life upon earth. The first—though here we are in shadowy and uncertain realms of prehistory with which this book does not deal—was the change from savage culture to patriarchal civilization, which occurred in the Mediterranean world in the dawn of the historical period. One of the features of prehistoric savage culture appears to have been a peculiar use of sexual relations for magical purposes. Nothing in archaic savage culture was more firmly established than the propriety of the religious sex orgy. Women were taught that it was holy to submit themselves to sexual intercourse with the Horned God, or rather with his masked magician-priest, for the purpose of encouraging the procreation of food-animals. This archaic sexual witchcraft became abhorrent to patriarchal civilization—the Horned God became the Devil of medieval Europe, and his worship was exterminated as an obscene heresy. But many of the tolerated or approved sexual practices of the patriarchal regime—the relegation, for instance, of hordes of women to prostitution, and the treatment of 'bastard' children—are now coming to seem to us as cruel, indecent, and silly as the orgies of savage devil worship. We have made a second great break with tradition. We have outgrown these patriarchal sex practices as the patriarchal regime outgrew sex witchcraft.

We do not seek to exterminate outworn patriarchal sex usages as heretical; that is not our modern way of doing things. We have learned the lesson of tolerance. We must be tolerant in order to understand, for it is only through understanding that we shall achieve our destiny. But unless we realize that our age has in truth made a break with the past, and that patriarchal sex compromises have no place in our modern world, we are not truly modern minded.

The savage usages of sex as witchcraft arose out of food anxieties. The patriarchal sex usages arose out of economic anxieties in general, and represented compromises of the property motive with the sexual instincts. As *magic* is the clue to savage distortions of sex, so is *property* the clue to patriarchal distortions of sex. And both distortions occur only through the halting of psychosexual development in an early stage. The savage use of sex as magic represents a halt at so very infantile a stage that when it occurs in modern life, as it does occasionally, it involves so complete a maladjustment to our civilized social scheme that it is classed as a psychosis, that is to say insanity. The patriarchal sex usages, still normal in patriarchal countries, appear in the more fully mechanized and liberated parts of Western civilization as neuroses. It will be shown in some detail that (1) these patriarchal usages are the products of a psychic growth halted in a preadult stage, (2) that the patriarchal economic system required these usages and demanded this halting of psychic development, and (3) that our modern world requires increasingly a full development to adult psychic life and a corresponding set of adult practices in love. The same things will be shown more briefly as regards work.

This will involve a discussion in which such practices as prostitution patronage and polite adultery, for example, will be shown as forms of timid compromise with the sexual instincts, and as being in modern life increasingly neurotic.

This will be followed by a detailed statement of the educational methods by which in the patriarchal regime children and young people were trained in permanently infantile attitudes. The chief of these patriarchal methods were compulsion, shame, and the permanent attachment of sexual emotions to the parents. It will be shown that these educational methods tend invariably to produce their patriarchal results in prolonged childishness, and hence neurotic maladjustment in a society which demands adult capacities. The different, nonpatriarchal method of education, dispensing with the mechanisms of compulsion, shame, and parental fixation—that is to say, a kind of child training which will enable children to grow up to psychic adulthood and fit them for love and work in the modern world—will be outlined.

It will also be necessary to deal with certain current social ideals of one and another sort of sexual "freedom," and show that they are not scientific prophecies, but ideological overcompensations against the emotional hurts of a transition era—and that when they are looked into carefully they are found to be simply the old patriarchal conventions and compromises and infantilities in a pseudomodern disguise.

The requirements of modern adult life will by this time have been made plain. For the generality of mankind these requirements will be in the nature of a liberation; unpoisoned by patriarchal training, most people would prefer to choose their own work and their own mates, and would enjoy the responsibilities which these choices bring. Mankind, however, has always a vision wider than its immediate opportunities of life; and there is a social need for the imaginative enlargements of our human destiny which art and heroism can furnish. One of the most neglected tasks of modern psychology has been that of tracing the ways in which in general the socially inacceptable impulses of mankind can be made acceptable by sublimation in art and ritual; and in particular, the tracing of this process with respect to outworn mores. Some space has therefore been devoted to showing that maladjustment of impulse and opportunity may lead, not to neurotic unhappiness, but to new social adaptations. The most of mankind can be happy in a simple biological fashion; but no precepts for civilized happiness and success in life are complete which do not include those for art and heroism. The artist may break all social rules in fantasy, the hero may break them all in fact. Why they may do this—what is the practical difference between art and neurotic fantasy-making, between heroism and crime—will be discussed.

The way will then be clear for a consideration of the practical needs of modern adolescence, as a period when boys and girls are to be helped to grow up, rather than detained in an ambiguous childhood. In our transition era, an important part of the growing-up process will be what is currently called *emancipation from the family*. Coincident with that, the positive aspect of the same process, is *the achievement of hetero-sexuality*, or full capacity for love of the other sex. Learning some socially approved mode of *earning a living* is another part of this process, and one which may be considered as a part of achieving sexual adulthood. For both boys and girls this sexual-economic development is complicated by the partial entrance of women into the world of work outside the home, and by the resultant conflict between the demands of love and family life and those of outside work upon women. The love-and-work tangle, however, when discussed in the light of our modern conceptions of psychic development toward adulthood, can be understood very simply as a soluble problem of courtship and family life. And finally, as part of the same growing-up process, there is the task of *achieving a philosophy of life*, gaining a view of things, however implicit, which will serve to explain to boy and girl their place in the human scheme and reconcile them to their destiny of struggle. The successful achievement of all these things—emancipation from the parental family, full heterosexuality, economic capacity for cooperation with other adults, and a satisfying philosophy of life—constitute (along with physical growth) the standard of modern adulthood.

It will be noted that none of these things were demanded or permitted by the patriarchal régime; nor can an education based upon patriarchal principles help young people to achieve such adulthood.

Patriarchal education, with the best intentions, imprisons youth in the parental home. Its *property*-precepts about "purity" or sex-fear, and its hostility to free courtship and love-choice, halt boys and girls in an infantile stage of development and doom them to inwardly compulsive careers of celibacy, or prostitution and prostitution patronage, to marriages made tragic by sexual impotence and frigidity or the compromise expedient of polite adultery. It hinders them from achieving the capacity for successful economic cooperation with others by limiting them to the patriarchal attitude of waiting for parental and quasi-parental favors. It bars them from finding their own philosophy of life by forcing upon them a traditional religion which contains no consolations for them, a traditional political formula which does not explain the workings of the world in which they have to live, and a traditional set of moral precepts to which nobody around them ever really conforms. Or, if unsuccessful in its negative effects, patriarchal education dooms these boys and girls to futile rebellions, to the prolonged waste of adult years in solving adolescent problems, and, if these remain unsolved, to the solaces of alcoholism and drug-taking, or even to the final confessions of inadequacy for adjustment to adult life in the infantile delusions of psychosis or the infantile revenge of suicide. The modern world needs modern education for its young people.

This, then, is the program of this book. It will be seen that it involves a discussion of love, marriage, children, education, work and economics in modern life, against a historical background. To build up this pyramid we now proceed, laying the historical groundwork. To encourage the reader to climb the pyramid, it is promised that the view from the top will be invigorating. To those to whom these views are but imperfectly known, the hope is extended that they will see their own lives and those of the younger generation in a new light; that dubious problems will be made simpler, and that they will be encouraged to deal with their tasks of adjustment in the belief that even in this confused transition age life offers the possibility of success and happiness to men and women of courage and understanding.

✿   ✿   ✿

The patriarchal system, being based on landed property, tended inevitably to restrict the privilege of socially protected parenthood to a limited number of inheriting sons and dowried daughters. The superfluous sons and daughters were in one fashion or other thrown overboard to sink or swim. This was less the case among the peasantry who worked their own lands, and could make use of the labors of a large family, than among the aristocratic classes and the city poor; hence the patriarchal family lingered in full strength among the peasantry for centuries after it had begun to break down among other classes. The superfluous sons of the respectable classes became, as we have seen, soldiers of fortune or priests, or members of a new middle class whose interests were hostile to the patriarchal system; and somewhat the same may be said for the superfluous sons of the poor, except that their opportunities as soldiers of fortune, not being socially privileged, tended to make them criminals and vagabonds. The superfluous daughters of the respectable classes might become nuns, and the superfluous daughters of the poor were always in demand as prostitutes—being thus in either case denied the privilege of socially protected maternity.

Yet the economic saving thus effected was in the long run entirely illusory. Many of those thus cast off from patriarchal family protection were unproductive as well as nonreproductive. Priests and nuns had to be provided for, and prostitutes, vagabonds and soldiers of fortune, respectable or poor, did their best to provide for themselves at the expense of others. To maintain them required goods, and what was provided willingly or unwillingly for their support was necessarily withdrawn from the support of families. The economics of the situation are perhaps most clearly to be seen as regards women. The nun on one side and the prostitute on the other took from the family a large proportion of the goods belonging prescriptively to the legitimate wife and mother. Thus her legal monopoly on childbearing was paid for at a heavy cost. Marriage and parenthood became an ever more severe burden upon both sexes, and in classical times they had already become so unpopular that they had to be urged as a "duty to the State."

When prostitution, at the height of the Roman Empire, had become for immense numbers of men and women a substitute for marriage, and when religious celibacy, in medieval times, had become the choice or the doom of other vast numbers of the population, it must be said that these "protections" of the family were in fact destroying it. The patriarchal family system and its basic mode of production were quite unable to cope with the population problem, except by relying upon war, famine, and pestilence to diminish the numbers of mouths to be fed. . . .

The patriarchal system was crashing in Europe when some of the superfluous population found a means of subsistence outside of landed property in trade and then in manufacture. These became a new class, the middle class, which in time was able to create a new kind of social security, offer new social guarantees to parenthood, and put the family upon a new economic basis. It reversed—within the middle class—the psychological relations of the family to property. The reproductive and parental impulses were no longer rigidly limited as to their expression by a static kind of wealth in the form of land; these emotions were rather used as the incentives to economic activities not merely of an exploitive but also of a productive sort. It thereby introduced the modern conception of "work." Labor had never been respectable in an aristocratic society in which it was derogated to slaves or serfs. An aristocrat obtained his privileges by inheritance or favor. Work as a respectable means of improving one's lot was introduced by the middle class. And the conception of the possible improvement of one's lot by work led in turn to a repudiation of the aristocratic ideal of castes fixed by birth. . . .

In spite of every effort of the triumphing middle class to take on all the cultural traits of the decaying aristocracy, it was unable to restore the broken powers of the patriarchal Church and the absolutist State; and, just as it had to free the slave and the serf, so it was obliged within the family to set the children free from paternal economic and social authority—thus establishing a legal age of majority beyond which parental rule must cease, and giving to sons and daughters the right to marry as they chose. It had to grant this legal and social adulthood to grown-up men and women, because it needed them to be psychologically grown up. It did not need to keep them in permanent emotional subservience to the parental family; it wanted them to have adult work ambitions and healthy adult heterosexual mating and family impulses as incentives to their activities. It was—for reasons which it did not fully understand—intolerant of the aristocratic compromises of prostitution, mistress-keeping, and polite adultery. It undertook to abolish permanent celibacy as an ideal. It established divorce, reinstituted romantic courtship and love-choice in marriage, and demanded sexual fidelity in marriage not only of women but of men.

An American woman, Gertrude Marvin Williams, writes of the Hindu form of the patriarchal family system, ... "The joint family system . . . is a device admirably suited to the timid man. He postpones indefinitely the wrench of growing up, putting his childhood behind him, and facing the responsibilities of adult life. Through the years he lingers, leaning on his parents and the reassuring intimacy of the family circle." This is the judgment of a new civilization upon an older one—of Western civilization upon a lingering and decadent remnant of the great patriarchal civilizations of the past. It represents the attitude of an age set free by machine power, toward not merely Brahmin India but all of the lingering and decadent remnants of patriarchal childishness in our Western world. Our modern civilization is not a refuge for the timid.

Marrying without love, courting prostitutes, keeping mistresses, scattering bastards and leaving them to their fate, and indulging in polite adultery, were patriarchal norms of conduct—are still patriarchal norms of conduct in patriarchal countries. However preposterous and undesirable they may seem to us, these practices had their sufficient social justification within the structure of patriarchal society. That was the way the patriarchal system worked. These practices could only become neurotic as the result of fundamental economic changes, which result in withdrawing social justification and approval from them. They are nowadays neurotic only insofar as they hamper social usefulness and prevent personal happiness.

Perpetual celibacy and chastity, for example, are not neurotic insofar as they still find shelter and justification in old patriarchal religious institutions, or in newer social-service formulas on the same model, which enable the celibate to be comparatively useful and happy. We are entitled, if we wish, to despise such ways of being useful, to smile at such ways of being happy; but we are not entitled to dismiss as neurotic any such usefulness and happiness as may be found to exist. The plain fact of our age, however, is that it does not afford such shelter and such justification to large numbers of celibates. Monasteries and nunneries are no longer centers of learning and art; no longer to any considerable extent avenues to power. So that most celibates are nowadays unable to feel proud of their celibacy. Nor is chastity in our middle-class world a permanent treasure; it is in general, in adult life, felt as a disability. The late patriarchal institutions which gave an honorable shelter and a real social function to celibacy and chastity have dwindled to a minor scope in modern society. Most of the world's work is now so arranged as to have simple sexual incentives and rewards in monogamic family life. It is increasingly true that the realm of social effort is comparatively meaningless to such people as are not appealed to by these incentives.

The same argument may be made with regard to prostitution and prostitution patronage. There are still submerged elements of our modern population who take these for granted as ways of life. To the behavior of individuals in that situation, it would be ridiculous and unjust to apply the term "neurotic." They have no choice of a more normal kind of sexual life; and in these symbolic substitutes for love they get the best satisfactions which life has to offer them. But with the growth of Western civilization, these submerged elements of our population are dwindling, and our generalizations apply more and more universally.

Our middle-class industrial and trading system (except in some of its less modern or more piratical forms of industrial exploitation, as for example in "seasonal" labor, cattle-herding, lumberjacking, the manning of ships, and a few others) takes a universal marriage and family life for granted, and is built directly around these institutions as a center. And not only does the modern system work best with a population which conforms emotionally to this sexual arrangement, but it is affected injuriously by almost every personal maladjustment in the sexual realm. The man who is happily mated and takes satisfaction in his family life is found to be the man who pays his debts, the man upon whom an extension of the credit system unprecedented in history can be built up. The disruption of an individual family represents almost invariably a series of economic losses and injuries to others. Marital disruption represents unpaid bills, loss of efficiency in industry, an addition to the turnover cost of labor, and it may mean among the economically insecure part of the population a temporary or permanent problem of vagrancy, as well as possibly requiring social assistance for the wife and children. When a poor family breaks up, it may take, as social workers have learned, the efforts of half a dozen state and social agencies, the court of domestic relations, the juvenile court, pensions, and institutional aid to repair the social damage. The institutional care of deserted children has been found in certain instances to take ten times as much money as was required in wages to keep the family going. Juvenile crime has also to be added to the bill. The fundamental importance of domestic and family happiness in our middle-class industrial and trading regime can hardly be overestimated.

And it is for these among other reasons that the patriarchal remnants of homosexuality, prostitution, polite adultery, and other forms of infantile sexuality are socially inconvenient—so much gravel in the delicate machinery of modern economics, so many obstructions in the realm of normal social expectations. In being such, they impair the social usefulness of the individual. And in lacking their ancient social justifications, they afford no plausible grounds for the individual self-respect which is essential to happiness.

We are, doubtless, not yet free enough from the effects of patriarchal repressions to be able to produce many triumphant illustrations of lives in which the concept of duty is not needed or used at all over long stretches of time—though everyone knows of happy aspects of his or her life to which such a concept would be ridiculously inapplicable. These aspects of life, momentary and fragmentary though they may be and however intermixed with failure, are the prophecies of a kind of life possible to a generation free from patriarchal repressions and able to become really grown-up.

Wholly adult lives lived from such almost wholly instinctive motives are, of course, not possible in a world still cluttered up in the realms of work and love with remnants of patriarchal tyranny. In the field of work, the population at large has little free choice of tasks and little opportunity to exercise the normal play instincts in the performance of these tasks. The patriarchal father, having been cast out from other fields, remains enthroned in economics in the form of the presumably all-wise and certainly all-powerful private owner of industry, and the workers are still supposed to content themselves with the role of obedient and loyal children. Their frequent inability when opportunity offers to take a more adult and responsible attitude toward their work is used as an argument for the necessity of maintaining the old patriarchalism in ownership and control. But the banishment of patriarchalism from industry will be required to complete the modernization of the world. The value of our new machine powers of production in freeing us from anxieties will not be fully realized until these powers are taken out of patriarchalistic class-control and put at the service of humanity. In the realm of love, too, there are vested interests of an institutional sort to delay progress. But we may look forward to a generation free to make its choices in love and able as adults to assume and enjoy the responsibilities which these choices bring.

But if the parental role of preaching duty to children may be expected to disappear, that will still leave parents with plenty to do for their children. Aside from the immense service of not lying to them, of answering truthfully and simply and without emotional attitudes the simple questions that children ask, there is a fundamental service which parents can perform for children: they can be healthily in love with one another. They will thus have no morbid need to exploit their children's love; and they will—without having to try—furnish their children examples of adult man-and-woman happiness. Their normal love for their children will be the natural encouragement to the children's progress in the task of growing up. And all this means that they, the parents, have to be really adult. That is what children need—parents who are emotionally adult: not parental preaching.

Such young people, not lied to by their parents or emotionally exploited by them but encouraged to grow up, will hardly need, it would seem, much of any explicit "philosophy of life" to help them through adolescence, to explain to them their place in the human scheme, and reconcile them to the destiny of struggle.

For the young people of today, less fortunately situated, an explicit philosophy of life of one sort or another is doubtless needed. In place of healthy instincts operating in a healthy social-economic world, we have partly crippled instincts operating in a partly sick world where privilege preys upon poverty and where property anxieties still too generally paralyze the love emotions. The young people of today do need encouragement in order to face bravely the tasks of adult life, work and mating.

They have a right to know that it is not altogether their fault if life seems difficult to them; they have a right to know how things got this way and what prospects there are of their getting better, before they are asked to adjust themselves as best they can to things as they are. A serviceable philosophy of life for adolescent youth is one which offers them the hope of ultimate health in society at large as well as in their individual lives. Such a philosophy will explain the fears of young people as due not merely to their individual shortcomings in adaptation but to our general social-economic backwardness. And in giving young people the knowledge upon which to bring themselves nearer to psychic adulthood, it will give them also the knowledge upon which they can base their endeavors to help bring the contemporary world a little nearer to social-economic health.

This means that the task of promoting mental hygiene must be courageously correlated with the task of promoting social-economic hygiene —not, Mrs. Partington-like, merely try to sweep back, wave by wave, the individual neuroses which are but the spume of the great social-economic tides of anxiety and despair which sweep from the past across our world.

17. The Lost Sex

In a sense the "woman question" perplexed and even bewildered Americans from the start—at least from the time when Anne Hutchinson made something of a nuisance of herself in Massachusetts Bay (1637). (There were, interestingly enough, at least three biographies of Mrs. Hutchinson published in the early 1930's!) The nature of femininity and the role and function of women in American life had been a persistent problem and many of the movements involved in achieving her "liberation" and independent development with her own place as citizen and worker in American society continued on into the postcrash period. Her "cause" was advanced by her greater role in social and governmental affairs during the New Deal and perhaps especially during World War II when she was urged to assume jobs and other responsibilities previously denied her. At the same time more and more analysts, basing their work on newer developments in psychology and psychiatry and even on supposed liberal or socialist grounds, began to offer what might appear to be more conservative solutions to the "problem."

Philip Wylie's vitriolic assault on the American woman, in *Generation of Vipers* (1942), added the word "momism" to our language. In *Modern Woman, the Lost Sex,* social historian Ferdinand Lundberg (born 1902) and psychiatrist Marynia F. Farnum (born 1899) summed up a considerable body of work throughout the period.

Mom
PHILIP WYLIE

Megaloid momworship has got completely out of hand. Our land, subjectively mapped, would have more silver cords and apron strings criss-

Philip Wylie, *Generation of Vipers* (New York, 1942), pp. 185–186, 186–187, 188–189, 203.

crossing it than railroads and telephone wires. Mom is everywhere and everything and damned near everybody, and from her depends all the rest of the U.S. Disguised as good old mom, dear old mom, sweet old mom, your loving mom, and so on, she is the bride at every funeral and the corpse at every wedding. Men live for her and die for her, dote upon her and whisper her name as they pass away, and I believe she has now achieved, in the hierarchy of miscellaneous articles, a spot next to the Bible and the Flag, being reckoned part of both in a way. She may therefore soon be granted by the House of Representatives the especial supreme and extraordinary right of sitting on top of both when she chooses, which, God knows, she does. At any rate, if no such bill is under consideration, the presentation of one would cause little debate among the solons. These sages take cracks at their native land and make jokes about Holy Writ, but nobody among them—no great man or brave—from the first day of the first congressional meeting to the present ever stood in our halls of state and pronounced the one indubitably most-needed American verity: "Gentlemen, mom is a jerk." . . . The machine has deprived her of social usefulness; time has stripped away her biological possibilities and poured her hide full of liquid soap; and man has sealed his own soul beneath the clamorous cordillera by handing her the checkbook and going to work in the service of her caprices.

These caprices are of a menopausal nature at best—hot flashes, rage, infantilism, weeping, sentimentality, peculiar appetite, and all the ragged reticule of tricks, wooings, wiles, suborned fornications, slobby onanisms, indulgences, crotchets, superstitions, phlegms, debilities, vapors, butterflies-in-the-belly, plaints, connivings, cries, malingerings, deceptions, visions, hallucinations, needlings and wheedlings, which pop out of every personality in the act of abandoning itself and humanity. At worst—i.e., the finis—this salaginous mess tapers off into senility, which is man's caricature of himself by reversed ontogeny. But behind this vast aurora of pitiable weakness is mom, the brass-breasted Baal, or mom, the thin and enfeebled martyr whose very urine, nevertheless, will etch glass. . . .

Mob got herself out of the nursery and the kitchen. She then got out of the house. She did not get out of the church, but, instead, got the stern stuff out of it, padded the guild room, and moved in more solidly than ever before. No longer either hesitant or reverent, because there was no cause for either attitude after her purge, she swung the church by the tail as she swung everything else. In a preliminary test of strength, she also got herself the vote and, although politics never interested her (unless she was exceptionally naive, a hairy foghorn, or a size forty scorpion), the damage she forthwith did to society was so enormous and so rapid that even the best men lost track of things. Mom's first gracious presence at the ballot box was roughly concomitant with the start toward a new all-time low in political scurviness, hoodlumism, gangsterism, labor strife, monopolistic thuggery, moral degeneration, civic corruption, smuggling, bribery, theft, murder, homosexuality, drunkenness, financial depression, chaos, and war. Note that.

The degenerating era, however, marked new highs in the production of junk. Note that, also.

Mom, however, is a great little guy. Pulling pants onto her by these words, let us look at mom.

She is a middle-aged puffin with an eye like a hawk that has just seen a rabbit twitch far below. She is about twenty-five pounds overweight, with no sprint, but sharp heels and a hard backhand which she does not regard as a foul but a womanly defense. In a thousand of her there is not sex appeal enough to budge a hermit ten paces off a rock ledge. She none the less spends several hundred dollars a year on permanents and transformations, pomades, cleansers, rouges, lipsticks, and the like—and fools nobody except herself. If a man kisses her with any earnestness, it is time for mom to feel for her pocketbook, and this occasionally does happen.

She smokes thirty cigarettes a day, chews gum, and consumes tons of bonbons and petits four. The shortening in the latter, stripped from pigs, sheep, and cattle, shortens mom. She plays bridge with the stupid voracity of a hammerhead shark, which cannot see what it is trying to gobble but never stops snapping its jaws and roiling the waves with its tail. She drinks moderately, which is to say, two or three cocktails before dinner every night and a brandy and a couple of highballs afterward. She doesn't count the two cocktails she takes before lunch when she lunches out, which is every day she can. On Saturday nights, at the club or in the juke joint, she loses count of her drinks and is liable to get a little tiddly, which is to say, shot or blind. But it is her man who worries about where to acquire the money while she worries only about how to spend it, so he has the ulcers and colitis and she has the guts of a bear; she can get pretty stiff before she topples.

Her sports are all spectator sports. . . .

I give you mom. I give you the destroying mother. I give you her justice—from which we have never removed the eye bandage. I give you the angel—and point to the sword in her hand. I give you death— the hundred million deaths that are muttered under Yggdrasill's ash. I give you Medusa and Stheno and Euryale. I give you the harpies and the witches, and the Fates. I give you the woman in pants, and the new religion: she-popery. I give you Pandora. I give you Proserpine, the Queen of Hell. The five-and-ten-cent-store Lilith, the mother of Cain, the black widow who is poisonous and eats her mate, and I designate at the bottom of your program the grand finale of all the soap operas: the mother of America's Cinderella.

The Reconstruction of the Home

FERDINAND LUNDBERG and
MARYNIA F. FARNHAM

In order to get to the very roots of the problem—and the economic diffi-culties in raising children under the new machine order represent one of the roots—society must recognize that women, as much as men, need to feel useful, necessary, of real worth. In the past, generally speaking, women acquired these feelings through work and achievement within the circle of the home and family. Now, as we have seen, they do not. With the coming of industrial civilization, woman lost her sphere of creative nurture and either was catapulted out into the world to seek for achievement in the masculine sphere of exploit or was driven in upon herself as a lesser being. In either case she suffered psychologically.

What woman has lost must in some way be recaptured. Society must recognize her need and make it possible for her to satisfy her healthy ego aims without sacrificing her instinctive desire for motherhood or the needs of her children.

Government subsidies that would remove the economic pressure which forces many women to seek work outside the home is at least a step in the right direction. But a far more overall attack is required. Further-more, the problem is not only to get women into the home but to get them there on a basis satisfactory to their own feelings and aspirations. The Nazis got women back into the home; they ordered them there. But it is highly doubtful that the order accomplished more than to raise the birth rate, thereby adding to the multitude of obvious neurotics that was Germany of the Third Reich (and of the Weimar Republic and the preceding Second Reich).

If, however, women could be *attracted* into organizing their lives more closely around the home and spheres of nurture, an important step would have been taken in making the home a place where children might grow up into well-balanced adults. The home, clearly, cannot be constituted exactly as it was prior to the Industrial Revolution, even if this were desirable. But we believe it could be reconstituted on the older and more satisfactory emotional basis within the framework of a machine technology.

There are several courses it seems that might help to bring this about.

Ferdinand Lundberg and Marynia Farnham, *Modern Woman, the Lost Sex* (New York, 1947), pp. 363–377.

In the first place, mothers should be given a larger role in the formal education of children to the age of eighteen. As matters stand now, they have little part in the education of their children from kindergarten age onward. Education has, largely, been made into the monopoly of professional spinsters. Jobs teaching in the school are still expressly reserved in most school districts as an economic perquisite of spinsterhood. Married women are widely barred by law or school board ruling from teaching. *We would suggest that this relic of a day when each county made this provision for its spinsters to keep them from becoming public charges be discarded and that all spinsters be barred by law from having anything to do with the teaching of children on the ground of theoretical (usually real) emotional incompetence. All public teaching posts now filled by women would be reserved not only for married women but for those with at least one child, with provision made for necessary exceptions.* The work day for each teacher would be reduced. More married mothers would be employed where now fewer unmarried women teachers are employed. There would be no reduction in the professional requirements of the teacher. Salaries would necessarily be reduced, but through the national mother's subsidy (operative even though the woman is employed and scaled only to the husband's earnings), there would be substantial restitution of the cut. Under such circumstances, of course, no woman teacher would earn so much as at present. As there are now about a million teachers in the United States (most of them women, most of them spinsters), there would be substantially more than a million married mothers employed as teachers, with considerable free time to devote to their own children and their households. They would be mothers with a sense of worthwhile occupation, of being paid for their work, of being concretely recompensed for their children, of having free time for their children. They would be women, in short, with strong evidence before them of social concern for their lives.

What would happen to the spinsters? They would, perhaps, be encouraged to marry. If they did not, they would have to seek other jobs on the ground that they had not met the basic requirements, for this particular, vital employment. A great many children have unquestionably been damaged psychologically by the spinster teacher, who cannot be an adequate model of a complete woman either for boys or girls. In higher educational institutions, such as colleges, it does not matter so much, if at all. By that time the die has been cast.

(From time to time it may have appeared in these pages that we are freely prescribing marriage for all persons. But we are by no means doing this any more than we are prescribing childbearing. Too many people today are unfit for both activities for such a recommendation to make any sense.)

Mothers not seeking economic support should be encouraged to take part in the schoolwork both as assistants to the paid teachers and as students. There is much of value to the community that they could learn by attending school in special adult day classes, where they might study subjects of special interest to women: biology, child and male psychology, the history of women and the home, anthropology, dietetics, anatomy, physiology, chemistry, general medicine, nursing or problems in retail buying. Such classes could not fail to pay social dividends.

But all along the line it is the married mothers, rather than the spinsters and bachelors, who should be encouraged to superintend and administer the entire social process of rearing and educating children. Mothers should not be divorced from this important part of their job.

The principle of part-time work, already put into operation by a number of women, might be recognized as desirable for more married women. The gain from part-time employment would be that women at present devoting most of their time to work or career would be enabled to devote some of it to homes and children. A reciprocal gain would be that other women, who at present are engaged in nothing more important than afternoon bridge playing, would be induced to take up some socially and personally useful work on a half-time, paid basis. The quota of paid jobs for women might be doubled if there were a general resort to this pattern.

Another step toward reestablishing the home on a sound emotional basis would involve public recognition of the fact that the psychically balanced woman finds greatest satisfaction for her ego in nurturing activities. Teaching, nursing, doctoring, social service work, guidance, catering, decorating, play direction, furnishing, are all entirely feminine nurturing functions, and there are many others. There is almost unlimited room for expansion in some of these fields—for instance, social service work. In psychiatry, this work needs to be greatly expanded.

As to the loss of functions by the home with the acquiescence of women, women might well ask themselves if the trend has been as much to their advantage as is popularly supposed. We are referring here, especially, to freedom from the "tyranny" of pots and pans. Women might observe and ponder the significance of the alacrity with which men have seized upon the food-preparing functions and institutionalized them in the form of restaurants, delicatessens, and preserving and packaging plants. They carried out the transition with characteristic male imaginativeness. Cooks were redesignated "chefs," so that we even have "short-order chefs" in roadside lunch counters. All along the line the refinement of French terminology was substituted for the homelier Anglo-Saxon. The improvement, if that is what it was, was purely verbal, for both in the palatability and nutritional value of the food there was a definite decline. In the variety of available foods, there has, thanks to transport and cultivation, been improvement over a period of a century, but in processing there has been marked deterioration. Commercial bread is a case in point. Overcooked, steamtable vegetables and canned vegetables and fruits provide another case. Men, however, while serving up foods less well prepared (the superiority of the male *chef* being a pure myth, based upon fancy sauces), have managed to acquire for themselves more prestige than women did performing the same task in the home. This is because men have invested their task with more embellishing overtones of *esprit*. Man as the suave *maître d'hôtel* or the genial host of the inn might well be contrasted here with the downcast, lack-luster female as the resentful "cook." She is obviously in need of stage direction, although some women have seen a way to restore themselves in this domain as "domestic scientists," "dietary specialists," and "nutritional analysts." We should say that once Mama in the kitchen were under-stood to be a food chemist, duly certified institutionally, with diploma hanging on the wall, the attitudes of the family and neighbors would undergo respectful change. Basic, however, is the function itself, and women must decide if they wish to be irrevocably deprived of it under guise of being liberated.

Men, Mephistopheles-wise, constantly advise women through adver-tising to "free" themselves of "drudgery" around the house by installing one new mechanism after the other. In other words, they counsel women to collaborate in increasing their own technological unemployment. Most women, when freed, find that they are doomed to sleeveless idleness or to routinized menial tasks in business or industry which carry with them no prestige whatever (selling, filing, typing, working on the production line in cigarette and canning factories, etc.). They are then in a position where the charge of incapability can be, and often is, seriously leveled at them. Neither can the perpetual window shopper, bridge player, and moviegoer make any valid claim to prestige. She may well be dismissed as a nonentity, for she is a nonentity.

Should woman collaborate in the not too subtle process which is con-verting her into a functional nonentity, an embellishment of dubious merit? Or, rather, should she not try to regain her functions and thereby her lost prestige? In theory, the freeing of women from "household drudgery" liberates them for "higher matters." Such as what, one may ask? In the cultivation of higher aims, as such aims are understood, many are called and few are chosen, among men no less than among women. A woman freed from "household drudgery" who repairs to a laboratory and there discovers a cure for a baffling disease or who makes some other cultural contribution may well have made a good ego bargain. But to few women is vouchsafed this distinction, as to few men.

Women, it seems to us, would do well to recapture those functions in which they have demonstrated superior capacity. Those are, in general, the nurturing functions centering around the home.

Not only in the culinary arts, women should observe, but in everything else pertaining to the home men are all too eager to replace them, and they do it while conferring upon themselves prestige. Women who had to stoke the furnace at one time complained bitterly. Men sympathetically heeded their complaint and took up the task, meanwhile styling themselves stationary engineers! Women deplored house painting, and men were happy to step into the breach, as decorators! Men, it is evident, are glad to take up any function in the home or to provide any product or appliance the woman asks for in her effort to push herself to one side. Does she find polishing her furniture tedious? A man will supply a liquid that is merely smeared on and it shines. The resulting luster, as everyone knows, is now no longer her doing but that of a remote male known as Mr. Johnson. Every new step she takes toward freedom, she finds, lands her higher and drier in nowhere. The men know that, for them, these functions will do until better ones come along. They aren't so eager for the "higher pursuits," for many of them sense that they are mainly illusory.

Men, collected in trade unions, have often resisted technological change that would deprive them of jobs. Men as functioning workers resisted the installation of machinery in general. Women, on the other hand, have briskly collaborated in their own technological unemployment and consequent diminution of prestige. Are we, in suggesting that women might of their own volition recapture some of their functions around the home, such as cooking, preserving, and decorating, trying to turn back the clock of progress? We think not. Eating better-tasting and more nutritive food, for example, is not unprogressive but progressive. Much of so-called progress, as the term is understood, is nothing but reaction of the most sable hue. In food quality, the world has never before known such reaction as we see today. If then, three-quarters of the canning plants and commercial baking establishments were to close overnight and food preparation and baking were to be restored to their one-time state in the home, the nation would leap forward about one hundred years or more nutritionally and in food enjoyment. That, we take it, would represent progress in the domain of human satisfaction. The cultivation of synthetic vitamins is a reflex to the loss of nutritional value in our commercially processed foods. Very possibly good food is no more susceptible of commercial exploitation than mother love. The two are, in sober fact, closely allied, and the decline of women's interest in food preparation parallels the decline in many of them of the capacity for affection.

As to the reputedly dirty and degrading nature of work around the home and kitchen, women might well observe that many of the occupations of men are not precisely genteel, yet cause no male outcry. The garage mechanic, plumber, miner, sandhog, stoker, professional dishwasher, surgeon, slaughterhouse worker, and sewer digger, nearly all of them men, have not fallen upon genteel or clean tasks. Yet none has lost social respect. The disproportionate odium that has come to be attached to household work and cooking in the home is the consequence not of anything inherently disagreeable in such work but of the repeated verbal fouling of their own nests by a long line of disordered female theorists and the disorganization of the feelings of women in general.

Women might therefore do well to reexamine the sphere of home tasks with a view to repossessing themselves of as many of them as possible. Running a household, it should be evident, requires more general capability than operating a typewriter, a bookkeeping machine or a filing system. A considerable number of women, we are aware, have not relinquished all these home functions, and in the face of increasing social difficulties manage to extract satisfaction from performing them. But the general trend is decidedly away from them, in part under the influence of a steady propaganda barrage.

Women should begin especially to look with critical eyes at the present physical framework of "home" as represented by the cramped, "efficient" apartment. The small apartment, set in a cell block of similar dwelling units, is an expression in bricks and stones of modern woman's reduced status.

It should be clear that we do not have in mind for women that anxiety-provoking bugaboo of the feminists: a lowly, inconspicuous role. On the contrary, we are suggesting a higher role than they have at present as poor imitators of men or as full-time slaveys in steam laundries, canning factories, and so forth. As the domain we suggest for women broadly includes all of biology, psychology, sociology, medicine, pedagogy, philosophy, anthropology, and several other systematic disciplines, it should be clear that there is ample room·for women intellectually equipped for more technical achievement than their sisters. However, women who might nevertheless be inclined to enter fields belonging to the male area of exploit or authority—law, mathematics, physics, business, industry and technology—should certainly be allowed to do so.

Government and socially minded organizations should, however, through propaganda, make it clear that such pursuits are not generally desirable for women. Solely in the public interest, the disordered fantasies of the masculine-complex women should be combated in so far as those fantasies are advanced as the proper basis for public policy toward women as a whole. The emphasis of prestige, honor, subsidy, and public respect should be shifted emphatically to those women recognized as serving society most fully as women. Discrimination all along the line should be shifted in their favor.

We propose that just as women should obtain status and prestige through motherhood, men should obtain it fundamentally by fatherhood. Bachelors of more than thirty, unless physically deficient, should be encouraged to undergo psychotherapy. They should also be subjected to differential tax rates so that they at least might enjoy no economic advantage over married men and fathers and might contribute to the social support of children. The bachelor, it might as well be recognized, is a dubious social quantity except in the fairly rare instances where he makes compensation by placing at the service of society some valuable skill. Most of them do not do this, and might just as well be bracketed in social esteem with the unmarried mother.

A program such as we have sketched, far from dividing men and women, would weld them closer together, would tend to make them complementary partners in a cooperative enterprise rather than competitors, as at present, in a junglelike struggle with the child buffeted about in between.

The force of such a policy would, it is probable, tend to increase the birthrate. What, then, of overpopulation? That might be a problem society would have to face in the future. It is not with us now. If it should ever arise, its solution would probably lie in imposing public controls to prevent the breeding of certain strains. With a full population, a country could afford to be more selective, could discourage certain types of people from propagating. Beyond that, the problem would have to be solved by some future generation on the basis of the facts as they presented themselves.

The plan proposed here is not beautifully simple. Neither is the problem. As to whether our suggestions will fully solve it, we cannot say. Anyone who has any better ideas should certainly put them before the public. What remedial steps are taken will depend on political and social action by the people. As a good section of the population is already disoriented, one may be certain that any sort of program will meet with only limited support. One might, if one wished to indulge in straw grabbing, invoke the aid of women's organizations, but as most of these are thoroughly imbued with penis-envy, women in the mass have not much to expect from them. Many such organizations will fight rather than support a rational program to reorient woman toward more satisfying goals in life.

Society will have to evolve out of its travail new values for living, values more in keeping with human needs, as the full significance of its experience becomes clear. Values arise from the exigencies of man's experience, and until he fully sees and understands his experience he cannot alter his values. For example, cultural values cannot be altered merely by rational, logical criticism. They must be *felt* as good or not good, healthy or unhealthy.

The values we live by come to us through several layers of historical soil. There are, to go back no further, the values enunciated by Jesus, terribly distorted and reshaped. Superimposed upon those are the values of the Renaissance, the Reformation, the economic revolution (capitalism), the scientific revolution, the Industrial Revolution, and romanticism. All these in turn have been filtered through the sieve of the home distorted by the Industrial Revolution, handed on in varying mood and temper by parents to children. In their transmission the most decisive, disastrous, and painful results have been obtained.

In addition to restoring order to his home, where his spirit is shaped, modern man is in urgent need of recasting every single one of his dominant values if he is to attain that which he always seeks: health and happiness. For it is these dominant values that have undermined the stability of the home, the postnatal socialized womb that is the corridor along which the individual must pass from his biological womb to the wider world of social man. Disquiet in this corridor, in the individual's tender years, spells trouble later in life, for the individual and for society.

What are the dominant values of which we speak, which have had so much to do with undermining the stability of the home and disorganizing the feelings of women? There is, first, the idea of progress, which cannot be regarded as without severe limits to its realization and which cannot be realized to any significant extent solely in material ways. There is, secondly, the idea dear to our times that human welfare is to be sought entirely in material and physiological pathways. There is, furthermore, the idea that much of human salvation is bound up with great emphasis on work and the endless production of goods, whereas what the world needs far more than goods is more skilled services of all kinds, particularly services bearing upon human relations and feeling. Put tersely, what the world needs is far more doctors, truly informed teachers and wise personal guides and far fewer engineers, salesmen and promoters.

Other ideas, frantically pursued, are those of personal success in a wide range of humanly doubtful achievement and the acquisition of wealth, as distinct from success in living in all departments of life; the quest for personal fame, celebrity and distinction; the undiscriminating celebration of knowledge, particularly in material spheres, as distinct from wisdom, and the idealization of the fundamentally destructive idea of competition as contrasted with the infinitely more rewarding idea of cooperation in all things. Cooperation, we often see, true enough, but always on a small scale; in the larger sweep of affairs today what we see is competition—that is, efforts directed to encompass the destruction of rivals.

Underlying these notions which we question so sharply is the idea of the primacy of rationality in human affairs over emotion, and the consequent cultivation of a grievously false rationality. Far from rationality ruling emotion, as scientists and mathematicians believe to be the case, in reality emotion directs rationality. The coolest mathematician or scientist, at work on the most complicated problem, is carried along in the main by self-aggrandizing emotion. He is as emotional, in fact, as an effusive schoolgirl, the difference being that in the scientist the emotional drive is far more powerful, is narrowly channeled so as to attain special ends, and is concealed from view because deeply repressed. The idea of a cool, powerful, and independent human intellect (which is only a sublimation of the idea of the phallus), will no doubt die a hard death. But the frenzied behavior of the physical scientists after the discovery of the atom bomb should do much to dispel the impression of them, sedulously fostered by science itself, as detached, wholly rational beings.

Various other ideas are also at work in our culture, diverting attention from solid reality—as, for example, the idea of the desirability of human equality in all things, the idea of individual freedom as attainable or desirable without group freedom, the idea of freedom as an end in itself without relation to other ends, and so on.

It is these values that in their overemphasis underlie the difficulties we have surveyed and analyzed. There is something of worth in all of them, but not so much as is insisted by schools, newspapers, political parties of Left and Right, and contemporary governments. Useful in limited degree, all these values are today pathological in their overemphasis. The key to ready understanding of the problem lies in this single word: overemphasis.

What is driving our culture toward the rocks of human disaster is not ambition so much as overambition; not acquisition but overacquisition; not rivalry but excessive rivalry; not progress but misunderstanding of what true progress entails; not work but overwork; not knowledge but overemphasis upon knowledge, particularly upon knowledge that is not humanly important; not striving but overstriving; not rationality but misconceived rationality that lacks knowledge of what the human animal really requires.

The best first step to be taken to reorganize in wholesale fashion the values people live by, it seems to us, would be for the government to sponsor a year-after-year series of radio lectures on the psychological as well as physiological requirements of the individual at all stages of growth. It would be one of the objects of such lectures to bring home to people that all socially approved ways of living, all socially approved goals, are not personally healthy ones or worthy ones. These lectures, it seems to us, should be given by leading psychiatrists, psychologists, philosophers, educators, sociologists and social workers, and it should always be made clear that they were factual, scientific in the best sense, not moralistic. The evenings hours with the heaviest listener-load should be chosen for the lectures, which should be strongly recommended by the President as of the greatest possible personal advantage to the public at large.

We should probably not be true citizens of our age if we did not, at some point, call for a revolution. We should, indeed, like to see a revolution take place. The revolution we believe to be required is a cultural revolution, a revolution that would drastically alter or modify the values by which we all live. Ours is a "sick culture"—a diagnosis that has been made in these or similar words by Howard Mumford Jones, T. S. Eliot, Pitirim Sorokin, Oswald Spengler, and a great many other artists and students. The supreme danger is that, living in a revolutionary age, a social revolution will take place before the cultural revolution. Then, as in Russia, we shall have social surgeons operating with contaminated instruments: the values to which we refer. There is nothing humanly constructive, per se, in the proliferation of bridges, dams, roads, factories, and public monuments. One can at most die in the most up-to-date electric chair. One can pine away in a model prison, fitted with the latest appliances.

What values should replace those we criticize? It seems to us that the fundamental value to be emphasized is that of human life, regarded all too cheaply today, particularly by the heavy-handed social surgeons commonly referred to as revolutionists. Next, emphasis should be placed on the importance of health, mental as well as physical. As the public is by now thoroughly convinced of the desirability of physical health, is willing to underwrite anything necessary to its attainment and is emphasizing the physical so much indeed as to defeat the ends of health in many ways, greater emphasis than ever before should be put upon the attainment of mental health. Next, emphasis should be placed, not upon the *pursuit* of happiness but upon its unfailing attainment when sought in the right ways. In its wholehearted commitment to the pursuit of happiness our age is seriously off the track. Blocking its attainment are the dominant values we have looked at. A serious confusion of this age comes from looking upon momentary pleasure as akin to happiness. History, if it proves anything, proves that those who ever seek pleasure never attain happiness.

After these new values there should be stressed those of skilled, humanly helpful service, of cooperation, of wisdom, and of the primacy of human feelings.

In one way, in particular, the present age leads itself seriously astray: in elevating convenience into a supreme end. An astonishingly large segment of the economic system is devoted to catering to convenience, although much of modern convenience is in fact highly inconvenient to the human spirit. Instead, there should be far more stress upon necessity, which today is underemphasized. Necessity should always precede convenience in human affairs. Indeed, convenience is related to necessity much as pleasure is related to happiness; in the common view they seem closely related but they are in fact poles apart. The cultivation of convenience (often self-defeating in its own terms) has represented since the seventeenth century an attempt to dispense with as much effort as possible. This age at the same time, contradictorily, sets a high value on work, overwork, striving. Its confusion in these respects is duplicated in many others.

The present age has only the dimmest possible idea of what it wants or where it is headed. The highly logical program it believes itself to be following is shot through with illogicality and self-defeat, distorted perspectives, and insufficient goals.

Neither exhortation nor coercion can win men over to new values. Both methods have been tried throughout history, particularly in the realm of ethics, without conspicuous success. Men and women follow the line of their conditioned inclinations, and whether or not they take to other values will depend on inclinations formed in the home. For this reason there seems to us to be necessary renewed emphasis on the primacy of the home, in its importance taking precedence over the affairs of any corporation, university, laboratory, school, stock exchange, political party, or legislative assembly. It is the home that is the source, the direct source, of most of the personal and social disorder of our time, although that disorder traces back to factors involved in the undermining of the home. The home, in fact, is in such poor condition that it merits a special government department devoted only to its affairs, and to the affairs of the sadly battered women and children in it. This remark applies to Europe as much as to the United States. Until the problem of the home is attacked seriously no real headway will be made in coping with the many social problems it creates.

Old complaints now rise to view. Aren't even the suggestions we are making for betterment fairly shallow and limited? Doesn't mankind have aspirations beyond worldly well-being? What, for example, of man's yearnings for immortality, for assurance that he is indestructible? What good does it do him even if he accepts the idea that his yearnings arise from reinforced infantile feelings of helplessness? Science is unable to answer this yearning with any facts positive and reassuring.

But science is entirely able to make clear to the individual that he is a single link in thousands of generations of individuals, the link perhaps to thousands of future generations that may perform wonders far outstripping those performed by man from Piltdown man to the present.

Here is a very definite sort of immortality that enables one to postulate human life as a high continuing value, and the present as fraught with vast significance.

In those that confess to seeking for something larger, outside themselves, upon which they can lean, psychoanalysis readily discerns the seeking after the original childhood or even prenatal condition of absolute dependency. However, in a very true and scientific sense, all persons are part of something larger than themselves, upon which their existence has depended: their line of descent. It is not very difficult to see, going back far enough, that this line of descent ultimately embraces the entire human race. In other words, scientifically, factually, all men are brothers, a profound *aperçu* when the conclusion was first arrived at and one that science completely supports. The human race, then, is something rather impressive to belong to.

In contrast to this rather breathtaking prospect and what it implies for action, the dominating values of the market place, which are the values of our culture, seem hideous and pitiful in their inadequacy. In the end people in the mass, guided by clinical insight into the depths of the tangled human personality, will have to decide which values are to be taken as codes for living. Man is either a being with inherent dignity deriving from the tragedy of his having attained to acute self-consciousness or he is, as all currently dominant schools of ideology proclaim, merely an insignificant consumer of oddments and bitments of merchandise in a capitalist or socialist political system. If the latter, he is surely fair game for the hawkers and demagogues. And if this is the case he can hardly regard himself as more than a disease, perhaps not worthy of his own serious consideration.

18. The Young

Those who remember the 1930's and the 1940's today happen—and this is the consequence of history that is always ongoing—to have been young during that period. And when they remember, somehow the recollection brings forward a set of images which recall what was indeed an apocalyptical age as one also in which the young adopted not only an apocalyptical mood but a politics to match. They think especially of college campuses and the development of a wide range of student organizations and movements representing a whole spectrum of left-wing sectarian attitudes. They do not remember falsely; there was—to use the title of a book the young James Wechsler (born 1915) wrote in 1935 while still an undergraduate at Columbia and editor of the campus newspaper—*Revolt on the Campus*. There were student strikes—some even ending in violence and police action; there was an outbreak of drugs (pot-smoking had previously been a feature only of the jazz musician, largely black subculture) among white middle-class students that created a furor which led to federal law and a whole system of law enforcement after a considerable scare literature in the press; there was, most significantly, toward the end of the prewar period a concentrated student peace movement that resulted in fierce debate and a vast number of signatures to a radical version of the so-called Oxford Pledge (initiated in England).

Yet as important as all these signs of radical discontent with the prevailing order were, the evidence from the period itself suggests a far different image of the young as a whole. Revolt, even on campus, was the property of a small element; New Deal liberalism was, finally, much more appealing. The sincere and often militant peace movement—fed by reading such popular and influential books as Walter Millis' *The Martial Spirit* (1931) and *The Road to War* (1935)—found itself divided by efforts of the various elements of the sectarian left to use the movement for its own purposes, and it seemingly collapsed soon after with the passage of the Selective Service Act and the coming of American entrance into the war itself. Sympathy for Loyalist Spain created momentary efforts to raise money and to organize but in no sense in ways that resemble, for example, the opposition to the war in Southeast Asia in the 1960's.

Maxine Davis, with long newspaper experience during the 1920's and early 1930's, undertook a four-months' journey over some 10,000 miles in the middle of the 1930's which resulted in a series of articles and a book, *The Lost Generation: A Portrait of American Youth Today* (1936). Unsystematic and journalistic as it is, an impressionistic and certainly not a sociological study, Miss Davis's book found wide support in a series of other studies in the period. Note she does not confine her analysis to college campuses.

What This Generation Wants
MAXINE DAVIS

We are constantly startled as we travel by the difference between this generation and ours at their age. They are earnest, but weren't we?

We were so solemn in discovering and asserting our rights.

There was that question of freedom. Oh dear, oh dear! Freedom was a *very* important matter to us.

For instance, there was freedom from duty and obligation to our parents. We discovered Samuel Butler. Brandishing the *Way of All Flesh* —almost twenty years after it was first published!—we confronted the family with the accusation that we didn't ask to be born, and why should we be grateful? It was usually disconcerting the way they were able to retain their poise in the face of this charge. They were about as agitated, we recall, as a glass of tepid milk.

There was that burning issue: should girls smoke? It is my definite recollection that we first took unto us the filthy weed, learned to enjoy it, and then courageously argued our divine right to line our lungs and tint our fingers and our teeth with nicotine.

Among ourselves we had pretty serious problems. With girls there was the question of whether we should kiss a man before we were engaged to him. We all did, of course, but under no circumstances would we admit it.

There were other issues: should a man or a woman Confess All to his mate-to-be, or was it best to lock the skeleton of the scarlet past in the closet and toss away the key?

Freedom was involved somehow in all of this. We wanted freedom to live by ourselves before we were married.

Maxine Davis, *The Lost Generation: A Portrait of American Youth Today* (New York, 1936), pp. 92–93, 108–113, 365–71.

We had a great many theories about freedom within marriage. For instance, we women wanted the right to earn our own money and spend our own money without any questioning by our husbands.

Men wanted the right to go where they pleased, when they pleased, without any necessity for a domestic accounting.

If one party or the other to a marriage had an irresistible urge to infidelity, his or her individual freedom bestowed an inalienable right to indulge it. If our mates' hearts wandered with their impulses, then we must nobly give way to our successors, and no recriminations or nasty remarks, either. We were to feel it was beautiful while it lasted, and everything has to end!

Æsthetically we were an unlovely lot. Out ears were tuned to the horrible dissonances of jazz bands. Whining saxophones and banging brasses were more beautiful than Brahms. We cut our hair like boys and shortened our skirts until we were ridiculous. That was part of the revolt against the past, and freedom from convention. James Branch Cabell was our Bible and Henry L. Mencken our Book of Common Prayer.

We wanted freedom; we wanted Life with a large L, and were hell-bent on having it. And life was summed up in the Greenwich Village of Floyd Dell.

As we look back, it wasn't a very heroic period. We were palpitating with trivialities.

Those of us who weren't in deadly earnest about our personal self-expression were crusaders for a cause. Some of us could raise our temperature to fever heat on the general subject of man's inhumanity to man. International cooperation was a shooting subject among us, so near were we to the fight on the League of Nations. Socialism was still the ultimate in radicalism, and George Bernard Shaw was its spokesman. Russia was a horror story, and we didn't discuss democracy; we had just made the world safe for it.

What a different picture today's children present!

After all, our raucous demand for freedom to think and act for our-selves was predicated on economic independence. We never doubted that we could find work. Youth was in demand. No matter how scanty our incomes were, we had them; they were our own; we earned them. So we thought we were exceedingly brave and clever when we went to live on them according to our own preferences. If we happened to forego our father's wholesale drygoods business for the adventure of art, or advertising, or engineering, we were valiant adventurers on uncharted seas, but always bolstered with the comforting knowledge that the whole-sale drygoods business was there. We would struggle and starve rather than run up the white flag, but it made a difference.

How brittle, how unreal, we seem beside the boys and girls we meet everywhere, every way, today.

There are, naturally, some even now who are untouched by the times. When the family income adds into five or six figures, realities impinge but gently. Poverty and unemployment are apt to seem academic to boys and girls who never feel or see it. Each season reaps its crop of debutantes, with their concomitant luxuries. We are interested in the 1935–36 winter necessities because they seem so far and so strange after our rambling.

Mrs. Joseph Bryan, III, in an article in the *Junior League Magazine*, gives minimum requirements. They consist of "at least five party dresses, two dinner dresses, a couple of tea gowns or dinner pajamas, and an evening wrap. For the daytime the debutante needs three wool or wool jersey dresses, two silk dresses, one street-length velvet or velveteen dress, one tailored suit, and as many sweaters and skirts as she can buy. She needs three coats: one fur, a tweed, and a rather dressy wool. The debutante wears very little jewelry . . . a pearl necklace to the base of the throat if possible."

We are resentful when we read over these items, remembering the little barber's daughter who wanted "only one or two dresses, with the proper accessories," and the motherless girl in Memphis who is happy to transmute seventy-nine cents into her spring wardrobe, that another girl may have one too! But there are always such inequalities, at any time, and there aren't many debutantes.

Indeed, we frequently find the sons of the very rich so conscious of their friends' problems that they themselves are shy of the accoutrements of wealth. For instance, one undergraduate Du Pont drives an old Ford, and another young Du Pont makes out with a motorcycle at college. There isn't the uneasiness manifest in those who have less when they are with those who have more that there used to be. That's because, we decide, there isn't such a sense of inferiority. The numerical strength of the less fortunate has increased even in milieus where money was a standard of value. If anything, the very rich boy or girl is the awkward one.

That's only a rare symptom of the change, however.

Today's children don't yammer for self-expression.

To them, freedom is a word in the dictionary.

They are not young radicals remaking a faulty society, because the problem of making something of their own lives is a Herculean task in the face of the difficulties they must surmount.

They either cannot earn their bread, or, for those a step up on the ladder of luck, there is nothing but a portion of dry bread.

So they are not concerned with abstractions. They are only dimly aware that they are a generation without faith, without tried standards.

They are terribly concerned with fundamentals. These fundamentals any one of them can list for us without hesitation: An education. A job. Marriage. And a little fun.

These are age-old requirements. Training for living. Work, a way of life, a means of preserving life. Marriage, as prime a need as the maintenance of life itself. It is axiomatic that self-preservation is the first law of nature, and that reproduction of the race is the second. And recreation, rest from work, follows naturally.

These needs have little to do with a civilization we like to regard as advanced. Primordial man, in his way, sought to satisfy them.

Thus the smug in spirit and the stuffed of stomach who like to orate with soap-box fluency, who like to tell the government and the people at large that they must "get back to basic principles" can watch a whole generation doing just that, if they will have the eyes to see.

We meet a good many such complacent souls as we journey through our country; and they are not always hard-boiled capitalists either. They are kind people who can't bear to pass a blind beggar with a tin cup and pencils and who would go to a lot of trouble to help the charwoman on the floor below the office because she has arthritis and a crippled son. But they make flowery speeches about tightening belts, and cultivating a few of the qualities that made this country great.

Well, that's what these boys and girls are trying to do. They are not concerned with Communism or Fascism. They'd rather have democracy if they had their choice. But they don't think about it much.

They can't go out and grow their beans and potatoes, most of them, because you can't even cultivate cockleburrs in a big city.

A boy who has learned to be a bookkeeper as a rule can't do odd jobs of carpentering and fence-mending, because he has never had an opportunity to learn.

They are not bothered much with ideas; they are after all luxuries. They are faced with the first necessities of living.

As we move along, we'll keep this in mind. This generation wants education, work, marriage, and fun.

If they secure these things for themselves, they will not build much of a superstructure. The years will be passing.

. . . They have a complete program for living happily ever after.

Young people tend to tackle the problems of marriage like this, practically and realistically. In the last few years schools and colleges have been here and there instituting courses in marriage. Class are uniformly crowded.

The best one which comes to our attention is conducted by Professor

Ernest R. Groves, at the University of North Carolina. The classes are open to men and women and taught separately. Students in the senior class, graduate students, and juniors in professional training, such as law and medicine, may elect them. These courses are among the most popular in the university.

This course developed eight years ago, at the request of the male students, and was an outgrowth of conventional sociological treatment of marriage and the family. The instruction now covers all of the larger legal, psychological, sociological, and physical problems of marriage.

Here is an interesting clue to the student reaction to this subject: the textbook in this course is Dr. Groves' five-hundred-page treatise. The manager of the largest secondhand bookshop in Chapel Hill reports that although he sells seventy-five or a hundred copies each year, thus far he has never been able to buy a secondhand copy, nor has he ever seen a secondhand copy advertised in the catalogues of the large secondhand stores, anywhere. Moreover, whenever we attempted to draw this volume from the public libraries of New York and Washington, or from the Library of Congress, every copy was always out!

At New York University, the Student Union offers a course in "premarital hygiene," given before members of the senior class. This Student Union secured the services of Dr. Marie P. Warner, assistant medical director of the Birth Control Clinical Research Bureau of New York City, for these courses.

Dr. Warner's lectures go deep into the problems most young people discuss among themselves, and on which they rarely have any scientific information. In addition to the sociological problems, they include the problems of the unmarried, covering personal physiological subjects such as continence, masturbation, and sexual relationships, combined in the same lecture with economic subjects such as budgeting, insurance, and old-age security; social problems, petting, education, family relationships, etc. They include discussion of accepted viewpoints on monogamy, family planning, birth control, emotional value training for parenthood; helpful factors leading to successful marriage such as age, education, mental equality, mutual pliability, similarity of tastes and standards, tolerance, and financial understanding. Dr. Warner discusses further actual preparation for marriage, such as engagements, marriage hygiene, the art of love.

Dr. Warner is a practicing physician, and undoubtedly some students consult her professionally because of the information they receive at her lectures.

All this should tend to reassure the viewers-with-alarm. Some of the less adaptable of the oldsters may shake their heads and mourn the premarital relations of this generation. They may be horrified, refuse to believe it of their own sons and daughters.

They needn't. Their own sons and daughters are clear-eyed and square in this matter.

＊　　＊　　＊

We have traveled long among the youth of our land. We have traveled far and wide: from the sun-topped towers of Manhattan to San Francisco's Embarcadero, shrouded in shimmering mist. From Nebraska's cornfields to the Texas range. We have met the boys and girls we went to see. We have listened to their stories, seen how they work, and live, and play.

It is time to cast up accounts.

We have found a problem unique to our times: young men and women with intelligence and personality, with ability and training—and no opportunity to exercise these qualities.

We have found unprecedented unemployment among the young. We have found that unemployment has afflicted them even more virulently than it has their seniors, and that the healing hand of recovery has touched them only lightly.

We know that such adverse economic conditions have been the cause of restlessness and revolt in European youth. Avidly it has swallowed patent medicines for its heartache, and thus poisoned become the backbone of the dictatorships.

The German situation is ever before us. In 1930 there were nearly eight million unemployed in Germany. Apprentices were being dismissed as soon as they finished their training, that employers, themselves impoverished, might hire more and younger men at apprentice wages. Enrollment in the universities increased, their halls filled with boys and girls learning for want of anything else to do. Forty thousand graduates, educated far beyond the American standards, sat in their homes, in the beer halls, with no hope of ever finding anything to do.

These young adults were still young. They were still healthy and eager. They still had youth's everlasting idealism, its need to serve, its willingness to suffer and sacrifice and fight, if only they might be active in their devotion.

Hitler offered them an outlet for their bursting emotions. We from this distance see them as an army of destruction of all we in this nation believe vital to the good life. We are likely to forget that they were a battalion of youth facing a future without meaning or light, and that Hitler gave them purpose and importance.

In Italy also youth is the strong right arm of Mussolini's Fascism. Bewildered, uncertain young men formed a large portion of the black-shirted troops that took over the government. Many of Il Duce's lieutenants were under thirty at the time of his march on Rome. Since then he has not forgotten the importance of the young. Lads step from the cradle into the Balilla organization, which teaches them to march almost before they can creep. Never a day from thence forward does the dictatorial grasp relax.

Russia too has marshaled its unwanted youth, stranded by famine and revolution. We remember the nightmare stories of the besprisoryni—the homeless children, a half-million of them, savage little vagabonds wandering over the land, stealing, begging, drinking.

These wild children were ultimately taken into camps, made one with the rest of Russian youth, all dedicated now heart and soul to the government which took them in, gave them work, made them a part of its far-flung program.

Which of these groups do unwanted young Americans resemble? Whither will their plight lead them? We set forth to examine and to assay if possible the character of the mutiny against their destiny buried in the breasts of our own unwanted boys and girls.

We never found revolt. We found nothing but a meek acceptance of the fate meted out to them, and a blind belief in a benign future based on nothing but wishful thinking.

We are not reassured. We cannot regard this patient waiting as aught but temporary. We have never been a nation of submissive cattle. Resignation has never been one of our characteristics, and we do not expect it to be developed very definitely in this generation.

Were it so, we should mourn, for this would hold as deep a danger as a passionate desire for revolution in a dynamic world.

This lack of revolt is more ominous than active radicalism, to our mind. Those potential Nazis were not protesters. They were merely sitting, enduring, quiescent. They were unaware of the fact that they were waiting for a leader to galvanize them into action. Youth doesn't think these matters out consciously, for itself.

Hitler did not arise overnight. For years, we remember, he declaimed and exhorted the German people.

In this country we can find no trace of any such magnetic messiah, for which we may give profound thanksgiving. The more conspicuous demagogues here have not studied Europe's lesson. They have made their appeals to old age, to cupidity, to hate, not to youth with its patriotism and its need to serve.

That leader may yet come. But the depth of his menace and the extent of his power is something we may control, if we will.

This generation has important assets. It is making some significant contributions to our life.

First and foremost is courage. Courage to do the work at hand no matter how trifling. These boys and girls see no labor at all as belittling regardless of their class and standards. They have no false pride, no self-importance.

Their sportsmanship is gallant. They neither whine nor whimper. "Smart cracks" shell fear and disappointment.

They have not conceded defeat, and they will not admit cynicism into their minds as they regard established institutions.

With them the basic social unit, the home, is safer, we think, than it has been in a long time. When they are able to marry, they value it; marriage is not as light a matter as it was in the easy-money era. With a code of practical premarital morality, they are losing sentimentality even while they retain youth's inherent romance. Because they have a deep need for emotional security, they are founding their families on enduring rock.

Their honesty makes a beginning toward a system of ethics related to practical experience and not to any taboos they know have no more relation to twentieth-century America than rainmakers or love potions. Their conclusions may be the same as their forefathers', but their reasons for adhering to them are based on experience. They are honest not because of a vague code handed down from father to son but because they know they need a sound basis for their relations with one another. In this they differ from our own postwar generation which rebelled against all old rules merely because they were old and they were rules.

These boys and girls we have been encountering from the rolling Alleghenies to the rugged Sierras know the golden calf for what it is. Money is not their yardstick. They are free from the snobbery of things.

Add to this the strength, the ebullience, the high spirit of the youth they still have, untarnished on the whole by any prescience of lasting defeat, and the fact that they have not lost their will to work or their desire for progress.

These are substantial assets in a people.

The list of their liabilities is food for thought. We have been discussing their apathy, which, once a sense of defeatism possesses them, makes them malleable material for a demagogue with an answer.

They are without faith and without belief. They are skeptical of the old-fashioned religions and the rewards of the old-fashioned virtues of thrift and industry. Their lives are without spiritual meaning. Youth wants to believe. A crusader, however subversive, who reveals to them a cause might find them ardent converts. The only reason we can find why Communism is not the menace it is advertised to be is that its proponents have not adapted it to the American mind and the American need, or phrased it in American terms. This is dangerous. It may find advocates not so stupid.

This generation does not think. While the level of intelligence is high, it is atrophied with inactivity. These young men and women do not think for themselves. They take what they like of what they hear, and reject by instinct rather than by reason. We need no clairvoyant to foretell what this tendency might mean under unscrupulous leadership.

They are utterly lacking in any sense of responsibility toward the conduct of this nation. Yet few of them are barren of that patriotism, that love of the homeland, that sense of possession of country which resides in normal human beings. Let someone translate that patriotism into a new philosophy and convince them of their obligation to the nation and the flag—he would not have a hard time. These young people have no old ties to slough off.

They want security. Isn't that what the dictators all promise? Don't they all guarantee freedom from want and woe, rest on the broad breast of the state?

Our boys and girls are not thinking of these things. They hear the economic problems discussed in terms of abstract principles, complex governmental activities. They are too hard for their unexercised minds. They laugh them off. They have personal problems, close and bitter. They evade them also, drugging themselves with vicarious amusements, with the escape media of movies, radios, fast motors, and alcohol. This does not add to their stability and their reliability.

They do know the older folk, the men and women who control the country today, are unaware of their problems. Their elders are contemptuous of them because they do not bring to life the versatility and the initiative which was characteristic of our people when there were still new frontiers, more space, more land, more opportunity for individual expression in the economic system than they see clearly for the moment.

We do not concede that there are no more frontiers. We believe that there is a whole world of work in fields of personal service as yet untouched, and whose existence no machine will ever challenge. We believe that we need not be dominated by the factory job. The girl who went home to the farm when the factory shut down in 1932 is happier selling the flowers she has weeded and watered in her garden and carried to her crossroads stands than ever she was standing all day long before a machine. We believe that there is a rich new world of culture and beauty and conservation to be explored by our citizens. But habits of mind and attitudes are hard to break. These things are just now rising above our horizon. For the first time they are beginning to have significance.

Still, the older generation does not fully grasp this, and the young folk are left to struggle with the traditional concepts, to modify and to change them without much sympathy or understanding.

This generation is straying aimlessly toward middle age. Soon it may be altogether lost. Then we as a nation will face a future dominated by a defeated citizenry, with nothing to lose and willing to try anything. It may be there will be nothing for it to try. It will remain then, a decadent, vitiated generation, a cancer in the vitals of our people, rearing its children in its own dun and dreary twilight.

These boys and girls are our responsibility. If we do not promptly assume it, some self-appointed piper may take it from us, and lead our youth God knows where.

This army of outsiders is not an abstract issue we can leave the politicians or the professional planners to deal with. These boys and girls are *ours*. Under prompt, competent handling, they may yet be transmuted into normal, busy, productive men and women.

Remember—this army moving with the shuffling feet of the faithless is our future—and mayhap our retribution.

PART SIX

THE WORLD OF TOMORROW AND TOMORROW THE WORLD

19. The Great Technology

Thus far in our brief survey we have come upon the question of the machine age in many forms. Here we propose to look most especially at one aspect of the cultural search of the period: those who believed that a great and good American culture could be created *by* the use of science and technology. "Can Science save us?" an American sociologist was to ask in 1947. For a great many American liberals in this period the answer seemed to be "Yes!" But not only did that positive and optimistic answer now suggest the development of particular skills and services that could and would solve social and economic problems; it actually implied a way to create a newer and richer *culture*. The belief in the positive virtues of science, planning, and technology were by no means new; American liberalism had especially become increasingly convinced that the very maintenance of its ideological hegemony depended on the incorporation of these elements in their thinking and program, in spite of the growing doubts of some like the Neo-Orthodox theologian Reinhold Niebuhr.

The precise position of science in cultural schemes did of course vary. Few perhaps were as enthusiastic about man's scientific potential as Buckminster Fuller. As early as 1928 he had designed a "Dymaxion House" which he felt to be a true machine for living, scientifically suited to man and his needs and built in terms of the newest technological tools. In his extraordinary book *Nine Chains to the Moon* (1938) he could redefine the nature of man himself:

a self-balancing, twenty-eight-jointed adapter-base biped; an electrochemical reduction plant, integral with segregated stowages and thousands of hydraulic and pneumatic pumps, with motors attached; 62,000 miles of capillaries; millions of warning signals . . . guided with exquisite precision from a turret in which are located telescopic and microscopic self-registering and recording range-finders. . . .

By 1936 *Scribner's Magazine* could offer its readers what it called "An Album of Recovery" stressing improvement in "our national plant." In 1937 Howard Aiken produced the first automated general-purpose digital calculator, part of a series of developments that was, by 1945, to create a whole new range of possibilities for machine functions.

In the discussion about the relationship between the machine and the development of an American culture few figures were as widely read as Stuart Chase (born 1888). Chase was an experienced accountant and economist before he became an outstanding writer on economic and social matters. By his own analysis a single theme runs through his large output of books and articles, the impact of the machine on human beings. No uncritical worshipper of the machine, Chase published a fascinating book—crucial in the central debate of the period over the nature of culture—which contrasted the folk culture of primitive and traditional Mexico and the urban-industrial culture of a community like Middletown. *Mexico, A Study of Two Americas* (1931) provided a critique of "our" way of life in terms of the virtues of traditional folk societies, but it also suggested in what ways a machine-oriented culture could be of use in that Mexican community.

The Marxists, too, refused to repudiate the machine and the kind of culture that could be built with its help: thus Robert Forsythe's "defense" in the New Masses. While there were, in fact, considerable efforts in the period to foster communitarian movements, agrarian retreats, and utopias of one kind or another, strong displays of hostility to an industrial-machine age order (Chaplin's masterful *Modern Times* of 1936 makes hilarious sport out of the absurdities of a machine age), and intellectual defenses of an older order, the key question could no more rest upon any notion of rejecting the machine. The issue, then, resolved itself around the problem of precisely what kind of machine culture this was to be.

Our Lock-step Culture
STUART CHASE

There are many machines in Western civilization. There are many standard behavior patterns. It is argued that there is a connection: that machinery is standardizing human life. There are practically no machines in China, although behavior patterns there are so rigid that they have persisted with little change for four thousand years. Here is an even stronger connection—save that it is upside down.

The Jeremiahs, notwithstanding, have prepared a moderately impressive exhibit. The machine-made character of George Folansbee Babbitt has been set before us in immensely documented detail. Mr. Mencken delivers one hundred pages of additional material every month. Mr.

Stuart Chase, "Our Lock-step Culture," *The Forum*, 81 (April 1929), pp. 238–242.

Upton Sinclair flings the goose step at our heads. One distinguished foreigner after another visits Mr. Ford's assembly line and a Rotary Club
at its luncheon ceremonies, and from thence departs on the next liner,
impatient to put upon a rotary press one more volume announcing that
machines are reducing Americans to automata. And many native philosophers, with ample time for observation, are, like Mr. John Dewey,
disturbed at what seems to be a growing regimentation in social life.

> They are our last frontier.
> They shot the railway-train when it first came,
> And when the Fords first came, they shot the Fords.
> It could not save them. They are dying now
> Of being educated, which is the same.
> One need not weep romantic tears for them,
> But when the last moonshiner buys his radio,
> And the last, lost wild-rabbit of a girl
> Is civilized with a mail-order dress,
> Something will pass that was American
> And all the movies will not bring it back.

Thus Mr. Stephen Vincent Benèt chronicles the passing of the Kentucky
mountaineer, and brings five specific mechanisms into his bill of charges.

This alleged leveling down, moreover, does not apply to the United
States alone. Mr. W. Redpath-Scott, writing in the London *Daily Mail*,
notes that a generation ago it was fairly easy to guess a man's occupation
by his appearance. Now the silk-hatted city clerk is as rare as the smock-
wearing farm laborer. The horsey-faced hostler has given way to a garage
man, with just a face. John Bull landlords with rosy gills are hard to find.
Where is the Durham miner with his shiny black broadcloth and queer
little round tasseled cap? Where is the shawl of the Lancashire mill girl?
Where is the navvy with his white felt hat, velveteen coat cut square,
spotted waistcoat, and blackened cutty clay pipe? Only his kerchief, and
that more subdued, survives today.

One could quote this sort of thing indefinitely, until a case of the first
magnitude had been compiled to prove the regimentation of Western
peoples. Nor am I disposed to doubt the general outline of the case. But
certain additional questions are in order before any final conclusion can
be drawn. Is the machine primarily responsible for this regimentation?
Is it more drastic than the regimentation enforced by the *mores* in other
civilizations, or among primitive peoples? Are the forms it enforces
better or worse than other historical forms?

The fact of culture, of group living, implies standardization. It always
has; it always will. Human beings submit well to the process. Standards
change, but standardization remains a perpetual element of all societies.

There is nothing, therefore, in the word itself to alarm us. The machine has certainly helped to cast our present mold, but it has not created the phenomenon. Nor, as I believe I can prove, has it enforced nearly such rigid standards as those promoted by ancestor worship in China; by the Church in medieval Europe; by the economy of the cocoanut, maize, wheat, or fish among peoples depending primarily upon these foods; by the caste system of India; by the state socialism of the Incas in ancient Peru; and by a score of other agents which might readily be named. One of the outstanding facts governing a machine culture is its restless and remorseless change. Look at the terrific shaking up the automobile alone has given us. Look at the enormous turnover in styles and fashions caused by too many machines in the textile industry. Machines create standards only to destroy them again.

In China, India, Samoa, standards crystallize century by century. In these countries a man hurled forward ten generations would find a world substantially unchanged. He could pick up his work, his love affairs, his marital arrangements, his religion, his games, with no astonishment and little effort. But imagine my grandsire of the tenth generation stepping into my shoes today. Even my grandfather used to shake his head sadly and ask what the world was coming to. Standards were changing faster than he could adjust himself to them. He would never read a magazine until he had first cut out all the advertising pages and thrown them into the fire.

Look at the fads which follow one another in crazy procession—bicycle riding, Ping-Pong, golf, bridge, Mah-Jongg, jazz, crossword puzzles, bobbed hair, antiques, prohibition cocktails. Look at the steady drift from the farm—where the *mores* have ever been powerful—to the cities— where they were always more tenuous. I repeat that the machine is probably the greatest destroyer of standards since the Goths sacked Rome.

Why, then, do we hear so much talk of modern regimentation? First, because regimentation is always a social fact; and second (a reason which I think is cardinal to the whole discussion), because the machine has destroyed so many of our habits with a devastating thoroughness that we have been left a people lost in the wilderness, our time-honored folkways scattered and dispersed. Such a thing is culturally unheard of, and obviously intolerable. Standards, customs, behavior patterns there must be. So, in a sort of frantic desperation, we have created one set after another, mainly temporary and not binding—in the sense that the corn-seeding ceremonies were binding—but at least serving as handholds for men who had lost their cultural balance. Like all ramshackle, temporary construction, they tend to be lopsided, ugly, and colorless. We have standards, and we do kneel by the millions before them; but as long as the tight pants of today become the plus fours of tomorrow, enduring crystallization on the Chinese model is not found among us. And I think it might be argued with some cogency that standards which do not outlast the season, metaphorically speaking, are nothing to be genuinely afraid of.

The varieties of standards are of course endless, but three great groups may be identified to make the discussion concrete. First, we may note technical standards for the use of science and for the operation of industry—the movement toward simplification. Second, commodity standards—the extent and variety of goods in a given culture. Third, social standards governing behavior patterns—the *mores* of sex, the family, worship, eating, drinking, playing, money, war, trade, work.

Industrial Standards. Mr. A. W. Whitney has developed a philosophy of industrial standardization, using an apt biological parallel. Nature, he says, continually experiments with new varieties and forms, and then, through natural selection, standardizes the most efficient. "If nature had no mechanism for fixing and holding the type, she would have no way of capitalizing her discoveries." Standardization is thus a liberator, relegating the problems already solved to their proper place—namely, the field of routine—and leaving the creative faculties free for problems still unsolved. "Standardization from this point of view is thus an indispensable ally of the creative genius"—akin to the reflex centers in man and animal which automatically guard the organism, leaving the mind free for unique and more experimental activity. When, after a long period of trial and error, an efficient and economical way to make automobiles, steel plates, or saucepans is evolved, then the process is crystallized in mass production, the commodities are manufactured according to standard routine, and invention is set free.

What is the objection, Mr. F. J. Schlink asks us, to standards for *units* of length, mass, time, temperature; to standard *sizes* for screw threads, bolts, nuts, invoice forms; to the *definition* of a horse power, a speed *rating* for locomotives; to *specifications* for cement, paint, steel bars, the fat content in milk; to a standardized *method* for the erection of steel bridges? No person in his senses can find the slightest objection.

Standards are cardinal in science and technology; they are implicit and often excellent in mass production. It is a waste of time to argue the bogey of "one deal level" in this category. Any specific project—say, the mass production of airplanes before the technique of safety has been achieved—is of course subject to argument (and in this case, one hopes, adverse decision).

Standards for Commodities. As good a starting point as any for the consideration of standardized articles is the Sears-Roebuck mail-order catalogue. It contains over one hundred thousand separate items. What other culture has ever provided such an exhibit? A well-to-do Chinese in the time of Confucius might have let his choice range among a thousand articles, more or less; the well-to-do American has the whole mail-order list to choose from, together with probably an equal number of items not comprehended in the list, but purchasable outside.

Furthermore, these goods are not limited to classes. Anyone may buy who has the money—billionaire, duke, or scavenger. Anyone may climb out of his social group if he has the money, or descend from Park Avenue to the gutter if he hasn't. There are no fixed classes in America, and this is becoming increasingly true of the whole Western world. Time-honored consumption standards for king, noble, soldier, merchant, peasant, craftsman are dissolving into spasmodic general standards, nebulous and endless in their variety. It is undoubtedly true that more people now dress alike and look alike than in any previous culture, because of these dissolving class distinctions. It is hard to tell a duchess from a coster girl. But at any moment skirts may begin to shorten, black trousers give way to knickerbockers. Men and women are not confined to uniformity over long historical periods, as was the coolie and the medieval villein.

Main Street towns may all look alike, but one cannot be sure from one year to the next in what that likeness is to consist. They sprout traffic signals, stupendously upholstered policemen, banks in the shape of Greek temples, magnificent high school buildings, sparkling drug stores, batteries of columnar street lights, memorial libraries—practically overnight. To keep pace with the changing skyline of our great cities would require a swift airplane perpetually on the wing.

Although "things are in the saddle" and may be bought in million-unit lots, the choices of today are dead tomorrow. To hold that our commodities increasingly seek a dead level is absurd. They seek altogether too many live, new levels—with the hand of the super-salesman always on the bellows. If this be standardization, make the most of it. It is the standardization of infinite variety and perpetual change—and thus uncomfortably close to a contradiction in terms.

Standards for Behavior. Since we machine peoples are coming more and more to look alike and to live the same kind of external lives, some observers jump to the conclusion that we are also tending more and more to act alike and think alike. This conclusion is the basis for all the tirades against modern standardization to which I referred at the beginning, and it is worth examining in some detail. All that we can be reasonably sure of in advance is that behavior, like the output of material commodities, is in constant flux. The machine, having destroyed the bulk of our old folkways, has forced us to experiment with a host of new ones, none of which have crystallized; and none of them can very well crystallize so long as our technology continues to change. No sooner do we adapt ourselves to traveling at the rate of thirty miles an hour on the earth than we are compelled to take to the air at two hundred miles an hour. And what is *this* going to do to the family, religion, the etiquette of visiting and entertainment, habits of recreation, education, relations with other races and nations?

Leaving the future to speak in its own due time, we must see that the present varieties of behavior patterns are legion, extremely difficult to fit into neat catalogues. We have no standard religious code. One may take one's pick between two Catholic Churches, more than one hundred Protestants sects, and heavens knows how many cults founded by prophets from the hinterland. If you rush up to a New York policeman and announce that you are an atheist, he will tell you to stop blocking traffic. In urban centers you can have One God, a whole pantheon, or none at all; and nobody particularly cares—unless you are running for high public office. How far this is from the unified pattern of worship in the Middle Ages, with its ordered procession of masses, fast days, feast days, penances, celestial bookkeeping for every variety of conduct with debits and credits all duly balanced, and cathedral bells tolling over even meadows proclaiming their eternal benediction upon the eternal unity of mankind!

If religious standards are in disorder, sexual standards are even worse. Unless we happen to live in the Bible Belt, we may select orthodox marriage, trial marriage, companionate marriage, marriage of convenience, or no marriage at all. We may divorce at random. We may practice birth control in all circumstances, in specific circumstances, in no circumstances—again with authority to sanction each decision. We are urged to have small families, large families, no families; to marry when we are young and poor, to wait until we are old and rich; to marry within our class, to marry above or below it. Nor is sanction altogether lacking for the advantages, cultural and economic, of a "sugar daddy." The psychoanalysts have lifted the curtain on a variety of matters long held suitable for discussion only in a brothel—if at all—and have made them current coin at every "modern" dinner table. In brief, the only dependable standard in sexual affairs seems to be that any sort of reticence connotes a serious, not to say perilous, internal conflict.

Education is in an equally contradictory state. Children should be disciplined; they should be permitted to run wild. They should be sheltered; they should be exposed. Parents are the ruination of their children. What is so beautiful as mother love? Public schools are bad for them; private schools are worse, while tutors are the most pernicious of all. They should be taught to work; they should be taught to play; they should not be taught anything. All children are little Leonardos; all children are little animals. Every child should go to college; no child should go to college—let him get his diploma in the university of hard knocks. In the center of this chaos stands the modern parent (I am one), praying with whatever vestiges of the *mores* of worship he can summon that somehow his child will survive his education.

Our occupational habits may be regimented in detail, but as a total phenomenon they are infinitely various. No good American believes that his place is anywhere but at the top. Nobody stays, if he can possibly avoid it, in the place it has pleased God to put him. The ladder of success is crawling with struggling forms. Few ascend, it is true, but who has not rushed for a higher rung and missed? In theory no man is fixed, however much he may be in fact; and because this doctrine is so generally held, the organized labor movement can make no great headway in America.

The outer evidence of these inner aspirations is a restless, moving population, forever on the march to higher things—which seldom come; forever drugging itself with correspondence school courses—some ninety per cent of which are given up before the first lesson is completed. Drifting youths and men come storming into accountancy when it is held to be a new and lucrative profession; into California and Florida real estate when booms are on; into brokers' offices when stocks are going up; into bootlegging when prewar stocks are going down. There is the constant migration from farm to city. There is the mass movement of Negroes from cotton fields to Harlem. And the variety of possible occupations—from deep-sea diving to flagpole sitting—is literally endless. A recent survey shows four hundred occupations in one Middle Western town. How different from the medieval village in which one was born and lived and died; where no one ever left his class; where everyone, normally, followed the trade of his father, and, at best, had hardly a dozen occupations from which to choose.

Through all this welter of modern life many old behavior patterns still survive, but the indirect effects of mechanization have shaken us loose from ancient mental certainties. We are never adequately prepared for change and resist it when it comes, but we are beginning to realize with some bewilderment that almost anything may happen. And that mental attitude is slippery ground on which to build a case for one dead level of behavior.

I believe I have overthrown the argument that the Western world is becoming rigorously standardized, by showing that on the contrary its *mores* are in flux and conflict, while many of its institutions and most of its commodities are becoming ever more complex. Yet, for all my reasoning, the pictures of the Kentucky mountaineer with his radio and the navvy shorn of his velveteens stubbornly refuse to fade. Local color *is* going out of life. How can my previous argument be reconciled with this obvious fact?

The two cannot be reconciled, but they can be brought somewhat closer together. Western civilization comprises perhaps half a billion people. They are tending to build certain structures alike, to dress alike on many occasions, to think alike on certain questions. The same area a century ago was split into hundreds of communities, each with its own set of customs, its own arts and crafts. Now, if we compare Western civilization as a unit today with, say, Cape Cod of a century ago, the latter is by far the more standardized community, in its morals, its arts, its behavior. But if we compare the total area now and then, Europe and America were more colorful a hundred years ago, by virtue of the differing communities. The complaint against modern standardization is usually made by travelers. But ask the traveler if he would prefer to live out his years in the Wales of the eighteenth century or as a citizen of the modern British Empire. Unless he is an incurable sentimentalist, he would choose the varied life of the modern man rather than the limitations of the premachine man—and put up with short skirts from San Francisco to Budapest as best he may.

But a last qualification is in order. We are not all free-roving citizens. Theoretically, the present choices before any individual are limitless. Practically, most of us never make these choices. We fall into a rut, and after a struggle or two stay there. Is the modern man in his rut more standardized than the average individual in other cultures? This is a knotty question. The taboos and *mores* which guide him are not as stringent as among primitive peoples, but his day-by-day behavior often tends to be more monotonous and dull. He has fewer vital things to do, fewer muscular adjustments to make, fewer problems to think about.

From all these baffling currents and cross currents, at least three conclusions emerge. (1) Machine civilization as a total culture is less standardized than any given former culture. (2) The life of a modern man is theoretically open to more variety, but practically may be less varied, than that of an individual in other cultures. (3) The machine is probably the greatest destroyer of old standards that the world has ever seen. New standards, to be sure, are springing up to fill the gap, but they are all too often ugly and unpleasant. There is no certainty, however, that they will last. Indeed, the only certainty is perpetual change, so long as science and the industrial arts continue to develop at their present pace.

In Defense of the Machine
ROBERT FORSYTHE

Among the major tenets of the intelligentsia of the nineteen-twenties was an abhorrence of the Machine. It revealed itself in the desire of those who could afford it to get away from the country entirely and in the effort of those left behind to retreat so far into the woods that a man could be known only by the wisp of straw behind his ear and the rich sweet loam pouring through his fingers. There was a great deal of nonsense in the thing but at bottom the intellectuals had hold of a sound idea. The Machine, when used as Ford uses it and as all exploiters use it, can be a terrible thing. Where they went astray was in assuming that a working man hated the thought of his tools and employment and was only driven to work by the pangs of hunger and the armed forces of capitalism.

The feeling still makes much of the writing and practically all of the reviewing of labor novels farcical. When it has to do with the Machine, one gets a picture of the man of labor tied to the wheels of industry until his brain reels with images of bolts and nuts. If it has to do with an even more fantastic occupation, mining, the average intellectual is completely alienated. The idea of a human being burrowed in the ground for his living is so abhorrent to one who has never worked in a mine that he can only assume that the miner has been driven to his job at the point of a bayonet.

Because so many left-wing critics have come over from the bourgeois intellectual group which I have mentioned, the fault has been particularly marked in their writings. What they have failed to do is distinguish between the Machine and its uses. The result is that they have left themselves unprotected on another flank. If the Machine is so horrible in America, how can they be so elated at the thought of Soviet Russia becoming mechanized? If the Machine is a brutalizing force, how can it ever be anything else whether used for social purposes or by the most ruthless of exploiters?

The problem should never have arisen. I once ran a turret lathe in a machine shop and I can testify that I have never had such a sense of achievement and power in my life. If it had not been that I was working a night shift of $13\frac{7}{12}$ hours at a wage of around 20 cents an hour, I would have enjoyed it. As for the coal mines, the evidence is even stronger. Strange as it may seem, coal miners like coal mining. What they

From *New Masses*, October 1, 1935.

don't like is intermittent work, low pay, company thugs, company stores, black lists and company mismanagement. I was born in a coal town and lived in one until my high-school days. My father went in the mines at the age of nine, with every reason to hate them. We lived in towns which would sicken the inhabitants of a tenement house. And yet I can to this day settle back into the most hideous coal-mining town with the thought that it is home and I belong there. My brothers all worked in the mines and I went in often to ride with the motorman or to carry rod with the surveyors. The horrifying feeling of being buried underground which brings such shudders to the ordinary observer, never enters into the matter. I am terrified by altitude and can't look out a high window without wanting to jump. I can't bear to look at structural workers tossing rivets about on sixty-story buildings, but I am certain the men walking about so casually up there on the string-like girders have no such twitterings. I understand, on the contrary, that they get a great kick out of it.

Tom Tippett's *Horse Shoe Bottoms* (Harper) is important because he shows these facts so clearly. Tippett is a coal miner who has come from a long line of miners. He knows their clannishness and pride, he knows the hold that coal mining can get on a family. It is the story of the miners who become conscious of the need of a union and of their fight for it. There is the hatred that all miners and all men have for owners who oppress them, but there is no hatred of the work itself. Without idealizing it and while showing it in all its horrors, he still manages to bring out the truth about it: miners are not miners out of compulsion.

What the intellectuals are eternally faced with—those who were sickened by the capitalistic picture of the twenties—is the conflict between two equally impossible desires: to escape it all by a retreat to a form of handicraft civilization which could just as easily continue reverting until it became a form of cave-dwelling civilization; and a machine civilization which would be used for benefits instead of profits. Because they were unaware of the causes of evils of the Machine under capitalism, or preferred not to admit them, they are still, even when they have become enlightened about the conflict of class forces, hampered by the notion that the Machine, by itself, is evil. That may be very well for Mr. Borsodi who wishes to return to an age of weaving our own clothes or for Mr. Stuart Chase who once yearned for the idyllic peace of Tepoztlan but it solves no problems for the workers and none for the world.

One of the troubles, I think, is that we have come to think of the Machine entirely in terms of the Ford assembly line. As one who has seen the belt line, I can testify that there is nothing more awful on this earth. But that is only a small part of industry. In a place such as Bethlehem Steel there is almost nothing of this kind. The work is hard and poorly paid and the workers are at the mercy of the owners but the work itself is not slavery. What makes it slavery are the conditions under which the men work and their hopelessness in the face of a ruthless economic system which has no mercy on its human equipment.

I am a laborer with a typewriter now and my work is drudgery when I do hack work and pleasure when I do something satisfactory. But from a strictly aesthetic viewpoint, I get no more satisfaction out of an article which I feel to be above the ordinary than I did in taking a round piece of steel and making it into a base plug for a 9.2 shell. It meant that I had to learn to grind my own tools, and to manipulate the carriage which ran the length of the lathe and another smaller carriage which bore the cutting tools. It meant that I had to make a base plug of such accuracy that it would fit into a shell to a thousandth of an inch.

As writers and critics we'll have to get over the notion that the Machine is an evil and that all workers are slaves of the Machine. It simply isn't true and it makes nonsense of our books and criticisms when we allow the hangover from the escapist days to affect our thinking about workers. The Machine can be an oppressor but it doesn't need to be. That fact makes all the difference in the world.

20. Designing the Future

One great new profession to emerge to stature and significance in this period was that of the industrial designer and with him concepts of efficiency, design, streamlining, modernism, and functionalism that had increasing importance, not simply in industry where he began, but for living and life-styles, thought and behavior among a wide-ranging middle-class public as well. Industrial design, Sheldon Cheney has told us, "is rightly determined by and geared to industry as it is. The machine is the foundation fact as well as the shaping tool; is influence and inspiration." But while these great engineering designers began in industry and served there, they were frequently not content to remain. They increasingly saw the consequence of their work in an expanded vision; they saw the whole world in need of redesign and believed fundamentally they could contribute to it.

R. Buckminster Fuller (born 1895) considers himself an engineer and a cosmic philosopher; both professions come largely out of his extraordinary experience and reading and little out of traditional formal education. Although he did attend Harvard, it was his apprenticeship in machine shops and industrial plants that really launched his exceptional career as inventor, engineer, designer, and educator.

Walter Dorwin Teague (1883–1960) was a designer of automobiles, railroads, appliances, buildings for Ford and other corporations; his list of corporate clients reads like a who's who in American industry. By 1940 (after service on the Design Board for the New York World's Fair where he created several buildings) he could write: "But I submit that better household equipment and better mechanical devices are of no real value unless they are first essays in the fundamental redesign of our world: harbingers of a wholesale reorganization of our chaotic scene. . . . What I have tried to do is outline . . . the technique that must be applied to the solution of any problem of design, whether it is a motor car or a new city or a new environment. If this technique is basically sound for one it will be sound for the others."

These are but two of the new professionals to emerge to prominence in the period. As social work was professionalized in the 1920's so industrial design was in the 1930's. These professionals—together with the architects, regional and urban planners, sociologists who had developed professionally earlier—were to play a major role in shaping the existing culture and in creating if not an ideology a structure of social beliefs and attitudes which might very well shape the future direction of liberal American culture.

Streamlining Society
R. BUCKMINSTER FULLER

Upon the premise that the sum-total of human desire to survive is dominant over the sum-total of the impulse to destroy, this book is designed. It does not seek to provide a formula to attainment. To do so would develop dogma and nullify the process of individual rationalization that is utterly essential for growth.

"Rationalization" is an act similar to walking through a half-frozen, marshy, unexplored country to mark out a trail that others may eventually follow. It involves not only the familiar one-two progression of shifting the weight and balance from one foot to the other, but an unknown quantity progression of selective testing to avoid treacherous ground before putting full weight upon the forward foot.

"Rationalization" is a time-word to replace "thinking," which is an ancient, mystically evolved word tentatively signifying an attempt to *force* the power of God into one's self. "Rationalization" connotes a constant, selective balancing of relative values, gained from experience, for the purpose of harmonious, inclusive *re*composition and subsequent extension.

It is central to my philosophy that everything in the universe is constantly in motion, atomically if not visibly, and that opposing forces throughout this kinetic picture are always in neat balance; furthermore, that everything invariably moves in the direction of least resistance.

The history of man's CREATIVE effort is the story of his struggle to control "direction" by the ELIMINATION of known RESISTANCES.

To the degree that the direction of least resistance is controlled by vacuumizing the advance and devacuumizing the wake, the course of society can be progressively better charted and eventually determinable with a high degree of certainty.

This creative control, or streamlining of society, by the scientific-minded (the right-makes-mightist) is in direct contrast to attempts by scheming

R. Buckminster Fuller, *Nine Chains to the Moon,* originally printed in New York, 1938, republished Carbondale, Illinois, 1968, pp. v–viii, 323–326.

matter-over-mindists (the might-makes-rightist) to control society by *increasing*, instead of lessening, *resistance* to natural flows through such devices as laws, tariffs, prohibitions, armaments, and the cultivation of popular fear.

By controlling direction, it becomes possible, scientifically, to increase the probability that specific events will "happen."

Preparation of the material herein set forth dates from the very beginning of my experience. Up to a point in that experience, I lived by the common code of loyalty and good fellowship with all of its convincing and romantic "tradition." Then, through my own particular quota of *important* slaps in the face, it became apparent that in "tradition" lies fallacy, and that to be guided in conduct and thought by blind adherence to tenets of tradition is, as said in slang, bravely to "stick the neck out." I realized that experience is the vital factor, and that, since one can think and feel consciously only in terms of experience, one can be hurt only in terms of experience. When one is hurt, then somewhere in the linkage of his experience can be discovered the parting of the strands that led to the hurt. Therefore, it follows that strict adherence to rationalization, within the limits of self-experience, will provide corrections to performance obviating not only for one's self, but for others, the pitfalls that occasion self-hurt. By cultivating the ability to rationalize in the absolute, one acquires the power of so ordering experience that truths are clarified and susceptibility to self-hurt is diminished to the point of negligibility. Through rationalization anyone may evolve solutions for any situation that may arise, and by the attainment of this ability through experience one obtains his license to be of service to mankind.

Rationalization alone, however, it not sufficient. It is not an end in itself. It must be carried through to an objective state and materialize into a completely depersonalized instrument—a "pencil." (Who knows who made the first pencil? Certainly not Eberhard Faber or "Venus.") The "pencil" not only facilitates communication between men, by making thought specific and objective, but also enables men, cooperatively, to plan and realize the building of a house, oxygen tent, flatiron, or an x-ray cabinet, by virtue of the pencil's availability. The inventor, alive or dead, is extraneous and unimportant; it is the "pencil" that carries over. Abstract thought dies with the thinker, but the mechanism was building for a long time before the moment of recognized invention.

The substance of this book develops my conviction of these truths. In a final chapter, I have recorded certain thought processes and results of abstract, intuitive thinking which would be obscure without reading the preceding sections. The reason for exposing myself to possible suspicion of "mysticism" is to show how important it is to transcribe the faint thought messages coming into our personal cosmos at the time of occurrence—sketchy and puzzling though they may be—because time, if well served, will turn them into monkey wrenches and gas torches.

The title *Nine Chains to the Moon* was chosen to encourage and stimulate the broadest attitude toward thought. Simultaneously, it emphasizes the littleness of our universe from the mind viewpoint. A statistical cartoon would show that if, in imagination, all of the people of the world were to stand upon one another's shoulders, they would make nine complete chains between the earth and the moon. If it is not so far to the moon, then it is not so far to the limits—whatever, whenever or wherever they may be.

Limits are what we have feared. So much has been done to make us conscious of our infinite physical smallness, that the time has come to dare to include the complete universe in our rationalizing. It is no longer practical to gaze at the surfaces of "named" phenomena, within the range of vision in the smoking car of the 5:15, with no deeper analysis of their portent than is derivable from a superficial exchange of complexed opinion-notions with fellow commuters.

"After all," Jeans said, "it is man who asked the question." The question is survival, and the answer, which is unit, lies in the progressive sum-totaling of man's evolving knowledge. Individual survival is identifiable with the whole as—extension or extinction. There is no good old country doctor on Mars to revive those, who, through mental inertia, are streamlining into extinction.

✻   ✻   ✻

Eventually the government, after surveying the enormous cost of the nonintegrated inefficiency of maintaining a population in hovels, will be forced, through ever persistent economy, into the transfer of unemployed city multitudes from such habitations to those of the highly modernized, efficient skyscrapers with which the government, willy-nilly, has been saddled by mortgage moratorium, *et cetera.*

The largest number of dwelling units ever built in the U. S. in one year by the combined building industries at peak load was 280,000, in 1925, and we are currently shy (this is admitted by the most conservative authorities) six million minimal-standard adequacy dwellings. Such seemingly prosocial legislation as the Wagner Housing Act, which at best might develop 20,000 new and, most questionably "low" cost homes in New York City *per annum* where 700,000 unemployed families or bachelors now "exist" without ability to pay rent, must be utterly futile. Such legislation is promoted, in reality, by the most selfish of the "conservative" finance interests to avoid even public mention of the one obvious method of wholesale relief of the housing problem, i.e., migration from the tenements to such buildings as the modernly equipped, relatively empty Empire State Building.

From a future viewpoint, there is rationality both in the skyscraper building of the city and in the mass-production dwelling for the urban and suburban community. They do not follow contradictory forces. The two forces involved are: (1) decentralization for physical activity, work or play, and (2) centralization for mental activity, work or play. The latter is primarily transient and the former primarily of long duration. . . .

By trial and error the professional and worker classes will ultimately learn that the current slum clearance project is a mirage and that the chief beneficiaries are the finance capitalists. This is mildly to be witnessed again by indirection of volition in Housing Administrator Strauss's policy, i.e., not to rebuild the old slum areas but to decentralize new mass housing to undeveloped marginal acres of cities. Once the technicians have mastered this fact, there will be an eventually-to-be-heard popular mandate for DOING the EFFICIENT thing. The C.I.O. unit, "The Federation of Architects, Engineers, Chemists, and Technicians," so rapidly gaining strength in revolt against professional stupidity, is a manifest of this approaching mandate.

When the city populace has moved into the skyscraper towers, they will blow up their slums wholesale with probably the most thrilling popular fiestas of all times and convert the land into vast parks. There will emerge from the present contradictory scene a clean, beautiful and orderly settlement of towers and gardens, with retention or restoration of all historically important tracery elements, knowledge of the latter having popularly developed through inadvertence of made-work writers and artists engaged in W.P.A. projects.

From these tower and garden cities the populace may progressively and efficiently be deployed to activity, in the for-years-to-come high manual effort employing industrial reproduction of scientifically evolved shelters and contiguous industries.

The swarms of oddly clad tenement dwellers will be incongruous when first transferred to their new environment of svelte skyscraper lobbies and elevators, but just as a transition in the stenographer's appearance from sloppiness or dowdiness to that of a "deb" occurred when she found herself in a skyscraper office, so slum dwellers will quickly avail themselves of first-class plumbing facilities, adequate warmth and fresh air, and will transform their outward appearance to conform to environment. There will be many a laugh, but that's what we are looking for: laughter and happiness.

It would not be efficient, however, simply to let slum exiles camp about the floors of Empire State buildings, along with their pots and pans, little cookstoves, and filthy clothing, using the windows for general refrigeration.

No! The efficient course will be to reclothe them completely and, in consideration of the fact that the skyscrapers are to be temporary hostelries until the slum exiles can be deployed to industrial service over the land, near or far, furnish them with food as would the hotel and with medical attention as would the hospital, giving as thoughtful care to the menu or diet in relation to intestinal habits as would be accorded hotel or hospital guests. Such efficient, nourishing feeding would be no more difficult than is the solution of the dietary problem of any great city hospital. It would be efficient, also, to furnish them with the best of education and amusement. All this would, of course, save more than the whole tax bill of N. Y. C. today wherein the "debt" service alone calls for $175,000,000 in the current year.

It is interesting that, whereas the professional planners of the would-be resuscitated housing industry look to and even go to Europe for precedent in the matter of emergency housing, there is in reality no compatibility between the housing problem of Europe and that of America. The comparative figures of population per room in Europe with 25 per cent of the world's population and in North America with 7 per cent of the world's population show that in Europe there is, throughout compound housing centers, even today a high room shortage. In Europe the figure is in the vicinity of 2.6 persons per decently dwellable room currently extant. In America on the other hand the average is only .9 persons per now-"available" dwelling room, not including potential skyscraper hotels. It is the decentralization-mobilization shift and rising "standard" progression that provokes "shortage" in America.

Relative only to the currently endured standard of housing, there is, so far as four walls and a roof go, actually no housing shortage in America. The need is for an efficient redeal of shelter, and rapid satisfaction of advancing standards of adequacy production, and service method. The true 100 per cent housing shortage in America and worldwide is of entirely new, highly mobile, scientific shelters that may be constantly and conveniently shifted from one to another currently important industrial or play sites. Relatively permanent shelters will be required, also, for the more scientific rehousing of the agricultural populace who, in the chemicomechanical industrialization of farming, will progressively become the mechanical supervisors of agricultural production rather than agricultural labor slaves.

Scientific, mobile shelters will be utilized, also, for the constantly moving placement or deployment of city-bogged, nonemployed people to play lands of the world where it would be possible for them to develop in health, strength, and intellectual ability. This might never completely rehabilitate the "lost" older generation, but would nurture its offspring into harmonious synchronization with and responsible continuance of the emergent age.

The trailer has already appeared as a gesture by small man for his need in this direction, but how sadly short of the goal it falls! The trailer, however, has its random element significance; it is forcing the automobile industry, which is SCIENTIFIC INDUSTRY itself, into efficient mobile housing design considerations and to the redesign of its interior mechanisms, an important baby. But more of this in the next chapter.

Not long ago a suggestion was made in a newspaper that all relief, popular and private, be immediately terminated; that all public schools be closed; that free hospitalization cease and that America be thrown on her "own" to prove her rugged manliness. If the suggester's impossible scheme were to be carried out, it is probable that he himself would be among the first to be eaten by the wolves. He probably was playing for a big role . . . as a "practical man." No! dear fellow, we are going to be truly practical and we are on the way. The way is scientific, and heavenly. Inherent in Disney's and his army of co-artists' *Snow White and the Seven Dwarfs* is the beauty and justification of the highly mechanized industrial age—just beginning.

Design This Day: A Program
WALTER DORWIN TEAGUE

To the modern man his physical environment is merely new material, an opportunity for manipulation. It may be that God made the world, but that is no reason why we should not make it over.   BERTRAND RUSSELL

In our times we have had a number of Five-Year and Three-Year Plans, which were going to make a notable increase in human happiness. But the specified period has passed with misery registering, if anything, a somewhat more painful level than before. Social reorganizations on a stupendous scale have been launched, based on widely different statements of principle, but all ostensibly aimed at achieving a more abun-

Walter Dorwin Teague, *Design This Day: The Technique of Order in the Machine Age* (London, 1946) pp. 204–215. Original New York edition published 1940. The London edition has some important changes and is therefore to be preferred as Teague's definitive statement.

dant life for everybody. Men feel an overpowering impulse to rebuild their world, and have been the dupe of any specious plan. The enormous energy generated in these movements by this high aim has been in every instance, sooner or later, concentrated on keeping a small group of exceedingly unattractive men in control of the lives and fortunes of their fellow citizens. The result of our experience to date is a deep and growing scepticism as to the adequacy of any man's brain for the task of planning society, and the adequacy of any man's moral stature for the task of putting a comprehensive plan into effect. All our planners and leaders have been fitting themselves rapidly and neatly to Santayana's definition of a fanatic—one who redoubles his efforts when he has forgotten his aim.

The trouble with our planning is that it is too comprehensive and too detailed, and too exactly programmed. More plans for human betterment have been wrecked on their own principles and programmes than on any overt opposition. We see only a little way into the future, and yet we lay out exact inflexible campaigns into this country whose terrain has never been seen or mapped. We assume that we shall reach our objective by seven league strides instead of by the careful step-at-a-time that is the inevitable method of human progress. Our headlong rashness lands us in ditches too wide for leaping and up against walls that bloody our heads. The duces and fuehrers and commissars and socials reformers of this kind and that rush noisily on ahead, each with his own banner of salvation and each into his own morass. Men grow increasingly doubtful of the possibility of finding our objective tied up in any compact formula, or of attaining it by any simple social bouleversement.

Yet all the time, while leaders shrieked and bombs fell, the builders have been at work. The vision of a rebuilt world has grown clearer to more men, and the step-by-step progress towards it does not falter even now. The builders feel into the future, groping carefully, aware of their own ignorance and ready like all good scientists—"knowers"—to adapt their plans instantly, at any moment, to the new truths and the unforeseen conditions that may be revealed as they progress. If they make a plan, it is one of objectives only, and these not too definite. It is impossible to say, "We will first do this, and then that, and afterwards that." We can only say, "We will do, as fast and as well as we can, the multitudinous tasks that lie around us, clearly to be seen, and crying to be done; as we accomplish these we will advance to the new tasks then revealed to us." All progress is opportunist, and all plans should be tentative.

So, when we list the possibilities that appear to us, today, to be realizable, it is obvious that no definitions can be precise and no sequence of achievements can be exactly forecast. We can see a little way, yes, because we have certain known factors that are still malleable, still waiting to be cast into their ultimate form. We can see certain needs that are inherent in human nature, certain circumstances that must exist if the gregarious human animal is to live happily together in large numbers on the surface of a subjugated world. And we have a long catalogue of very tangible and immensely potent tools ready to be used in the making of a better world. But scientists and engineers are at work in countless laboratories and shops, ready to surprise us at any moment with new resources that may require a recasting of our plans. Our advance must be along a very wide front, slowly, moving up one division here, supporting it with another there.

Any continuing advance depends, of course, on whether constructive work can continue without the interruption of further catastrophic war. And it is clear now that peace depends on whether we succeed in passing from a complex of communities segregated by national prejudices into a single community of the world. There is reason to hope that what we are suffering now are the pains of such a transmutation. We are overwhelmingly conscious of the interdependence of all men in these modern times, aware that the methods of exchange, transportation, and communication we have created are knitting the world into one social and economic network. Against this realization a last wave of nationalism is fighting a vicious counteraction. It must collapse before the fact that men can no longer live apart from other men, even in great national groups, or we shall have to abandon the system of specialized production and general exchange we have been evolving and relapse into barbarism for lack of an alternative. We can't yet see the issue, but our system is still so young, so expansive, so productive that it is hard to conceive of its nonsurvival.

Most formidable obstacle to unity is the ideological conflict splitting world thought to its roots. Military victory brought no ideological peace, because in the late war the ideological lineup did not conform to the military lineup. Men have proved thousands of times in the past that their beliefs are more precious than their lives, especially the beliefs that have to do with their concept of life's purposes and obligations. We see great national groups committed to the belief that the citizen possesses certain rights and responsibilities which the State, his servant, has no authority to curtail, and these groups have demonstrated in practice the validity of such a concept of social and political organization. We see other great national groups committed to a system in which the individual has no rights or responsibilities except as the State allocates them to him, and these groups have maintained such a system authoritatively in their own special circumstances. Here is a cleavage not easily bridged. Men will not readily accept in a World State a concept of either authority or liberty which they have never been willing to accept in their own Nation States.

Perhaps here, too, the exigencies of the times will prove more effective than either argument or force in bringing about a worldwide meeting of minds. At present an impenetrable wall of censorship isolates the Statist groups, completely barring a free flow of thought and information both inwards and outwards. Distrust and animosity inevitably flourish on both sides of such barriers. But if all nations must associate in international organizations, exchange their goods and share in systems of international credit, it is hard to see how breaches in these artificial dikes can be prevented indefinitely.

Meanwhile those who believe in the right of the individual to think, speak and act on his own initiative, accepting an equivalent responsibility for his course, face a challenge to prove all over again that their system is most fruitful of well-being, both for themselves and the world. They must demonstrate that the energy and ingenuity released from multitudinous individual sources is more effective in creating wealth—using the word in its root meaning—than the energy of the millions directed by the will of the few. If they succeed in this test, they will let loose in the world forces of unity against which totalitarian barriers cannot stand; and they will create in their own lands a setting of increasing rightness in which life can be lived with greater dignity and felicity than the human race has ever enjoyed in the past. It should be a convincing demonstration.

The material means we have available for the accomplishment of such an advance are ample. We are faced with the heavy responsibility of using these resources effectively. We shall deserve great credit and enjoy vast benefits if we succeed, but we shall suffer greater ignominy and distress if we don't.

1. The motive force of modern civilization is mechanical power under precise control. The comfort and well-being, even the health and serenity, of mankind in the sort of world to which we have committed ourselves depend on the extent to which we can supplement our own feeble strength and perceptions with others more ample. There have been occasional halcyon oases where this was not true, but in the world of today a poverty of mechanical power reduces life to the precarious level we observe at present in huge stretches of China and India.

The production of power has increased with astonishing acceleration in modern times. To cite the United States as an example, sources of mechanical power have expanded in fifty years from a potential of seventeen million horse-power to two-and-a-quarter billion horse-power today—from one-quarter horse-power per capita in 1896 to an average of eighteen horse-power per capita of the much larger population in 1946. This is an almost fantastic extension of our ability to control our environment and augment our welfare. It is not enough, and both we and the rest of the world must expand our power resources with concentrated energy in the years to come. This we can do.

The intense effort exerted during the war has made the task easier than before. Much of the swift modern increase in power production has been due to the development of the internal combustion principle. In the past few years molecular reconstruction has created—literally created— new super-fuels such as high octane gas and triptane which will make internal combustion engines immensely more powerful. At the same time the swift development of gas turbine and jet engines has produced new and simple methods of using low-grade fuels with unprecedented effectiveness. Every type of engine from steam to diesel is now yielding more power per pound of weight and pound of fuel, and the generation and transmission of electrical energy has steadily gained in economy and efficiency.

As innumerable automobiles, airplanes and ships drain the world's oil supplies, we shall replace them from man-made sources. Oil can be produced from coal by hydrogenation, and the world's supply of coal is sufficient for this purpose for a thousand years. Oil shale contains much more oil than all the original oil deposits of the world before they were tapped—and we know how to extract it. We also know that oil can be synthesized directly from carboniferous vegetable matter by the application of heat and power, as nature did it. All these techniques are more expensive now than pumping oil from underground lakes, but they will not remain so when we are forced by circumstances to perfect them.

We may never be driven to these recourses, since we have tapped the original source of all power. In achieving man's age-long dream of releasing atomic energy, we have liberated a force that, if it is not kept under rational administration, may be used to destroy civilization, the human race, the world itself. But it is also capable of accomplishing man's final emancipation from the natural conditions of life, if he applies it to the doing of useful work. When we realize that the energy that can be released, even by the early unperfected techniques of atomic fission, from one pound of Uranium 235 is equal to the energy released by the burning of 1350 tons of coal, we see that we have penetrated new levels of capability. Atomic engines are in a crude stage of development but their evolution will be swift, and if we concentrate on the constructive utilization of atomic energy instead of applying it to racial suicide there is practically nothing we cannot do in manipulating matter, remodelling the face of the earth, regulating even the weather.

2. All power is potentially dangerous: its value to us is directly proportionate to our ability to control it, and the delicacy and precision with which we can apply it. Here again we have acquired fabulous

resources. Whoever is contemptuous of machine production today is simply not acquainted with it, either its existing mechanical equipment or its capacity for beautiful and beneficent performance. Modern machinery is science realized in material complexes, abstract knowledge made operative. And in spite of its amazing proliferation, we have not yet begun to realize its immense potentials for human betterment.

The boundaries of possible achievement in the use of energy have been burst by the newest and most fundamental of sciences—the same which has given us its awesome offspring, nuclear fission. It is not possible here to give even a hint of what electronics is contributing to our powers by its incredible versatility in transmitting, transforming and controlling energy. But we should realize that our sensitivity, our vision, and the tardy tempo of our nervous reactions have acquired, in electronics, a series of aids that in time will leave none of the mysteries of matter, not even the mystery of life itself, beyond our penetration.

What electronics is contributing to knowledge, health and wealth production is only dimly realized, if at all, by most of us. We are somewhat more aware of its services in communication, but even here the final implications of radio, television, radar, and facsimile transmission are still beyond our grasp. They serve an immense number of practical ends, but ultimately they will be the means of bringing the whole world together into a single community of thought. One of the most critical battles to be fought in these times is for the freedom of the ether waves, the abolition of all political censorship on what people may choose to receive by radioactive transmission; so that electronics cannot become the agency of propaganda without correctives, and there can be no arbitrary barrier to universal intercommunication. When this basic liberty is won throughout the world, we shall have established a primary condition for human unity.

Electronics, in its nucleonic subdivision, has scored the first successes in the actual transmutation of elements, but the creation of wholly new combinations of elements by means of molecular reconstruction is becoming a commonplace of physiochemistry. By rearrangement of the atoms in molecules we have acquired a long list of invaluable new fuels, drugs, materials, and alloys, and we are entering an era when, if we need a substance of properties not found in any natural combination, we can create it. The man who designs and builds in the future world need never be handicapped by lack of materials exactly suited to his purpose, and no man need suffer from a lack of natural products necessary to his health, comfort and freedom of action. An exquisitely exact control of unlimited power; an armoury of tools that will accomplish practically any physical operation the mind of man can conceive; an inexhaustible store of materials exactly patterned to our needs—with this equipment there is no barrier, outside the mind and character of man himself, to universal abundance.

3. It is necessary not only to produce wealth: in a united world it is necessary that needed goods shall be moved freely from the places where they can best be produced to the places where they can best be used; and it is necessary that men themselves shall be able to move about the earth as their work and interests demand. Here again we are acquiring ample means of transport by land, sea, and air.

Where the automobile has come into common use, it has enormously expanded the orbit of the individual. In the United States, before the war, we had an automobile for every four-and-one-half people, which meant an average of about one per family. This has had the effect of emancipating millions of people from confinement to locales and circumstances in which the accidents of fortune deposited them and allowed much greater latitude in locating industries and planning communities. It has brought serious problems of readjustment, naturally, but if we assume that the aim of human progress is the freeing of the individual from irrational restraints, so that he can plan and conduct his life under ethical compulsions alone, then the automobile provides one important phase of his emancipation.

The airplane promises another, of greater range. Today no two important centers of population on the globe are as far apart as London and Edinburgh were in 1800, and soon we shall have reduced that maximum separation to a mere ten hours or so. The airways will soon be crowded with pressurized cabin planes, guarded by radio and radar, cruising the stratosphere with cargoes of one hundred passengers and many tons of freight, at speeds above three hundred and fifty miles an hour. The network of their routes will cover the earth.

When we remember that man's first flight in a heavier-than-air machine was made at Kittyhawk on December 17, 1903, we should be deeply impressed by the swift progress of an art that for thousands of years had seemed an unattainable dream. A modern heavy-duty plane is a technological marvel, and an airplane engine of high horsepower is an incredibly complex although dependable mechanism. Now it seems that the turbine and jet principles may restore a large measure of simplicity and economy to aviation power plants, at the same time that they carry us beyond sonic speed. And it is not safe to say that in a few years atomic engines adapted to airplanes will not solve the fuel problem for all time, with immense expansion in range of flight and carrying capacity. Looking back over what has been accomplished in a mere forty-three years, we should be confident that the old phrase about the annihilation of time and space will pass from the status of a cliché to become a mere statement of commonplace fact.

Flying will not all be on this colossal, professional scale—far from it. Private planes will take to the air by the million, and the automobile will be supplemented by a general use of helicopters and roadable planes. We shall have need of a system of airfields and landing strips as comprehensive as the system of multilaned motor highways we already have begun and must complete in the next few years.

The shifting of huge quantities of fast freight and passenger traffic to the airways and public highways calls for drastic revision of the railways. They must see their usefulness restricted to the hauling of heavy freight in bulk, or they too must adopt a lighter, more flexible method of conveyance than the locomotive-powered, flanged-wheels-on-steel-rails system to which they were committed by the technological limitations of the early nineteenth century. The railways occupy what in many respects are the finest available routes: their gradients are slight, their lines are straight or curved on generous radii, cross traffic already has been largely eliminated. It should be possible to convert them, at least in part, to paved roadways barred to private usage and operated under signal control as high-speed commercial arteries, integrated at points of departure and delivery with the public highway system. In this way they could be launched on a new career of usefulness.

It will be many a day before the merchant marine is eliminated as a carrier of transoceanic heavy freight, and we enter the postwar epoch with a world tonnage equal to prewar totals, and with improved methods of shipbuilding. Gas turbine engines will greatly enhance the carrying capacity and reduce the cost of operation of marine vessels, and when atomic engines are developed for this application the ultimate economies will be realized.

Our resources for the creation of wealth are matched by our means for its physical distribution over the face of the earth. As electronic communication can bind the world together in thought, modern transport can bind it together in an indispensable reciprocity of production and service.

4. Human life is conditioned largely by the homes in which men live and the work they do. In these phases of life we are offered a new freedom.

Aviation and motor highway transport have removed most reasons for industries to cluster along the railway lines, and for workers to live in the neighborhood of their employment. The motorization of the railways and their integration with the public highways will further accelerate the decentralization of industry. Huge populations will be able to abandon city slums forever and recover the pleasure in life and in work to which all men are entitled.

Light, cleanliness, order, healthful conditions are already the accepted objectives of intelligent industrial planning. Many factories in recent years have risen in a form worthy of a civilization more advanced than ours. The elimination of smoke and dirt and the prompt utilization of waste products are making these factories acceptable in any setting. They are acquiring the bright, metallic, orderly aspect that thrills us in so many of their own products, but they are only forerunners of the shining factories of the future. From these workshops drudgery and mere burden-bearing will have disappeared: machines will do all the work of beasts, men will do the work that only rational animals can do. The laboratories, engineering departments, and drafting rooms will dwarf anything we can see today. Creating, discovering, planning, designing, operation, and maintenance of subtle mechanisms will overshadow all other activities in the industrial world. Work will be creative.

With greatly expanded range of travel and more leisure, the men of tomorrow can live amid quiet and beauty and cultivate their gardens with Voltairean equanimity. The city will become a place of business, barter, intellectual and artistic exchange, social enjoyment and amusement, rather than a place of residence. Large numbers of people are necessary to support these phases of life, they must exist at focal points of population. But the city will be more sparsely built, a collection of tall towers separated by gardens and greensward, crossed by transport systems moving on different levels. The city air will be clean, for coal will not be burned within its limits and wood will be burned only in fireplaces—for pleasure. Our internal combustion engines will actually complete their combustion internally and the air will be free of their gases and fumes. The city will be a place of wide spaces, sunlight, greenery in summer and clean snow in winter. It will be quiet, urbane, civilized beyond anything the world has ever before accomplished in the line of city-building.

The country as a whole will become urbanized. That is, population will spread more evenly over its surface, but without impairing its beauty and without rusticating its inhabitants. Large areas of forest, plain, lake and ocean front will be preserved uninvaded by building, so that wild life may flourish and the pleasures of solitude may be enjoyed. Agriculture, intensively practised as chemurgy, will require less land but will yield more abundant and better results. Integrated with other industrial activities it will become a scientific method of producing foodstuffs and chemical raw materials, instead of the picturesque but archaic and frequently abortive craft it is today.

At wide intervals over the populated countryside, steel and glass towers will rise in glistening brilliance above the tree tops and rolling lawns. They will accent communities of single dwellings, served but not penetrated by arterial highways and resting in what will seem to be remote seclusion. The houses, even the towers, will be fabricated by the technological methods which have not yet been fully imported into building construction as into all other phases of modern production. As a result they will be not only cheaper but better, more gracious, more complete than anything the man of moderate income can obtain today. And they will be equipped for a degree of physical comfort and gracious living that only substantial wealth makes possible now: because, in fact, they will be the evidence of the enormously expanded total wealth of society as a whole.

There is a pseudophilosophic attitude which assumes that possessions are a handicap and a burden, and it is true that they may become so. But possessions may also be a liberating force, essential to real freedom of thought and action. Modern civilization is predicated on an assumption of a balanced and varied diet, adequate heating, cooling and lighting, abundant hot and cold water, ubiquitous bathtubs and water closets. Where these advantages are common they recede into the background and are given no thought, but they free their possessor from appalling discomfort and disease, and from futile preoccupations with his bodily functions. The trouble is that they are *not* common, not in any society as yet. They will not fulfill their mission until they become the normal equipment of all living.

A great many things, still rarer, must also become universal possessions before human life can proceed on its proper plane: a well-furnished mind; interesting, stimulating, creative work; emancipation from drudgery and a pleasant setting for daily life; leisure and recreation; freedom of movement, free exchange of thought; bodily health and mental equanimity; a sense of confidence in the future. A few people enjoy these advantages now: they should be attainable by all diligent and prudent men.

This kind of living may not be achieved in this age, in spite of its imminent feasibility. To accomplish it requires a continued, great, and uninterrupted expansion and improvement of our productive equipment, in the fields of wealth creation, transportation, exchange, communication, housing, education, health. It demands the removal of staggering quantities of debris, the wreckage of past abortive efforts now cluttering the mental and physical landscape, hampering our activities and warping our intentions. It depends on the creation of a rational order, convenience and rightness, so that the physical organization of life becomes a facile aid to mental freedom and a source of satisfaction instead of an irritation and a defeat. It depends, in short, on that reconstruction of our environment, in stability and peace, that we have been talking about from the beginning of this book.

If this reconstruction could be accomplished only through the loss of individual liberty it would not be worth attempting. Antisocial activities must be eliminated, but the field of constructive opportunity must be enlarged by a general polarization of endeavor. Greater freedom of action, broader scope for individual initiative, are among the major objectives of any rational effort, and to sacrifice them at the outset is to admit that our task is impossible before we start. Utopia by fiat is a contradiction in terms. Our better world will be built because men envision it, will it, unite without organization or compulsion to create it. Individual initiative cannot be sacrificed: it must be focused on a common end through individual acceptance of a common standard of rightness.

We have the means for the task already in our hands. For the first time in history the possibility of a good life for all men is conditioned only by our own discretion and intelligence in ordering our affairs, our energy and acumen in utilizing the tools we possess, our goodwill in defining our objectives. We have attempted here a tentative outline of the technique that must be applied to one important phase of the work— the phase of physical design. This would have been a too ambitious undertaking except for our deep conviction of the unity of all design— that we may learn from minor efforts how to accomplish major ones. The major efforts await our will. We believe we see this will clarifying, focusing, gathering up its mighty strength.

21. Housing and the New Society

Given the centrality of the concern for community and family and their survival in a machine age, it is not at all exceptional that those interested in what became increasingly known as "design for survival" should concentrate more and more attention on the key problem of housing. It was perhaps because in this field a whole array of major issues—economic, political, social, aesthetic, moral—became inexorably intertwined that discussions of the house itself and housing more generally became the focus of extended discussion, not only in professional journals but in a wide range of popular journals as well. The idea of the modern house with its technological improvements, its increased utilization of new gadgets and devices for ease and efficiency in the home led to obvious and significant changes in life-style; the modern kitchen alone created striking changes in family living and relationships within the family itself. And patterns of housing development were to have consequences politically and economically. This is why from its very beginnings *Fortune* devoted considerable space to systematic studies of these changes and their effects. (It offered a prize for articles on industrial design, including housing studies.)

One writer to win an early *Fortune* prize in this area was Catherine Bauer (1905–1964). Daughter of a New Jersey highway commissioner who instituted the first modern superhighways that bypassed major towns, and the wife of an able architect, she first pursued architectural studies at Cornell but later transferred to Vassar to continue more general studies. In 1930 she was associated with the Regional Planning Association and pursued additional studies, here and abroad, in planning and housing. Her book, *Modern Housing* (1934), is regarded as a classic in the field, a "study in the origins and methods and purposes of modern workers' housing."

Modernism: The House That Works
FORTUNE

Along about the year 1923 there was a building boom in the U.S. Citizens still alive remember quite clearly the sound of the riveting machines and the odor of wet cement. That building boom flourished to produce $13 daily in the pants pockets of the nation's carpenters, silk stockings on the knees of its masons' wives, automobiles ten deep in the vacant lots behind the construction jobs, and an all-time record in architectural ineptitude and uninventiveness. Generations will pass before the fashionable suburbs and the real estate developments of America are cleared of the false, faked, footling inconveniences erected to the glory of France or the glory of Spain or the glory of Isador Lefkowitz in the decade of the twenties.

Along about the year 1936 there will sprout in the U.S. a second building boom. It will probably be less of a boom than its predecessor. Its mother will be necessity, not the stock market. Its wage scales may be lower, its silk stockings skimpier, and it automobiles more battered than the wage scales, silk stockings, and automobiles of the decade before. But its architecture, by and large and with all proper allowance for the intransigence of millionaires and the caution of speculative real-estate developers, will surpass the architecture of the school of Coolidge. For the characteristic (though not necessarily the most common) architecture of the boom of the thirties (and the forties) will be inventive, not imitative, rational, not faked. The characteristic architecture of the thirties, in other words, will be Modern.

Why it will be Modern is a matter of some interest involving, first, a consideration of the meaning of the word. The word is best defined with reference to what it is *not*. Modernism is *not* an architectural style. Modernism is a basic idea. The content of that idea is this: a building, whether it be a dwelling or a factory or a post office, is a tool. That is to say, it is an instrument fabricated for a purpose. The one and only law of its being is that it should accomplish the purpose for which it exists. Everything else, including most specifically its appearance, is incidental to, and dictated by, its accomplishment of its purpose. Just as the shape of an ax, of a wrench, of a pitchfork, is fixed once and for all by the work it has to do, so the shape of a building is fixed once and for all by the work it has to do. And just as the shape of a tool will be more beautiful

"The House That Works," *Fortune* 12 (October 1935), pp. 59–65, 94.

as it approximates more nearly to a perfect appropriateness of its function, so the shape of a building will be more beautiful as it approximates
more nearly to perfect appropriateness. The corollary to this proposition
is, of course, that any attempt to prettify a building by applying to it
external, arbitrary decoration can only result in a falsification of its being.
Like the woman who brings to the useful loveliness of her hips the
adventitious bulbousness of a bustle, the well-built building which drapes
itself in Gothic cascades merely succeeds in looking artificial.

For all this there is a name, a slogan, and a history. The slogan came
first. It was the pronouncement of an unfashionable Chicago architect
named Louis Sullivan who worked in the first decades of steel construction. To Louis Sullivan, looking upon a naked girder and finding it
beautiful, it was revealed that "form follows function; function creates
form." From that phrase there was derived the name Functionalism by
which the movement came to be known in the studios. And for the
movement known as Functionalism there developed in America, over a
long generation, a meager history enlivened by the one great name of
Frank Lloyd Wright and illuminated by a very small amount of actual
building and a very great deal of talk.

The talk, because it has determined to a considerable extent the
popular impression of Functionalism, deserves a word in passing. Functionalism, like certain other movements in the arts, has suffered ironically
at the hands of its apostles. To Louis Sullivan the word was a fighting
word—a declaration of war upon the Paris-trained, Beaux-arty architects
of his generation and a declaration of faith in the tough, resourceful
engineering of the American shops. As time passed however the movement has been taken over by the very group at whom it was originally
aimed. It has been taken over by the drawing rooms and the dilettantes,
it has become a languid, salon topic for epigrammatic conversation, and
it has supplied a fashionable British playwright with a fashionable British
phrase. If Louis Sullivan, throwing his World's Fair Transportation
Building in the face of the fashionable world of the nineties, could hear
the voices which now apply Noel Coward's "Design for Living" to his
theories and his works he would stammer in the grave.

As for the actual buildings which now give Modernism form they are
far and few enough. There are, at the present time, no more than fifty
residences in the United States which show an honest and devoted
acceptance of the law of Louis Sullivan and these fifty are so scattered
over the country's two billion acres as to exert little if any concentrated
influence. The eastern states have a bare dozen: no more than four in
the entire city of New York. The West Coast has more, but the greatest
concentration (in the Los Angeles area) is barely twelve. Four only are
big enough to impress the impressionable with their size; the rest are

middle-sized or definitely small—the most recent and radical of the Los Angeles crop falling below $5000. As for the architects involved, they are even fewer than the houses. Wright is responsible for about a score of the fifty and the only other names to appear with any frequency are those of the Viennese, Richard J. Neutra, and the Swiss, William Lescaze.

In addition to the houses there are the office buildings. Or, rather, there are two office buildings. The popular belief that all large office buildings are Modern because they are all of recent construction has no basis in fact. Many skyscrapers are handsome, simple, and explicit but most are anything but Modern. The New York Central Building apologizes for its honest steel with a seventeenth-century gilt French roof. The Chicago Tribune Tower, like many a Chicago millionaire of the stockyards era, forgets its iron past in a false front of Gothic buttresses and romantic stones. The Bankers Trust Building in New York, like the Hollywood successors to the kings of beef, diverts attention from its rugged beginnings with a Roxyish roof of Babylonian inspiration. The Empire State, more up-to-date in its romanticisms, thrusts a silvered nipple at the sky in mute invitation to a Zeppelin which never comes. Only Howe and Lescaze's Philadelphia Saving Fund Society Building and Hood and Fouilhoux's McGraw-Hill Building in New York rigorously obey the Sullivan decrees. And only a few others like the Starrett-Lehigh Building of Cory and Cory in New York and the New York Daily News Building of Hood have valid secondary claims.

Beyond these major accomplishments there are perhaps a dozen theaters—the interior (but not the indistinguishable exterior) of Radio City Music Hall in New York, a few neighborhood houses, a handful of newsreel shows. There are three schools—Joseph Urban's New School for Social Research in New York and two country schools by Howe and Lescaze. There are four small clubs. There are perhaps two airports. And there is little else. With that unimpressive roster the record of Modern construction in America is complete.

Any man who undertakes to support the proposition that Modernism will dominate the next American boom has therefore two questions to answer. Why, if Modernism is inevitable, has Modernism made no more progress than it has? And why, if Modernism did not make progress in the boom of the twenties, is there any reason to suppose it will make progress now?

The answer to both questions is the same. Aeschylus framed it some centuries ago. It is this: "The voice of the People is a mighty voice." Artists may invent but the people choose. It is not enough that a new mode in music or a new purpose in architecture should be conceived. It is not enough even that it should be practiced. Before it can alter the life of a nation it must be accepted. And the people accept not when they might but when they please. Moreover the people accept according to their habits and in consonance with their nature.

Nothing could prove the point more neatly than a comparison of the European and the American experiences of Modernism in the years that followed the War. In Europe, as everyone knows, Modernism made spectacular advances. Here, as we have seen, it made next to none. The difference is not a difference in European and American architectural skill. The difference lies in the citizens. Both continents were faced with housing crises. In Europe, as a result of the prevalent postwar Socialism, the crisis was met on social terms. In this country, as a result of the traditional individualism of the people, it was met in individualistic terms. To the European states, with their minds set upon the improvement of the living conditions of the masses and particularly upon the provision of sunlight and air and recreational opportunities, Modernism was a gift from God: Modernism conceived of the house precisely in such terms. To America, with no such social objective, and with a problem definable in cubic feet and potential purchasers, Modernism had nothing whatever to say. The consequence was block after block of functional housing in Hamburg and precisely none in New York.

Europe, in other words, came to Modernism by way of political theory. America did not. And nothing that occurred during the following decade served to change the American point of view. Not even when Le Corbusier dubbed the functional house a "machine for living" was the American housebuilder stirred. The phrase intrigued him since he loved machines. But it intrigued him only as a metaphor. For in the early twenties—and therein lies the key to an understanding of the American attitude—very few Americans had learned to think of houses as machines or of machines as bearing any relation to houses. The machine, in the middle twenties, had not been domesticated. In 1924 the automatic refrigerator was a clumsy, noisy, and painfully expensive contraption which had driven the old-fashioned icebox out of relatively few homes. There were only 65,000 mechanical refrigerators in the country in that year as against 7,000,000 in 1934. In 1924 the oil burner was an experimental gadget not yet out of its awkward adolescence. There were 101,800 oil burners in the country in that year as against 879,900 ten years later. In 1924 air-conditioning was an innovation. Domestic installation was practically unknown and commercial installation reached considerable proportions only in 1928. The whole story is told by the figures which indicate that the average consumption of electricity in homes in 1924 was 378 kwh as against 631 in 1931. A Swiss author architect who called a home a machine for living in the first term of Calvin Coolidge was talking pure literature. The idea that the entire house might become a mechanized tool for living seemed purely fanciful. And lacking that idea there was nothing left of Modernism but its apparently arbitrary difference from traditional architecture.

The housebuilder of the twenties preferred what we still see about us —the imitation French *manoirs*, the half-timbered drugstores; all the sad, wistful, pathetically shoddy attempts of hundreds of thousands of honest American voters to prove (and how they proved it) their good taste.

But if the reasons for the failure of Modernism in the twenties are clear, the reasons for the probable success of Modernism in the thirties are even clearer. Indeed they are the same reasons underlined and in reverse. Between 1924 and 1934, as the figures cited above would indicate, the machine was domesticated in America. Not only that but the machine was domestically perfected. Men grew accustomed to the machine in their homes and in their garages and they grew accustomed to expecting more of the machine. Specifically they were accustomed by their automobiles to expect more in matters which they could not help but relate to their domestic experiences. Their automobiles, in the late twenties and early thirties, advanced amazingly in coachwork. They acquired doors which latched perfectly and easily, windows which opened and shut smoothly and without effort, ventilation which ventilated without drafts, dials and instruments which eliminated all useless decorations and stood out with greater beauty because they confessed their purpose. To a man who rides in a 1937 car the phrase "machine for living" is no longer literary metaphor. He already possesses a machine for living in transit—a tool of which the principal parts are increasingly designed with a view to efficient operation.

Briefly what has happened in the last decade is this. The various domesticated machines like the automatic oil heater, the automatic electric refrigerator, the all but automatic electric stove and washing machine, the automatic air-conditioning machine, together with all the lesser mechanical gadgets which have bred in the home, have predisposed urban Americans to think of the domestic services as primarily mechanical and as properly handled by automatic or semiautomatic devices. And at the same time the automobile with its perfected coachwork and ingenious controls of ventilation and light has predisposed them to expect of the shell of the house an efficiency in operation and a suitability to purpose which their fathers, struggling with the clumsy wooden window frames of the nineteenth century, never permitted themselves to think about. In combination the two influences have operated to prepare the minds of the citizens for the engineering of their houses and the reconstruction of their shelter in terms of workability. And minds so prepared are prepared for Modernism.

It may be objected that neither of these considerations, concerned as both of them are with gadgetry, has much to do with architectural taste and that neither of them is weighty enough to affect the living habits of a great people. As to the second objection, all that can be said is that a great people changes its habits in its own way and that the Americans are much more apt to change their homes to match their machines than they are to change their homes to match their politics. Modernism in Europe is largely gadgetless (a functional shell without functional works) because Europe came to its Modernism socially and politically. Modernism in America will be full of gadgets because Modernism in America will be the gadget's child. The difference is racial, not moral. As to the first objection, the complete and satisfactory answer is that although gadgetry may have nothing to do with architectural taste it has everything to do with Modernism. A housebuilder who approaches his problem from the point of view of the efficient operation of that house as a congeries of machinery—who builds his house in imagination from the air-conditioning system outward to the roof—is already halfway to Modernism. It merely remains for him to learn that floors, walls, chairs, exposure, etc., are as important to efficient operation as window frames, door jambs, and heat control. And to take, thereupon, the final intellectual leap which lands him in Louis Sullivan's arms: "Let her look like what she is."

That final leap has one considerable hurdle to clear: the hurdle of habit. The average American, however predisposed in 1930-odd to treat his house as a machine, still nourished his doubts about the modern "style." Ten years ago those doubts were mountainous. The flat roof, the boxlike shoulders, the bare façades were not at all what he had meant by "house." Today, however, owing to an assortment of causes, the doubts have shrunk. First and foremost among those causes must be listed the Paris Exposition of 1925. It it highly doubtful whether a more meretricious exposition was ever held on this earth than the Paris Exposition of 1925. It was an exposition of the "modernistic." The "modernistic" is the Modern deprived of its manhood and perverted into decoration. The effect since 1925 of the "modernistic" has been prodigious. It has swept the world. It styled the *Ile de France* and forestyled the *Normandie*. It filled the foyers of New York hotels and skyscrapers. It got into glassware and lipstick holders. It affected store fronts and restaurant counters. It altered advertising and the packaging of vegetables. It deformed automobiles. It riddled the drug business. It changed hats. It was a fad, a falsehood, and a bitter laugh. But it served a purpose. By discouraging the average man with everything it prepared the average man for anything. Having once seen the queer, meaningless geometric shapes which idle fashion imposed on his wife's dinner table he could no longer be shocked by the queer but meaningful geometric shapes which logical architecture imposed upon his friend's house.

And by the time the movies went modernistic his defenses were down. If the inevitable symbol of female smartness, whether in gangster's moll, banker's wife, or novelist's mistress, was a bed without posts, a chair without feet, and a mirror without a frame, then American antiques and Louis Quinze imitations were valueless and a man must swim with the rest. The only difficulty at that point was the expensiveness of the swimming. For some years after the Paris Exposition the designing of modernistic interiors had fallen into the hands of style profiteers and art exploiters who turned out their precious simplicities like objects of *grand luxe*. But with time even the obstacle of cost has been removed. Grand Rapids makes modernistic beds as cheaply as Colonials. And as for the real thing, the Modern, which the modernistic apes, prices there are well below the level of period work. A Modern house may be built for about thirty per cent less than a comparable house in a traditional style.

The Paris Exposition of 1925 prepared the way for Modern architecture by preparing the eye for stranger sights. Other influences operated more directly. There is no occasion in this article to investigate the secret life of the American soul over the last decade but there can be little doubt in anyone's mind but that the American soul has traveled far. It has lost a number of conventional garments on the way. As a result of the snatching and tearing of H. L. Mencken and Sinclair Lewis and their likes, the American soul no longer goes arrayed in conventional notions of morality and conduct. It has put on, in place of these capes and veils, a covering which serves it well and which Louis Sullivan would have approved—the covering of workability. If there are no moral laws then let love be governed by pragmatic sanctions. If there are no æsthetic laws then let women's clothes be easy. Obviously, to a soul thus bedizened, Modern architecture, which sets workability as its first principle, must be a sympathetic object.

It is not necessary however to indulge in philosophic speculation in order to suggest that the American soul is more amenable to Modernism than it was. One has only to consider the patent and obvious fact that America, in the last decade, has discovered the sun. And to recollect that nothing about the Modern house, with its flat roofs and its broad glass, is more characteristic than its sunworthiness. The discovery of the delights of sunbathing dates from the last decade. It had become necessary before the depression began to legislate against excessive human exposure on the beaches north of Boston and east of New York City. Farmers in rigid Franklin County, Massachusetts, began to appear in their fields, and later on the roads, with their shirts off before the thirties were well under way. Ladies took sun baths on the cindery roofs of New York hotels while Hoover was still President. And as time has passed the passion for sunlight has further increased. There is hardly a road west of Amarillo, Texas, which will not yield at least one maiden in eight-inch shorts and brassière on a dusty summer afternoon.

But it is not alone in terms of influence and possibilities that the future of Modernism must be discussed. There are the straws which show that a wind is already blowing. One such was the late Century of Progress Exposition in Chicago. The Exposition buildings were not Modern throughout: they did not even include the work of America's foremost Modernist Frank Lloyd Wright. They were not purely functional. But they were frankly and simply exposition buildings, they were adequately adapted to their purposes, and some of them were beautiful. Another was the great General Electric Architectural Competition of 1935. Over 2000 architects from all parts of the U.S. submitted designs for this contest. Neither in the rules nor in the known preferences of the sponsor was there anything to indicate that functional houses would be preferred. And yet over half the entries avoided period design, one Grand Prize went to a house clearly embodying Modern principles, the other went to a Modern house with southern modifications, three of the four first prizes went to plans without period implications, one second prize was a radically Modern solution of the problem, two second prizes might be labeled "progressive," eighteen of the forty honorable mentions were frankly Modern, and only ten were in open period style. Moreover a number of these plans have since been built for house owners, and about twenty-five per cent of the plans thus constructed are Modern.

Beyond, and in support of, these indications there is one final consideration which any man interested in the problem must bear in mind. If prefabrication of houses is ever to come it must come in terms of Modernism because only the Modern, functional house lends itself to prefabrication. That is to say, only the Modern functional house with its flat roofs, bare walls, and absence of adornment can be cut up into standard shapes for easy reassembly on the job. The consequence is that success in prefabrication would necessarily mean an architectural revolution. Some years ago in a series of articles on housing, *Fortune* referred to the building industry as the industry which the industrial revolution forgot. It is not without interest to consider that if the industrial revolution eventually arrives in that industry, and if it arrives in terms of prefabrication, it will accomplish by mere technical necessity what the theorists of architecture were unable during thirty years to bring about.

Slums Aren't Necessary

CATHERINE BAUER

For decades "housing" has been urged by small groups of Americans, occasionally with a concrete program, more often as a vague but somehow essential adjunct to the Good Life. Their cause seemed for long to be making no progress whatever. Today, however, after four years of the depression, it has gained a multitude of converts—though at the moment the Good Life as a reason for good housing seems to have been superseded by a whole battery of other purposes. Economists, both conservative and otherwise, urge "housing" as a means of providing emergency employment and as one of the few potentially self-liquidating forms of Public Works. Cities and various sections of the financial interest see in it a chance to rehabilitate economically blighted urban areas. Architects and engineers are inclined to feel that housing is their one glimmer of hope in a drab future. A sizable group of big-time industrialists is fascinated with the notion that the prefabricated dwelling might, like the automobile industry after the war, provide an entirely new boom market to exploit. Romantic reactionaries hail it as a means of putting restless urban unemployed safely "back on the land" in hand-made homesteads with vegetable gardens. A few of the more forward-looking see in government-assisted community housing a real tool for regional planning and industrial recentralization. Still others, not so vocal, perhaps, see in it new sources for municipal graft.

This chaos is accurately mirrored in the recent history of our official housing policy. Introduced in the first place primarily as an emergency measure to provide employment and not as a housing policy *per se* at all, it has tended to get steadily more and more enmeshed in various side issues. The avowed purpose, originally fairly constructive and ambitious, has been pared down and compromised until now it appears to be little more than a halfhearted desire to tear down a few central slums, but only if this can be done without hurting anyone's feelings or really changing anything important.

The simple fact which underlay even the most special agitation still stands: all the old methods of providing houses for people of average income or less have miserably failed. There is a whole shelf of recent literature for proof, and a whole gallery of exhibitions and charted

Catherine Bauer, "Slums Aren't Necessary," *The American Mercury*, 31 (March 1934), pp. 296–305. [I have omitted considerable material relating to housing developments in Europe.—Ed.]

surveys for evidence. Briefly stated, it all amounts to the same thing. The average new dwelling has been steadily growing more expensive, more wasteful, and less adequate to the real needs of the individual, the family, the city and the nation. The combined efforts of speculative builders, building and loan associations, and individuals building for themselves cannot supply a new dwelling at a price which even half the population can pay. And such buildings as they do construct are for the most part either built-in slums, or so badly laid out and constructed as to constitute an incipient "blighted area" from the start. The net result is that the American standard of living today, even in times of "prosperity," is one of the lowest in the Western world with respect to light, air, facilities for group living, and even basic sanitation.

Moreover, quite a large number of people have begun to realize that there is a better way to do things—that the jostling small builders and the front-foot lots and the miserable straggling suburbs and the ideology of individual Home Ownership must go. And in their place must come a technique for building complete communities, designed and administered as functional units and constructed by large-scale methods. And finally, that only governments can make the decisive step.

Any orthodox radical could explain in five minutes exactly why good modern housing at low rentals cannot conceivably be achieved, even on an experimental scale, in the capitalist chaos. And, looking around at the current and apparently insoluble contradictions, one is almost inclined to believe it. Nevertheless, it *has* been done. In England and Germany and Holland and Austria alone—not to mention many other European countries—there are today at least four million new dwellings which are essentially modern in plan and community layout, and better in every important respect than almost all the dwellings ever erected in this country, and which are rented to people who have never before been able to afford a new or a decent home.

It may be well to recognize first of all that the heritage of most European cities is not fundamentally very different from that of our own. They all had the same period of bustle and growth after the industrial revolution, and the vast majority of their buildings were erected under conditions of land speculation, exploitive competition, small-scale enterprise, and aimless centralization identical with conditions here.

What we may call the nineteenth-century environment (though it is still dominant in America) was a truly "international style." Its distinguishing characteristics were dirt, congestion, disorder, and waste, all overlaid with a film of empty and frustrated pretentions. Its archeology is the classification of slums, and its focal point is a railroad station surrounded by tenements, smokestacks, and beetling facades. Whole regions were squeezed into a gridiron network regardless of geography or any other science, and carved up into salable front feet, into twelve- to twenty-foot lots, into solid blocks of tenements, into an ugliness and tastelessness never before produced with such relentless energy on the face of the earth.

True, the nineteenth century had its Romantic reaction. A steady stream of the more adventurous individuals kept moving to the outskirts, into straggling villas and bungalows, there to raise a small piece of green lawn and perhaps a few cabbages, if not, or not for long, to contemplate the primeval. But for the most part the inhabitants of the By-Law Streets and the Old and New Law tenements and the grim respectable suburbs, clipped their vague desires to the shape of their condition, and concentrated on more pressing matters. The typical figure of the nineteenth century is nothing if not busy. As for the admitted slum dwellers, the submerged half or two-thirds of the population, they remained exactly where they were (only more crowded), paying a little more rent for a trifle more dilapidated quarters, and without benefit of even the most fleeting notion of escape.

So much for the cosmopolitan environment of the nineteenth century. It continued in full force on both continents, with merely a few interior improvements for the upper classes, straight through until the world war. But then there is a cleavage. In America the old pattern still went on, merely adding unto itself more expensive gadgets and a heavier burden of waste. Skyscrapers, subways, and sprawling speculative suburbs— these have all served merely to intensify the congestion, to speed up the cycle of blight and bankruptcy, and to make even the bad new dwellings too expensive for all but a small minority.

But in Europe, for one reason or another, there has been a real break with the past. The hiatus in all civil construction during the war brought on a critical shortage as soon as the war was over. And the shortage was met, not as in America by applying artificial respiration to the old building agencies, but by developing an entirely new housing technique on an entirely new hypothesis.

Even the most casual traveler in Europe during the past half-dozen years must have noticed some signs of the change, some evidence of a new layer of civilized environment essentially as different from the typical nineteenth-century background as that was from the eighteenth or even the fifteenth. The city centers themselves, bulwarks though they are of the old order of things, show considerable evidence here and there of this new deposit. In all continental towns there are gleaming glass-and-metal department stores, airy ungilded cafés, handsome new post offices, subway stations, art galleries, and shops. Here and there are expensive hotels and apartment houses dedicated to *licht, luft, und öffnung*. And already our American traveler, with his weakness for classification, has learned to call these buildings "modern."

But the new stratum goes deeper than this. It is no mere surface style, tacked on to the sacred rigmarole which reads Louis Treize, Louis Quatorze, Louis Quinze, Biedermeyer, and so on. It is no mere matter of facades—of ornament or lack of ornament, of window and door arrangement, of symmetry or asymmetry—nor yet of materials and manner of construction. Indeed, a large proportion of this newest layer of environment is quite lacking in the more obvious tags of "modernism."

But, looking out of the window as the train approaches Frankfurt or Karlsruhe or London or Rotterdam or Vienna—or, better still, looking down from an airplane (for the railroad has made its own environment and most trunk lines do not provide ideal modern housing sites along their banks), this traveler must have noticed something obviously quite new and not explicable on any of the old terms. Here were residential communities that were orderly, but not mechanical like the By-Law streets or the gridiron blocks; neat and regular and obviously "planned," but neither grandiose like the Renaissance avenues nor grim like the factory villages; spacious and putting the site to its fullest use, but not faked "picturesque" like the romantic zig-zags prescribed in the City Beautiful era.

The best of them show not only "taste" but positive aesthetic form, though without any evidence of individual display, or of competition between individual dwellings. Our traveler may also have seen parks which were neither "classic" nor "romantic," nor yet merely high-pressure playgrounds, and schools and churches and shops and vegetable gardens and perhaps a few factories which clearly formed organic parts, both aesthetically and usefully, of the communities in which they were located.

All of these phenomena belong in one way or another to the postwar housing movement, which has already left its mark across the face of Europe. Modern housing is much more than houses, and that is one reason why the results of the movement even now point to an entirely new layer of civilization. For the technique of modern housing implies a whole new conception of human environment, beginning with land and sun and air, and extending—in purpose at least—to include the daily routine of the last working-class housewife. And, although the results vary enormously in character and degree of success, its achievements are already so considerable that in England and Holland and Germany and Austria, at least, one housewife out of every six or seven may be said to be living within the new pattern, her routine, and the health and happiness of her family, influenced by the new standards.

Six or seven million new dwellings have been constructed in northern

Europe since the war, most of them during the past decade, most of them for the lower-income half of the population, and almost every one completely different from anything produced in the nineteenth century.

It is not merely that the dwelling standard of one class of people has been hauled up a few notches nearer the next most privileged group, and the bill grudgingly underwritten by the taxpayers. Far more important than any mere scaling-up within the old pattern is the fact that the average working-class cottage or flat of the past ten years has certain built-in qualities which even the upper middle-class residence of before the war rarely achieved. And the community of which this average new dwelling is a part offers a permanent amenity which the richest house builder would hardly have known how to command.

Do not mistake me. I do not mean merely bathtubs and electricity. I mean sun and air and outlook and convenience and facilities for recreation. I mean compact planning and scientific construction which lessens the burden of housekeeping and house-maintaining. I mean a kind of neighborhood layout and control which forever prevents blight—or boom —from descending on one section at the expense of the other sections. And I mean entirely new building forms, growing, on the one hand, out of the new standards and materials and methods and functions, and related on the other just as clearly to that quickening and renewal of aesthetic sensibility which we call "modern" in the best twentieth-century painting and sculpture and photography. A new human environment! . . .

How was it done? How was it possible for chaotic, bankrupt, unstable postwar Europe to have a great era of building? Obviously the actual mechanics—political, legal, financial, technical—cannot be dealt with here, but some of the fundamental premises are not difficult to state. In the first place, housing in Europe has become a *public utility*. The right to live in a decent dwelling has taken its place among what Sydney Webb calls the National Minima—the right to good and abundant water, to sanitation, to adequate fire and police protection, to the use of paved and lighted roads, to education, to a certain amount of medical care, and, in most European countries, to various forms of social insurance against illness, unemployment and old age.

Now the corollary to this is that, if dwellings of a certain minimum standard are not and cannot be provided for all individuals by their own or other private efforts, the responsibility devolves upon the community as a whole, or the state or some other public authority. And, as a matter of fact, practically the entire output of low-cost housing in Europe since the war has been achieved through the direct assistance and regulation of governments. Governmental assistance has taken two general forms: one investment, and the other subsidy. The principle behind such assistance has been about as follows: money is loaned on duly approved projects, at a rate just high enough to cover the cost of the money to the government. If this does not make it possible to charge rents low enough for those who need the housing, the government further offers a subsidy, either in interest rebates or in outright cash, or perhaps in the form of free land or tax-exemption. Municipal land-purchase policies have played a very important part in the whole movement as also have social insurance funds. Government regulation is designed to insure high standards and the safety of the public investment.

The actual constructing and owning agencies have been, in the main, either the local authorities themselves or one form or another of non-profit housing society. In some cases, and with due control, private builders have been assisted as well.

Naturally, it has been an essential interest of the governments—and of the public at large—that such housing investment should be financially as sound as possible—infinitely sounder than any ordinary speculative project has ever been or ever could be. The houses had not only to be economically constructed and laid out, but had to be proof against all forms of insidious blight and decay, and had to be planned in efficient relation to the rest of the city organism—for the future as well as the present.

Out of this fact grew the second fundamental axiom in the technique of modern housing: the *community unit*. In order to take full advantage of mass-production methods, in order to provide all necessary equipment as economically and efficiently as possible, and most important of all, in order to insure permanent amenity and economy, the complete neighborhood was adopted as the minimum unit for planning, construction and management. The result is that there is not a single old-fashioned gridiron street layout in any modern housing development in Europe: streets are organically planned for definite and permanently differentiated use, not for releasing salable front feet for speculation.

Another result of the neighborhood planning unit is—modern architecture. An aesthetic of architectural design has' developed which frankly makes use of standardized units, which makes a positive virtue of precision and simplicity and economy, and which is able to consider the group as an organic whole instead of as an infinite series of individually competitive structures. An aesthetic of design solidly based on economics, technology, and human functions, instead of a veneer applied afterwards if you can afford to show off, it is the first vernacular of domestic design since the eighteenth century which is really entitled to be called "architecture." Perhaps it is the first one since the Middle Ages whose implications are organic and complete.

"Functionalism" has been a popular descriptive term for the new forms

—and it is as good as any one-dimensional slogan ever succeeds in being. . . .

But behind all this—behind the legislation, the public control, the subsidies, the planning technique, even the modern architecture—was, not philanthropic "reform" and not surface politics, but as practical and realistic a piece of subconscious collective reasoning as any that modern history can show—perhaps the *only* one of the past ten or fifteen years. One might paraphrase it, with some temerity, about as follows:

Bad houses are a public evil. They create enormous and unproductive public expense through endless battling against disease, crime, dirt, ugliness, fire, degeneracy, waste. They undermine any possible prosperity by making potentially intelligent workers either inefficient or criminal, and by turning people who might have been merely relatively inefficient into paupers and public charges.

Nine-tenths at least of a city is devoted to living quarters. If the dwellings are bad, the city is bad. If the dwellings are wastefully constructed, chaotically laid out, unrelated to the city organism, ugly, and too expensive for the people who must live in them, then it is the community as a whole that is penalized and eventually bankrupted thereby. The Blighted Area, that spreading insidious disease which is gradually ruining most cities on both sides of the Atlantic, is directly due to planless construction, to neighborhoods which can deteriorate almost overnight, because they were designed for quick individual profits and not for efficient use.

Hardly a single really decent dwelling for the average person, except under very special circumstances, was erected during the entire century up to the war. All of these substandard dwellings were the product of either the individual building for his own use, or the speculative builder seeking speedy profits. Both of these agencies, as far as average shelter for the average citizen is concerned, have nothing but a history of progressive failure to show for their efforts.

Their failure is inherent and not accidental. Neither restrictive legislation (building codes, zoning laws, etc.) nor "reform" (by individual philanthropists, cooperative experiments, well-meaning industrialists and the like) have proved in the least successful. History shows that such remedial measures usually end by merely producing a new kind of slum (for example, the New Law tenement in New York, the By-Law street in London). Efforts to relieve congestion and get around exorbitant land values—subways, skyscrapers, spreading suburbs—have only intensified the speculation and increased the area and degree of congestion.

The individual home builder failed because a custom-made house with a Machine-Age standard of equipment and service is an economic anachronism—a luxury, like a custom-made automobile or an individually tailored refrigerator, that none but the wealthiest can afford.

The speculative builder failed because he got caught in a vicious circle. His insistence on quick returns (and he had to have them, for no one could judge ten years ahead what was likely to happen to any given section of a city) produced a shoddy product. This made financing costs excessively high, which in turn put the cost of even the bad dwelling out of reach of all but a very small minority of the population—until it had deteriorated below any standard of decency.

Both the individual home builder and the speculative builder failed because of the high land costs resulting from their own greed, and because a modern dwelling is not in any sense a self-sufficient unit, physically, economically, or any other way. A man's house can no longer be his castle, complete with moat and drawbridge. The success or failure of a dwelling depends essentially on its relation to a thousand other buildings, to hundreds of different service lines, to streets and parks and open country and the whole social organism.

But (and here was the real stroke of creative genius in this process of subconscious reasoning) *bad dwellings are not an unavoidable necessity.* Something can be done about it. If an age which knows as much as this one does about the economies of large-scale production, about hygiene and convenience and amenity, about human habits and the nature of cities, cannot produce a good inexpensive dwelling in pleasant surroundings for everybody, then it has reached a strange and tragic impasse indeed.

But there must be a complete break with past methods. The modern problem is so complicated, the necessary controls and planning techniques so integral in the whole social pattern, that private efforts cannot be expected to solve it alone. The entire future of our cities and our states depends on the method which we now set up to deal with housing and its related problems. The responsibility, and the initiative, must come from the public as a whole. And with the proper controls over land and location and planning and financing, it is cheaper to build good houses than bad ones.

Thus realistically was the first step taken. And when certain possible side effects were pointed out to them—such as the depreciation of central real-estate values, the dampening of private initiative or the decline of individual home-ownership—those who followed the process of subconscious reasoning did not allow themselves to be readily swayed into compromise. Instead, they looked at their new houses, found them remarkably good on the whole, and decided that compromises and readjustments would better come from the other side.

In this way, while surface politics and international economics have been almost solely occupied with this or that shifting of power within the old scheme of things, with pegging old values and reinforcing negative defenses, the new technique of housing and land planning has slowly begun to create new values, new purposes for politics and for social struggles, even for revolutions.

Within fifteen years, European housing has evolved from chaos to some semblance of science, from "reform" to at least a promise of New Form, from remedial restrictions to positive construction, from slum panaceas and pauper philanthropy to a practical working standard of modern environment for everybody.

However, if there has been any implication that the housing problem has actually been *solved* in Europe, or that it can be solved under present circumstances, it must be hastily disposed of. A few million dwellings are merely a drop in the bucket. And when one considers that a large number of these are still too expensive for unskilled workers, and that all houses good or bad are too expensive for the unemployed, and that the vast field of regional and economic planning of which housing is merely one small department has barely been scratched, one must admit that the accomplishment is small indeed by contrast with the need. Moreover, the various labor and social-democratic governments which were largely responsible for the most active housing policies are for the most part quite dead, as a result of their flabby stupidities in other fields. What even the immediate future holds in store no one can say.

But still, there it is for all to see, a new standard of human environment, and a new way to achieve it. And, although it is not true that any government which could carry through a modern housing policy would be *ipso facto* a good government, it is certainly true that any government which cannot do so is a reactionary and antisocial one.

22. The World
of Tomorrow

No more self-conscious "document" ever existed to demonstrate forcefully the effort to create a culture on the basis of the Great Technology than the World's Fair that opened in Flushing Meadows in 1939. Optimistic in the midst of depression that a new and yet democratic culture could be created with the aid of science and modern technology, a distinguished group of planners, designers, sociologists, architects, social theorists, public administrators met in the winter of 1935–1936 to propose a plan for The Fair of the Future. Their proposal was in large measure carried through when the Fair came into being during the dark days that were to see the European continent plunged into war. The Fair not only demonstrated what the World of Tomorrow might be; it served as a means of educating visitors to the Fair, indeed *preparing* them for the new world the designers and planners hoped to bring about. It was a Fair with a precise social theme; it was a symbolic attempt to bring about a consciousness of key social values that might well lead to a transformation of American culture by a commitment to these new values. Creating for the public a "Democrocity" as a key new social, economic, political, and cultural form, the Fair in its official literature argued for "unity without uniformity." The Fair itself was to be "a machine for display"; its product, a new set of social attitudes and understanding. Some of this is spelled out in even clearer detail by Robert D. Kohn, active in the field of public housing, who served as Chairman of the Fair's Committee on Theme and as a member of the Board of Design.

Social Ideals in a World's Fair

ROBERT D. KOHN

Many of us have been bored by endless praise of the wonders of mechanical inventions, lauded for their contributions to unity and peace in the world. Time is annihilated; consequently, peoples are no longer kept apart by difficulties of communication. The foreigner is no longer the man who lives on the other side of the mountain, as a century ago. Misunderstandings can no longer arise between individuals, between groups of people or nations who now get into touch with one another so easily.

All this, however, appears to be hopeless nonsense at this time of the world's distress. No one questions the opportunities for progress in human relations which science offers to man, but to congratulate ourselves because of the results of their use is blinding ourselves to the truth. And our failure to understand other nations only two seconds distant is no more noticeable (if more dramatic) than is my ignorance of what motivates the opinions and actions of the man upstairs or out on the farm, who is working at something different than I.

We have all heard of factory workers who growl about the farmers' constant wails for help. Why don't they take care of themselves? Why must the city pay to help them out? And, similarly, I have heard a Nebraska farmer curse the city as an aggregation of Wall Street gamblers—leeches on the hard-working agriculturalist. There is, of course, an unavoidable relation between the welfare of the workers of both classes. They simply do not know that they cannot escape it. The mason goes about his work, indifferent to what the steel erector has done and he cares little, in turn, for the carpenter's problems or the latter of the electrician's; each looks out for his own kind. Another kind of technician has to coordinate their work. The functional isolation of each craft from the others is complete.

Yet people say that we know one another better than in the days when communication and travel were difficult! The trouble lies in the fact that as these facilities increase and our contacts become more universal, the freedom based on self-sufficiency has to give way to a new freedom based on understanding cooperation of many functions—an independence to be worked out in full recognition of our interdependence.

It was a recognition of the immediate importance of presenting this

Robert D. Kohn, "Social Ideals in a World's Fair," *The North American Review*, 247 (March 1939), pp. 115–120.

idea as the basis of a forward-looking rather than a retrospective fair that moved the directors of the 1939 New York World's Fair to approve a "World of Tomorrow" theme. There is so much necessary publicity about the magnitude of any coming world's fair that the public can hardly be made to believe that a serious social purpose can permeate both the plan and the execution of what is, after all, a colossal business venture. The celebration of an historical event (in this case the 150th anniversary of the assumption of the Presidency by George Washington) and the national and international trade objectives are taken for granted. But from the start of this particular project it appeared to us that the time had come when so great an expenditure of work and money must justify itself by something more than a vainglorious exhibition of the mechanical achievements of a century and a half. The economic and political distress of the present day suggested rather that we orient ourselves toward the future and ask ourselves, "What way do we go from here?" We would do something toward progress if we recognized our mechanical blessings as tools whose use we have not yet learned.

What we designers started off with was to ask ourselves, "How can we make the average visitor to the Fair realize the import of some of the serious thought of the day?" The world of progressive social ideas is ordinarily restricted, in print, to editorial columns and the pages of magazines and weeklies rarely ever looked at by ninety per cent of our citizens. What an opportunity a fair might have to present dynamically some of these ideas to millions of "men in the street." We are always showing them things in isolated categories. Why not exhibit the forces that connect them—the living ideas that alone make things useful or harmful?

Accordingly, the Fair designers could not divide it into such categories as science, art, agriculture, manufactures—the classic divisions of fairs for centuries. That would only perpetuate divisions convenient for technicians but not illuminating to laymen. We chose to make our major divisions more or less functional, the things with which the average man comes in contact in his everyday life—food, shelter, clothing, communications, education, transportation, etc. What is more, instead of isolating science and art, the planners would attempt to show them permeating all of these other things, as illustrations of their interpenetration into the functions of modern life.

At the entrance to each sector, there is to be a noncommercial "focal" or "key" exhibit illustrating to modern man its import, its connections with other sectors and the contributions to social service which it renders. As an illustration, the key exhibit in the Food Sector can show how the country family of a century ago was almost independent of urban activities. Living on a farm it had helpful cooperation from neighbors but, with the exception of books and luxuries, its members were able to produce almost everything needed—clothing, food, transportation, shelter, and light. Moreover, because of its manifold activities the home afforded all the necessary training in the arts that were needed, while the contacts with the neighboring community made for the human relations that were part of the economic and political scene.

Today, by contrast, whether the family lives in mansion or tenement house, the immediate neighborhood means nothing. A small part of one function is performed by each worker in the family, but everything else comes from some far distant point or is done for it by people the family does not know. The supplies for the simplest breakfast come to the family from a dozen sources—the milk on the doorstep from a farm a hundred miles away, the bread from wheat grown a thousand miles away, the pepper from the Far East. An infinite number of people near and far and marvelous mechanical appliances serve the family, so that instead of the 16-hour day's work which was required from each worker to sustain the family we are freed to the extent of 8 hours. But for what? The Key Exhibit asks the question and attempts to give the answer, but it also asks if men are aware that the new freedom requires for its perpetuation a recognition of the involved community of interests which makes it possible.

This broad purpose was described to Mr. H. G. Wells during his visit some months ago, after he had made a tour of the grounds. He was told that we had attempted an arrangement based on function—that we wanted the Fair to mean something understandable to the man who is ordinarily indifferent to serious discussion; and that the apparent isolation of science, art, commerce, and agriculture would disappear in our plan. "In the modern world," we explained, "science is everywhere— commerce is everywhere—art should be in everything. These things for the layman cannot be isolated. They must be shown as interpenetrating. Why not, therefore, provide exhibits in categories that mean something to this average man—shelter, clothing, food, communication, transportation, production, and distribution? If we can only make the average citizen understand that back of every practical application of science to his everyday needs, there is a world of nonobjective research; men digging away at the discovery of some new truth without any idea of its immediate or remote application—if that could be done in the field of science, for instance, how much more willing would legislatures be to support pure research." He was told that we are by no means trying to mirror what he had done in his books, namely to picture the actual form of the world of tomorrow; that any attempt at a physical portrayal of such an ideal would be a mistake. The designers of the Fair this year are only trying to show the average visitor what things are available to him and, above all, what ideas and forces are at work which he should recognize as potential tools with which he, with his fellow men, would build it.

Mr. Wells praised these objectives. "In what I have just heard there is more commonsense than has been spoken in my presence for many a year."

The most striking, perhaps, of the many illustrations of the Fair's theme will be found in a dramatic exhibit being built into the great Perisphere at the center of the project. The spectator will find himself on one of the two galleries which gradually revolve as they move the visitor from the entrance to the exit. As he is moved around he will be looking down on a panorama showing an imaginary settlement of the immediate future formed by a group of settlements. Immediately below will be a city with its centers of culture, education, and government. In the near distance, yet separated by belts of green, will be satellite settlements devoted to manufacturing, mining, milling, shipping, and other industries, each of these with suitable housing for its workers and management. In the further distance, almost at the horizon, he will see the areas of farm and cattle-raising country. Between all of these will be the suggestion of road and transport interconnections. The aim is an illustration of the fact that the city is producing many necessaries for the farmer and the farmer for the city, and that each of the areas of the new integrated life is dependent on all of the others for the welfare of the individuals engaged in any one of the functions that comprise it.

To what extent these ideas will impress Fair visitors remains to be seen. Whatever may be the success of the attempt to do more than produce an exciting exposition of international scope, it will repay the effort even if a modest percentage of the millions of visitors get an inkling of the basic democratic idea which has inspired much of the project—the idea of illustrating in a popular way a vision of an approach toward economic and political peace.

23. The Social Scientist and the Social Order

It was not only the industrial designer who moved from the factory and machine shop to practice his trade in a larger social arena; the industrial psychologist, too, proposed ways in which his skills and knowledge might be applicable in the solution of larger-scaled social problems. During the first world war and after, an increasing number of social scientists had been called upon by industrial management to help them find solutions to the problems they faced—problems of human relations and organization—within the new productive systems of mass machine-line industry. One of the most famous experiments instituted for these reasons was conducted in the 1920's at the Hawthorne Works of Western Electric and one of the leading research social scientists there was a Professor of Industrial Research from the Harvard Business School, Elton Mayo (1880–1947).

Called into the Hawthorne Works to investigate, initially, the problem of fatigue which affected production, he soon found himself dealing more generally with questions of boredom, a common problem of the new industrial order, and what amounted to the question of morale. Morale was, in fact, becoming a word of more and more significance; by the time of the second world war the maintenance of high morale and techniques to achieve this were to be key social issues; the whole depression-war experience had made quite clear the problem of psychological attitudes essential to the stability of the social system itself. Mayo's studies and those of others at Hawthorne and elsewhere (most of these published throughout the 1930's) convinced him of the importance of human relations in achieving successful social systems whether that be a factory or a nation. It convinced him too that science could be applied by skilled and trained practitioners to enable social conflicts to be avoided or resolved through effective counseling; thus the problem of morale could be handled by skillfully adjusting men and situations within the system and the attention given to individual men could itself provide a new sense of worth and position within the order. When he came to give the famous lectures that formed the basis of *The Human Problems of an Industrial Civilization* he felt quite willing to suggest the meaning of his inquiries for areas outside the confines of the small social system of a factory.

The Problems of the Administrator

ELTON MAYO

The industrial inquiry nevertheless makes clear that the problems of human equilibrium and effort are not completely contained within the area controlled by factory organization and executive policy. Certain of the sources of personal disequilibrium, and especially the low resistance to adverse happenings in the ordinary workroom, must be attributed to the developing social disorganization and consequent *anomie* which is in these days typical of living conditions in or near any great industrial center. This developing *anomie* has changed the essential nature of every administrative problem—whether governmental or industrial. It is no longer possible for an administrator to concern himself narrowly with his special function and to assume that the controls established by a vigorous social code will continue to operate in other areas of human life and action. All social controls of this type have weakened or disappeared—this being symptomatic of the diminished integrity of the social organism. The existing situation, both within the national boundaries and as between nations, demands therefore that special attention be given to restatement of the problem of administration as the most urgent issue of the present. . . .

It must, however, be confessed that leaders of society the world over have shown very little perspicacity or foresight in the present serious crisis. It is "as if" the necessary "circulation" of administrators of which Pareto speaks had been interrupted. Brooks Adams, writing in 1913, prophesied the advent of just such a crisis. He points out that a modern society can hope to maintain a stable equilibrium in the midst of rapid change only by ensuring that it has amongst its administrators (of both types—governmental and nongovernmental) a sufficient number who possess "a high order of generalizing mind—a mind which can grasp a multitude of complex relations—but," he adds, "this is a mind which can, at best, only be produced in small quantity and at high cost." He proceeds to claim that our educational system has not sufficiently raised its standards "save in science and mechanics, and the relative overstimulation of the scientific mind has now become an actual menace to order because of the inferiority of the administrative intelligence." That is to say, we are suffering from . . . "lopsidedness" in the development of

Elton Mayo, *The Human Problems of an Industrial Civilization.* Originally published by Harvard University Press, 1933. Reprinted New York, 1960 (Compass Books–Viking Press), pp. 165, 167–168, 169–179. [Footnotes omitted.]

an *élite*. We have developed scientific research and the training of scientists admirably; we have failed utterly to promote any equivalent educational development directed to the discovery and training of administrators of exceptional capacity. These considerations led Brooks Adams to infer that "the extreme complexity of the administrative problems presented by modern industrial civilization" was "beyond the compass" of the mentality of the administrators of his time. "If this be so," he adds, "American society as at present organized . . . can concentrate no further and, as nothing in the universe is at rest, if it does not concentrate, it must, probably, begin to disintegrate. Indeed we may perceive incipient signs of disintegration all about us. . . ." Who shall say that this prophecy, made twenty years ago, has not found some fulfillment in the present crisis? . . .

. . . The primary difficulty is a human complication of the mechanical and economic; the latter indeed, the mechanical and economic, apart from the human complication present no serious problem at all. But "confidence" and "economic nationalism" are merely phrases; they indicate, it is true, but they do not describe or explain. We are faced with the fact, then, that in the important domain of human understanding and control we are ignorant of the facts and their nature; our opportunism in administration and social inquiry has left us incapable of anything but impotent inspection of a cumulative disaster. We do not lack an able administrative *élite*, but the *élite* of the several civilized powers is at present insufficiently posted in the biological and social facts involved in social organization and control. So we are compelled to wait for the social organism to recover or perish without adequate medical aid.

The first problem is that of the failure of collaborate effort within the nation. This failure, considered as a symptom of social disorganization, is far more significant than the emergence of black spots of crime or suicide upon the social geography. It is illustrated in the developed misunderstanding between employers and workers in every civilized country; this has persisted for a century without any sign of amelioration. It is, however, only the name of the problem which has persisted; the problem itself has, I think, completely changed its form since, for example, the England of 1832. At that time . . . it was essentially a problem of wages and working conditions; long hours of work and low wages were the rule. Since then wages have risen considerably, the conditions of work have much improved; the worker's standards of consumption are higher, he has established for his children a right to education and to freedom from the worse forms of exploitation. Communist Russia has not yet been able to establish, in respect of real wages and satisfactory working conditions, an equivalence with the countries she calls "capitalist." This is not fair criticism, but merely passing comment; the new Russia is too newly born for her achievements to be assessed. The idea that Russia will necessarily do better by her workers in the future, immediate or remote, than we do by ours is, however, equally unwarranted. For the moment she is obsessed, as we are, with the need of developing better methods for the discovery of an administrative *élite*, better methods of maintaining working morale. If the actualities of the situation be considered, and mere words such as capitalism and Bolshevism for the moment set aside, then it must be admitted that the present problems of Russia, on her own confession, are remarkably like the present problems of Detroit.

Better methods for the discovery of an administrative *élite*, better methods of maintaining working morale. The country that first solves these problems will infallibly outstrip the others in the race for stability, security, and development. There is one important aspect of the employer-employee problem which has persisted through a century of change in industrial organization, in wages and in working conditions. This is the problem which was tentatively stated in the final phases of the interview study at Hawthorne. It may be briefly expressed in a claim that at no time since the industrial revolution has there been, except sporadically here and there, anything of the nature of effective and wholehearted collaboration between the administrative and the working groups in industry. To "take sides" immediately on an issue such as this and to assign heavy blame to one side or other is useless. The failure is due to our incapacity to define the actual problem with sufficient precision. And until such definition is attempted, public discussion of the issues will do little except to load upon an already complicated situation an added burden of mutual suspicion and distrust. Such a method of procedure can only make the existing difficulties more acute, and the solution more unlikely. Dispassioned understanding, for us as for Russia, is the greatest need.

These problems for a century have been defined in terms of economics and the clear logic of economics; social and human factors have been disregarded. If we seek to know more of the part played by such factors, the simplest situation that we can first inspect is the collaboration in work which has been studied in primitive peoples by anthropologists— Malinowski, A. R. Brown, Lloyd Warner. Amongst the Australian aborigines their method of living involves an almost perfect collaboration drilled into members of the tribe in such a fashion that a kinship relation, a social ceremony, an economic duty become signals or commands to act or respond in a certain manner. I say "drilled into" members of a tribe, because although individual actions, as with a regiment of soldiers, are intelligently related to the actions of others and to the situation, yet no member of the tribe can expound the system and its grounds as a logic. The tribe responds to situations as a unit; each member knows his place and part although he cannot explain it. The analogy with military discipline and drill must not, of course, be pushed to an extreme; primitive collaboration is rather the effect in action of a primitive social code. From the point of view of its simple effectiveness, however, it is more like a "drilled" and military evolution than like our civilized inter-relationships.

A century of scientific development, the emergence of a considerable degree of social disorganization—these and certain effects of education have led us to forget how necessary this type of nonlogical social action is to achievement and satisfaction in living. Before the present era, changes in method of living tended to come gradually, usually there was no sudden disruption of slowly evolved methods of working together. Even now one can witness in Europe the successful accomplishment of a necessary economic duty as a purely social function, comparable with the ritual performances of a primitive tribe. The vintage activities and ceremonies of the French peasantry, for example, in the Burgundy district present features essentially similar to the activities of the primitive, although at a higher level of understanding and skill. In the United States we have traveled rapidly and carelessly from this type of simple social and economic organization to a form of industrial organization which assumes that every participant will be a devotee of systematic economics and a rigid logic. This unthinking assumption does not "work" with us, it does not "work" in Russia, it has never "worked" in the whole course of human history. The industrial worker, whether capable of it or no, does not want to develop a blackboard logic which shall guide his method of life and work. What he wants is more nearly described as, first, a method of living in social relationship with other people and, second, as part of this an economic function for and value to the group. The whole of this most important aspect of human nature we have recklessly disregarded in our "triumphant" industrial progress.

In England, trade unionism no doubt came into being as a necessary defense of working class interests. But it developed for a time as an attempt to adapt and modernize social organization and the social code. As the tempo of industrial development became faster and the scientist and engineer—logicians both—established their grip of industrial procedures, the possibility of comprehension, or any element of control, by workers in the mass receded infinitely. The trade union thus came to represent in many localities the very essence of conservative reaction— the resistance of a dying social code to innovation. There was nowhere amongst the administrative group a sufficient appreciation of the human values contained in a social code of behavior; so the battle between an attempt to conserve human values and economic innovation developed.

In the United States changes finally came with such rapidity that any attempt to save the nonlogic of collaboration became futile. It was as if one were to drill a regiment with a new set of commands and a new drill book every day. The result was not discipline and collaboration but disorder and resistance. The rapid pace of industrial development, uninformed by human research or knowledge, dispersed the last possibilities of collaborate and social effort and imposed upon the workers a low level of human organization from which social participation and social function were excluded. This low-level organization, like trade unionism, also represents a conservative and reactionary attempt to conserve human values; its chief symptom is "stalling," a procedure apparently resented as much by the workers themselves as by management. Since this seems to be as characteristic of Russia as of the United States, it is probable that the human problems involved are fundamental and contain no "political" element. Again it may be said that the question is not who is to control, but, rather, what researches are essential to the development of intelligence in control.

Socialism, Communism, Marxism would seem to be irrelevant to the industrial events of the twentieth century. These doctrines probably express the workers' desire to recapture something of the lost human solidarity. Russian Communism, however, although it claims this purpose, seems to be expressive of twentieth-century methods rather than of an ideal of human solidarity. The violent uprooting of peasants and workers to take them to a distant scene, the quick and final determination of disputes, are in part perhaps Slavonic and in part due to the critical nature of the present developmental phase. But the conceptions of work and industrial organization which such methods express are more nearly related to the engineering logic of the twentieth century than to Marx's dictatorship of the proletariat. Indeed, if the predictions of engineers have any value, we are about to enter upon an era in which our material production will be accomplished by machines directed by engineers, and the worker, as we at present conceive him, no longer needed by industry. If this is to be, then history will record not the triumph but the extinction of the proletariat. And Communist theories of revolution will be superseded by the profoundest revolution mankind has ever contemplated—the development of a society in which there will be no place for the illiterate or the ignorant.

But these ideas are fantastic. The urgent problem of the present is that our administrative élite has become addict of a few specialist studies and has unduly discounted the human and social aspects of industrial organization. The immediate need is to restore effective human collaboration; as a prerequisite of this, extension of the type of research I have reported is the major requirement. An administrator in these days should be qualified as a "listener"; many of our élite are so qualified, but are not able to relate the various "echoes" they catch in conversation to anything beyond their own experience. However wise the man, however wide his experience, the limitation to his own experience and his own reflective powers makes him illiterate in comparison with what he might have been with knowledge of the relevant researches. . . . The most melancholy fact of our time is that the appropriate inquiries—biological, anthropological—are so little developed that their findings are relatively unavailable for the training of an administrative *élite*. England has for some time required her younger colonial officials to study anthropology—and that is all that can be reported for the world of the twentieth century.

A human problem which is at present even more urgent than that of the general relationship between management and employee is that indicated in the word "confidence." If confidence can be restored the normal consumption of commodities will be resumed, the price level will rise, the wheels of industry will again begin to turn. But the devices suggested for such restoration are either those which presume an expert knowledge of economics in everyone, or else are of the nature of tricks and shifts which bear a remarkable resemblance to primitive magic. Here again there is a problem in human cooperation which our administrative leaders do not understand. Yet there is evidence available with respect to the locus of the difficulty. When England went off the gold standard in September 1931, there was much excitement outside England but none in England itself. Confidence was not disturbed, the price level of commodities for the householder remained steady at the time and has been stable since. The cost of living has not changed in England itself—this in the face of considerable variations in the foreign exchange value of the pound. Does anyone believe that an unexpected abandonment of the gold standard in the United States would have so little effect, would cause no visible tremor in the social life of the country? In what respect do the two great nations differ? One cannot answer this except to say that in England to a much larger extent than in the United States the social code is still undamaged. There has been no high mobility of labor, no problem of alien "colonies" and cultures. In spite of a certain *anomie* the social life has not lost its inertia—its capacity to go on—a disadvantage when quick industrial adaptation is required, an advantage in times of social crisis.

Yet the assumption that social codes anywhere, even in England, will continue to operate in their effective nonlogical fashion is not justifiable. The world over we are greatly in need of an administrative *élite* who can assess and handle the concrete difficulties of human collaboration. As we lose the nonlogic of a social code, we must substitute a logic of understanding. If at all the critical posts in communal activity we had intelligent persons capable of analyzing an individual or group attitude in terms of, first, the degree of logical understanding manifest; second, the nonlogic of social codes in action; and, third, the irrational exasperation symptomatic of conflict and baffled effort; if we had an *élite* capable of such analysis, very many of our difficulties would dwindle to vanishing point. Our leaders tend to state these problems in terms of systematic economics, and since the gravamen of the issue is human and social and not primarily economic their statements are not relevant. But no university in civilization offers any present aid to the discovery and training of the new administrator.

In the field of international relations . . . a similar situation exists. In every national group the leaders decry the rising tide of "economic nationalism"—the attempt of every political unit to become economically self-sufficient and independent of the others. Yet the tendency develops unchecked; our leaders, interrupted in speeches deploring the disharmony, are forced to act in a manner that accentuates it. The very descriptions published of the economic consequences of this social malady seem to develop the malady. Here also attention is being given to tariffs, currencies, price level, to anything rather than the discovery of means whereby the human capacity to collaborate may be restored.

The statement of this problem in the international field immediately suggests Geneva and the League of Nations. An ardent supporter of the League, Professor Alfred Zimmern, in a book published in 1928 when League affairs were more promising than now, says:

Has the establishment of a League of Nations ensured the peace of the world? Has it mastered the forces making for disorder? Has it set to work to deal methodically, in the spirit of Science, with the germs of future conflict? Every well informed observer of international politics must reluctantly answer these questions in the negative.

A little later, Zimmern adds:

Every three months some of the leading statesmen of the world assemble at Geneva. What do they do there? Are they free to consider the general interests of mankind? Can they plan how to recover control over events? Can they set to work to transform civilization from an appearance to a reality? No doubt, as men of reason and feeling, they would earnestly desire to do so; but, as every one knows, in actual fact they are obliged to spend their efforts upon matters of far lesser significance.

Zimmern's reasons for this ineffective outcome of a gallant attempt are odd. He attributes the failure in some rather incomprehensible fashion to Science. He says, "The control that Science has so carelessly abandoned has found no one equipped to accept it." And in this connection he speaks of "the abdication of Mind." Elsewhere he claims that Science has given all her attention to the "how" and has forgotten the "why" that science has confused "means" with "ends." What he is probably trying to say is that Geneva would have done better to create and foster scientific research— biological and social—than to institute political secretariats. France's reiterated demand for "security," for example, has always been interpreted politically in the environs of Geneva as intended to restrict German activity and growth. No doubt the claim has often had this intent, especially in the years immediately after 1918. But the prime source of the French claim is to be found in the nature of French society. In a recently published book, Mr. E. D. Schoonmaker says:

> Somehow in France, to a degree unequaled in any other country, the unity of life has been preserved. And this unity has been achieved with no loss of variety. It is not a unity brought about by conformity, but a unity of elements held together by the ideal. The colors are there, but there is also harmony. . . .

This is a literary expression, but is descriptive of the fact that France, better than any other civilized country, has held her social integrity against the modern drive towards social disorganization. The writer further illustrates this by pointing to the surprising continuity of French foreign policy through extensive changes of political organization during two hundred years. It is this tenacity of social integration which gives the individual Frenchman his feeling of security and solidarity with his group. This tenacity of social integration is the only real source of security, "confidence," and "solidarity" for any people; it is not surprising that the French, uneasy at the signs of social disorganization in the world outside, should preach to others the doctrine of solidarity and its consequent "security." Zimmern probably intends to claim that Geneva has done little or nothing to extend our knowledge by research into, for example, the sources of national attitude. These sources are rooted in unreason as in reason; both are important to the administrator.

The accomplishment of Geneva must not be belittled. The League has, it is said, provided "a clearinghouse of opinion"; it has insisted upon international political discussion. It remains a tragedy that limitation of its appointments to diplomatic and civil-service persons has prevented it from doing more. Our administrative *élite*, at Geneva as elsewhere, is the *élite* of yesterday. It faces the problems of the present with the outworn weapons—political and economic theories—of yesterday. The chief difficulty of our time is the breakdown of the social codes that formerly disciplined us to effective working together. For the nonlogic of a social code, the logic of understanding—biological and social—has not been substituted. The situation is as if Pareto's circulation of the *élite* had been fatally interrupted—the consequence, social disequilibrium. We have too few administrators alert to the fact that it is a human social and not an economic problem which they face. The universities of the world are admirably equipped for the discovery and training of the specialist in science; but they have not begun to think about the discovery and training of the new administrator.

24. The Modern Corporation

The 1920's and 1930's witnessed the most prolific outpouring of empirical studies of the state of the American social and economic order. The definition of an American culture depended increasingly on knowledge of the changes that had occurred, of the state of things as they were in fact, of the consequences of such knowledge in building a new order in America. Perhaps no study, however, had quite the ideological impact as that undertaken under the auspices of the Social Science Research Council and carried out at Columbia University by a young professor of law and a research associate in economics, A. A. Berle (1885–1971) and Gardiner C. Means (born 1896). Both men had had traditional training in their fields at Harvard University. Both were later to serve in various capacities in government service during the New Deal. But in the publication of their extensive scholarly study they did something few such studies can claim: they introduced (and thereby altered old ways of thinking) a new view of the crucial institution of the American capitalist system, the corporation. Their fundamental reassessment of the nature and role of property within American capitalism has not had the attention it deserves, for its implications changed the thinking about the very nature of our culture and the relationships within it, posing new problems, it is true, but at the same time redefining the fundamental structure underlying the culture itself, challenging both Marxist contentions and traditional capitalist ones as well.

The New Concept of the Corporation
A. A. BERLE and GARDINER C. MEANS

Though the American law makes no distinction between the private corporation and the quasi-public, the economics of the two are essentially

Adolf A. Berle, Jr., and Gardiner C. Means, *The Modern Corporation and Private Property* (New York, 1932), pp. 6–9, 352–357.

different. The separation of ownership from control produces a condition where the interests of owner and of ultimate manager may, and often do, diverge, and where many of the checks which formerly operated to limit the use of power disappear. Size alone tends to give these giant corporations a social significance not attached to the smaller units of private enterprise. By the use of the open market for securities, each of these corporations assumes obligations towards the investing public which transform it from a legal method clothing the rule of a few individuals into an institution at least nominally serving investors who have embarked their funds in its enterprise. New responsibilities towards the owners, the workers, the consumers, and the State thus rest upon the shoulders of those in control. In creating these new relationships, the quasi-public corporation may fairly be said to work a revolution. It has destroyed the unity that we commonly call property—has divided ownership into nominal ownership and the power formerly joined to it. Thereby the corporation has changed the nature of profit-seeking enterprise. This revolution forms the subject of the present study.

. . . Here we are concerned only with a fundamental change in the form of property, and in the economic relationships which rest upon it. . . . Outwardly the change is simple enough. Men are less likely to own the physical instruments of production. They are more likely to own pieces of paper, loosely known as stocks, bonds, and other securities, which have become mobile through the machinery of the public markets. Beneath this, however, lies a more fundamental shift. Physical control over the instruments of production has been surrendered in ever growing degree to centralized groups who manage property in bulk, supposedly, but by no means necessarily, for the benefit of the security holders. Power over industrial property has been cut off from the beneficial ownership of this property—or, in less technical language, from the legal right to enjoy its fruits. Control of physical assets has passed from the individual owner to those who direct the quasi-public institutions, while the owner retains an interest in their product and increase. We see, in fact, the surrender and regrouping of the incidence of ownership, which formerly bracketed full power of manual disposition with complete right to enjoy the use, the fruits, and the proceeds of physical assets. There has resulted the dissolution of the old atom of ownership into its component parts, control and beneficial ownership.

This dissolution of the atom of property destroys the very foundation on which the economic order of the past three centuries has rested. Private enterprise, which has molded economic life since the close of the Middle Ages, has been rooted in the institution of private property. Under the feudal system, its predecessor, economic organization grew out of mutual obligations and privileges derived by various individuals from their relation to property which no one of them owned. Private enterprise, on the other hand, has assumed an owner of the instruments of production with complete property rights over those instruments. Whereas the organization of feudal economic life rested upon an elaborate system of binding customs, the organization under the system of private enterprise has rested upon the self-interest of the property owner —a self-interest held in check only by competition and the conditions of supply and demand. Such self-interest has long been regarded as the best guarantee of economic efficiency. It has been assumed that, if the individual is protected in the right both to use his own property as he sees fit and to receive the full fruits of its use, his desire for personal gain, for profits, can be relied upon as an effective incentive to his efficient use of any industrial property he may possess.

In the quasi-public corporation, such an assumption no longer holds. As we have seen, it is no longer the individual himself who uses his wealth. Those in control of that wealth, and therefore in a position to secure industrial efficiency and produce profits, are no longer, as owners, entitled to the bulk of such profits. Those who control the destinies of the typical modern corporation own so insignificant a fraction of the company's stock that the returns from running the corporation profitably accrue to them in only a very minor degree. The stockholders, on the other hand, to whom the profits of the corporation go, cannot be motivated by those profits to a more efficient use of the property, since they have surrendered all disposition of it to those in control of the enterprise. The explosion of the atom of property destroys the basis of the old assumption that the quest for profits will spur the owner of industrial property to its effective use. It consequently challenges the fundamental economic principle of individual initiative in industrial enterprise. It raises for reexamination the question of the motive force back of industry, and the ends for which the modern corporation can be or will be run.

The corporate system further commands attention because its development is progressive, as its features become more marked and as new areas come one by one under its sway. Economic power, in terms of control over physical assets, is apparently responding to a centripetal force, tending more and more to concentrate in the hands of a few corporate managements. At the same time, beneficial ownership is centrifugal, tending to divide and subdivide, to split into ever smaller units and to pass freely from hand to hand. In other words, ownership continually becomes more dispersed; the power formerly joined to it becomes increasingly concentrated; and the corporate system is thereby more securely established.

This system bids fair to be as all-embracing as was the feudal system in its time. It demands that we examine both its conditions and its trends, for an understanding of the structure upon which will rest the economic order of the future.

✿   ✿   ✿

Most fundamental to the new picture of economic life must be a new concept of business enterprise as concentrated in the corporate organization. In some measure a concept is already emerging. Over a decade ago, Walter Rathenau wrote concerning the German counterpart of our great corporation:

> No one is a permanent owner. The composition of the thousandfold complex which functions as lord of the undertaking is in a state of flux. . . . This condition of things signifies that ownership has been depersonalized. . . . The depersonalization of ownership simultaneously implies the objectification of the thing owned. The claims to ownership are subdivided in such a fashion, and are so mobile, that the enterprise assumes an independent life, as if it belonged to no one; it takes an objective existence, such as in earlier days was embodied only in state and church, in a municipal corporation, in the life of a guild or a religious order. . . . The depersonalization of ownership, the objectification of enterprise, the detachment of property from the possessor, leads to a point where the enterprise becomes transformed into an institution which resembles the state in character.[1]

The institution here envisaged calls for analysis, not in terms of business enterprise but in terms of social organization. On the one hand, it involves a concentration of power in the economic field comparable to the concentration of religious power in the medieval church or of political power in the national state. On the other hand, it involves the interrelation of a wide diversity of economic interests—those of the "owners" who supply capital, those of the workers who "create," those of the consumers who give value to the products of enterprise, and above all those of the control who wield power.

Such a great concentration of power and such a diversity of interest raise the long-fought issue of power and its regulation—of interest and its protection. A constant warfare has existed between the individuals wielding power, in whatever form, and the subjects of that power. Just as there is a continuous desire for power, so also there is a continuous desire to make that power the servant of the bulk of the individuals it affects. The long struggles for the reform of the Catholic Church and for the development of constitutional law in the states are phases of this phenomenon. Absolute power is useful in building the organization. More

---

[1] "Von Kommenden Dingen," Berlin, 1918, trans. by E. & C. Paul ("In Days to Come"), London, 1921, pp. 120, 121.

slow, but equally sure is the development of social pressure demanding that the power shall be used for the benefit of all concerned. This pressure, constant in ecclesiastical and political history, is already making its appearance in many guises in the economic field.

Observable throughout the world, and in varying degrees of intensity, is this insistence that power in economic organization shall be subjected to the same tests of public benefit which have been applied in their turn to power otherwise located. In its most extreme aspect this is exhibited in the Communist movement, which in its purest form is an insistence that *all* of the powers and privileges of property, shall be used only in the common interest. In less extreme forms of socialist dogma, transfer of economic powers to the state for public service is demanded. In the strictly capitalist countries, and particularly in time of depression, demands are constantly put forward that the men controlling the great economic organisms be made to accept responsibility for the well-being of those who are subject to the organization, whether workers, investors, or consumers. In a sense the difference in all of these demands lies only in degree. In proportion as an economic organism grows in strength and its power is concentrated in a few hands, the possessor of power is more easily located, and the demand for responsible power becomes increasingly direct.

How will this demand be made effective? To answer this question would be to foresee the history of the next century. We can here only consider and appraise certain of the more important lines of possible development.

By tradition, a corporation "belongs" to its shareholders, or, in a wider sense, to its security holders, and theirs is the only interest to be recognized as the object of corporate activity. Following this tradition, and without regard for the changed character of ownership, it would be possible to apply in the interests of the *passive* property owner the doctrine of strict property rights, the analysis of which has been presented above in the chapter on Corporate Powers as Powers in Trust. By the application of this doctrine, the group in control of a corporation would be placed in a position of trusteeship in which it would be called on to operate or arrange for the operation of the corporation for the *sole* benefit of the security owners despite the fact that the latter have ceased to have power over or to accept responsibility for the *active* property in which they have an interest. Were this course followed, the bulk of American industry might soon be operated by trustees for the sole benefit of inactive and irresponsible security owners.

In direct opposition to the above doctrine of strict property rights is the view, apparently held by the great corporation lawyers and by certain students of the field, that corporate development has created a new set of relationships, giving to the groups in control powers which are absolute and not limited by any implied obligation with respect to their use. This logic leads to drastic conclusions. For instance, if, by reason of these new relationships, the men in control of a corporation can operate it in their own interests, and can divert a portion of the asset fund of income stream to their own uses, such is their privilege. Under this view, since the new powers have been acquired on a quasi-contractual basis, the security holders have agreed in advance to any losses which they may suffer by reason of such use. The result is, briefly, that the existence of the legal and economic relationships giving rise to these powers must be frankly recognized as a modification of the principle of private property.

If these were the only alternatives, the former would appear to be the lesser of two evils. Changed corporate relationships have unquestionably involved an essential alteration in the character of property. But such modifications have hitherto been brought about largely on the principle that might makes right. Choice between strengthening the rights of passive property owners, or leaving a set of uncurbed powers in the hands of control therefore resolves itself into a purely realistic evaluation of different results. We might elect the relative certainty and safety of a trust relationship in favor of a particular group within the corporation, accompanied by a possible diminution of enterprise. Or we may grant the controlling group free rein, with the corresponding danger of a corporate oligarchy coupled with the probability of an era of corporate plundering.

A third possibility exists, however. On the one hand, the owners of passive property, by surrendering control and responsibility over the active property, have surrendered the right that the corporation should be operated in their sole interest—they have released the community from the obligation to protect them to the full extent implied in the doctrine of strict property rights. At the same time, the controlling groups, by means of the extension of corporate powers, have in their own interest broken the bars of tradition which require that the corporation be operated solely for the benefit of the owners of passive property. Eliminating the sole interest of the passive owner, however, does not necessarily lay a basis for the alternative claim that the new powers should be used in the interest of the controlling groups. The latter have not presented, in acts or words any acceptable defense of the proposition that these powers should be so used. No tradition supports that proposition. The control groups have, rather, cleared the way for the claims of a group far wider than either the owners or the control. They have placed the community in a position to demand that the modern corporation serve not alone the owners or the control but all society.

This third alternative offers a wholly new concept of corporate activity. Neither the claims of ownership nor those of control can stand against the paramount interests of the community. The present claims of both contending parties now in the field have been weakened by the developments described in this book. It remains only for the claims of the community to be put forward with clarity and force. Rigid enforcement of property rights as a temporary protection against plundering by control would not stand in the way of the modification of these rights in the interest of other groups. When a convincing system of community obligations is worked out and is generally accepted, in that moment the passive property right of today must yield before the larger interests of society. Should the corporate leaders, for example, set forth a program comprising fair wages, security to employees, reasonable service to their public, and stabilization of business, all of which would divert a portion of the profits from the owners of passive property, and should the community generally accept such a scheme as a logical and human solution of industrial difficulties, the interests of passive property owners would have to give way. Courts would almost of necessity be forced to recognize the result, justifying it by whatever of the many legal theories they might choose. It is conceivable—indeed it seems almost essential if the corporate system is to survive—that the "control" of the great corporations should develop into a purely neutral technocracy, balancing a variety of claims by various groups in the community and assigning to each a portion of the income stream on the basis of public policy rather than private cupidity.

In still larger view, the modern corporation may be regarded not simply as one form of social organization but potentially (if not yet actually) as the dominant institution of the modern world. In every age, the major concentration of power has been based upon the dominant interest of that age. The strong man has, in his time, striven to be cardinal or pope, prince or cabinet minister, bank president or partner in the House of Morgan. During the Middle Ages, the Church, exercising spiritual power, dominated Europe and gave to it a unity at a time when both political and economic power were diffused. With the rise of the modern state, political power, concentrated into a few large units, challenged the spiritual interest as the strongest bond of human society. Out of the long struggle between church and state which followed, the state emerged victorious; nationalist politics superseded religion as the basis of the major unifying organization of the western world. Economic power still remained diffused.

The rise of the modern corporation has brought a concentration of economic power which can compete on equal terms with the modern state—economic power versus political power, each strong in its own field. The state seeks in some aspects to regulate the corporation, while the corporation, steadily becoming more powerful, makes every effort to avoid such regulation. Where its own interests are concerned, it even attempts to dominate the state. The future may see the economic organism, now typified by the corporation, not only on an equal plane with the state, but possibly even superseding it as the dominant form of social organization. The law of corporations, accordingly, might well be considered as a potential constitutional law for the new economic state, while business practice is increasingly assuming the aspect of economic statesmanship.

25. "The First Great American Century"

If the media played a crucial role in defining and shaping American culture and commitment perhaps no single figure in the history of the media in America was quite as significant as Henry Robinson Luce. Born of missionary parents in China in 1898, educated at Yale and Oxford, the brilliant young Luce not only "reached the conclusion that most people were not well informed and that something should be done about it . . ." but also did several things about it that reshaped the very media and quite possibly the culture in which it developed. Beginning with the new-style newsmagazine *Time* in 1923, Luce went on to build an influential media empire. While analyzing American culture in every aspect, his magazines tried to mold that culture as it informed it. In 1930 Luce launched *Fortune,* aimed at what was beginning to be called the "business and financial community." Especially designed to find and express the "technological significance of industry," the magazine remains, because of its superbly researched and carefully selected subjects, one of the best single sources for a study of the culture history of the period since 1930. In 1931 "March of Time" first appeared as a radio series, one of the great educational ventures in the history of the medium and so popular that some have claimed only "Amos and Andy" attracted a greater audience. (There was to be a film version beginning in 1935.) In 1936 Luce pioneered again with *Life* which brought photo-journalism to the status of a fine art and provided extraordinary documentation of the emerging culture, a careful elaboration of developing life-styles among Americans and others throughout the world. Luce's publications provided a way of reading, hearing, and seeing the world around the millions of middle-class Americans who came to rely increasingly on them as a way of understanding the world.

Concerned always because, as he was frequently quoted as saying, "the expanding machine" had "slowly deadened our aristocratic sense," Luce in his editorials in *Life* called for the creation of an American culture and an American commitment that would serve the world in the twentieth century. Certainly no editorial of his and possibly none in the whole period under review was of greater significance or created more debate than "The American Century," an effort to define our war aims. It is part of our story, not because of its political implications but because, like an earlier nineteenth-century call for "Manifest Destiny," it is a cultural statement of profound meaning as Americans sought to define their culture and define their commitments.

The American Century
HENRY R. LUCE

We Americans are unhappy. We are not happy about America. We are not happy about ourselves in relation to America. We are nervous—or gloomy—or apathetic.

As we look out at the rest of the world we are confused; we don't know what to do. "Aid to Britain short of war" is typical of halfway hopes and halfway measures.

As we look toward the future—our own future and the future of other nations—we are filled with foreboding. The future doesn't seem to hold anything for us except conflict, disruption, war. . . .

. . . And how can we tell ourselves for what purposes we seek allies and for what purposes we fight? Are we going to fight for dear old Danzig or dear old Dong Dang? Are we going to decide the boundaries of Uritania? Or, if we cannot state war aims in terms of vastly distant geography, shall we use some big words like Democracy and Freedom and Justice? Yes, we can use the big words. The President has already used them. And perhaps we had better get used to using them again. Maybe they do mean something—about the future as well as the past.

Some amongst us are likely to be dying for them—on the fields and in the skies of battle. Either that, or the words themselves and what they mean die with us—in our beds.

But is there nothing between the absurd sound of distant cities and the brassy trumpeting of majestic words? And if so, whose Dong Dang and whose Democracy? Is there not something a little more practically satisfying that we can get our teeth into? Is there no sort of understandable program? A program which would be clearly good for America, which would make sense for America—and which at the same time might have

Henry R. Luce, *The American Century* (New York, 1941), pp. 3, 20–40. [So popular was the editorial that it was reprinted in volume form with critical comments from several distinguished journalists. The passage above is taken from this version.—Ed.]

the blessing of the Goddess of Democracy and even help somehow to fix up this bothersome matter of Dong Dang?

Is there none such? There is. And so we now come squarely and closely face to face with the issue which Americans hate most to face. It is that old, old issue with those old, old battered labels—the issue of Isolationism versus Internationalism.

We detest both words. We spit them at each other with the fury of hissing geese. We duck and dodge them.

Let us face that issue squarely now. If we face it squarely now—and if in facing it we take full and fearless account of the realities of our age—then we shall open the way, not necessarily to peace in our daily lives but to peace in our hearts.

Life is made up of joy and sorrow, of satisfactions and difficulties. In this time of trouble, we speak of troubles. There are many troubles. There are troubles in the field of philosophy, in faith and morals. There are troubles of home and family, of personal life. All are interrelated but we speak here especially of the troubles of national policy.

In the field of national policy, the fundamental trouble with America has been, and is, that whereas their nation became in the twentieth century the most powerful and the most vital nation in the world, nevertheless Americans were unable to accommodate themselves spiritually and practically to that fact. Hence they have failed to play their part as a world power—a failure which has had disastrous consequences for themselves and for all mankind. And the cure is this: to accept wholeheartedly our duty and our opportunity as the most powerful and vital nation in the world and in consequence to exert upon the world the full impact of our influence, for such purposes as we see fit and by such means as we see fit.

"For such purposes as we see fit" leaves entirely open the question of what our purposes may be or how we may appropriately achieve them. Emphatically our only alternative to isolationism is not to undertake to police the whole world nor to impose democratic institutions on all mankind including the Dalai Lama and the good shepherds of Tibet.

America cannot be responsible for the good behavior of the entire world. But America is responsible, to herself as well as to history, for the world-environment in which she lives. Nothing can so vitally affect America's environment as America's own influence upon it, and therefore if America's environment is unfavorable to the growth of American life, then America has nobody to blame so deeply as she must blame herself.

In its failure to grasp this relationship between America and America's environment lies the moral and practical bankruptcy of any and all forms of isolationism. It is most unfortunate that this virus of isolationist sterility has so deeply infected an influential section of the Republican Party. For until the Republican Party can develop a vital philosophy and program for America's initiative and activity as a world power, it will continue to cut itself off from any useful participation in this hour of history. And its participation is deeply needed for the shaping of the future of America and of the world.

But politically speaking, it is an equally serious fact that for seven years Franklin Roosevelt was, for all practical purposes, a complete isolationist. He was more of an isolationist than Herbert Hoover or Calvin Coolidge. The fact that Franklin Roosevelt has recently emerged as an emergency world leader should not obscure the fact that for seven years his policies ran absolutely counter to any possibility of effective American leadership in international cooperation. There is of course a justification which can be made for the President's first two terms. It can be said, with reason, that great social reforms were necessary in order to bring democracy up-to-date in the greatest of democracies. But the fact is that Franklin Roosevelt failed to make American democracy work successfully on a narrow, materialistic, and nationalistic basis. And under Franklin Roosevelt we ourselves have failed to make democracy work successfully. Our only chance now to make it work is in terms of a vital international economy and in terms of an international moral order.

This objective is Franklin Roosevelt's great opportunity to justify his first two terms and to go down in history as the greatest rather than the last of American Presidents. Our job is to help in every way we can, for our sakes and our children's sakes, to ensure that Franklin Roosevelt shall be justly hailed as America's greatest President.

Without our help he cannot be our greatest President. With our help he can and will be. Under him and with his leadership we can make isolationism as dead an issue as slavery, and we can make a truly *American* internationalism something as natural to us in our time as the airplane or the radio.

In 1919 we had a golden opportunity, an opportunity unprecedented in all history, to assume the leadership of the world—a golden opportunity handed to us on the proverbial silver platter. We did not understand that opportunity. Wilson mishandled it. We rejected it. The opportunity persisted. We bungled it in the 1920's and in the confusions of the 1930's we killed it.

To lead the world would never have been an easy task. To revive the hope of that lost opportunity makes the task now infinitely harder than it would have been before. Nevertheless, with the help of all of us, Roosevelt must succeed where Wilson failed.

. . . Consider the twentieth century. It is ours not only in the sense that we happen to live in it but ours also because it is America's first century as a dominant power in the world. So far, this century of ours has been a profound and tragic disappointment. No other century has been so big with promise for human progress and happiness. And in no one century have so many men and women and children suffered such pain and anguish and bitter death.

It is a baffling and difficult and paradoxical century. No doubt all centuries were paradoxical to those who had to cope with them. But, like everything else, our paradoxes today are bigger and better than ever. Yes, better as well as bigger—inherently better. We have poverty and starvation—but only in the midst of plenty. We have the biggest wars in the midst of the most widespread, the deepest and the most articulate hatred of war in all history. We have tyrannies and dictatorships —but only when democratic idealism, once regarded as the dubious eccentricity of a colonial nation, is the faith of a huge majority of the people of the world.

And ours is also a revolutionary century. The paradoxes make it inevitably revolutionary. Revolutionary, of course, in science and in industry. And also revolutionary, as a corollary in politics and the structure of society. But to say that a revolution is in progress is not to say that the men with either the craziest ideas or the angriest ideas or the most plausible ideas are going to come out on top. The Revolution of 1776 was won and established by men most of whom appear to have been both gentlemen and men of common sense.

Clearly a revolutionary epoch signifies great changes, great adjustments. And this is only one reason why it is really so foolish for people to worry about our "constitutional democracy" without worrying or, better, thinking hard about the world revolution. For only as we go out to meet and solve for our time the problems of the world revolution, can we know how to reestablish our constitutional democracy for another 50 or 100 years.

This twentieth century is baffling, difficult, paradoxical, revolutionary. But by now, at the cost of much pain and many hopes deferred, we know a good deal about it. And we ought to accommodate our outlook to this knowledge so dearly bought. For example, any true conception of our world of the twentieth century must surely include a vivid awareness of at least these four propositions.

First: our world of 2,000,000,000 human beings is for the first time in history one world, fundamentally indivisible. Second: modern man hates war and feels intuitively that, in its present scale and frequency, it may even be fatal to his species. Third: our world, again for the first time in human history, is capable of producing all the material needs of the entire human family. Fourth: the world of the twentieth century, if it is to come to life in any nobility of health and vigor, must be to a significant degree an American Century.

As to the first and second: in postulating the indivisibility of the contemporary world, one does not necessarily imagine that anything like a world state—a parliament of men—must be brought about in this century. Nor need we assume that war can be abolished. All that it is necessary to feel—and to feel deeply—is that terrific forces of magnetic attraction and repulsion will operate as between every large group of human beings on this planet. Large sections of the human family may be effectively organized into opposition to each other. Tyrannies may require a large amount of living space. But Freedom requires and will require far greater living space than Tyranny. Peace cannot endure unless it prevails over a very large part of the world: Justice will come near to losing all meaning in the minds of men unless Justice can have approximately the same fundamental meanings in many lands and among many peoples.

As to the third point—the promise of adequate production for all mankind, the "more abundant life"—be it noted that this is characteristically an American promise. It is a promise easily made, here and elsewhere, by demagogues and proponents of all manner of slick schemes and "planned economies." What we must insist on is that the abundant life is predicated on Freedom—on the Freedom which has created its possibility—on a vision of Freedom under Law. Without Freedom, there will be no abundant life. With Freedom, there can be.

And finally there is the belief—shared let us remember by most men living—that the twentieth century must be to a significant degree an American Century. This knowledge calls us to action now.

. . . What can we say and foresee about an American Century? It is meaningless merely to say that we reject isolationism and accept the logic of internationalism. What internationalism? Rome had a great internationalism. So had the Vatican and Genghis Khan and the Ottoman Turks and the Chinese Emperors and nineteenth-century England. After the first world war, Lenin had one in mind. Today Hitler seems to have one in mind—one which appeals strongly to some American isolationists whose opinion of Europe is so low that they would gladly hand it over to anyone who would guarantee to destroy it forever. But what internationalism have we Americans to offer?

Ours cannot come out of the vision of any one man. It must be the product of the imaginations of many men. It must be a sharing with all peoples of our Bill of Rights, our Declaration of Independence, our Constitution, our magnificent industrial products, our technical skills. It must be an internationalism of the people, by the people, and for the people.

In general, the issues which the American people champion revolve around their determination to make the society of men safe for the freedom, growth, and increasing satisfaction of all individual men. Beside that resolve, the sneers, groans, catcalls, teeth-grinding, hisses, and roars of the Nazi Propaganda Ministry are of small moment.

Once we cease to distract ourselves with lifeless arguments about isolationism, we shall be amazed to discover that there is already an immense American internationalism. American jazz, Hollywood movies, American slang, American machines and patented products, are in fact the only things that every community in the world, from Zanzibar to Hamburg, recognizes in common. Blindly, unintentionally, accidentally and really in spite of ourselves, we are already a world power in all the trivial ways—in very human ways. But there is a great deal more than that. America is already the intellectual, scientific and artistic capital of the world. Americans—Midwestern Americans—are today the least provincial people in the world. They have traveled the most and they know more about the world than the people of any other country. America's worldwide experience in commerce is also far greater than most of us realize.

Most important of all, we have that indefinable, unmistakable sign of leadership: prestige. And unlike the prestige of Rome or Genghis Khan or nineteenth-century England, American prestige throughout the world is faith in the good intentions as well as in the ultimate intelligence and ultimate strength of the whole American people. We have lost some of that prestige in the last few years. But most of it is still there.

No narrow definition can be given to the American internationalism of the twentieth century. It will take shape, as all civilizations take shape, by the living of it, by work and effort, by trial and error, by enterprise and adventure and experience.

And by imagination!

As America enters dynamically upon the world scene, we need most of all to seek and to bring forth a vision of America as a world power which is authentically American and which can inspire us to live and work and fight with vigor and enthusiasm. And as we come now to the great test, it may yet turn out that in all our trials and tribulations of spirit during the first part of this century we as a people have been painfully apprehending the meaning of our time and now in this moment of testing there may come clear at last the vision which will guide us to the authentic creation of the twentieth century—our Century.

Consider four areas of life and thought in which we may seek to realize such a vision:

First, the economic. It is for America and for America alone to determine whether a system of free economic enterprise—an economic order compatible with freedom and progress—shall or shall not prevail in this century. We know perfectly well that there is not the slightest chance of anything faintly resembling a free economic system prevailing in this country if it prevails nowhere else. What then does America have to decide? Some few decisions are quite simple. For example: we have to decide whether or not we shall have for ourselves and our friends freedom of the seas—the right to go with our ships and our oceangoing airplanes where we wish, when we wish and as we wish. The vision of America as the principal guarantor of the freedom of the seas, the vision of America as the dynamic leader of world trade, has within it the possibilities of such enormous human progress as to stagger the imagination. Let us not be staggered by it. Let us rise to its tremendous possibilities. Our thinking of world trade today is on ridiculously small terms. For example, we think of Asia as being worth only a few hundred millions a year to us. Actually, in the decades to come Asia will be worth to us exactly zero—or else it will be worth to us four, five, ten billions of dollars a year. And the latter are the terms we must think in, or else confess a pitiful impotence.

Closely akin to the purely economic area and yet quite different from it, there is the picture of an America which will send out through the world its technical and artistic skills. Engineers, scientists, doctors, movie men, makers of entertainment, developers of airlines, builders of roads, teachers, educators. Throughout the world, these skills, this training, this leadership is needed and will be eagerly welcomed, if only we have the imagination to see it and the sincerity and goodwill to create the world of the twentieth century.

But now there is a third thing which our vision must immediately be concerned with. We must undertake now to be the Good Samaritan of the entire world. It is the manifest duty of this country to undertake to feed all the people of the world who as a result of this worldwide collapse of civilization are hungry and destitute—all of them, that is, whom we can from time to time reach consistently with a very tough attitude toward all hostile governments. For every dollar we spend on armaments, we should spend at least a dime in a gigantic effort to feed the world— and all the world should know that we have dedicated ourselves to this task. Every farmer in America should be encouraged to produce all the crops he can, and all that we cannot eat—and perhaps some of us could eat less—should forthwith be dispatched to the four quarters of the globe as a free gift, administered by a humanitarian army of Americans, to every man, woman and child on this earth who is really hungry.

But all this is not enough. All this will fail and none of it will happen unless our vision of America as a world power includes a passionate devotion to great American ideals. We have some things in this country which are infinitely precious and especially American—a love of freedom, a feeling for the equality of opportunity, a tradition of self-reliance and independence and also of cooperation. In addition to ideals and notions which are especially American, we are the inheritors of all the great principles of Western civilization—above all Justice, the love of Truth, the ideal of Charity. The other day Herbert Hoover said that America was fast becoming the sanctuary of the ideals of civilization. For the moment it may be enough to be the sanctuary of these ideals. But not for long. It now becomes our time to be the powerhouse from which the ideals spread throughout the world and do their mysterious work of lifting the life of mankind from the level of the beasts to what the Psalmist called a little lower than the angels.

America as the dynamic center of ever-widening spheres of enterprise, America as the training center of the skillful servants of mankind, America as the Good Samaritan, really believing again that it is more blessed to give than to receive, and America as the powerhouse of the ideals of Freedom and Justice—out of these elements surely can be fashioned a vision of the twentieth century to which we can and will devote ourselves in joy and gladness and vigor and enthusiasm.

Other nations can survive simply because they have endured so long—sometimes with more and sometimes with less significance. But this nation, conceived in adventure and dedicated to the progress of man—this nation cannot truly endure unless there courses strongly through its veins from Maine to California the blood of purpose and enterprise and high resolve.

Throughout the seventeenth century and the eighteenth century and the nineteenth century, this continent teemed with manifold projects and magnificent purposes. Above them all and weaving them all together into the most exciting flag of all the world and of all history was the triumphal purpose of freedom.

It is in this spirit that all of us are called, each to his own measure of capacity, and each in the widest horizon of his vision, to create the first great American Century.

PART SEVEN

TOWARD AN ICONOGRAPHY OF THE PERIOD 1929-1947

26. An Album of Images

It was an age increasingly self-conscious of itself; it sought increasingly to define itself in a series of images, often even contradictory ones, by which it hoped to understand and realize and even identify itself as a culture. Some of these images readily became symbols. A careful study of these images, often widely known and reproduced, help us to understand as well that search for a culture, its nature, its fundamental tensions, its commitments.

Illustrations

1. Signs of the Times: In the Midst of Depression the Assertion of the American Dream
   (a) Dorothea Lange, "U.S. Highway 99 in California" (1937). Farm Security Administration. *Library of Congress.*
   (b) John Vachon, "National Association of Manufacturers" Sign, Dubuque, Iowa" (1940). Farm Security Administration. *Library of Congress.*

2. Nature in Disruption: A Subject of Special Fascination for Writers and Artists in an Apocalyptical Age
   (a) Arthur Rothstein, "Dust Storm—Cimmarron County, Oklahoma" (1935). Farm Security Administration. *Library of Congress.*
   (b) Still from *The River* (1937). Produced by the Resettlement Administration, U.S. Government. Written and Directed by Pare Lorentz. Photographed by Willard van Dyke. A Paramount Release. *Film Stills Archive of the Museum of Modern Art.*

3. Monsters: Man and Nature in Strange Relationship
   (a) Still from *Frankenstein* (1931). Directed for Universal Studios by James Whale with Boris Karloff as the "monster." *Reproduced from the Film Stills Archive of the Museum of Modern Art.*

(b) Still from *King Kong* (1933). Produced by David O. Selznick for RKO Pictures. Conceived and Directed by Merian C. Cooper and Ernest B. Schoedsack; trick photography by Willis H. O'Brien. With Fay Wray. *Brown Brothers.*

4. The "New" Landscape

(a) Charles Burchfield, *November Evening* (1934). The Metropolitan Museum of Art, George A. Hearn Fund, 1934. (Oil on canvas, 32⅛ x 52 inches.) Burchfield himself said of this painting: "I have attempted to express the coming of winter over the Middle West as it must have felt to the pioneers—great black clouds sweep out of the west at twilight as if to overwhelm not only the pitiful human attempt at a town, but also the earth itself."

(b) Edward Hopper, *Gas* (1940). *Museum of Modern Art.*

5. . . . And the Automobile: The Automobile, itself a newly defined symbol for the age, transforms life-style and even landscape.

(a) Highway in Massachusetts built by the state. *Brown Brothers.*

(b) The Clover Leaf: You Turn Right to Go Left. New Jersey. *Brown Brothers.*

6. Urban Environment: Planned and Unplanned

The advocates of planned environment dominated much of the social thinking of the period: Robert Moses and his highway systems and great planned public parks (Jones Beach is a stunning example); the planned communities of the Resettlement Administration and the Greenbelt Idea, the model Broadacre City of Frank Lloyd Wright, the New York World's Fair of 1939.

(a) The Child in the Unplanned Slum. Still from American Documentary Films Production (1939) directed and photographed by Ralph Steiner and William Van Dyke. Outline scenario by Pare Lorentz supposedly based in Lewis Mumford's *The Culture of Cities. Film Stills Archive of the Museum of Modern Art.*

(b) Planned Environment for Children: Jane Addams Houses, Chicago, John A. Holabird, Chief Architect. Low-rental housing development on former slum site: 1027 dwelling units on 22 acres, coverage 27 per cent. *Brown Brothers.*

7. The Way West: Two Versions

Spatial mobility, both forced by environmental circumstances and increasingly made attractive by new means of transportation, new design, new systems of highways, new institutions developed to meet the needs of the ever-traveling American.

(a) Dorothea Lange, "Family of 9 from Ft. Smith, Ark. on Road from Phoenix to Yuma" (1937). The famous characteristics "Okies" of the era. Farm Security Administration. *Library of Congress.*

(b) "The Rocket," famous "Streamliner" of the period, built by Edward G. Budd Manufacturing Company for the Chicago, Rock Island and Pacific Railroad. Went into service August, 1937. "Streamlining" of design a characteristic of the whole new field of design engineering, a major new field of activity. *Culver Pictures, Inc.*

8. Temporary Towns: Two Versions

It was an era of new towns, planned and unplanned, new communities the result of enforced dislocation, and voluntary mobility the result of new transportation facilities and the constant American characteristic movement through space and place.

(a) Characteristic "Hooverville" (ca. 1931). *Brown Brothers.*

(b) Characteristic "Tourist City" (this one in Dade City, Florida, 1936) for the newly popular "trailers." These "Tin-Can Tourists" were part of a movement that created not only the Trailer Park but also the Motel, the Tourist Cabin, and other "Roadside" innovations in the new era of the automobile and the highway. *Brown Brothers.*

9. Design for Living: Two Visions

(a) The more permanent new town was the housing development, often suburban, and often in spite of the fascination with streamline and modern design, with the application of modern technology. The model was the so-called "Williamsburg" house, presumably influenced by the Rockefeller reconstruction in Virginia. Typical housing development of the period. (This particular suburb was on Long Island, New York.) *Brown Brothers.*

(b) Yet Americans were also attracted to what was felt to be the height of elegance in modern interior design, anything but Williamsburg in inspiration or feeling. Not uncharacteristic of this modern interior design was this Men's Lounge on the Third Mezzanine of Radio City Music Hall, Rockefeller Center, one of the great show places and tourist attractions of the period. *Radio City Music Hall, Rockefeller Center.*

10. The Mighty Machine: Two Versions

No analysis of the period can fail to deal with the enormous technological triumphs and the fascination with technology and its achievements. Such achievements often became monuments and even symbols of the era. Yet there remained those whose vision did not see in the machine a golden tomorrow but a threat.

(a) Hoover Dam as well as Hoovervilles characterize the period. At the Arizona–Nevada border on the Colorado River, this major work was initiated in 1928 by the Federal Government and dedicated in 1935. One of the largest dams in the world. (Known during much of the period as Boulder Dam.) *Brown Brothers.*

(b) Charlie Chaplin's *Modern Times* (1936). United Artists Film. *Film Stills Archive of the Museum of Modern Art.*

11. The Machine as Game: Machines that didn't "sew, drill, boil or kill," as Lenny Bruce suggested

(a) The Juke Box: Recorded Music for a Coin. (Note other icons as well, the ever-present "Coke" bottle, for example.) *Brown Brothers.*

(b) The Pin-Ball Machine: A Game of Chance. *Brown Brothers.*

12. Leisure: The Cultural Meanings of Entertainments

(a) *Monopoly:* A Real Estate Trading Game, Parker Brothers. A most popular board game of the period.

(b) The Radio as Home Altar. Russell Lee, "Tenant Purchase Clients at Home, Hidalgo County, Texas" (1939). Farm Security Administration. *Library of Congress.*

13. Toward a New Domestic Order: The Machine and the Home

(a) Russell Lee, "Home of Oklahoma Migrants Who Have Returned from the West" (1939). Farm Security Administration. *Library of Congress.*

(b) Russell Lee, "Kitchen Detail in Migrant Labor Camp, Robstown, Texas" (1940). Farm Security Administration. *Library of Congress.*

(c) Walker Evans, "Floyd Burrough's Wash Stand, Hole County, Alabama" (1935). Farm Security Administration. *Library of Congress.*

(d) Russell Lee, "Bathroom of Tenant Purchase House, Hidalgo County, Texas" (1939). Farm Security Administration. *Library of Congress.*

14. The Line: Two Versions

(a) Reginald Marsh, *Breadline.* Etching (1932). *Courtesy Prints Division, The New York Public Library, Astor, Lenox and Tilden Foundations.*

(b) The Rockettes. A Special Feature of the new (in the 1930's) Radio City Music Hall which has become a tradition. Precision dancing with stress on mechanical formations. *Radio City Music Hall.*

15. Rallies and Rituals: Some Events as Symbolic Actions

While certainly nothing new to American history, the use of events as symbolic actions broadened and intensified in the period. From dramatic Sit-Down Strikes in Michigan to Eleanor Roosevelt's sponsorship of a Marian Anderson concert at the Lincoln Memorial in Washington, D.C. (when Miss Anderson had been denied the use of other facilities because of her race) a wide range of events became treated most self-consciously as symbols. A few examples:

(a) N.R.A. Rally in Times Square, New York City. *Brown Brothers.*

(b) Swing Addicts Swarm on Stage of Paramount Theater unable to Resist Benny Goodman's Music (1938). *Brown Brothers.*

(c) Harrisburg "Hunger Marchers" (July 1936). *Brown Brothers.*

(d) Jack Delano, "Pickets at Textile Mill, Greensboro, Georgia" (1941). Farm Security Administration. *Library of Congress.*

16. Monuments for an Era

(a) George Washington Bridge. Opening Day (1931). Cass Gilbert, consulting architect and O. H. Ammann, chief engineer of the Port Authority of New York. *Port of New York Authority.* For other "visions" of Washington, see below.

(b) Rockefeller Center. Built 1931–39, an extraordinary complex of fourteen buildings between 48th and 51st streets and Fifth Avenue and the Avenue of the Americas. Key designers Raymond Hood and Wallace K. Harrison. *Thomas Airviews. Rockefeller Center, Inc.*

(c) Rockefeller's Other Monument: Williamsburg Restoration. A view of the restored Capitol Building (1936). *Brown Brothers.*

(d) The Pentagon, Arlington, Virginia. *Brown Brothers.*

17. The Nation in History: Two Visions of an Historic Leader

(a) The Monumental View: Mt. Rushmore National Memorial, South Dakota. Gutzon Borglum, sculptor. *Brown Brothers.*

(b) The Minuscule View: Grant Wood, *Parson Weems' Fable* (1939). *Associated American Artists.*

18. The Nation's Leaders

(a) Walt Disney's Mickey Mouse. Copyrighted by Walt Disney Productions. *Brown Brothers.*

(b) The President of the United States: F.D.R. made himself into a symbol with characteristic smile and trade-mark cigarette holder. He was brilliantly aware of the value of symbolic action. *Photograph (April 1939) World Wide Photos.*

19. The Social Surrealism of David Smith: An American Sculptor Tries to Find the Proper Means to Express His Deep Anger at a World of Social Injustice in a Fusion of Symbolism and Realism not Uncommon in the Art of the Period.

Four *Medals for Dishonor* (from a series of fifteen he struck in bronze in three years between 1938–40). Originally exhibited Willard Gallery, New York, 1940. Accompanying text his own from the catalog for that show. *David Smith Estate, Marlborough–Gerson Gallery Inc., 41 East 57th Street, New York.*

(a) *Diplomats: Fascist and Fascist Tending* (1938).

(b) *Private Law and Order Leagues* (1939).

(c) *Food Trust* (1938).

(d) *Munitions Makers* (1939).

20. The American Family: Two Versions

(a) Still from *Judge Hardy's Children*. Produced by Metro–Goldwyn–Mayer with Lewis Stone, Cecilia Parker, Mickey Rooney, and Fay Holden. The film's "typical American family" in a "typical Middlewestern small town." *Brown Brothers*.

(b) Walker Evans, "Bud Fields and Family—Hole County, Alabama" (1936). Farm Security Administration. *Library of Congress*.

21. Middle-Class Visions of the Folk

In addition to the various searches for the authentic American folk traditions in art, design, and music and the genuine persistence of that tradition in, for example, living American folksingers like Pete Seeger and Woody Guthrie, there was another more commercial effort to render folk materials in acceptable forms especially in the American lyric theater.

(a) Catfish Row as it appeared in original 1935 production of George Gershwin's *Porgy and Bess*. *Brown Brothers*.

(b) "Surrey with the Fringe on Top" from *Oklahoma!* (1943). *World Wide Photos*.

22. Heroic Images

(a) Superman. © National Periodical Publications, Inc.

(b) Popeye. © King Features Syndicate, 1938.

(c) A Special Champion: Joe Louis. *Brown Brothers*.

(d) Edward G. Robinson as *Little Caesar*. Warner Brothers, 1930. Directed by Mervyn LeRoy. The Gangster as Hero was a popular theme in fiction, pulps, and most especially, films. *Brown Brothers*.

(e) But law and order had its own special heroes as well: Dick Tracy in the comics who brought science, intelligence, and remarkable integrity to his work against a fantastic array of unusual criminal types, and J. Edgar Hoover who seemed almost chiseled from the same block of granite. He and his G-Men became a special part of our institutional life and our "folk culture" in the period. *Brown Brothers*.

23. The Era's Most Popular and Award-Winning Hollywood Director Finds a Special Hero and a Special Theme: Frank Capra

Life defined the classic Capra film: "You have a naive and idealistic hero thrown suddenly in contact with a shrewd professional woman, who first holds him up to the contempt of newspaper photographers, then repents and attempts to help our dumb-but-honest hero as he gets involved in Crooked Politics, High Finance, and the difficulties of Love." Always the innocent, nonconforming individualist against the easily misled mob; always a kind of ritual humiliation must precede his ultimate vindication.

(a) Still from *Mr. Deeds Goes to Town* (Academy Award 1936), Columbia Pictures. Longfellow Deeds (Gary Cooper) is a tuba-playing country boy who inherits a fortune and is then set upon by those who make their parasitical living by attaching themselves to those with wealth. When Deeds proposes to give all his money away, to set up farms to aid the economy (film makers of the 1930's like simple solutions to economic problems) he is almost judged insane by the courts in a scheme by wicked sophisticated city lawyers to keep the books from being audited. *Film Stills Archive of the Museum of Modern Art.*

(b) Still from *Mr. Smith Goes to Washington* (1939), Columbia Pictures. Idealistic young man goes to the Senate; realistic girl reporter believes him too good to be true. He fights for a noble cause (involving conservation of resources) and is betrayed by the elder senator he most admired (Claude Rains) because of corrupting influence of political boss. With aid of reporter, he launches a filibuster —virtually standing alone—and of course is ultimately vindicated. *Film Stills Archive of the Museum of Modern Art.*

24. The War: Two Versions
    (a) Bill Mauldin's Classic G.I.'s. This famous cartoon won him the Pulitzer Prize. *Drawing copyrighted 1944 by United Features Syndicate, Inc. and reproduced by courtesy of Bill Mauldin.*
    (b) Arthur Sasse, "She'll be so nice to come home to" (1944). *UPI Photo.*

25. Mothers and Children: Thirties Versions
    (a) Arshile Gorky, *The Artist and his Mother* (1926–36). Oil on canvas, 60 × 50. Gift of Julien Levy for Maro and Natasha Gorky in memory of their father. *Whitney Museum of American Art, New York.*
    (b) Dorothea Lange, "Destitute Pea Picker in California, Migrant Mother of 6" (1935). *Library of Congress.*

26. The Female Image: Heroines of the Era
    What follows is only a sampling of ideal types. A more complete iconographic record would surely want to deal with the ladies ever the butt of cartoon humor characteristic in the period: James Thurber's ominous, always threatening, dominating wife; Helen

Hokinson's *New Yorker* middle-class club ladies so interested in world affairs and the arts; William Steig's aggressive housewives who regard their husbands as interested only in sex; Art Young's housewives who see themselves more exploited than their husbands; the President's wife, always fair game because of her extensive and unusual involvement in public affairs—it is a fascinating and extensive list. But here are some more obvious key female images:

(a) Shirley Temple in *Rebecca of Sunnybrook Farm* (1938). 20th Century Fox. Miss Temple is eight and a half and literally the nation's darling because of her sweet innocence. *Brown Brothers.*

(b) Marlene Dietrich. The period doted on Glamour Girls and Cafe Society; it responded to women of obvious sensuality like Mae West but was even fonder of exotic and mysterious women. Miss Dietrich may also have delighted the nation, but *not* because of her sweet innocence.

(c) War-Time Image: "Rosie the Riveter." She was immortalized as a special kind of romantic wartime heroine in Norman Rockwell's humorous yet heroic *Saturday Evening Post* cover for May 29, 1942, where she appeared as a new version of Michelangelo's *Isaiah*. *Brown Brothers.*

(d) War-Time Image: The Pin-Up Girl. Miss Betty Grable in the famous picture that adorned G.I. footlockers, Gob seabags, barracks' walls, and ships' bulkheads all over the world during World War II. *United Press International.*

27. Dreams and Fantasies: New and Other Worlds

(a) Hollywood may have done it best: The brilliantly futuristic settings for great numbers in musical comedies, the Science Fiction world of things to come, the fantasy visit to the dream world of Oz, but most especially the bringing to "life" of James Hilton's novel *Lost Horizon* by Frank Capra (1937), which gave us even a new coinage for the land of our dreams: Shangri–La. Columbia Pictures. *Film Stills Archive of the Museum of Modern Art.*

(b) Symbol for the World of Tomorrow: Trylon and Perisphere. *Culver Pictures, Inc.*

1. (a) Dorothea Lange, "U.S. Highway 99 in California" (1937).

1. (b) John Vachon, "N.A.M. Sign, Dubuque, Iowa" (1940).

2. (a) Arthur Rothstein, "Dust Storm—Cimarron County, Okla." (1935).

2. (b) Still from *The River* (1937).

3. (a) Still from *Frankenstein* (1931).

3. (b) Still from *King Kong* (1933).

4. (a) Charles Burchfield, *November Evening* (1934).

4. (b) Edward Hopper, *Gas* (1940).

5. (a) Highway in Massachusetts (1938).

5. (b) The Clover Leaf: You Turn Right to Go Left. New Jersey.

6. (a) The Child in the Unplanned Slum.

6. (b) Planned Environment for Children: Jane Addams Houses.

7. (a) Dorothea Lange, "Family of 9 from Ft. Smith, Ark. on Road from Phoenix to Yuma" (1937).

7. (b) "The Rocket" (1937).

8. (a) "Hooverville (ca. 1931).

8. (b) "Tourist City," Dade City, Florida (1936).

9. (a) "Williamsburg" house, Long Island, New York.

9. (b) Men's Lounge, Third Mezzanine of Radio City Music Hall.

10. (a) Downstream Face of Hoover Dam.

10. (b) Still from *Modern Times* (1936).

11. (a) Juke Box (ca. 1930s).

11. (b) Pin-Ball Machine (1936).

12. (a) *Monopoly*.

12. (b) Russell Lee, "Tenant Purchase Clients at Home, Hidalgo County, Texas" (1939).

13. (a) Russell Lee, "Home of Oklahoma Migrants Who Have Returned from the West" (1939).

13. (b) Russell Lee, "Kitchen Detail in Migrant Labor Camp, Robstown, Texas" (1940).

13. (c) Walker Evans, "Floyd Burrough's Wash Stand, Hole County, Alabama" (1935).

13. (d) Russell Lee, "Bathroom of Tenant Purchase House, Hidalgo, County, Texas" (1939).

14. (a) Reginald Marsh, *Breadline* (1932).

14. (b) The Rockettes, Radio City Music Hall (1948).

15. (a) N.R.A. Rally in Times Square, New York City.

15. (b) Benny Goodman at Paramount Theater (1938).

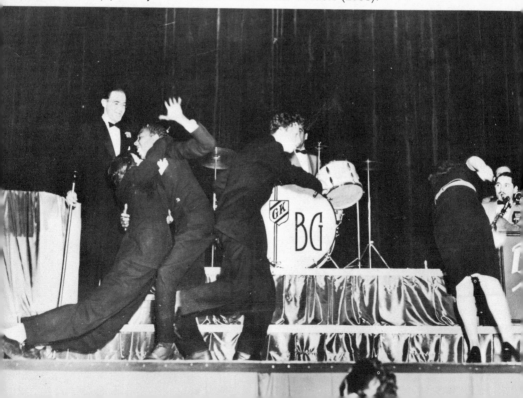

15. (c) Harrisburg "Hunger Marchers" July 1936).

15. (d) Jack Delano, "Pickets at Textile Mill, Greensboro, Ga. (1941).

16. (a) George Washington Bridge. Opening Day (1931).

16. (b) Rockefeller Center. Built 1931–39.

16. (c) Rockefeller's Other Monument: Williamsburg Restoration (1936).

16. (d) The Pentagon, Arlington, Virginia.

17. (a) The Monumental View: Mt. Rushmore National Memorial, South Dakota. Gutzon Borglum, sculptor.

17. (b) The Minuscule View: Grant Wood, *Parson Weems' Fable*.

18. (a) Walt Disney's Mickey Mouse.

18. (b) The President of the United States: F.D.R. made himself
into a symbol with characteristic smile and trade-mark cigarette holder.

19. (a) David Smith, *Diplomats: Fascist and Fascist Tending* (1938).

19. (b) David Smith, *Private Law and Order Leagues* (1939).

19. (c) David Smith, *Food Trust* (1938).

19. (d) David Smith, *Munitions Makers* (1939).

20. (a) Still from *Judge Hardy's Children*.

20. (b) Walker Evans, "Bud Fields and Family—Hole County, Alabama" (1936).

21. (a) Catfish Row as it appeared in original 1935 production of George Gershwin's *Porgy and Bess*.

21. (b) "Surrey with the Fringe on Top" from *Oklahoma!* (1943).

22. (a) Superman.

22. (b) Popeye.

22. (c) Joe Louis.

22. (d) Edward G. Robinson as *Little Caesar* (1930).

22. (e) J. Edgar Hoover.

23. (a) Still from *Mr. Deeds Goes to Town* (1936).

23. (b) Still from *Mr. Smith Goes to Washington* (1939).

"Fresh, spirited American troops, flushed with victory, are bringing in thousands of hungry, ragged, battle-weary prisoners . . ."
(News item)

24. (a) Bill Mauldin's Classic G.I.'s (1944).

24. (b) Arthur Sasse, "She'll be so nice to come to" (1944).

25. (a) Arshile Gorky, *The Artist and his Mother* (1926-29).

25. (b) Dorothea Lange, "Destitute Pea Picker in California, Migrant Mother of 6" (1935).

26. (a) Shirley Temple in *Rebecca of Sunnybrook Farm* (1938).

26. (b) Marlene Dietrich.

26. (c) Wartime image: "Rosie the Riveter"

26. (d) Betty Grable

27. (a) Still from *Lost Horizon* (1937).

27. (b) Trylon and Perisphere, New York World's Fair (1939).

Selected Bibliography

Aaron, Daniel. *Writers on the Left*. New York. Harcourt, Brace and World, 1961.

Aaron, Daniel and Bendiner, Robert, editor. *The Strenuous Decade*. Garden City, New York. Anchor Books, Doubleday and Company, 1970.

Agee, William C. *The 1930's: Painting and Sculpture in America*. New York. Whitney Museum, 1969.

Alexander, Charles C. *Nationalism in American Thought, 1930–1945*. New York. Rand, McNally and Company, 1969.

Allen, Frederick L. *Since Yesterday*. New York. Harper and Brothers, 1940.

Barnouw, Eric. *The Golden Web: A History of Broadcasting in the United States, 1933–1953*. New York. Oxford University Press, 1968.

Battersby, Martin. *The Decorative Thirties*. New York. Walker and Company, 1971.

Baxter, John. *Hollywood in the Thirties*. New York. A. S. Barnes and Company, 1968.

Bendiner, Robert. *Just Around the Corner*. New York. Harper and Row, 1967.

Bird, Caroline. *The Invisible Scar*. New York. David McKay Company, Inc., 1966.

Clurman, Harold. *The Fervent Years*. New York. Hill and Wang, 1957.

Cowley, Malcolm. *Think Back On Us*. Carbondale, Illinois. Southern Illinois University Press, 1967.

Eisinger, Chester E., editor, *The 1940's: Profile of a Nation in Crisis*. Garden City, New York, Doubleday and Company, 1968.

French, Warren. *The Social Novel at an End of an Era*. Carbondale, Illinois. Southern Illinois University Press, 1966.

————, ————, editor. *The Thirties*. Delano, Florida. Everett Edwards, Inc., 1967.

Geist, Sidney. "Prelude: The 1930's," *Arts*, Vol. 30, No. 12. September 1956, pp. 49–55.

Gurko, Leo. *The Angry Decade.* New York. Dodd, Mead and Company, 1947.

Harmon, Jim. *The Great Radio Heroes.* Garden City, New York. Doubleday and Company, 1967.

Higham, Charles and Greenberg, Joel. *Hollywood in the Forties.* New York. A. S. Barnes and Company, 1968.

Howe, Irving and Coser, Lewis. *The American Communist Party.* Boston. Beacon Press, 1957.

Hoyt, Edwin P. *The Tempering Years.* New York. Charles Scribner's Sons, 1963.

Leuchtenberg, William. *Franklin D. Roosevelt and the New Deal, 1932–1940.* New York. Harper and Row, 1963.

Lynd, Robert S. and Helen. *Middletown in Transition.* New York. Harcourt, Brace and Company, 1937.

Madden, David, editor. *Proletarian Writers of the Thirties.* Carbondale, Illinois. Southern Illinois University Press, 1968.

———, ———, editor. *Tough Guy Writers of the Thirties.* Carbondale, Illinois. Southern Illinois University Press, 1968.

Matthews, Jane D. *The Federal Theater, 1935–39.* Princeton, New Jersey. Princeton University Press, 1967.

Mellers, Wilfrid. *Music in a New Found Land.* New York. Alfred A. Knopf, 1965.

"Modern Architecture Symposium: The Decade 1929–1939," *Journal of the Society of Architectural Historians,* Vol. XXIV, No. 1. March 1965. Note especially article by Robert A. M. Stern, "Relevance of the Decade," pp. 6–10.

Pearson, Norman H. "The Nazi–Soviet Pact and the End of a Dream," in Daniel Aaron, editor, *America in Crisis.* New York. Alfred A. Knopf, 1952, pp. 324–48.

Phillips, Cabell. *From the Crash to the Blitz: 1929–1939.* New York. The Macmillan Company, 1969.

Phillips, William. "What Happened in the 30's." *Commentary,* Vol. XXXIV, September 1962, pp. 204–12.

Rogers, Agnes and Allen, F. L., editors. *I Distinctly Remember: A Family Album of the American People, 1918–1941.* New York. Harper and Brothers, 1947.

Schickel, Richard. *The Disney Version.* New York. Simon and Schuster, 1968.

Simon, Rita, editor. *As We Saw the Thirties.* Urbana, Illinois. University of Illinois Press, 1967.

Susman, Warren I. "The Thirties," in Stanley Coben and Lorman Ratner, editors, *The Development of an American Culture.* Englewood Cliffs, New Jersey. Prentice-Hall, Inc., 1970.

Swados, Harvey, editor. *The American Writer and the Great Depression.* Cleveland. The Bobbs–Merrill Company, 1966.

Tanner, Louise. *All the Things We Were.* Garden City, New York. Doubleday and Company, 1968.

Terkel, Studs. *Hard Times.* New York. Pantheon Books, 1970.

"The 1930's: A Symposium," *The Carleton Miscellany.* Winter 1965, pp. 6–104.

"Thirty Years Later: Memories of the First Writers Congress," symposium in *The American Scholar,* Vol. XXXV, Summer 1966, pp. 495–516.

Time-Life Books. *The Fabulous Century,* Vol. IV, 1930–1940. New York. Time, Inc., 1971.

Wecter, Dixon. *The Age of the Great Depression.* New York. The Macmillan Company, 1948.

Wilson, Edmund. *Classics and Commercials. A Literary Chronicle of the Forties.* New York. Farrar, Straus and Company, 1950.

———, ———. *The Shores of Light. A Literary Chronicle of the Twenties and Thirties.* New York. Farrar, Straus and Young, 1952.